SHINOBU OHTAKA

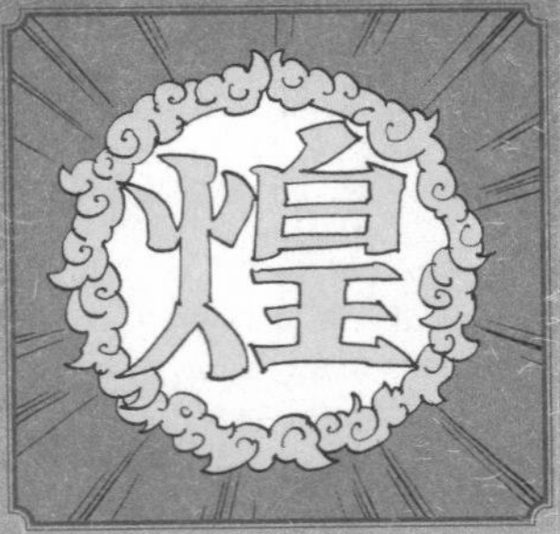
煌

The Kou Empire story arc begins!!!

MAGI

Volume 25

Shonen Sunday Edition

Story and Art by
SHINOBU OHTAKA

MAGI Vol.25
by Shinobu OHTAKA
© 2009 Shinobu OHTAKA
All rights reserved.
Original Japanese edition published by SHOGAKUKAN.
English translation rights in the United States of America, Canada, the United Kingdom,
Ireland, Australia and New Zealand arranged with SHOGAKUKAN.

ORIGINAL COVER DESIGN / Yasuo SHIMURA+Bay Bridge Studio

Translation & English Adaptation ◆ John Werry

Touch-up Art & Lettering ◆ Stephen Dutro

Editor ◆ Mike Montesa

Printed in Canada

Published by VIZ Media, LLC
P.O. Box 77010
San Francisco, CA 94107

10 9 8 7 6 5 4 3 2 1
First printing, August 2017

PARENTAL ADVISORY
MAGI is rated T for Teen.
This volume contains
suggestive themes.
ratings.viz.com

www.viz.com

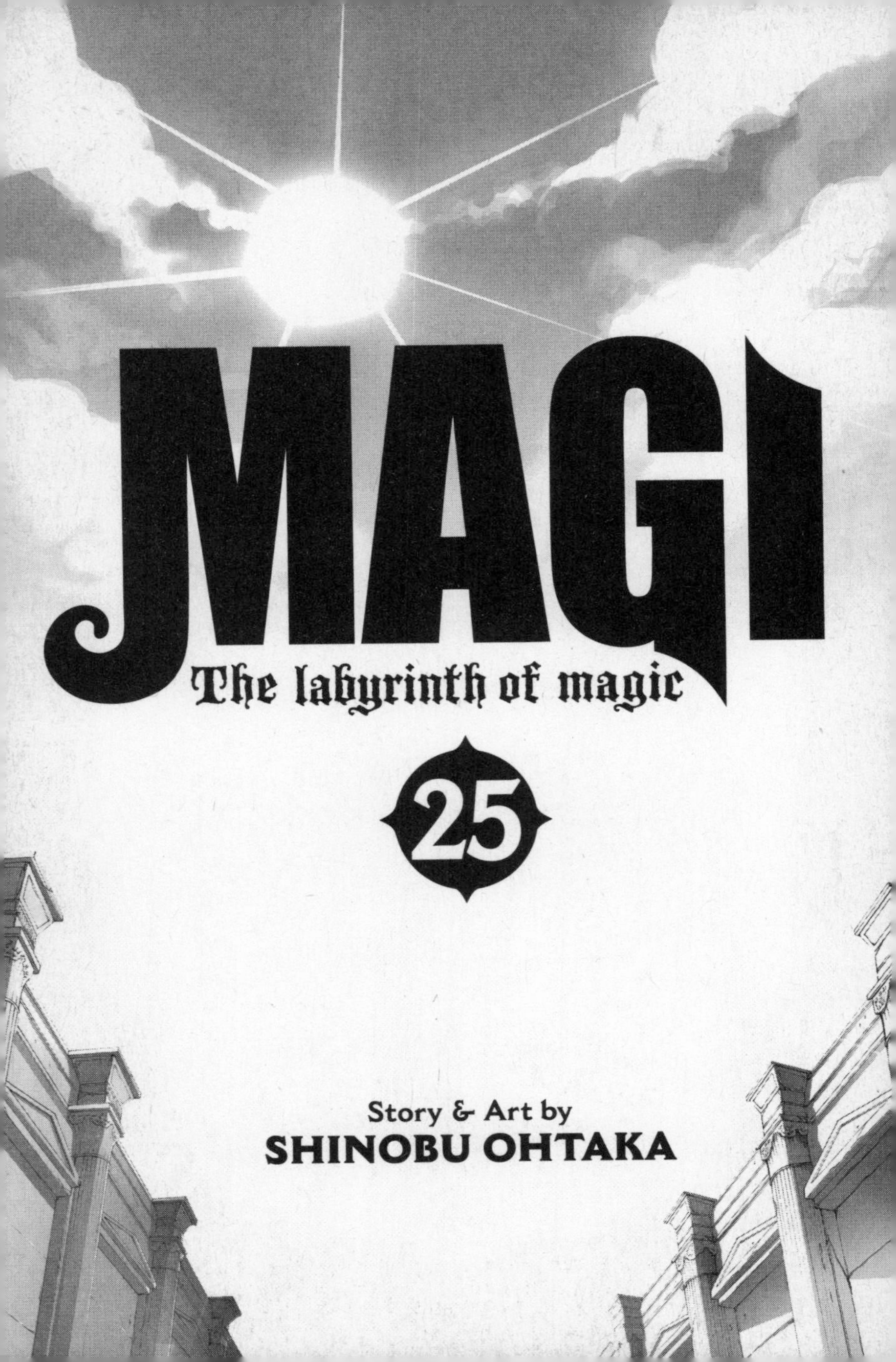

MAGI

The labyrinth of magic

25

Story & Art by

SHINOBU OHTAKA

MAGI
The labyrinth of magic

25

CONTENTS

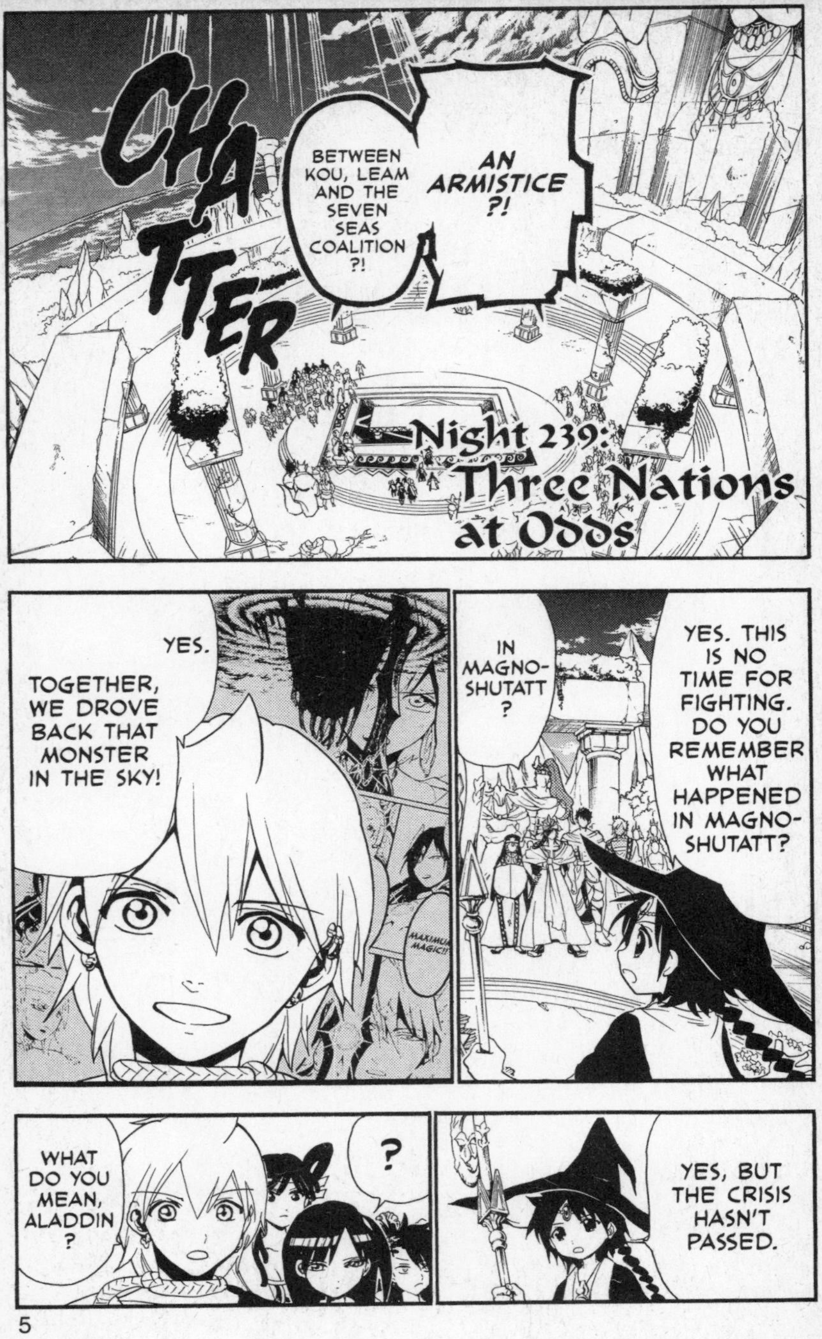

CHATTER
AN ARMISTICE ?!
BETWEEN KOU, LEAM AND THE SEVEN SEAS COALITION ?!
Night 239: Three Nations at Odds
YES. THIS IS NO TIME FOR FIGHTING. DO YOU REMEMBER WHAT HAPPENED IN MAGNO-SHUTATT?
IN MAGNO-SHUTATT ?
YES.
TOGETHER, WE DROVE BACK THAT MONSTER IN THE SKY!
MAXIMUM MAGIC!!
YES, BUT THE CRISIS HASN'T PASSED.
?
WHAT DO YOU MEAN, ALADDIN ?

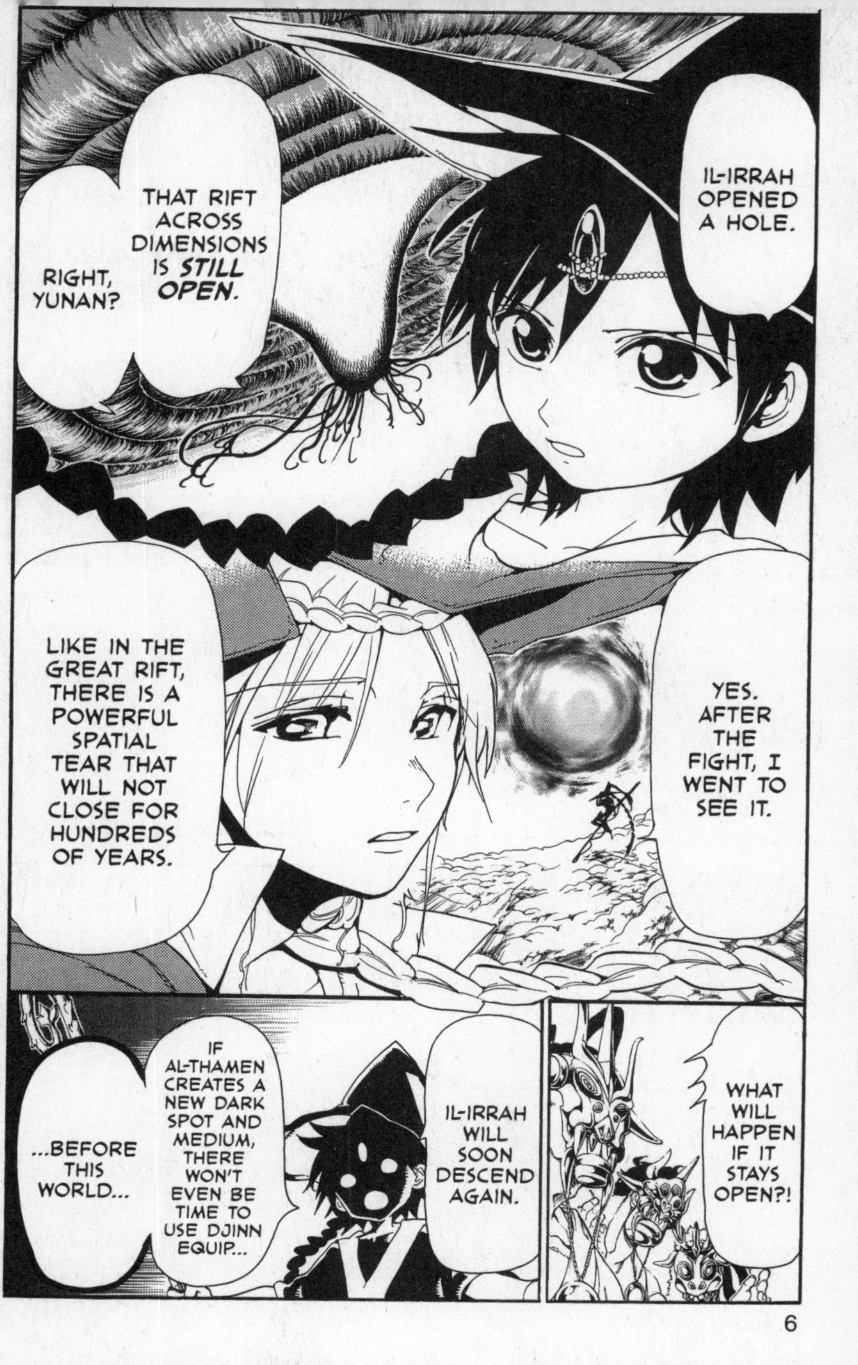
IL-IRRAH OPENED A HOLE.
THAT RIFT ACROSS DIMENSIONS IS STILL OPEN.
RIGHT, YUNAN?
YES. AFTER THE FIGHT, I WENT TO SEE IT.
LIKE IN THE GREAT RIFT, THERE IS A POWERFUL SPATIAL TEAR THAT WILL NOT CLOSE FOR HUNDREDS OF YEARS.
WHAT WILL HAPPEN IF IT STAYS OPEN?!
IL-IRRAH WILL SOON DESCEND AGAIN.
IF AL-THAMEN CREATES A NEW DARK SPOT AND MEDIUM, THERE WON'T EVEN BE TIME TO USE DJINN EQUIP...
...BEFORE THIS WORLD...

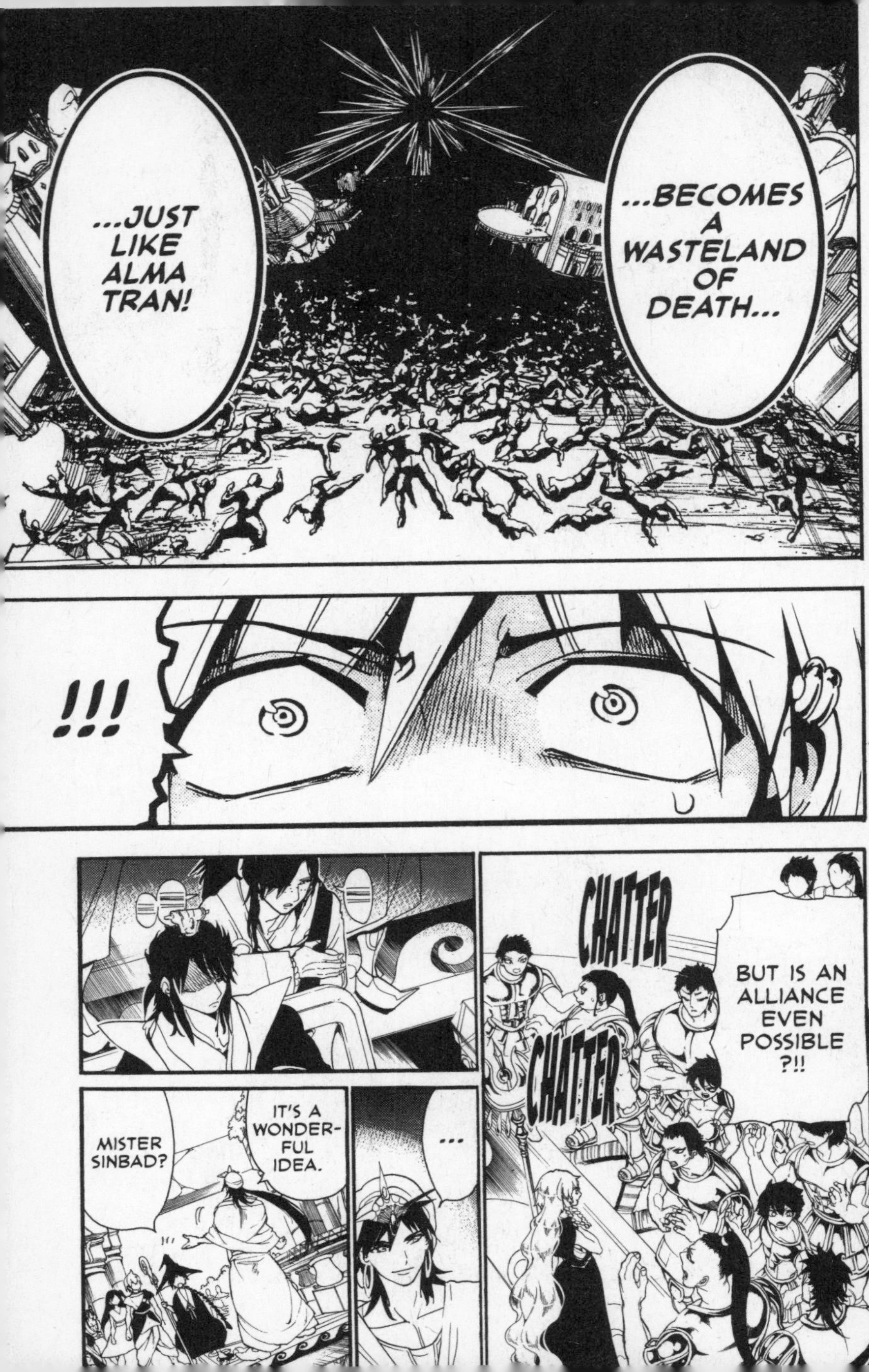
...BECOMES A WASTELAND OF DEATH...
...JUST LIKE ALMA TRAN!
!!!
CHATTER
CHATTER
BUT IS AN ALLIANCE EVEN POSSIBLE?!!
...
IT'S A WONDERFUL IDEA.
MISTER SINBAD?
!!!

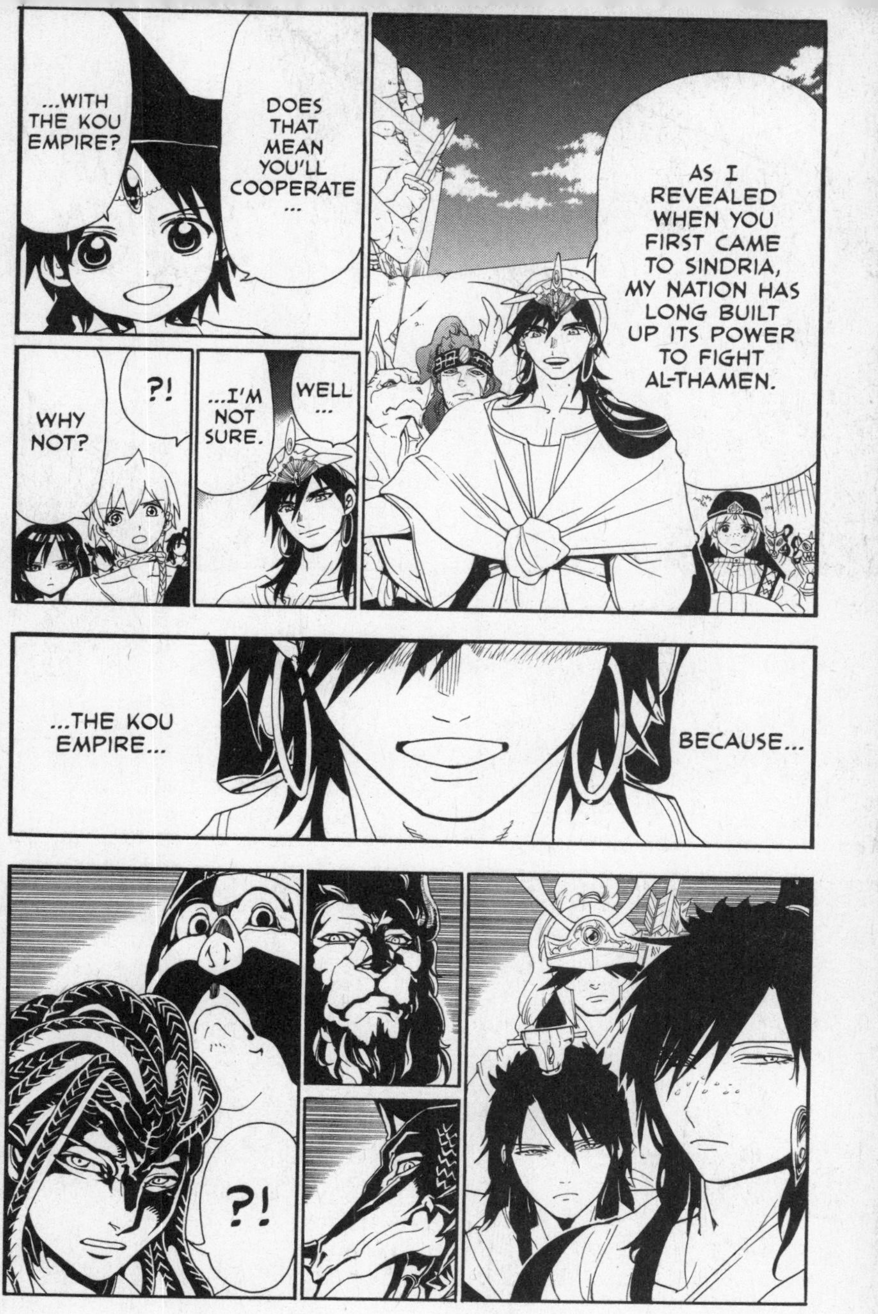
AS I REVEALED WHEN YOU FIRST CAME TO SINDRIA, MY NATION HAS LONG BUILT UP ITS POWER TO FIGHT AL-THAMEN.
DOES THAT MEAN YOU'LL COOPERATE ...
...WITH THE KOU EMPIRE?
WELL ...
...I'M NOT SURE.
?!
WHY NOT?
BECAUSE...
...THE KOU EMPIRE...
?!

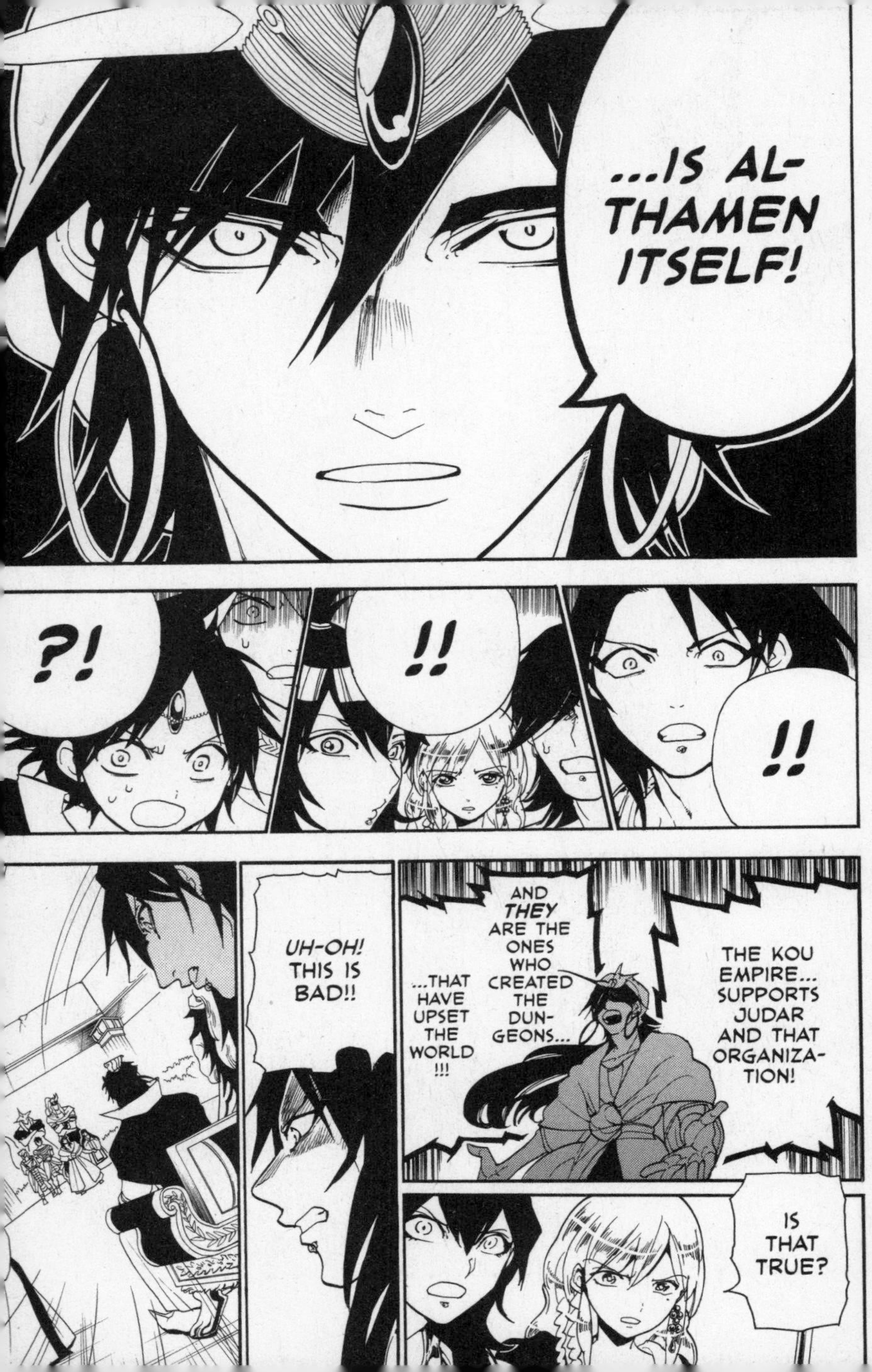
...IS AL-THAMEN ITSELF!
!!
!!
?!
THE KOU EMPIRE... SUPPORTS JUDAR AND THAT ORGANIZATION!
AND *THEY* ARE THE ONES WHO CREATED THE DUNGEONS...
...THAT HAVE UPSET THE WORLD!!!
IS THAT TRUE?
UH-OH! THIS IS BAD!!

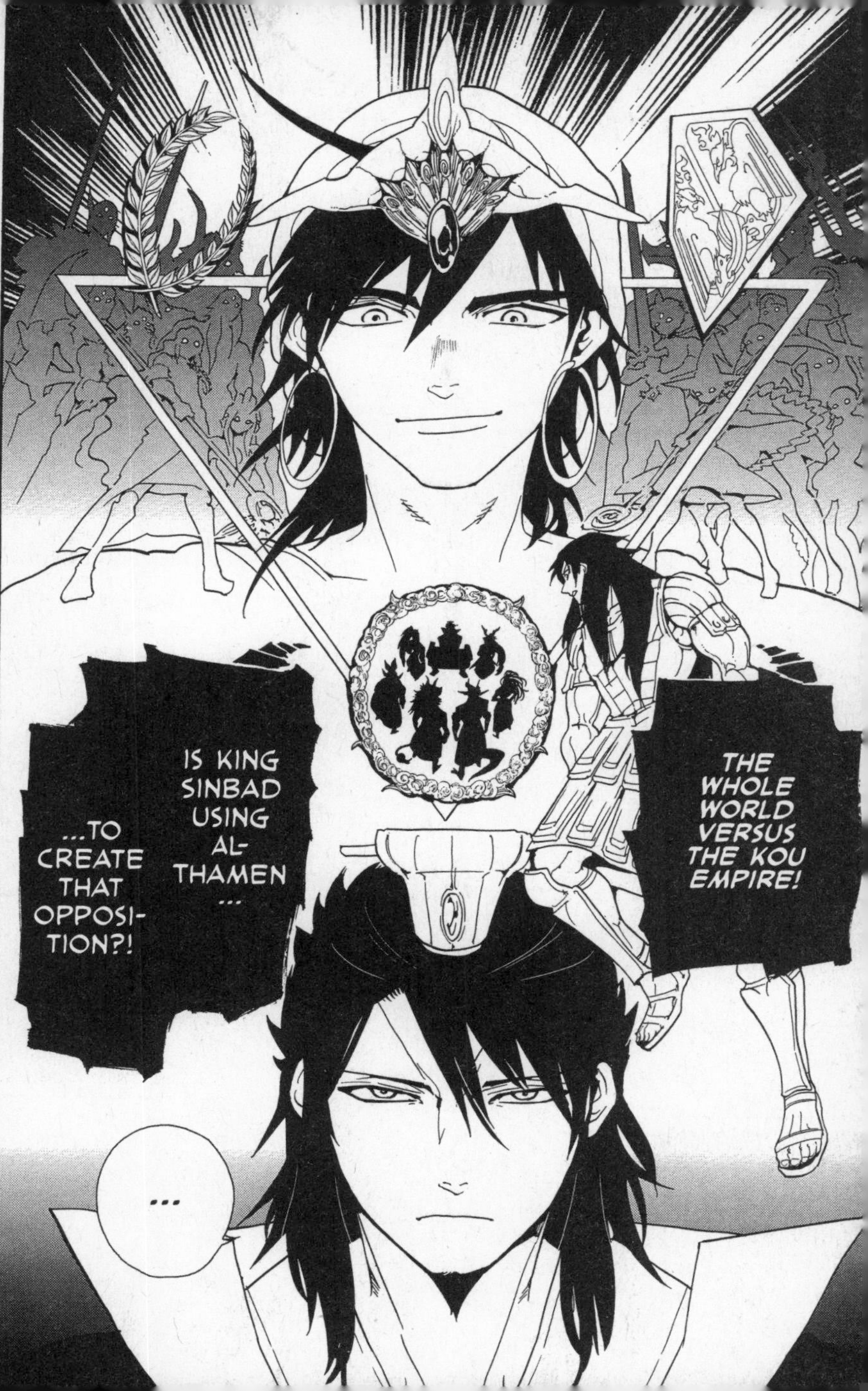
THE WHOLE WORLD VERSUS THE KOU EMPIRE!
IS KING SINBAD USING AL-THAMEN ...
...TO CREATE THAT OPPOSITION?!
...

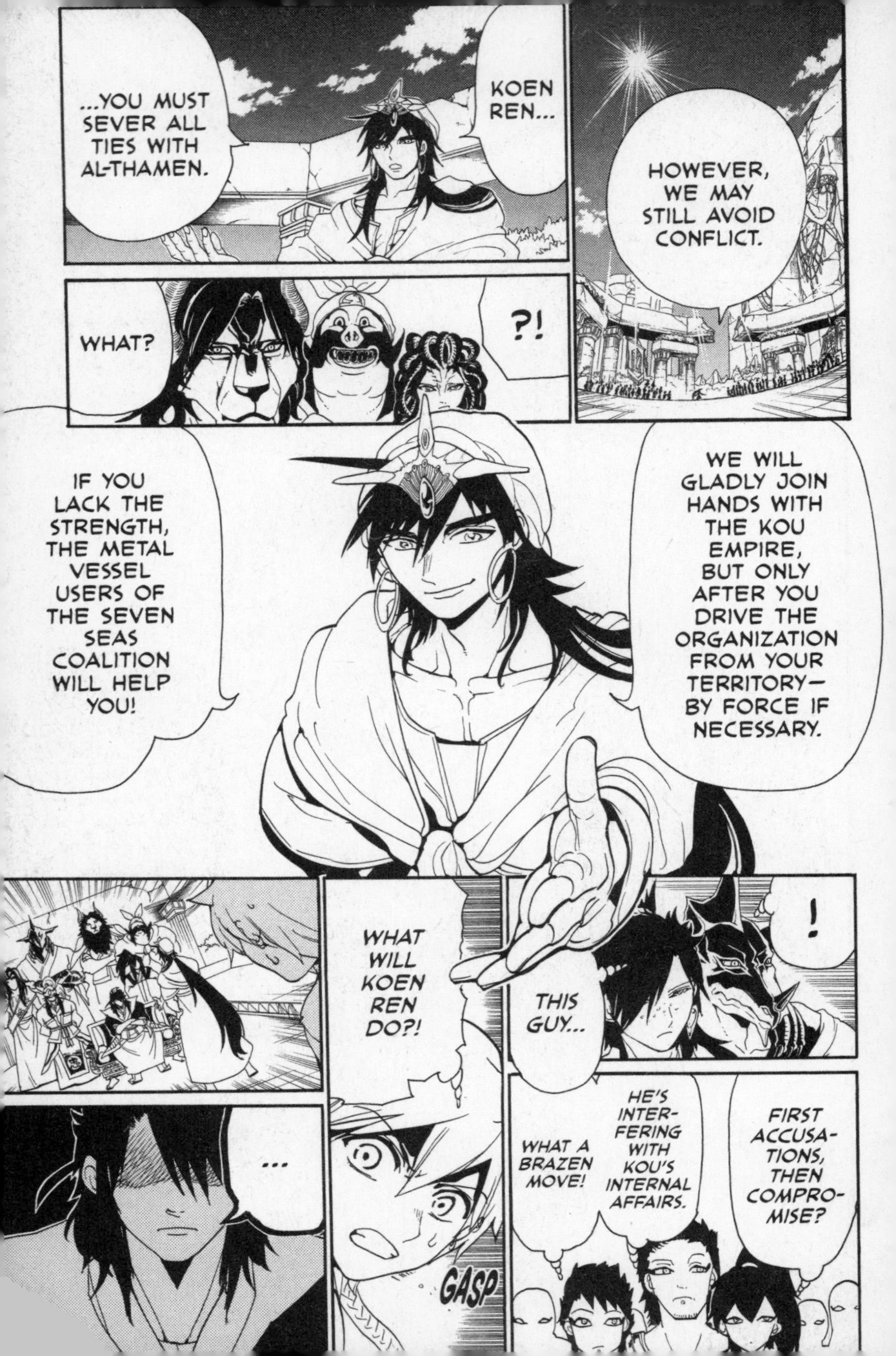
HOWEVER, WE MAY STILL AVOID CONFLICT.
KOEN REN...
...YOU MUST SEVER ALL TIES WITH AL-THAMEN.
?!
WHAT?
WE WILL GLADLY JOIN HANDS WITH THE KOU EMPIRE, BUT ONLY AFTER YOU DRIVE THE ORGANIZATION FROM YOUR TERRITORY— BY FORCE IF NECESSARY.
IF YOU LACK THE STRENGTH, THE METAL VESSEL USERS OF THE SEVEN SEAS COALITION WILL HELP YOU!
!
THIS GUY...
WHAT WILL KOEN REN DO?!
FIRST ACCUSA-TIONS, THEN COMPRO-MISE?
HE'S INTER-FERING WITH KOU'S INTERNAL AFFAIRS.
WHAT A BRAZEN MOVE!
GASP
...

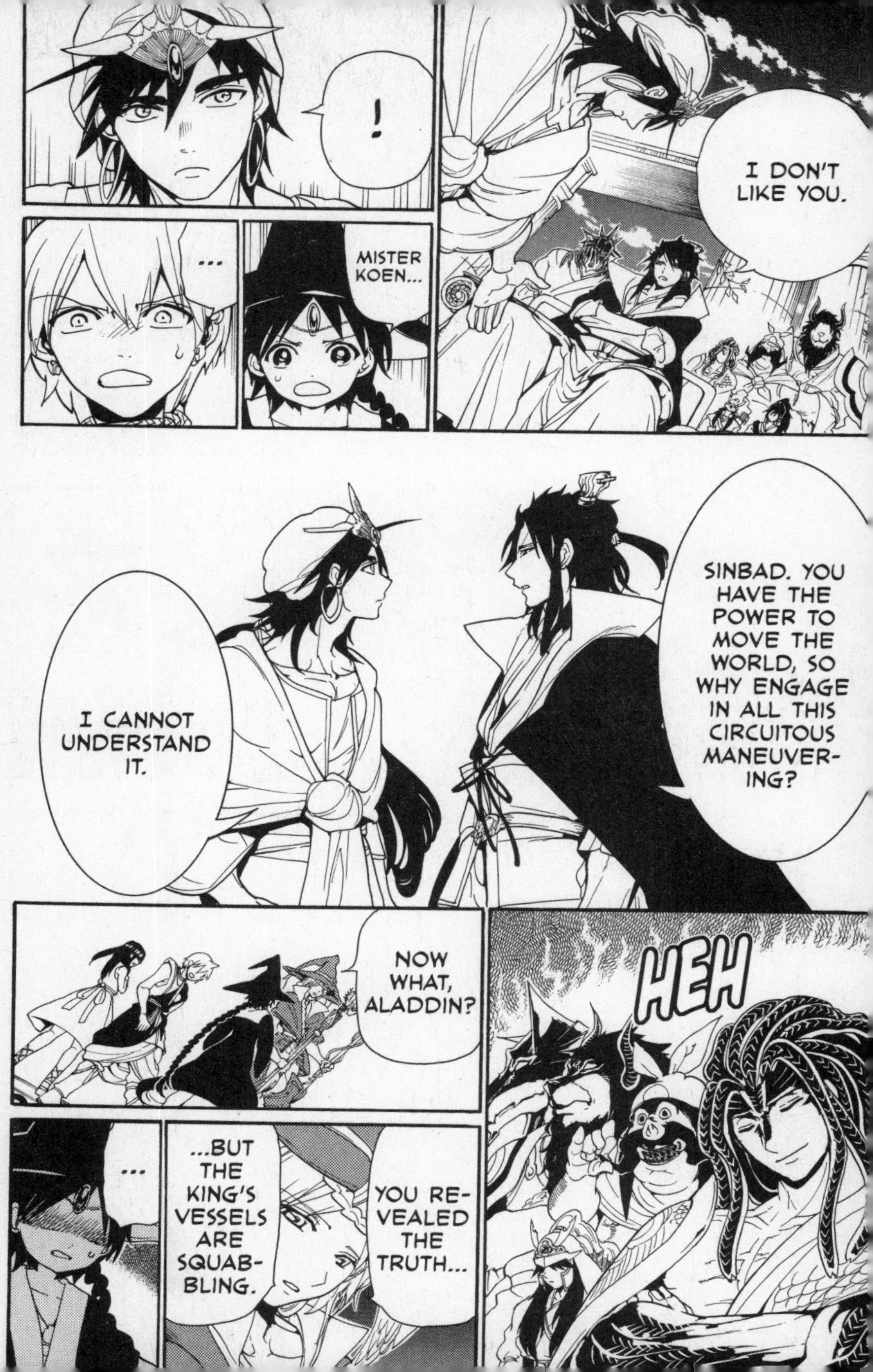
I DON'T LIKE YOU.
!
MISTER KOEN...
...
SINBAD. YOU HAVE THE POWER TO MOVE THE WORLD, SO WHY ENGAGE IN ALL THIS CIRCUITOUS MANEUVERING?
I CANNOT UNDERSTAND IT.
HEH
NOW WHAT, ALADDIN?
YOU REVEALED THE TRUTH...
...BUT THE KING'S VESSELS ARE SQUABBLING.
...

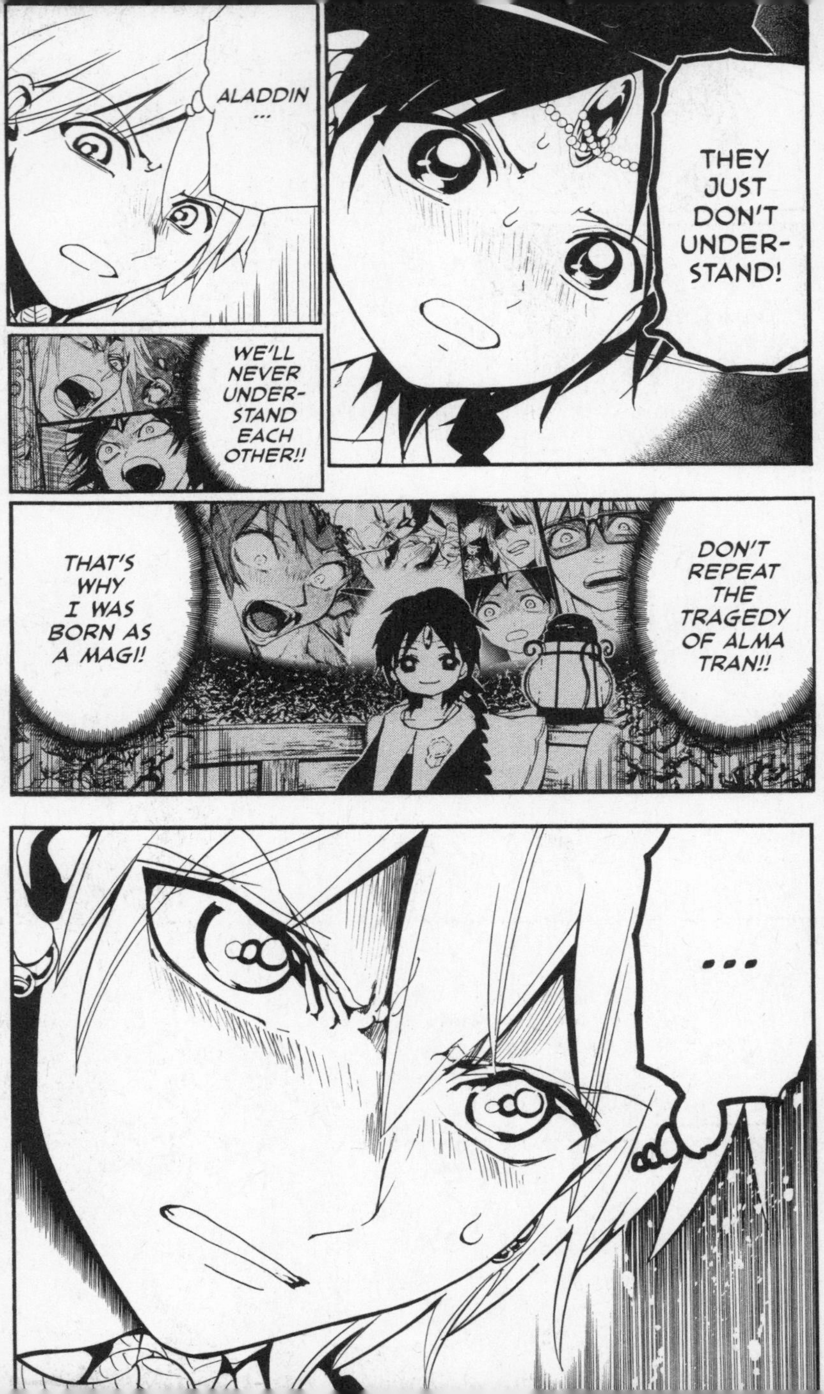
THEY JUST DON'T UNDERSTAND!
ALADDIN...
WE'LL NEVER UNDERSTAND EACH OTHER!!
DON'T REPEAT THE TRAGEDY OF ALMA TRAN!!
THAT'S WHY I WAS BORN AS A MAGI!
...

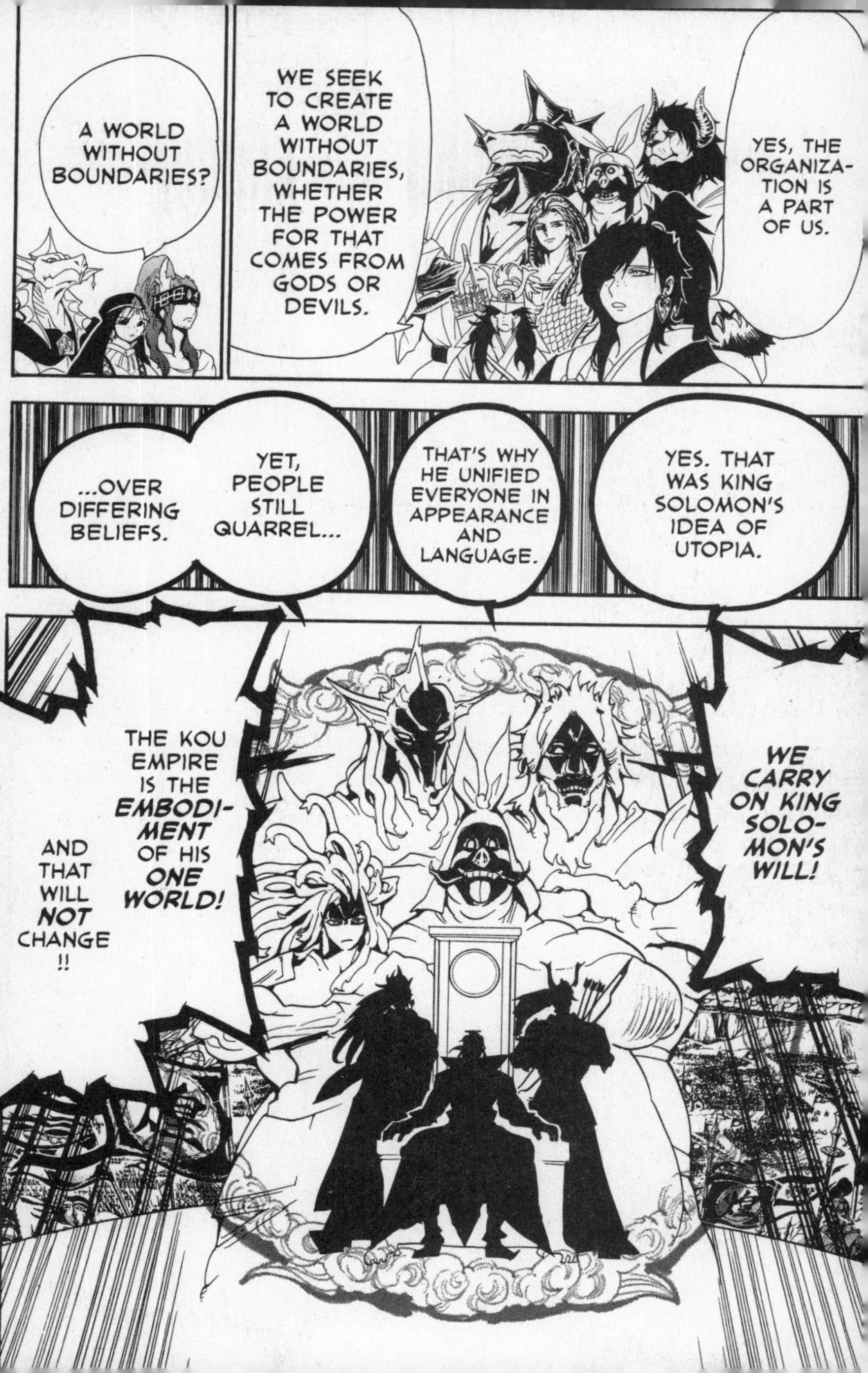
YES, THE ORGANIZATION IS A PART OF US.
WE SEEK TO CREATE A WORLD WITHOUT BOUNDARIES, WHETHER THE POWER FOR THAT COMES FROM GODS OR DEVILS.
A WORLD WITHOUT BOUNDARIES?
YES. THAT WAS KING SOLOMON'S IDEA OF UTOPIA.
THAT'S WHY HE UNIFIED EVERYONE IN APPEARANCE AND LANGUAGE.
YET, PEOPLE STILL QUARREL...
...OVER DIFFERING BELIEFS.
WE CARRY ON KING SOLOMON'S WILL!
THE KOU EMPIRE IS THE *EMBODIMENT* OF HIS *ONE WORLD!*
AND THAT WILL *NOT* CHANGE !!

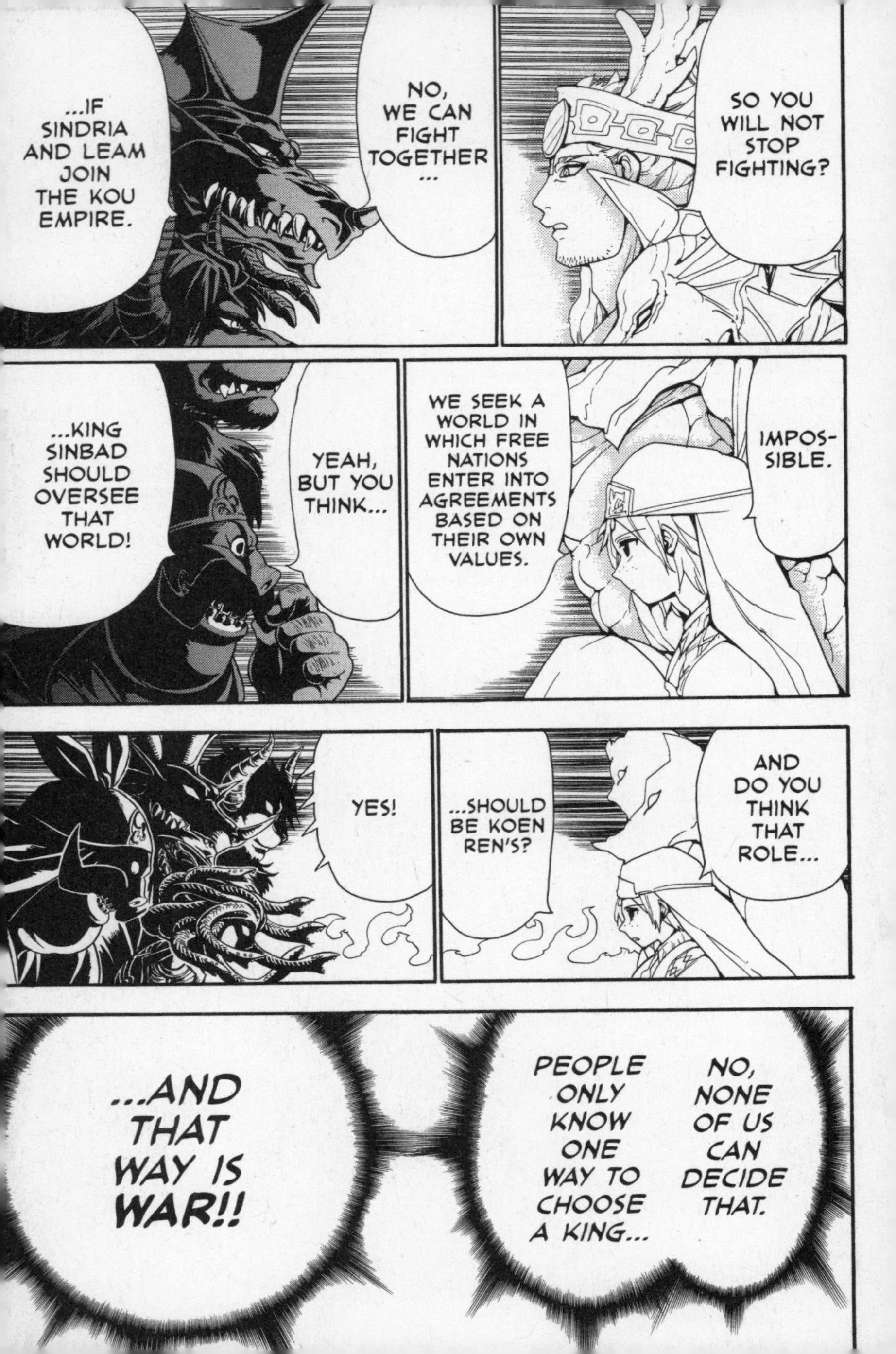
SO YOU WILL NOT STOP FIGHTING?
NO, WE CAN FIGHT TOGETHER ...
...IF SINDRIA AND LEAM JOIN THE KOU EMPIRE.
IMPOS-SIBLE.
WE SEEK A WORLD IN WHICH FREE NATIONS ENTER INTO AGREEMENTS BASED ON THEIR OWN VALUES.
YEAH, BUT YOU THINK...
...KING SINBAD SHOULD OVERSEE THAT WORLD!
AND DO YOU THINK THAT ROLE...
...SHOULD BE KOEN REN'S?
YES!
NO, NONE OF US CAN DECIDE THAT.
PEOPLE ONLY KNOW ONE WAY TO CHOOSE A KING...
...AND THAT WAY IS WAR!!

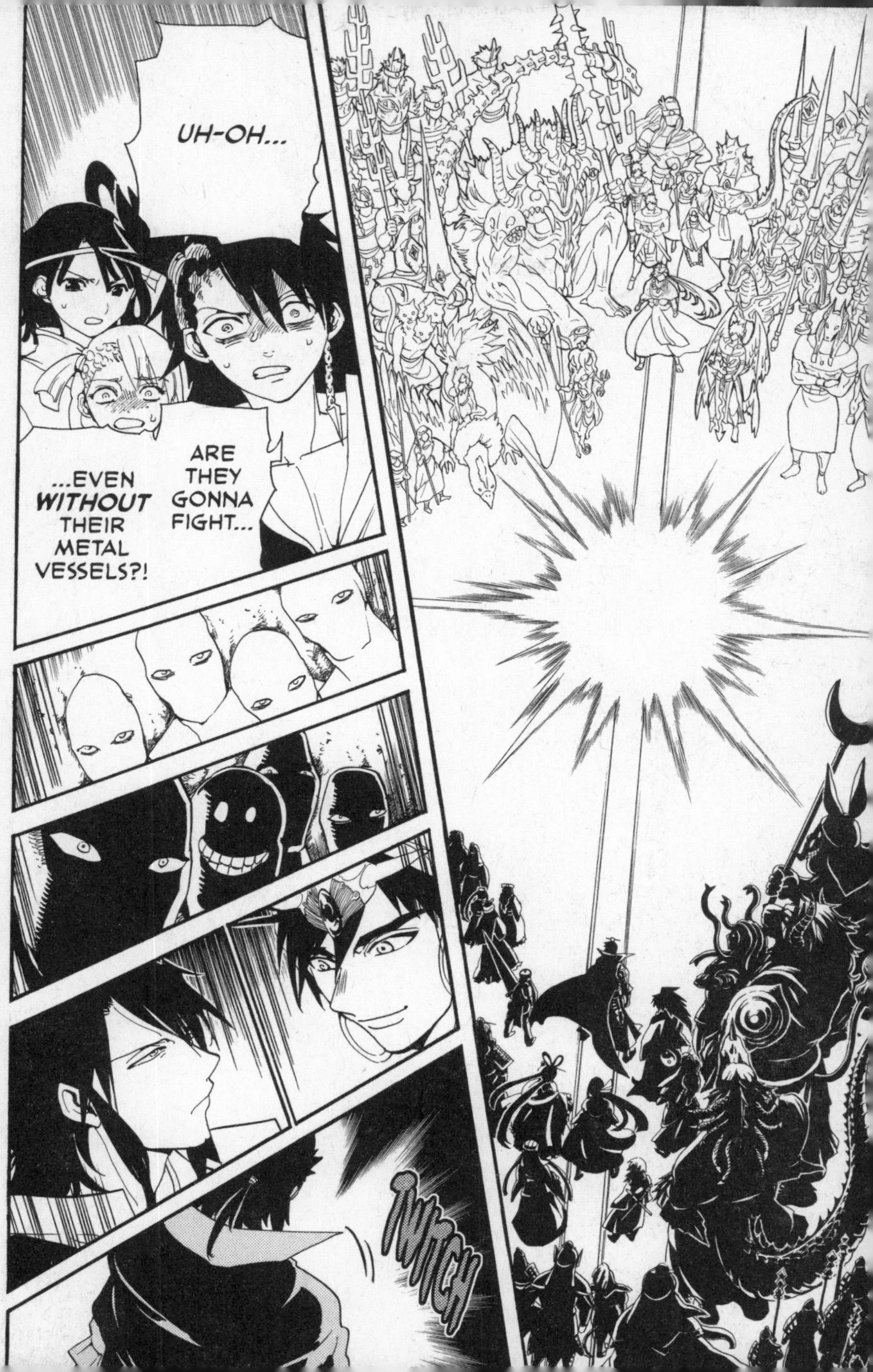
UH-OH...
ARE THEY GONNA FIGHT...
...EVEN WITHOUT THEIR METAL VESSELS?!
TWITCH

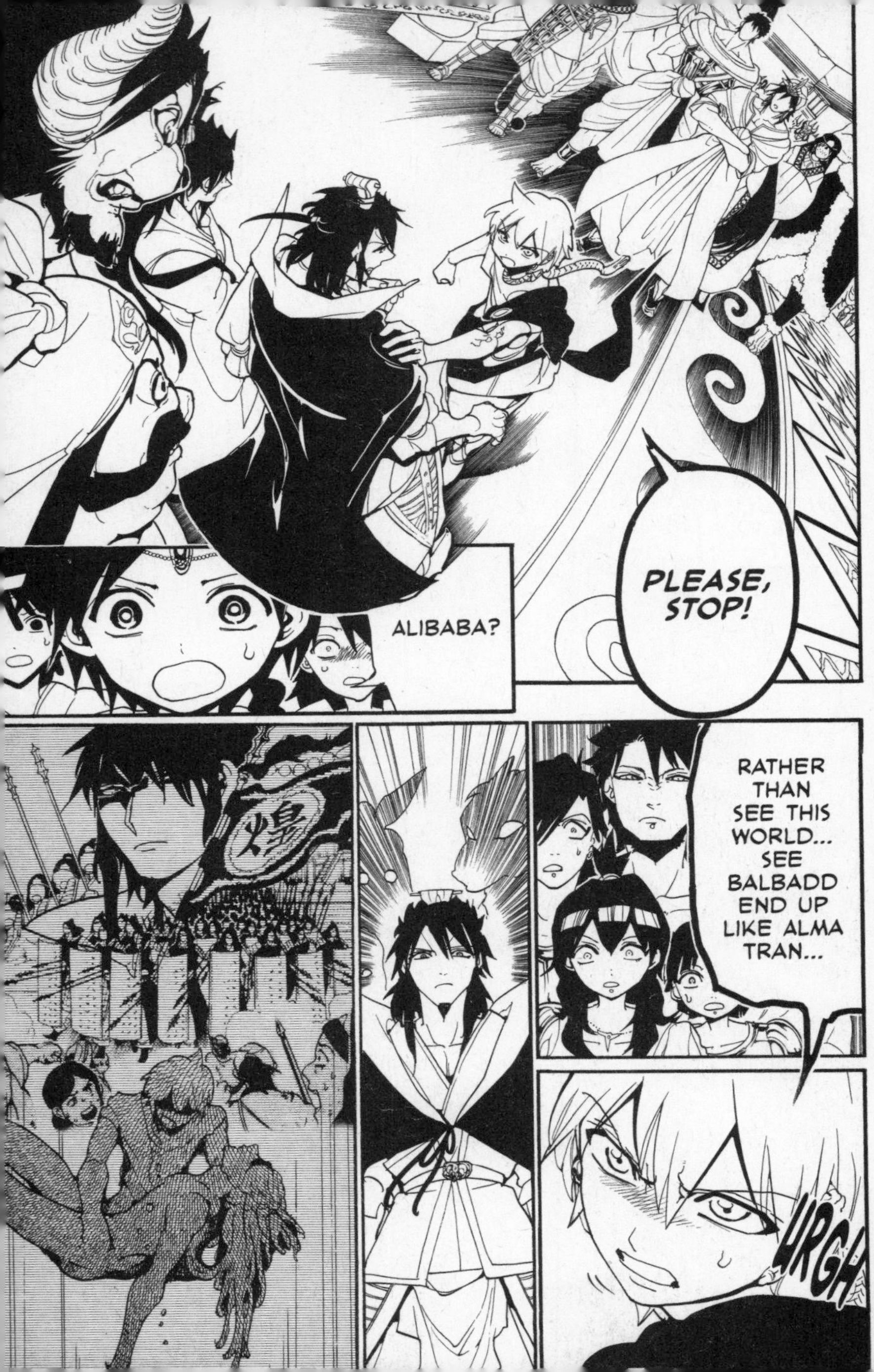
PLEASE, STOP!
ALIBABA?
RATHER THAN SEE THIS WORLD... SEE BALBADD END UP LIKE ALMA TRAN...
URGH

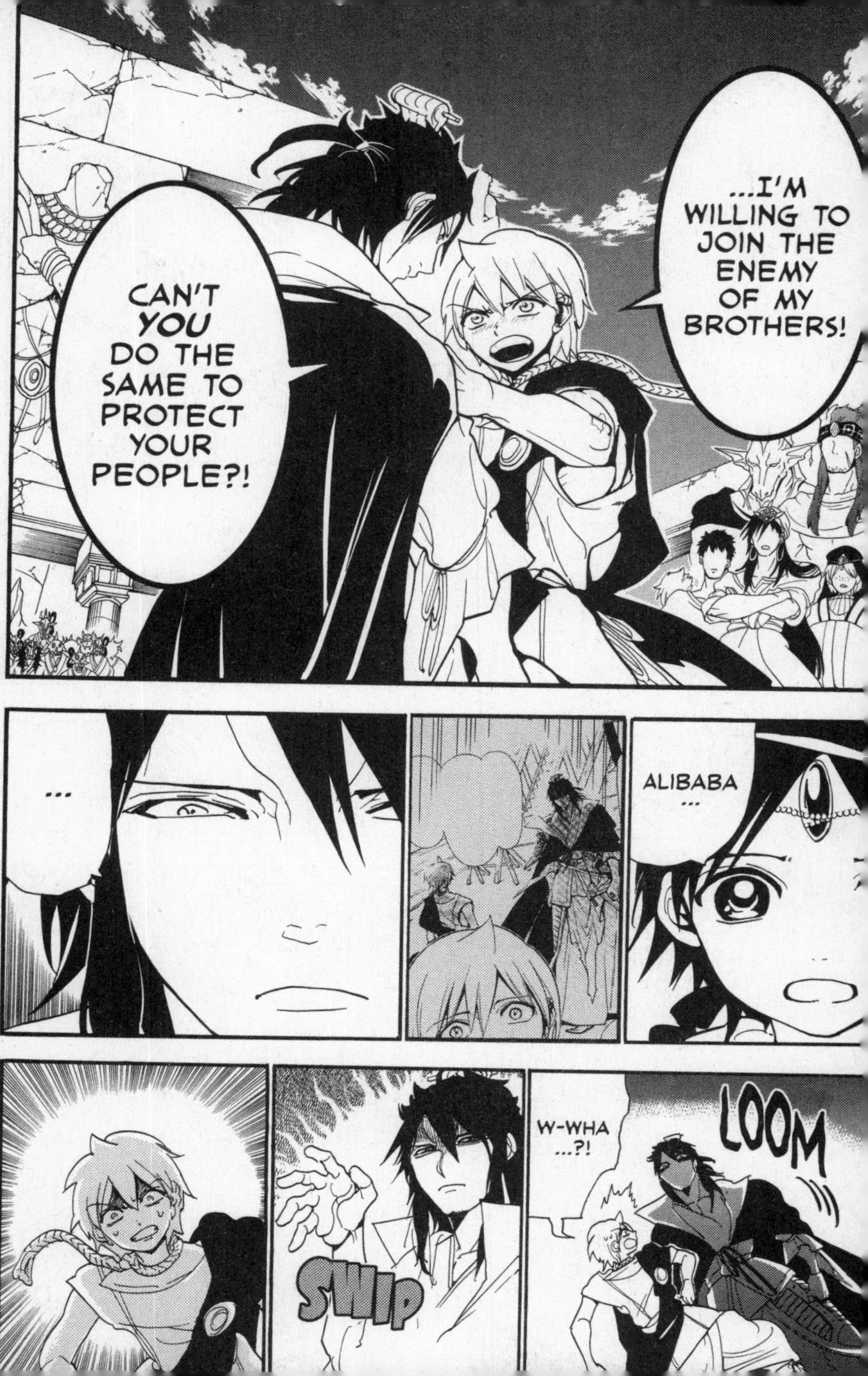
...I'M WILLING TO JOIN THE ENEMY OF MY BROTHERS!
CAN'T *YOU* DO THE SAME TO PROTECT YOUR PEOPLE?!
ALIBABA ...
...
LOOM
W-WHA ...?!
SWIP

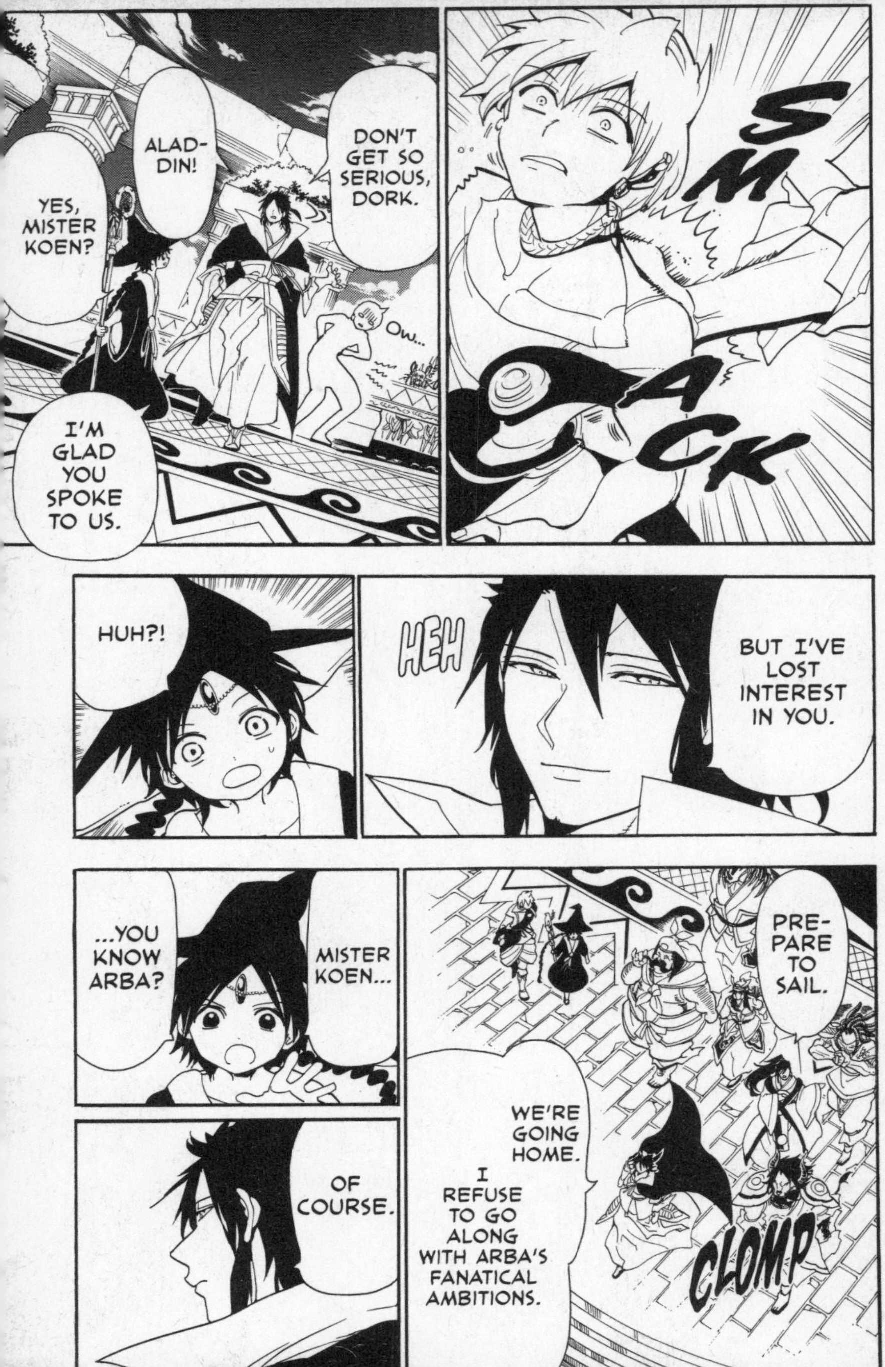
SMACK
DON'T GET SO SERIOUS, DORK.
ALAD-DIN!
YES, MISTER KOEN?
Ow...
I'M GLAD YOU SPOKE TO US.
HEH
BUT I'VE LOST INTEREST IN YOU.
HUH?!
PRE-PARE TO SAIL.
WE'RE GOING HOME.
I REFUSE TO GO ALONG WITH ARBA'S FANATICAL AMBITIONS.
CLOMP
MISTER KOEN...
...YOU KNOW ARBA?
OF COURSE.

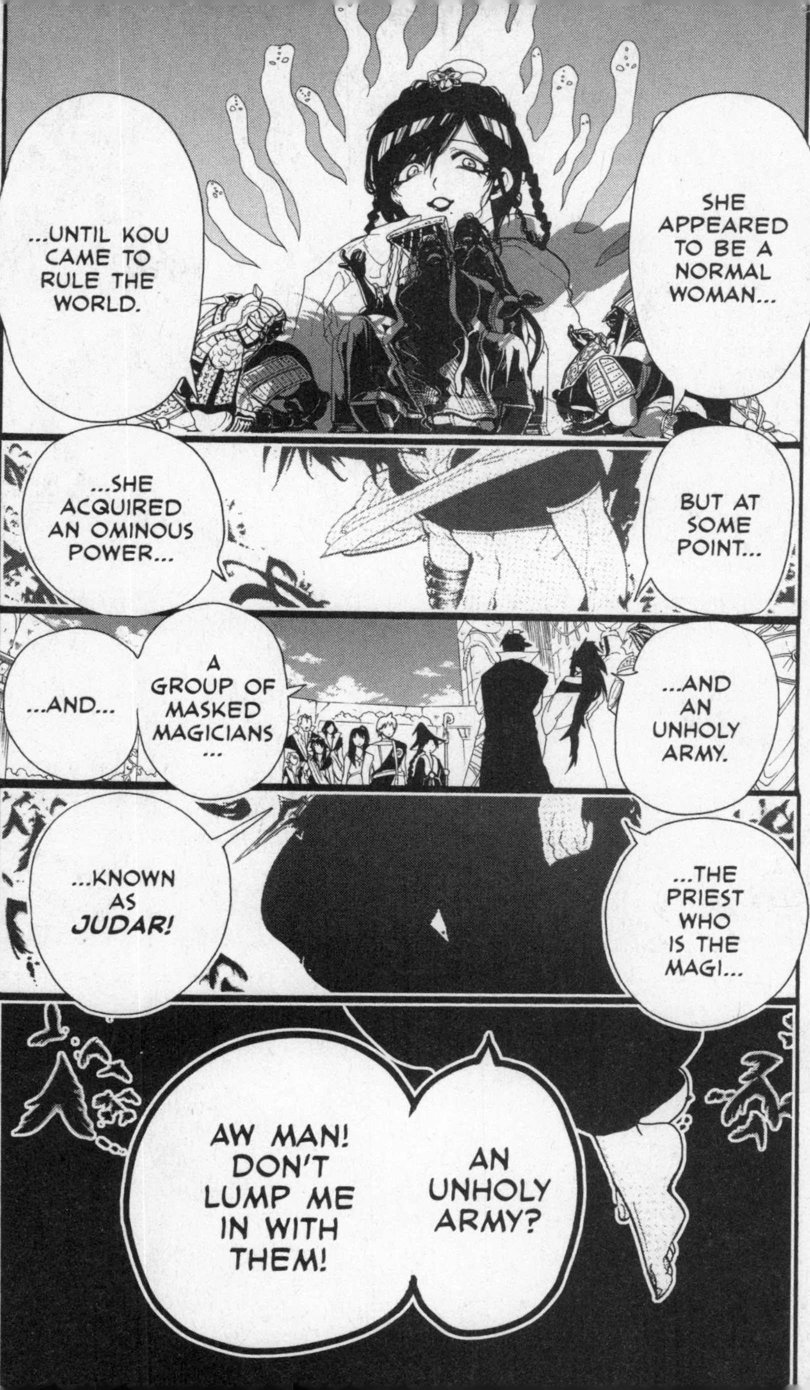
SHE APPEARED TO BE A NORMAL WOMAN...
...UNTIL KOU CAME TO RULE THE WORLD.
BUT AT SOME POINT...
...SHE ACQUIRED AN OMINOUS POWER...
...AND AN UNHOLY ARMY.
A GROUP OF MASKED MAGICIANS ...
...AND...
...THE PRIEST WHO IS THE MAGI...
...KNOWN AS JUDAR!
AN UNHOLY ARMY?
AW MAN! DON'T LUMP ME IN WITH THEM!

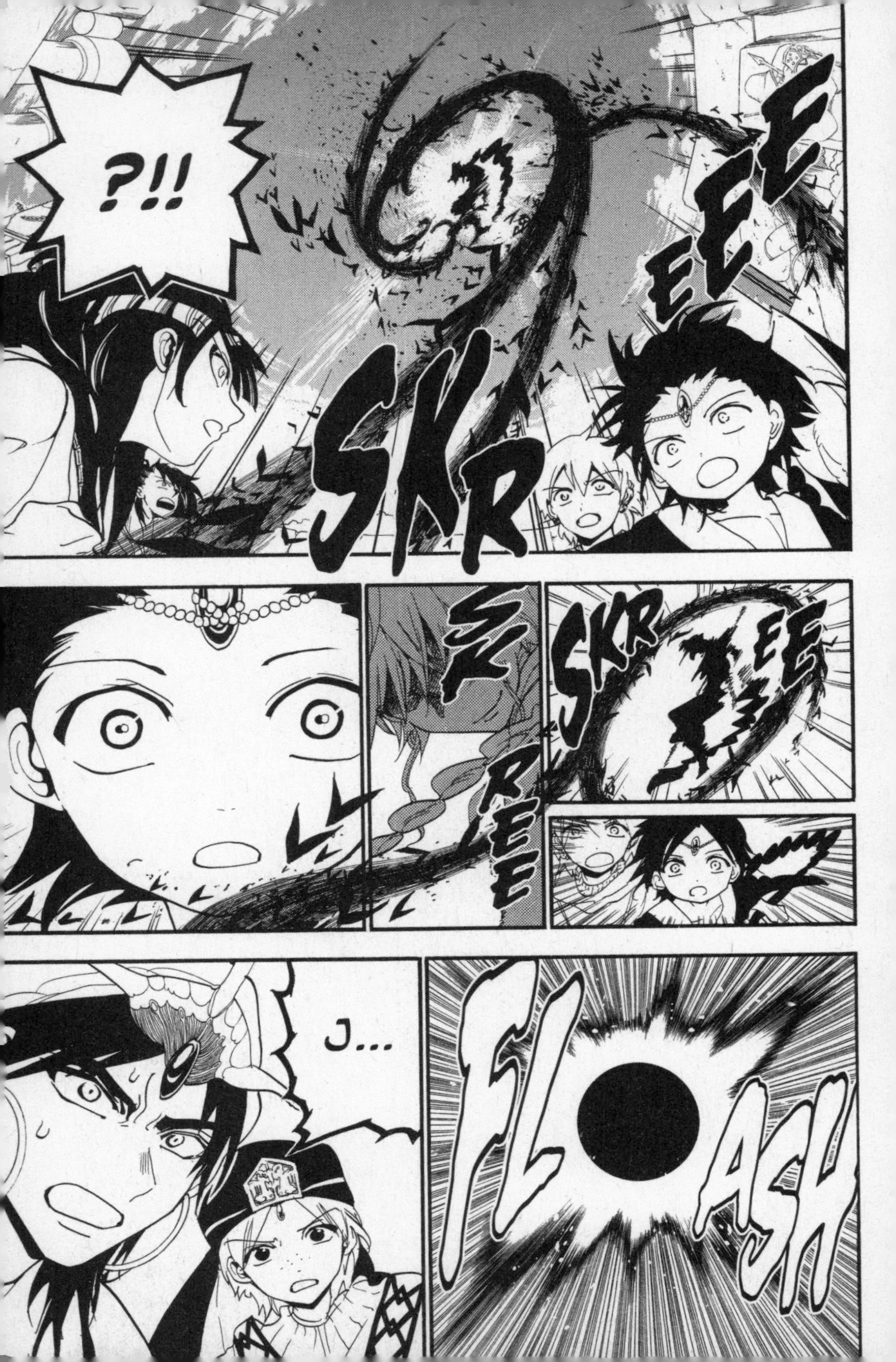

SKREEE
?!!
SKREE
SKREE
J...
FLAACH

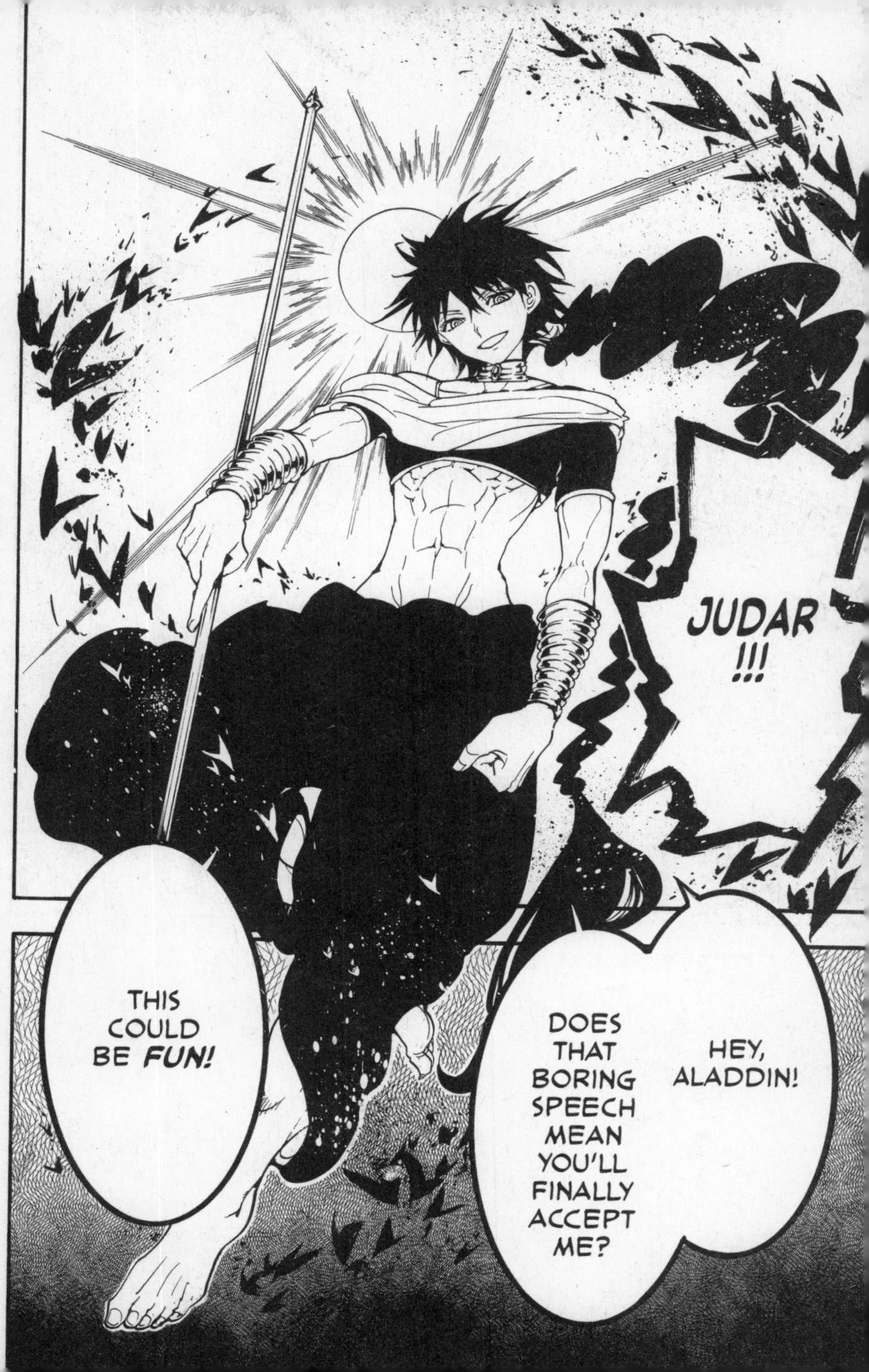
JUDAR !!!
HEY, ALADDIN!
DOES THAT BORING SPEECH MEAN YOU'LL FINALLY ACCEPT ME?
THIS COULD BE *FUN!*

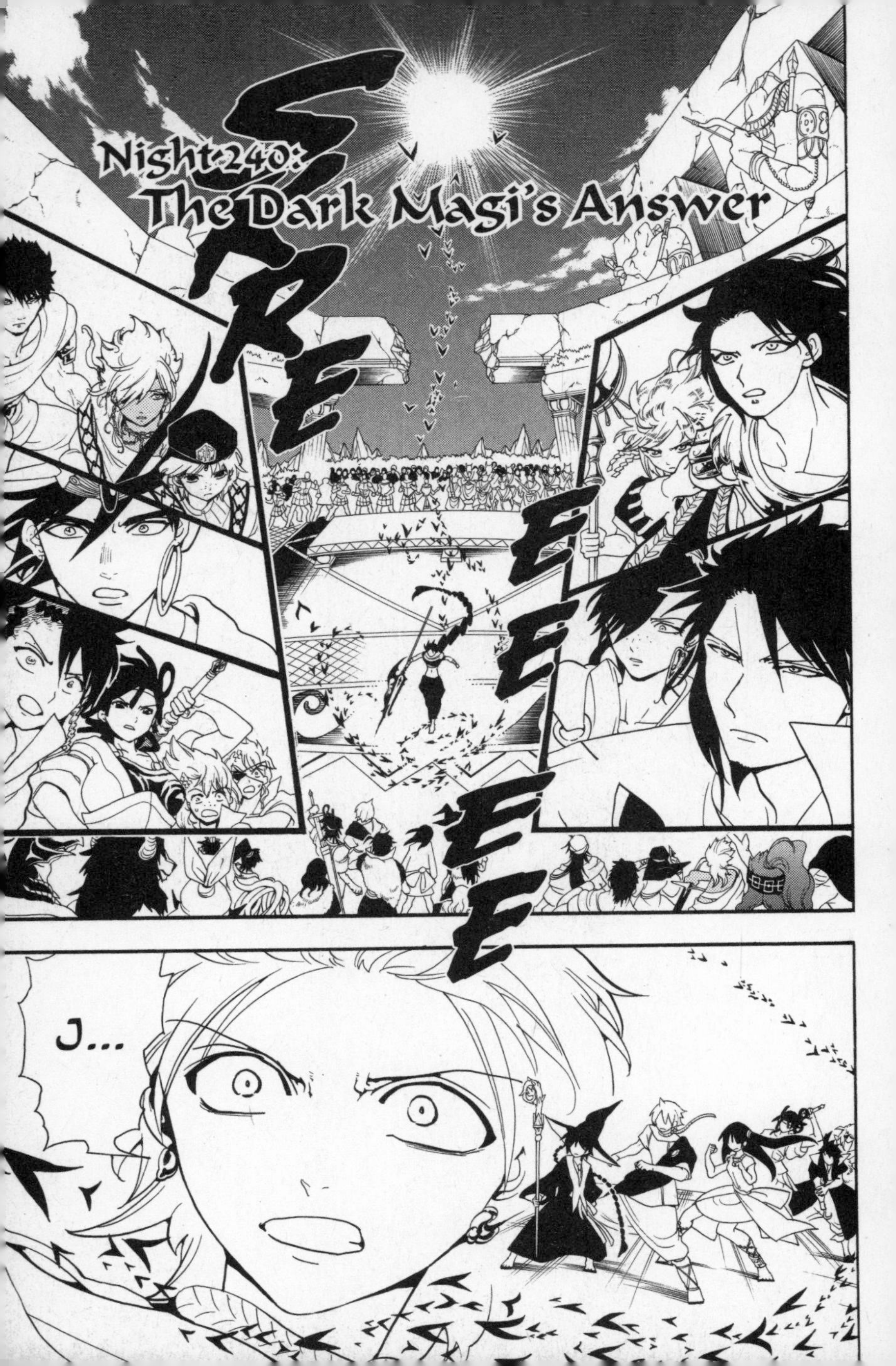
Night 240: The Dark Magi's Answer
SKREEEEEE
J...

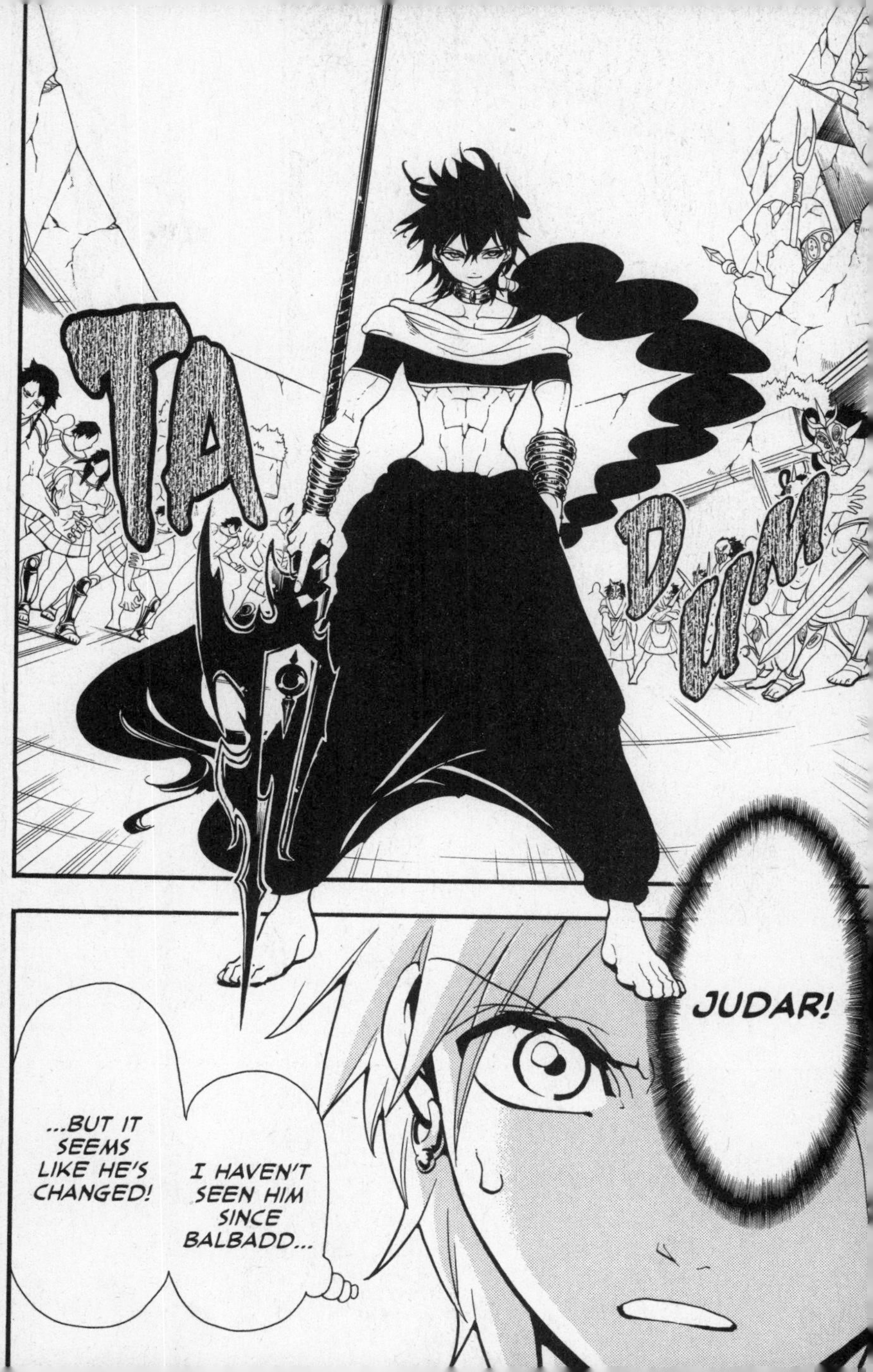
TA
DUM
JUDAR!
I HAVEN'T SEEN HIM SINCE BALBADD...
...BUT IT SEEMS LIKE HE'S CHANGED!

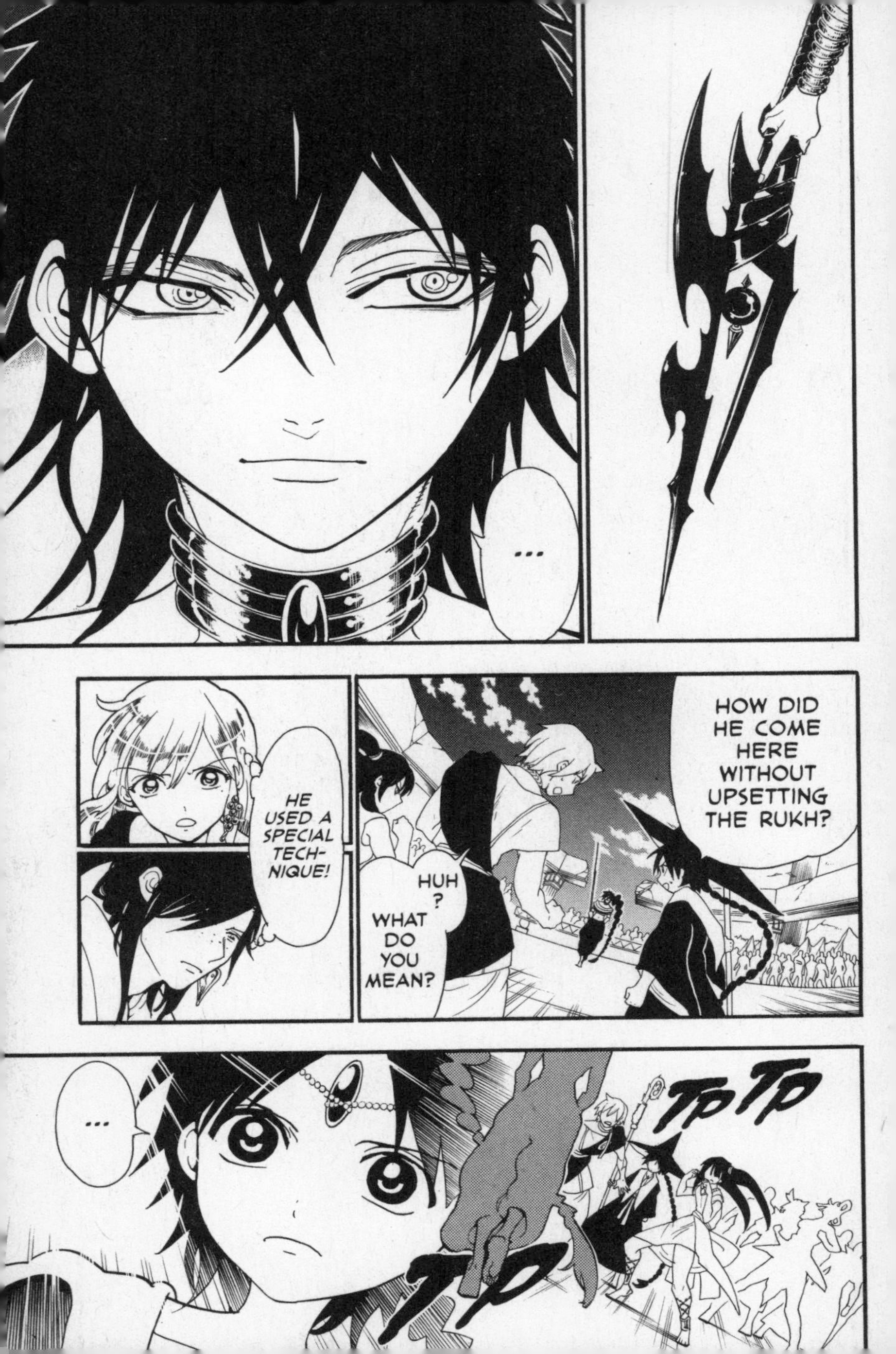
...
HOW DID HE COME HERE WITHOUT UPSETTING THE RUKH?
HUH? WHAT DO YOU MEAN?
HE USED A SPECIAL TECH-NIQUE!
Tp Tp
...

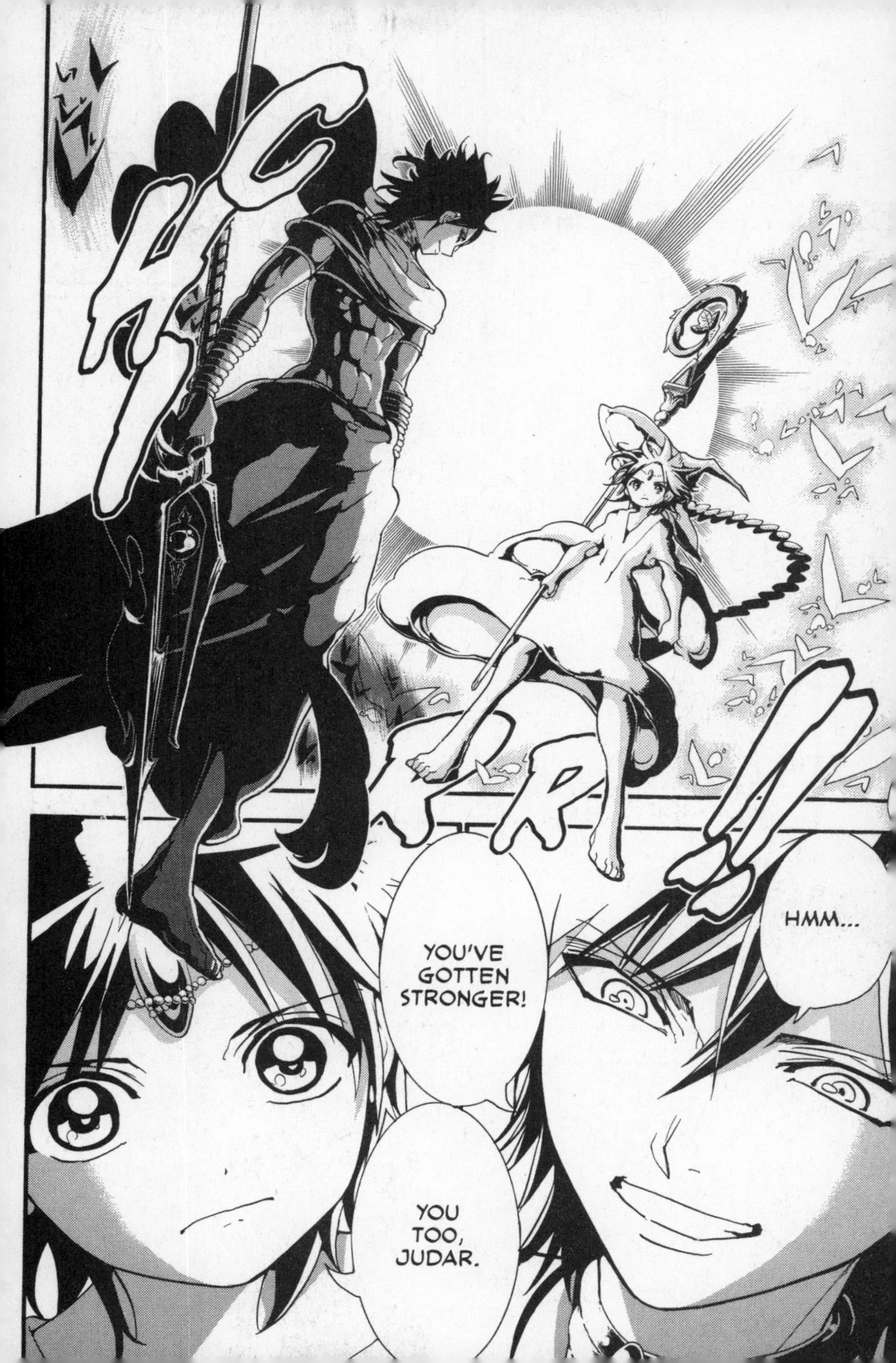
HMM...
YOU'VE GOTTEN STRONGER!
YOU TOO, JUDAR.

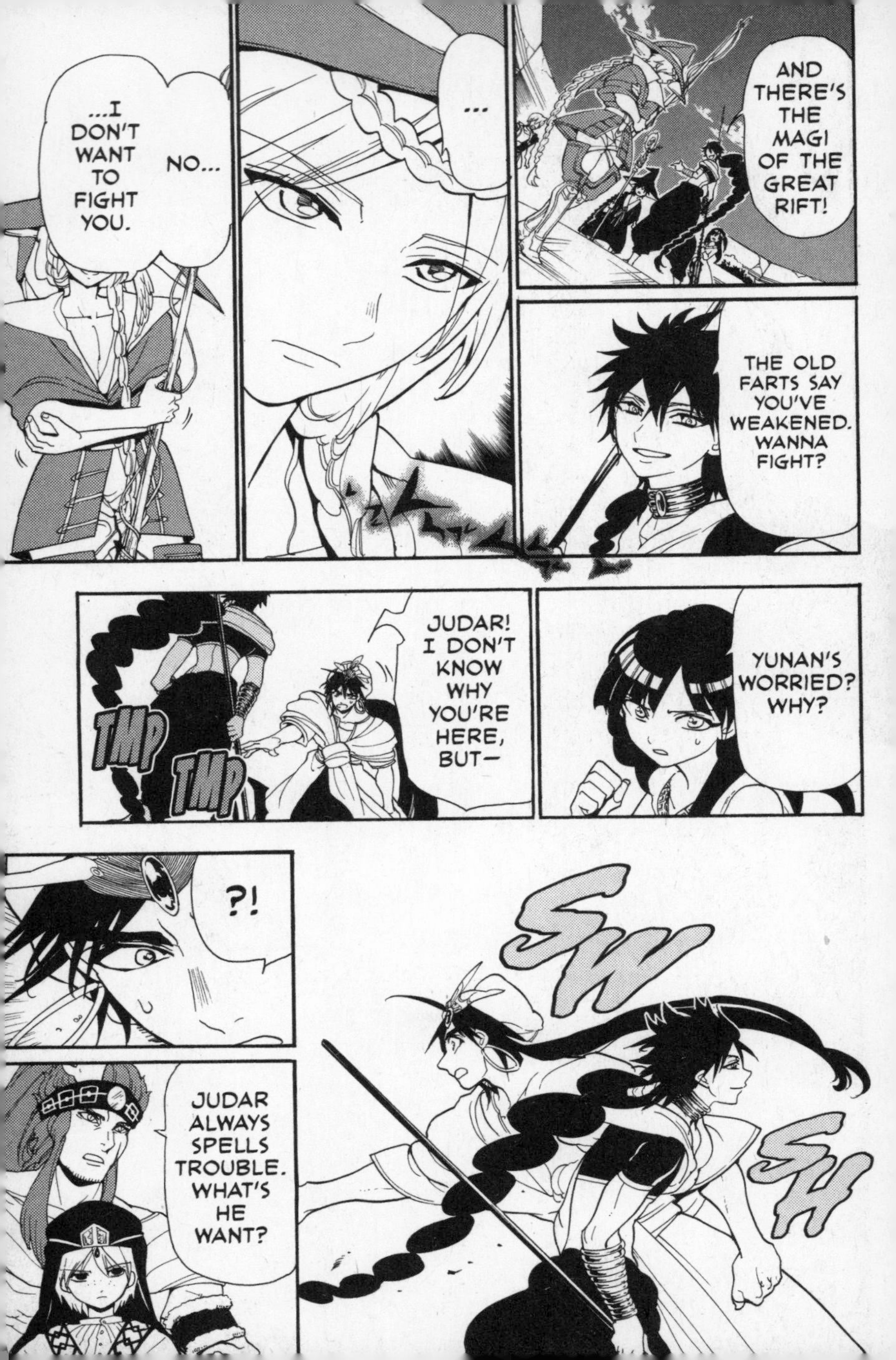
AND THERE'S THE MAGI OF THE GREAT RIFT!
THE OLD FARTS SAY YOU'VE WEAKENED. WANNA FIGHT?
...
NO...
...I DON'T WANT TO FIGHT YOU.
YUNAN'S WORRIED? WHY?
JUDAR! I DON'T KNOW WHY YOU'RE HERE, BUT—
TMP
TMP
SW
SH
?!
JUDAR ALWAYS SPELLS TROUBLE. WHAT'S HE WANT?

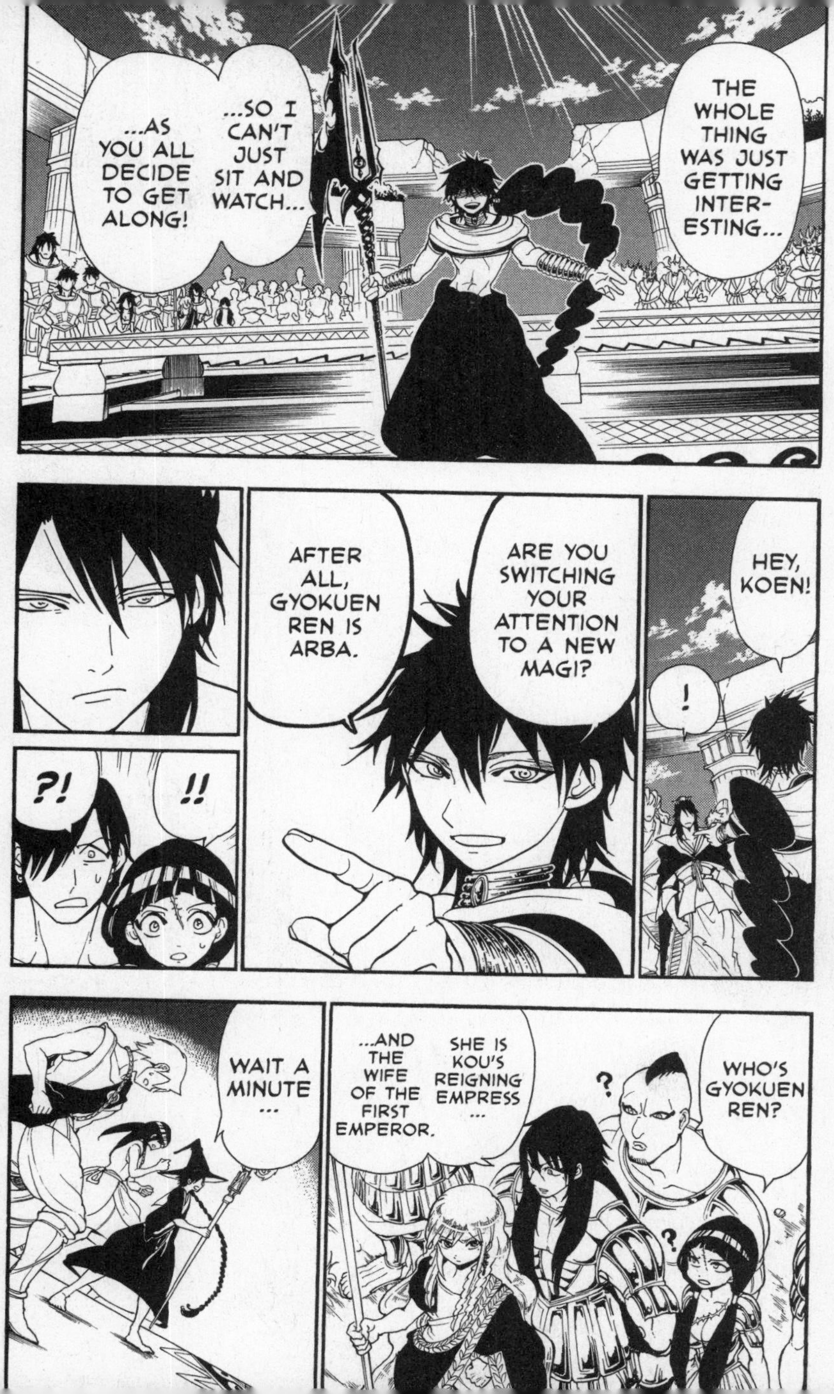
THE WHOLE THING WAS JUST GETTING INTER-ESTING...
...SO I CAN'T JUST SIT AND WATCH...
...AS YOU ALL DECIDE TO GET ALONG!
HEY, KOEN!
!
ARE YOU SWITCHING YOUR ATTENTION TO A NEW MAGI?
AFTER ALL, GYOKUEN REN IS ARBA.
!!
?!
WHO'S GYOKUEN REN?
?
SHE IS KOU'S REIGNING EMPRESS ...
...AND THE WIFE OF THE FIRST EMPEROR.
?
WAIT A MINUTE ...

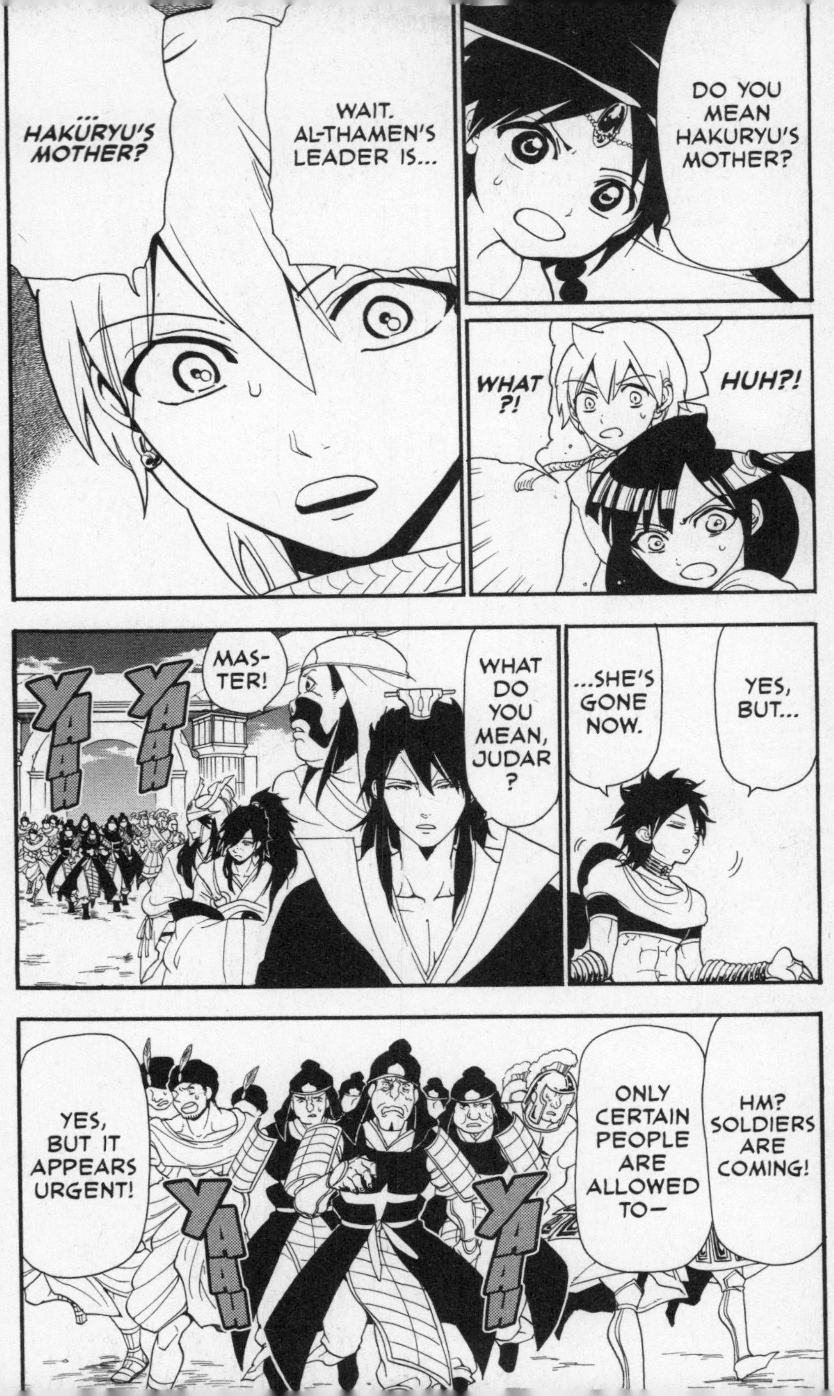

DO YOU MEAN HAKURYU'S MOTHER?
HUH?!
WHAT?!
WAIT. AL-THAMEN'S LEADER IS...
...HAKÜRYU'S MOTHER?
YES, BUT...
...SHE'S GONE NOW.
WHAT DO YOU MEAN, JUDAR?
MASTER!
YAAAH
YAAAH
HM? SOLDIERS ARE COMING!
ONLY CERTAIN PEOPLE ARE ALLOWED TO—
YAAAH
YES, BUT IT APPEARS URGENT!
YAAAH

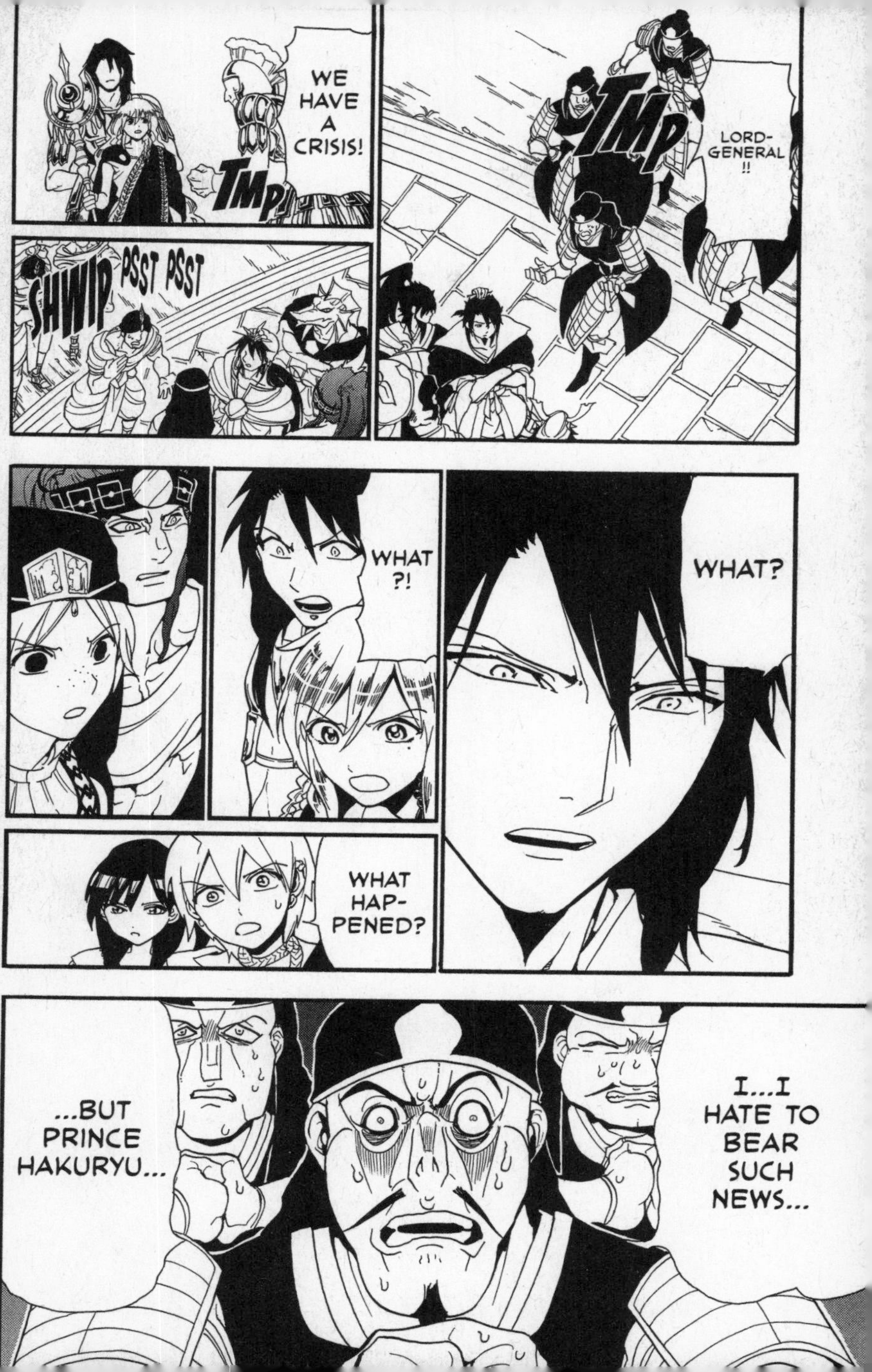

TMP
LORD-GENERAL !!
WE HAVE A CRISIS!
TMP
PSST PSST
SHWIP
WHAT?
WHAT ?!
WHAT HAPPENED?
I...I HATE TO BEAR SUCH NEWS...
...BUT PRINCE HAKURYU...

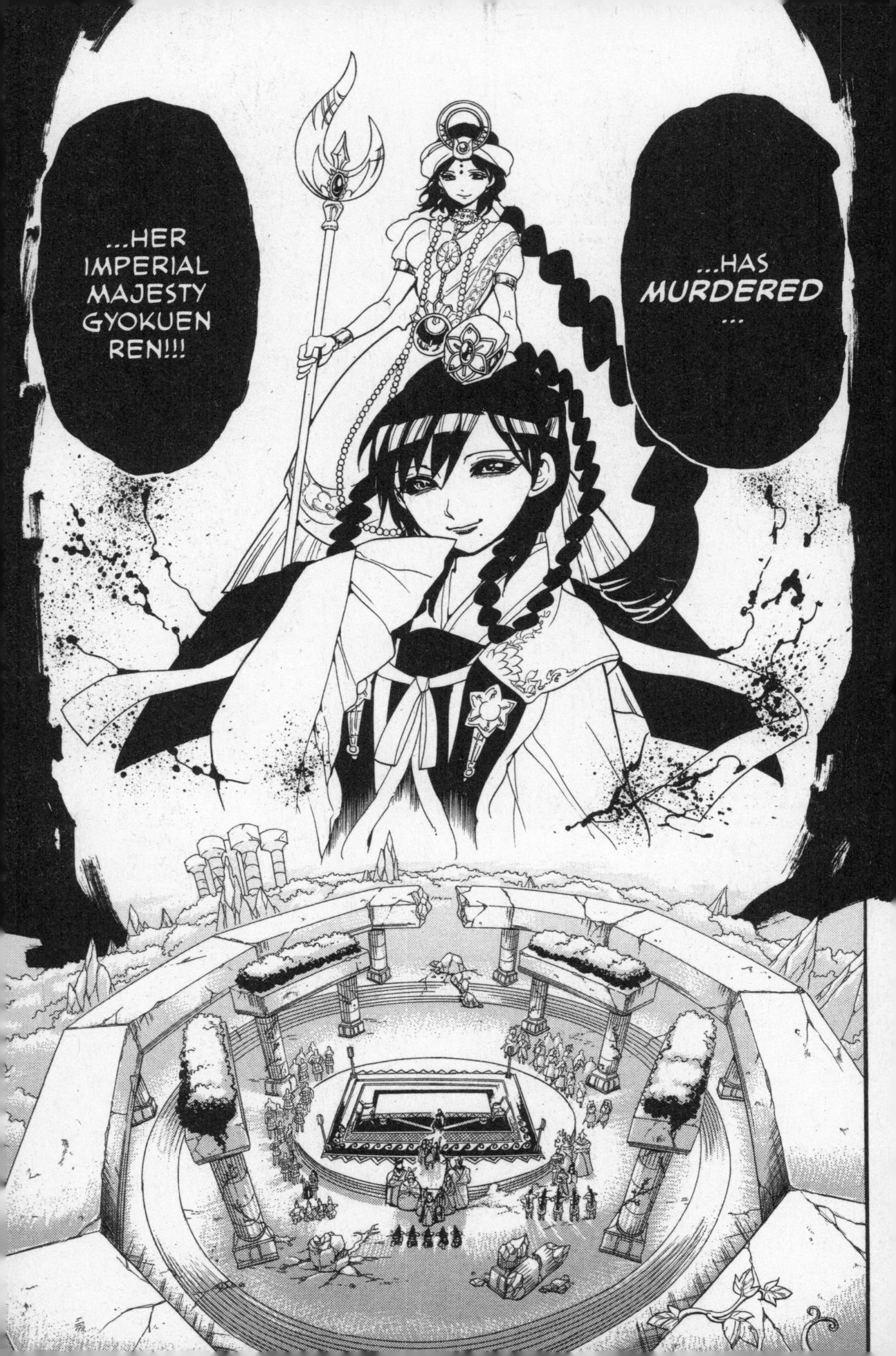
...HAS MURDERED ...
...HER IMPERIAL MAJESTY GYOKUEN REN!!!

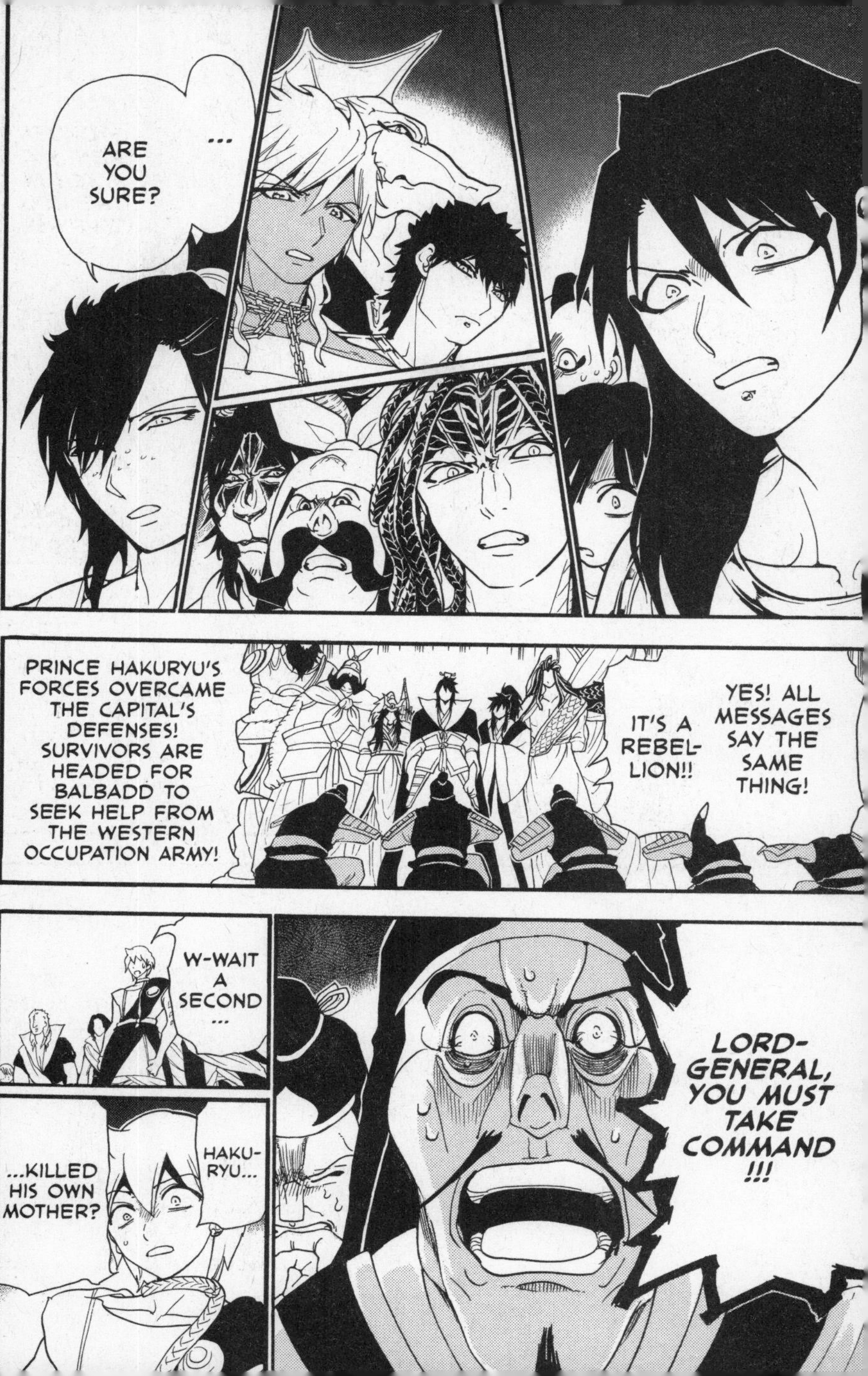
...
ARE YOU SURE?
YES! ALL MESSAGES SAY THE SAME THING!
IT'S A REBEL-LION!!
PRINCE HAKURYU'S FORCES OVERCAME THE CAPITAL'S DEFENSES! SURVIVORS ARE HEADED FOR BALBADD TO SEEK HELP FROM THE WESTERN OCCUPATION ARMY!
LORD-GENERAL, YOU MUST TAKE COMMAND!!!
W-WAIT A SECOND...
HAKU-RYU...
...KILLED HIS OWN MOTHER?

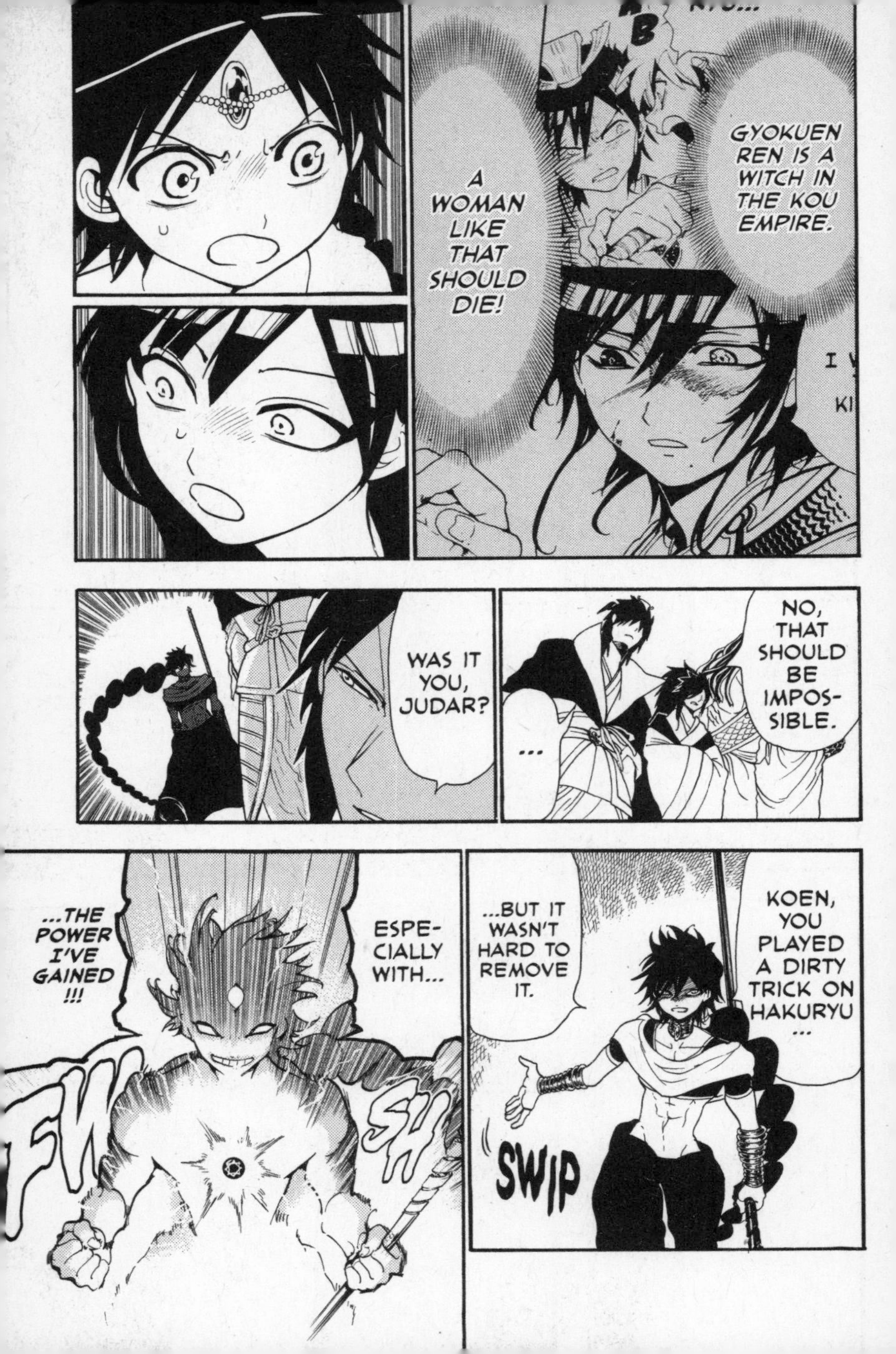
GYOKUEN REN IS A WITCH IN THE KOU EMPIRE.
A WOMAN LIKE THAT SHOULD DIE!
NO, THAT SHOULD BE IMPOSSIBLE.
...
WAS IT YOU, JUDAR?
KOEN, YOU PLAYED A DIRTY TRICK ON HAKURYU ...
...BUT IT WASN'T HARD TO REMOVE IT.
SWIP
ESPE-CIALLY WITH...
...THE POWER I'VE GAINED !!!
FWSH

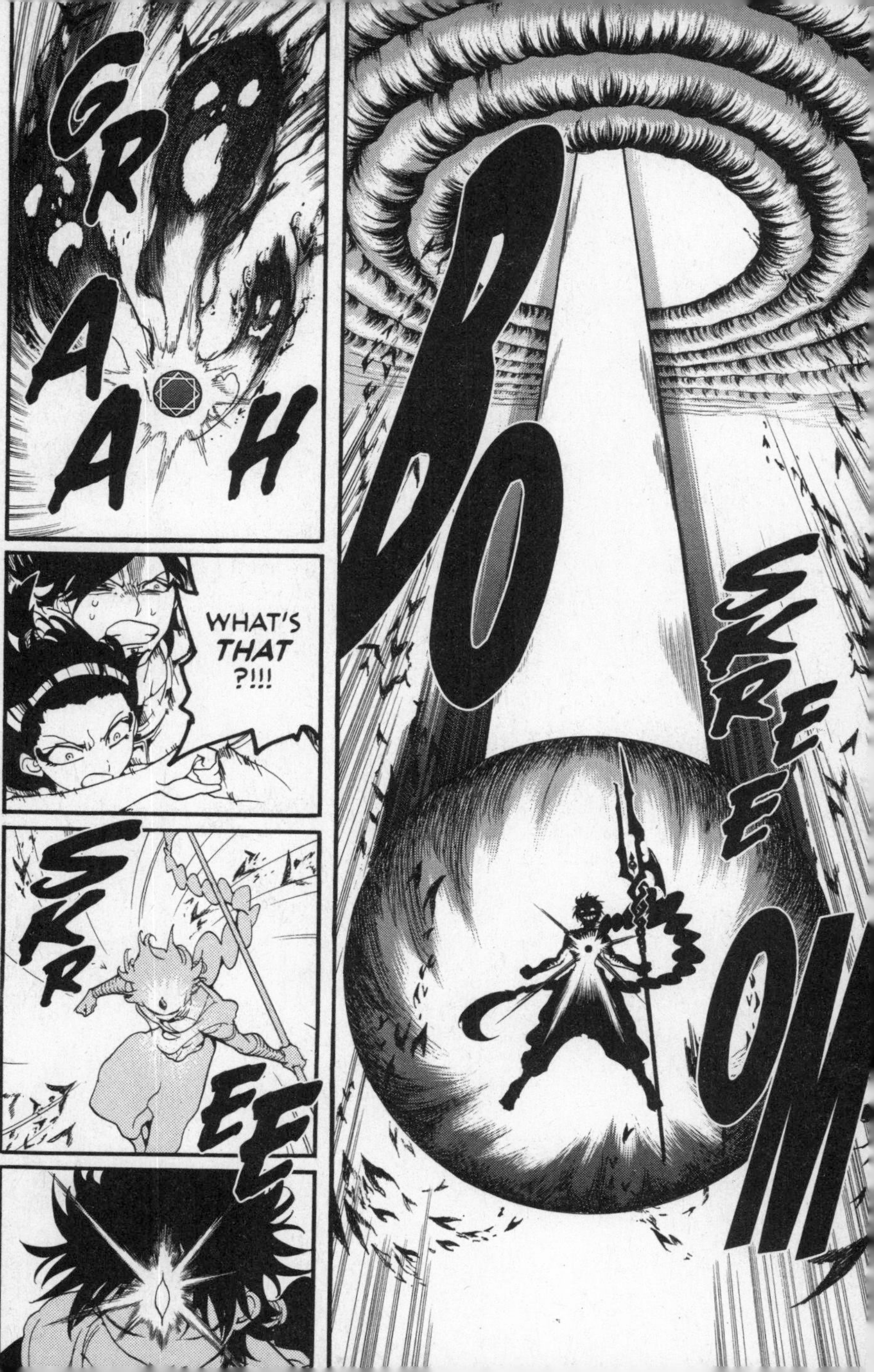
SKREEE
GROAAH
WHAT'S THAT?!!!
SKREE

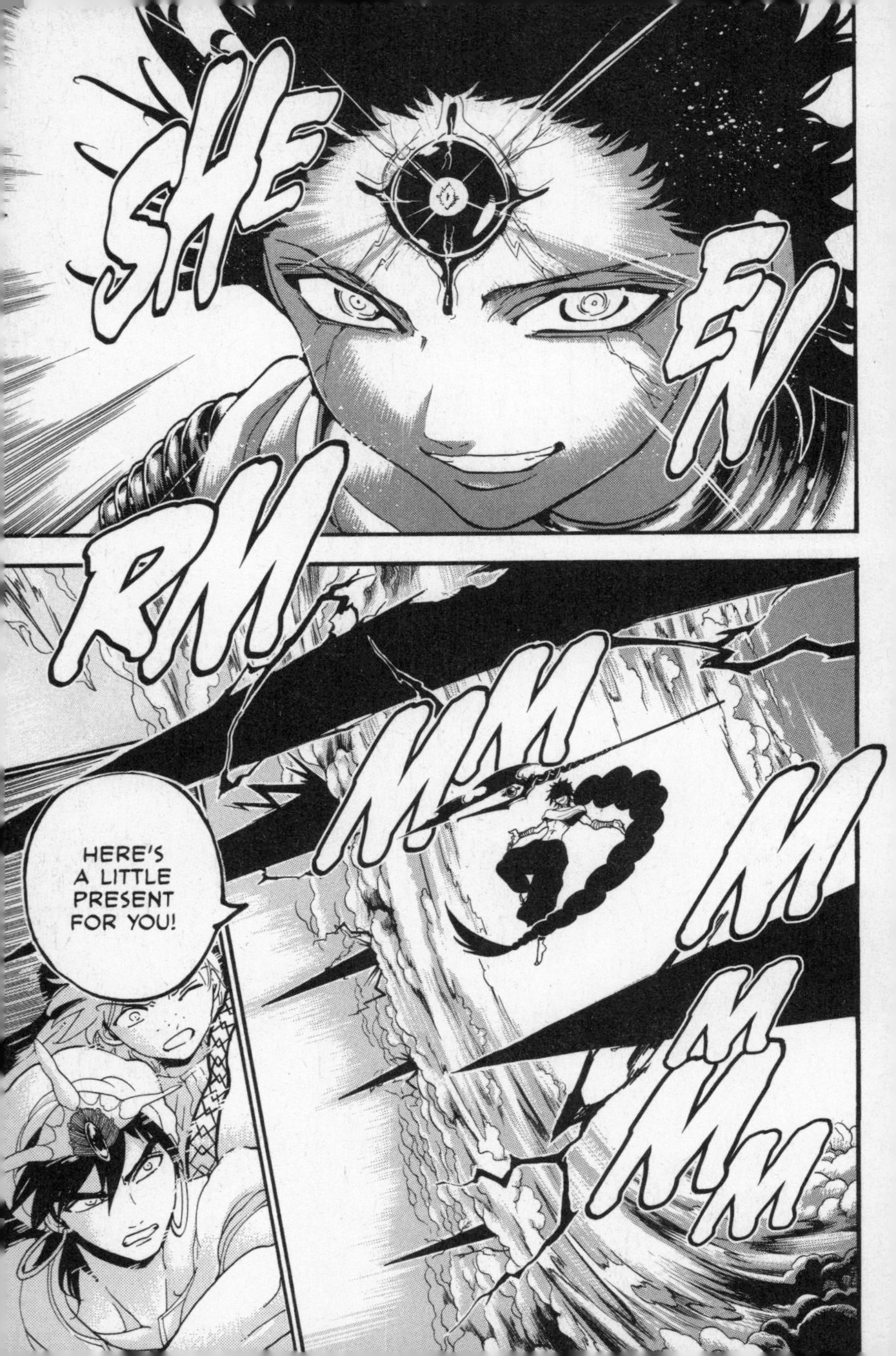
HERE'S A LITTLE PRESENT FOR YOU!

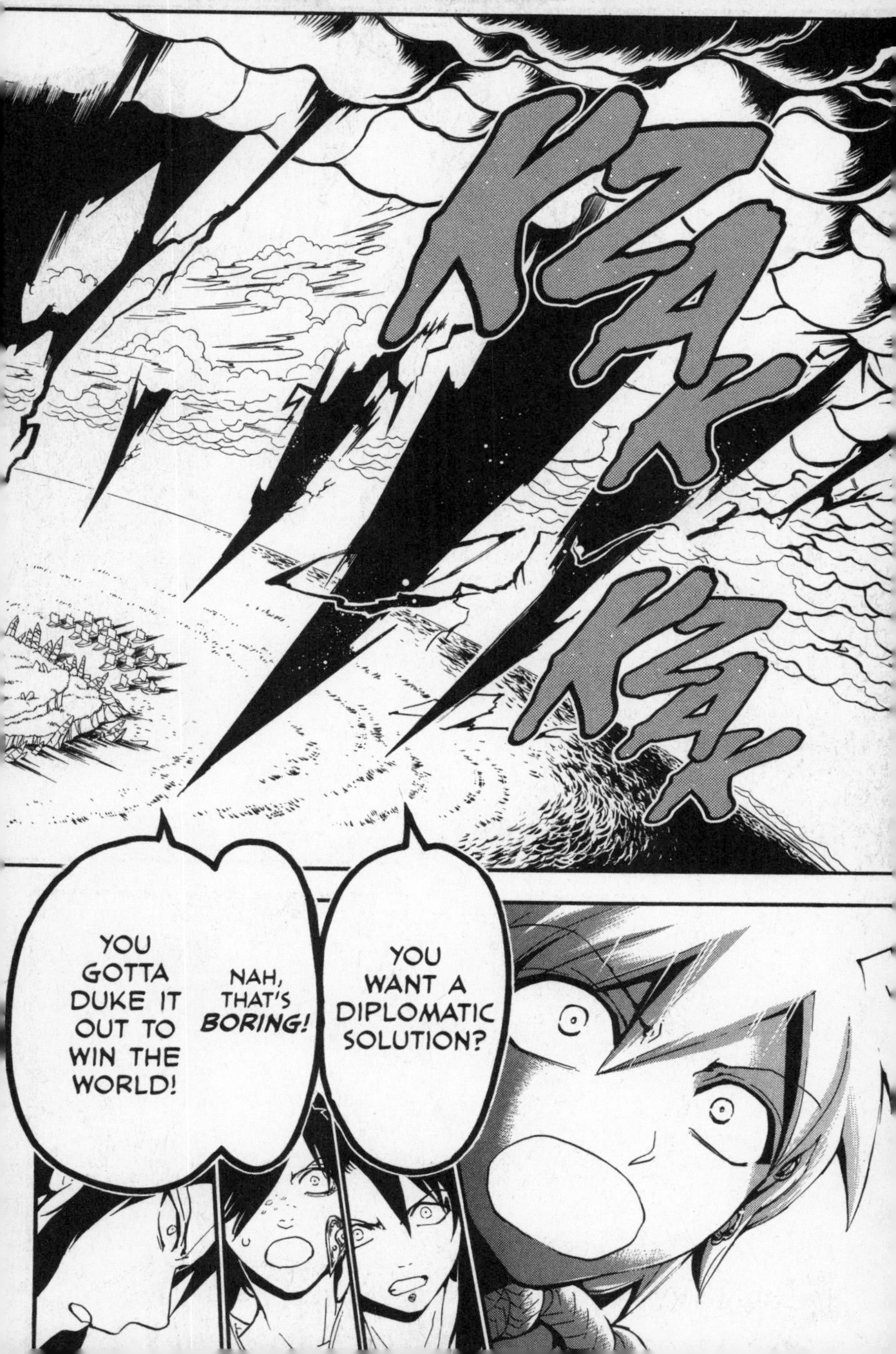
YOU WANT A DIPLOMATIC SOLUTION?
NAH, THAT'S *BORING!*
YOU GOTTA DUKE IT OUT TO WIN THE WORLD!

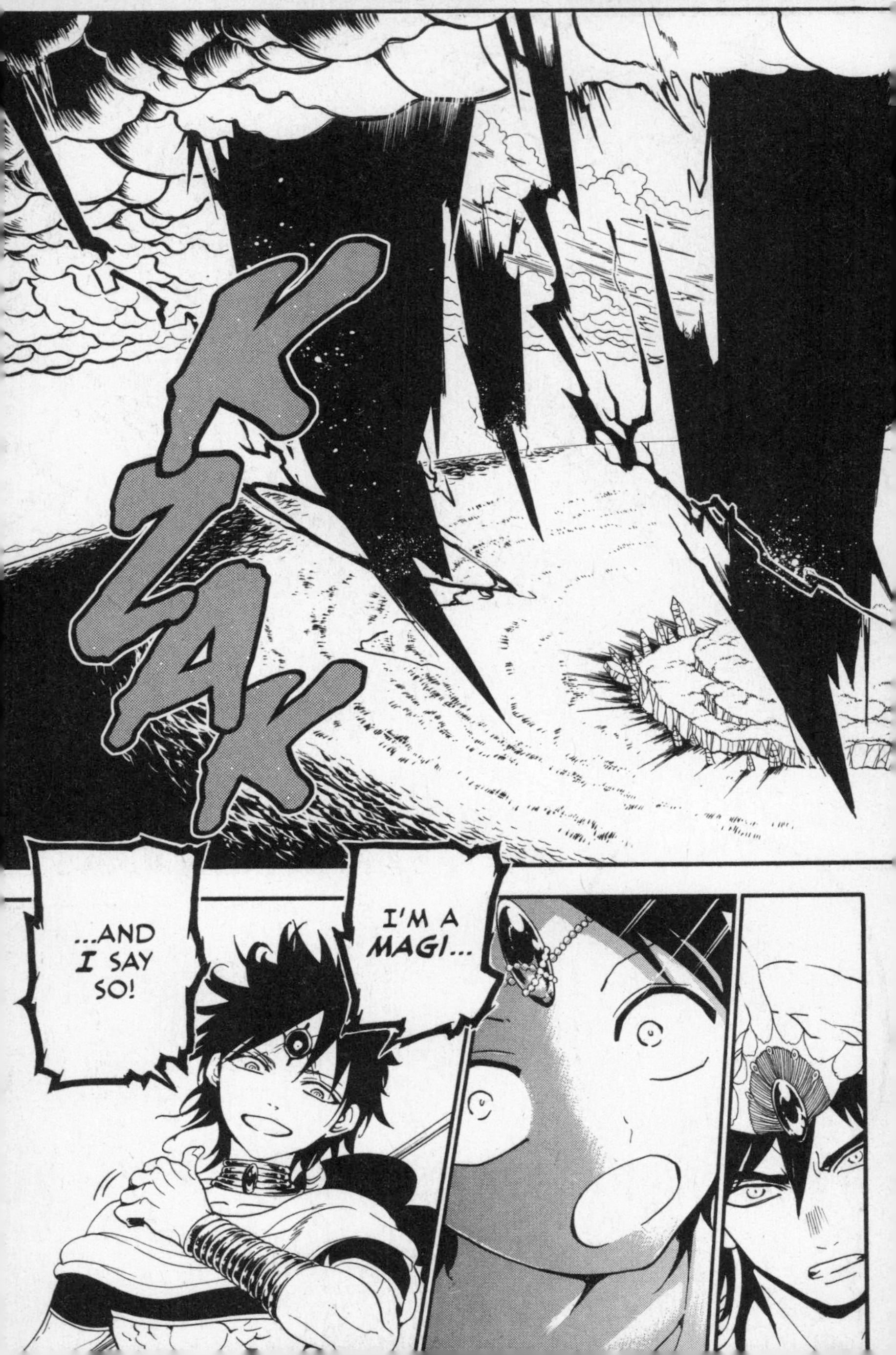
I'M A MAGI...
...AND I SAY SO!

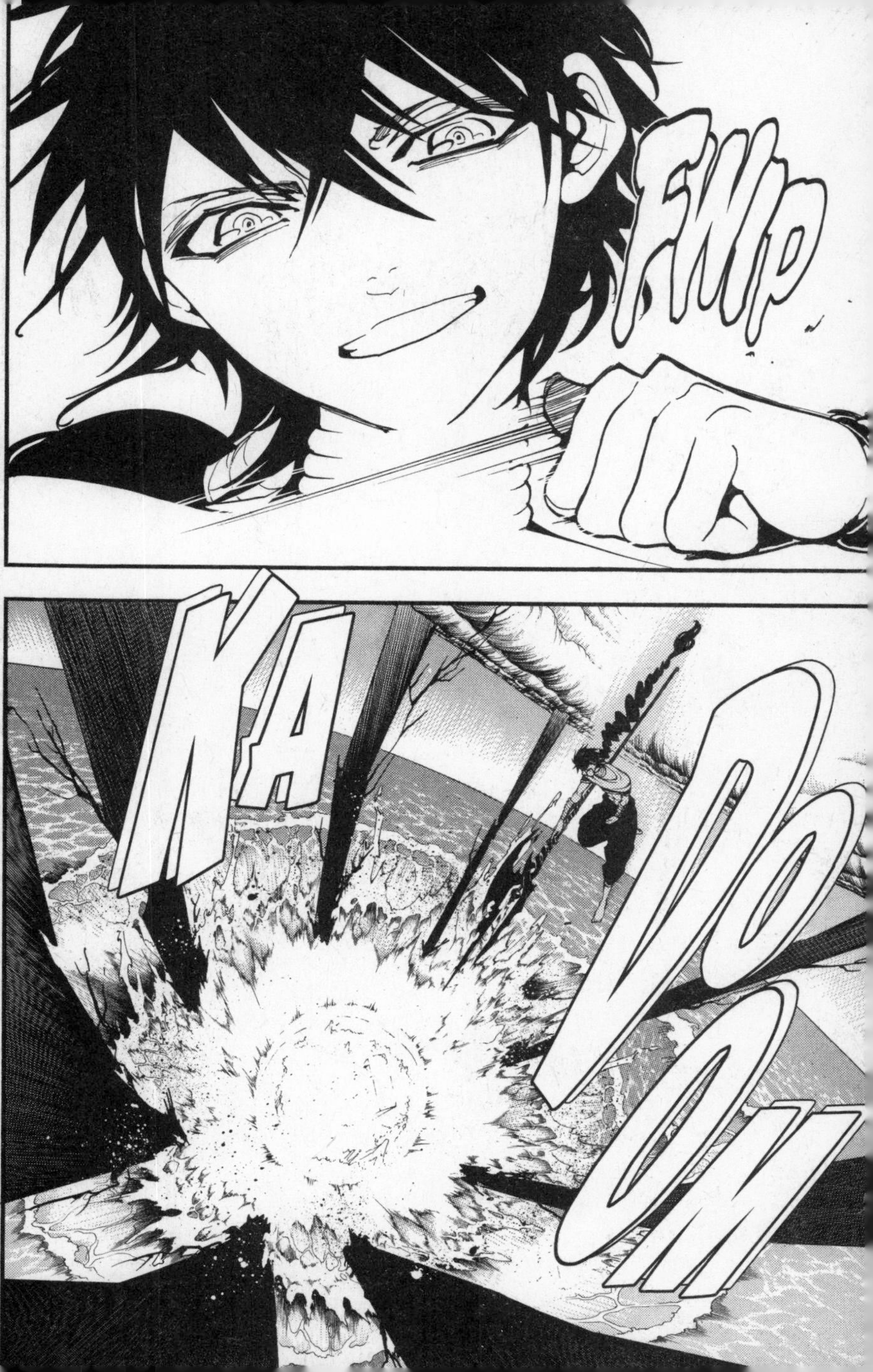
FWIP
KABOOM

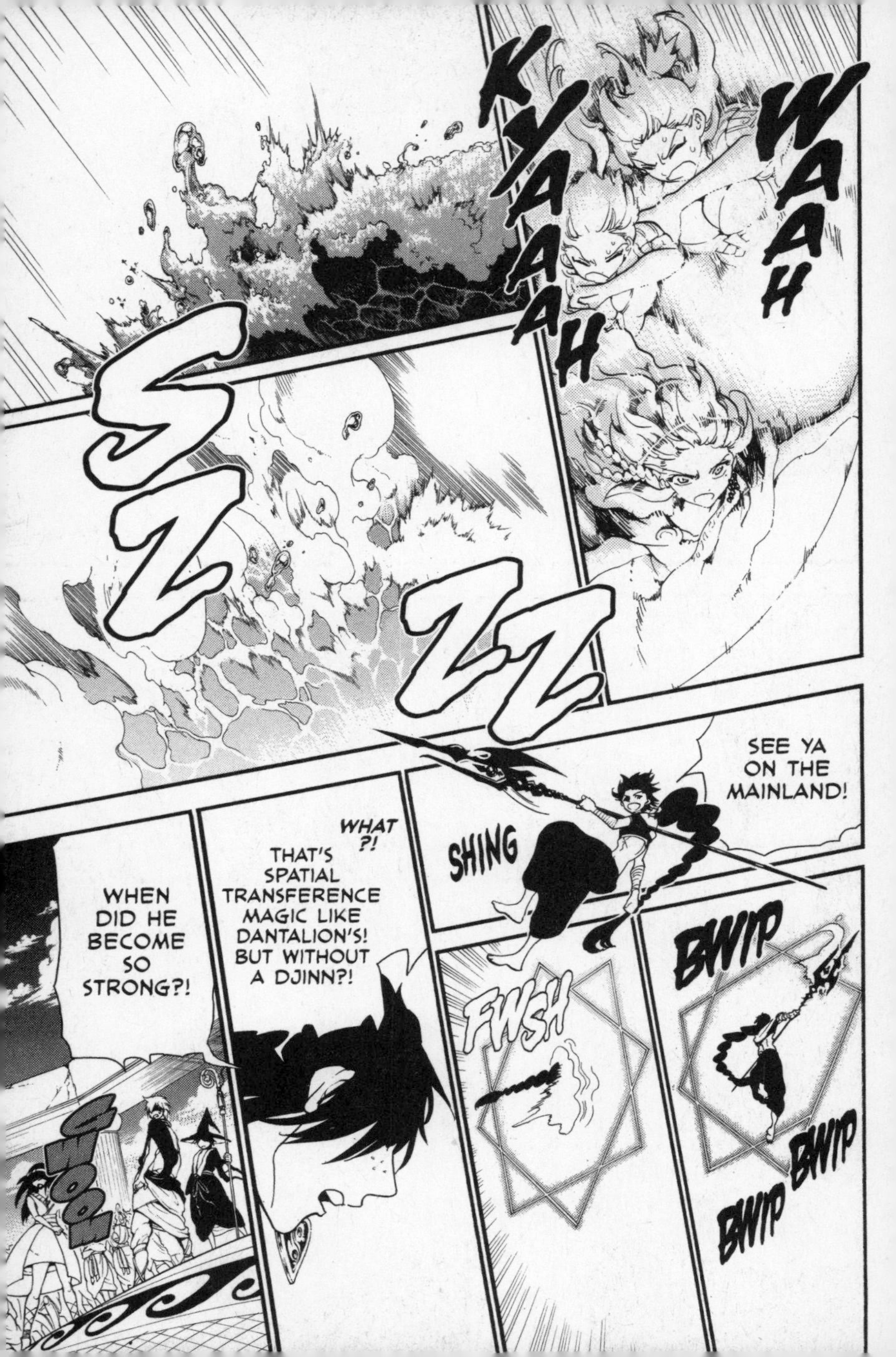
WAAH
KYAAAH
SZZZ
SEE YA ON THE MAINLAND!
SHING
BWIP
BWIP
BWIP
FWSH
WHAT?!
THAT'S SPATIAL TRANSFERENCE MAGIC LIKE DANTALION'S! BUT WITHOUT A DJINN?!
WHEN DID HE BECOME SO STRONG?!
WHOOOM

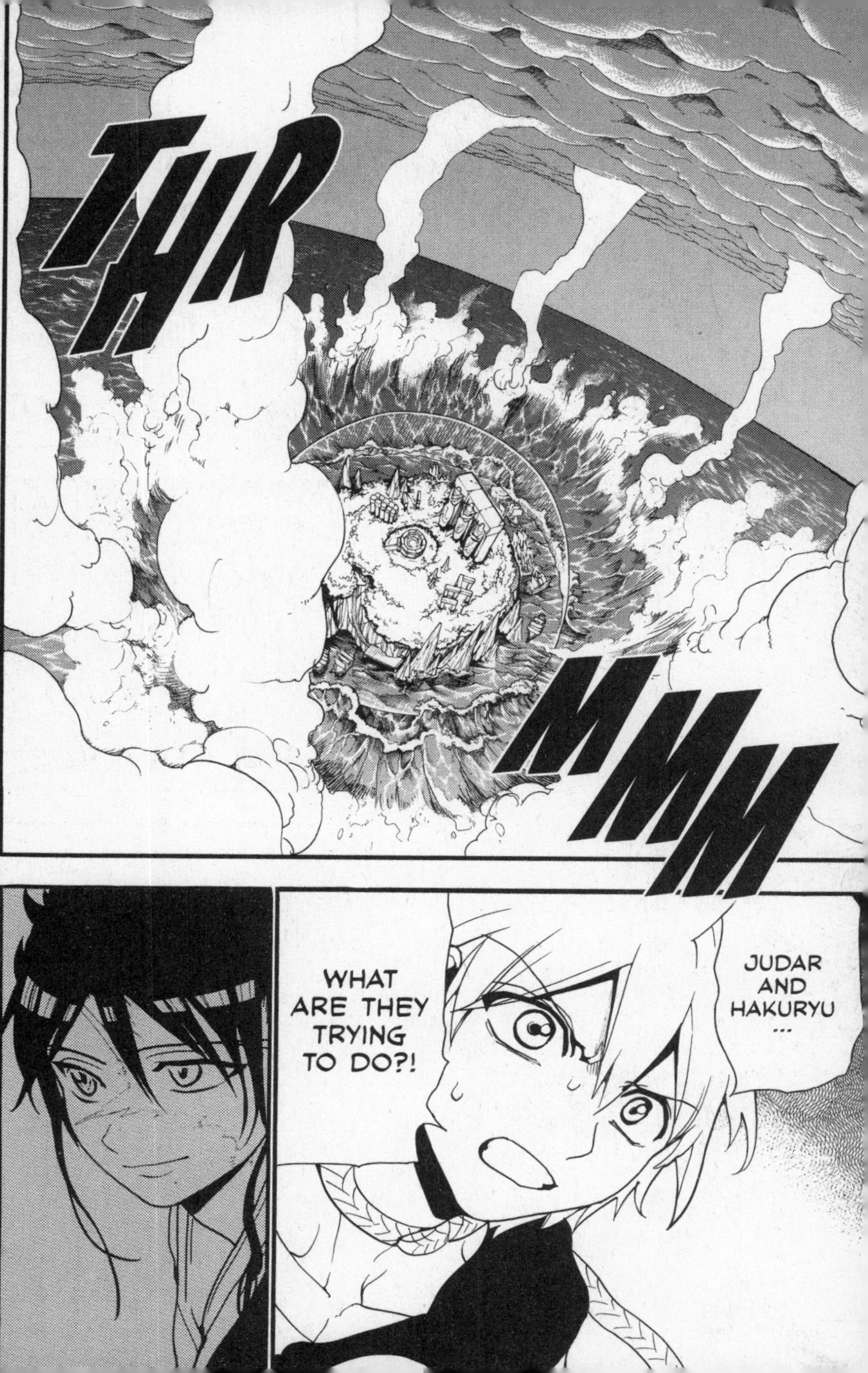
THRMMM
JUDAR AND HAKURYU ...
WHAT ARE THEY TRYING TO DO?!

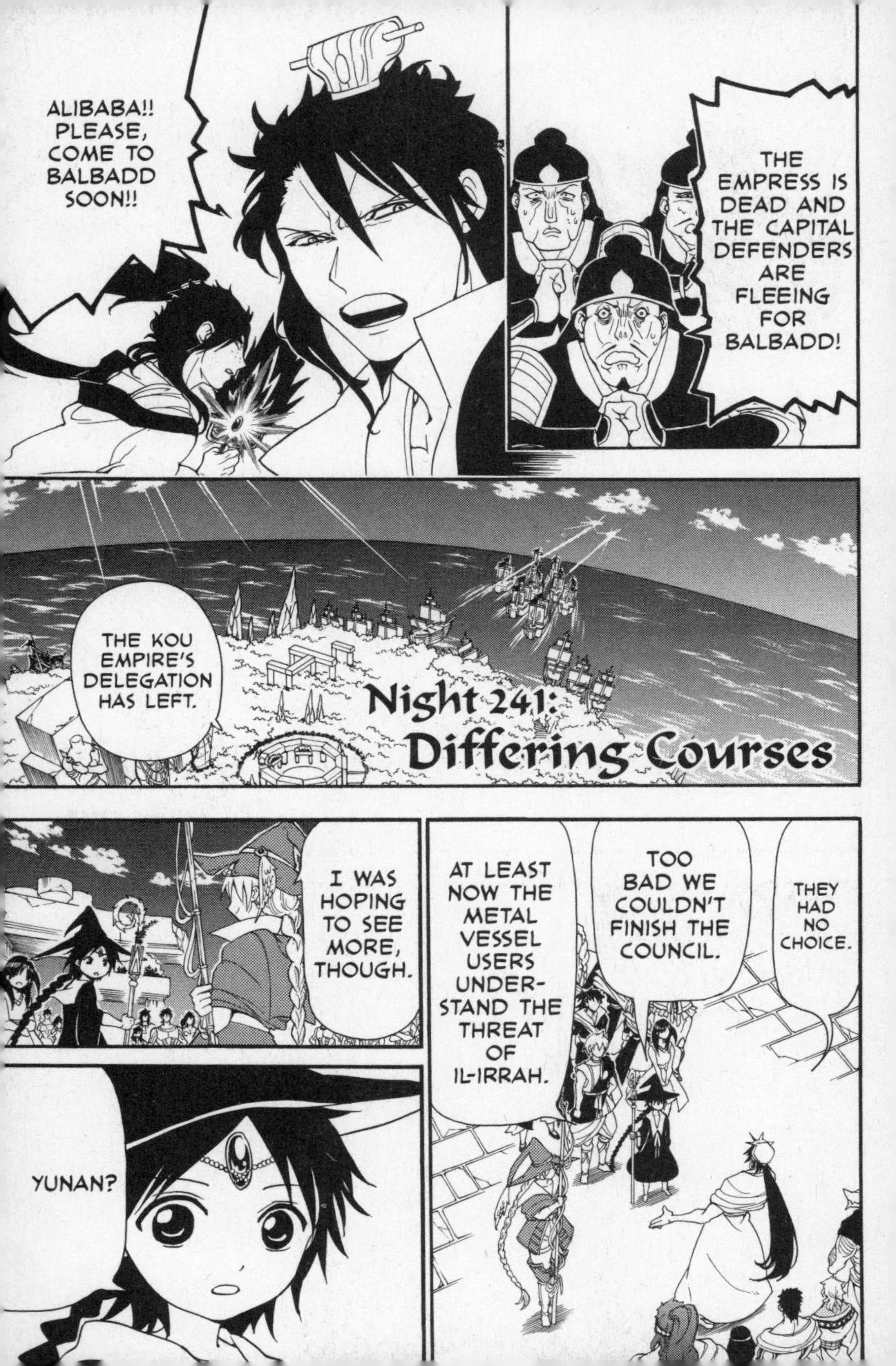
THE EMPRESS IS DEAD AND THE CAPITAL DEFENDERS ARE FLEEING FOR BALBADD!
ALIBABA!! PLEASE, COME TO BALBADD SOON!!
THE KOU EMPIRE'S DELEGATION HAS LEFT.
Night 241: Differing Courses
THEY HAD NO CHOICE.
TOO BAD WE COULDN'T FINISH THE COUNCIL.
AT LEAST NOW THE METAL VESSEL USERS UNDER-STAND THE THREAT OF IL-IRRAH.
I WAS HOPING TO SEE MORE, THOUGH.
YUNAN?

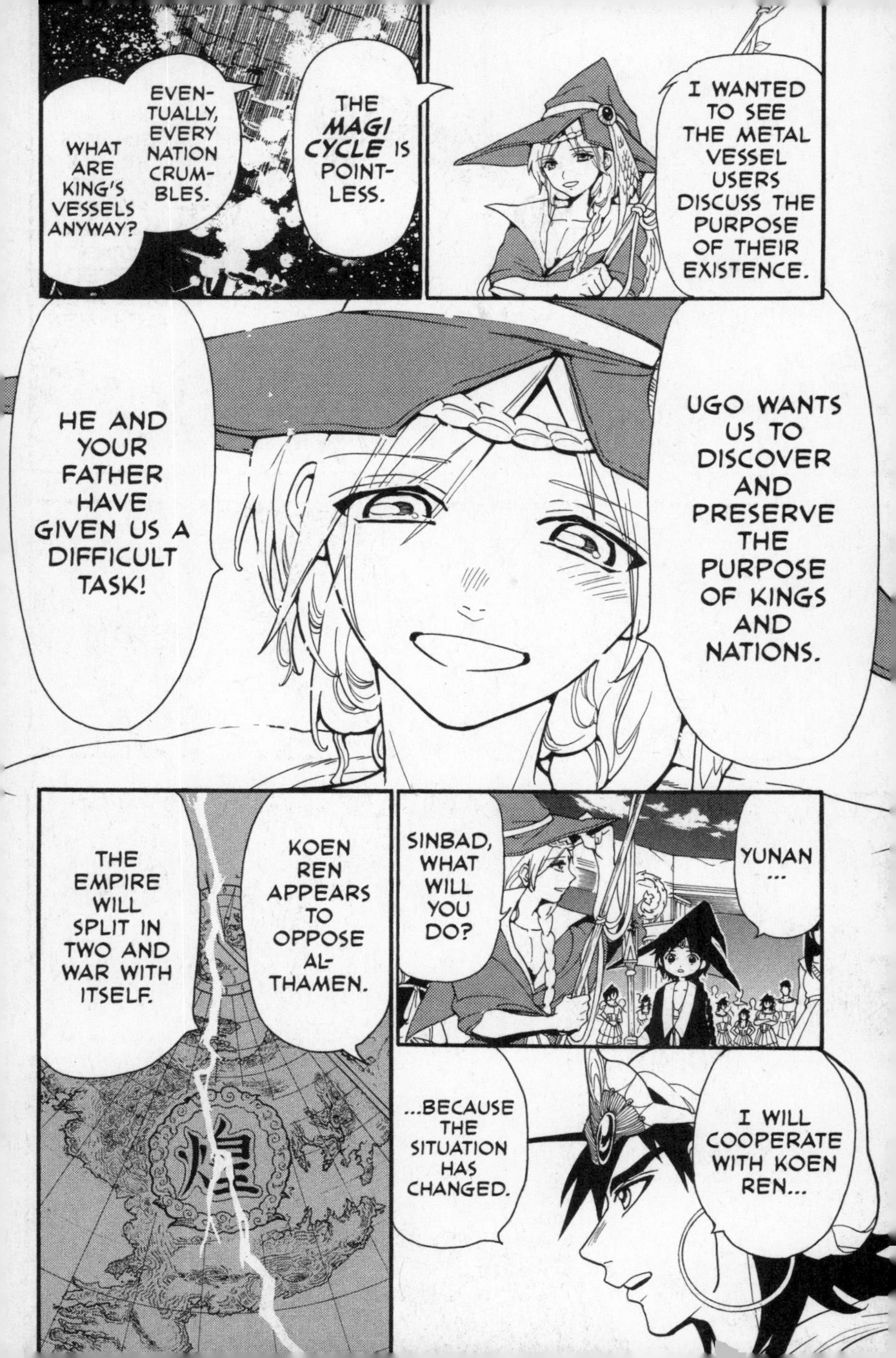
I WANTED TO SEE THE METAL VESSEL USERS DISCUSS THE PURPOSE OF THEIR EXISTENCE.
THE *MAGI CYCLE* IS POINTLESS.
EVENTUALLY, EVERY NATION CRUMBLES.
WHAT ARE KING'S VESSELS ANYWAY?
UGO WANTS US TO DISCOVER AND PRESERVE THE PURPOSE OF KINGS AND NATIONS.
HE AND YOUR FATHER HAVE GIVEN US A DIFFICULT TASK!
YUNAN...
SINBAD, WHAT WILL YOU DO?
I WILL COOPERATE WITH KOEN REN...
...BECAUSE THE SITUATION HAS CHANGED.
KOEN REN APPEARS TO OPPOSE AL-THAMEN.
THE EMPIRE WILL SPLIT IN TWO AND WAR WITH ITSELF.
煌

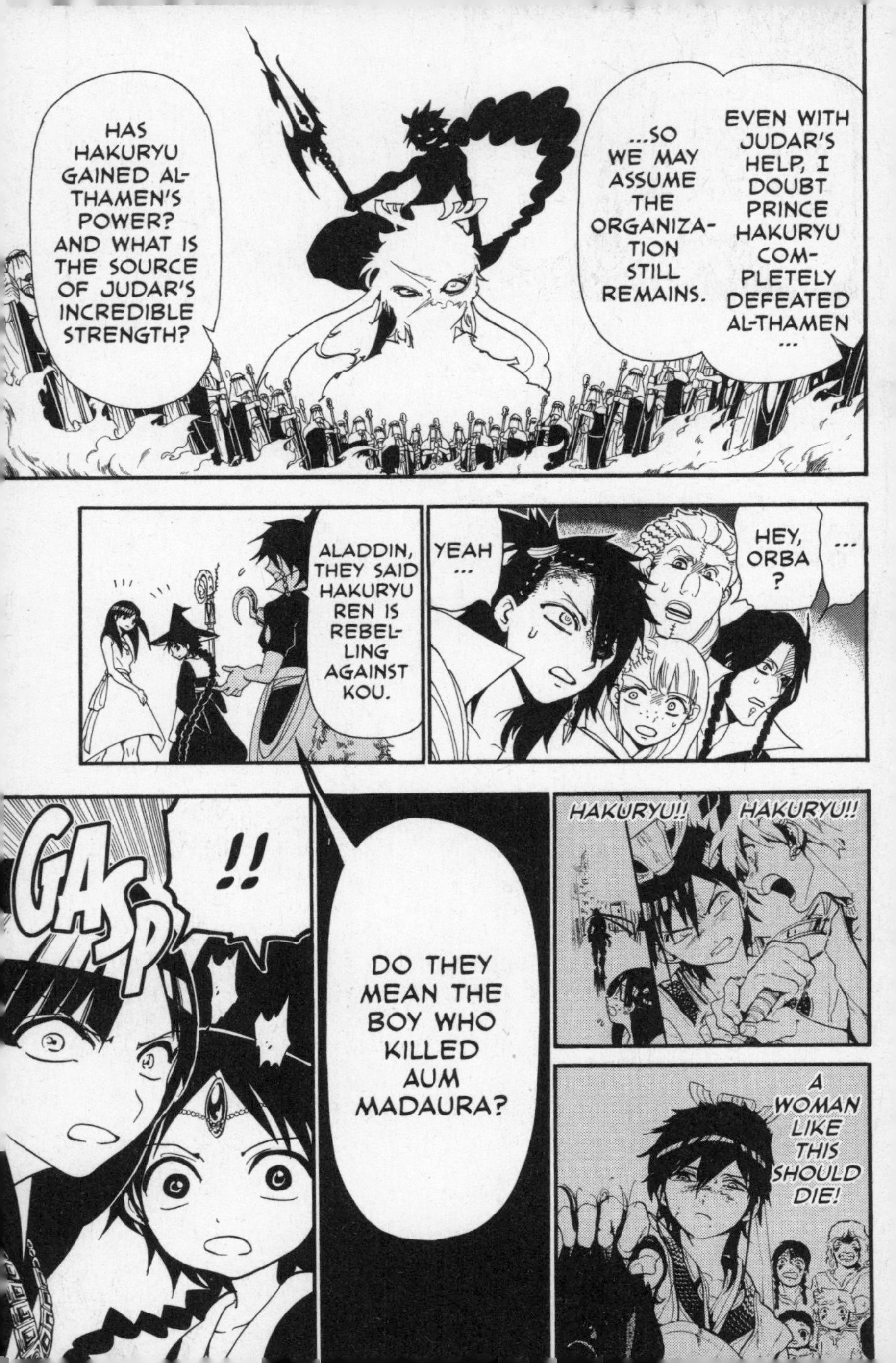
EVEN WITH JUDAR'S HELP, I DOUBT PRINCE HAKURYU COMPLETELY DEFEATED AL-THAMEN...
...SO WE MAY ASSUME THE ORGANIZATION STILL REMAINS.
HAS HAKURYU GAINED AL-THAMEN'S POWER? AND WHAT IS THE SOURCE OF JUDAR'S INCREDIBLE STRENGTH?
...
HEY, ORBA?
YEAH...
ALADDIN, THEY SAID HAKURYU REN IS REBELLING AGAINST KOU.
HAKURYU!!
HAKURYU!!
A WOMAN LIKE THIS SHOULD DIE!
DO THEY MEAN THE BOY WHO KILLED AUM MADAURA?
GASP!!

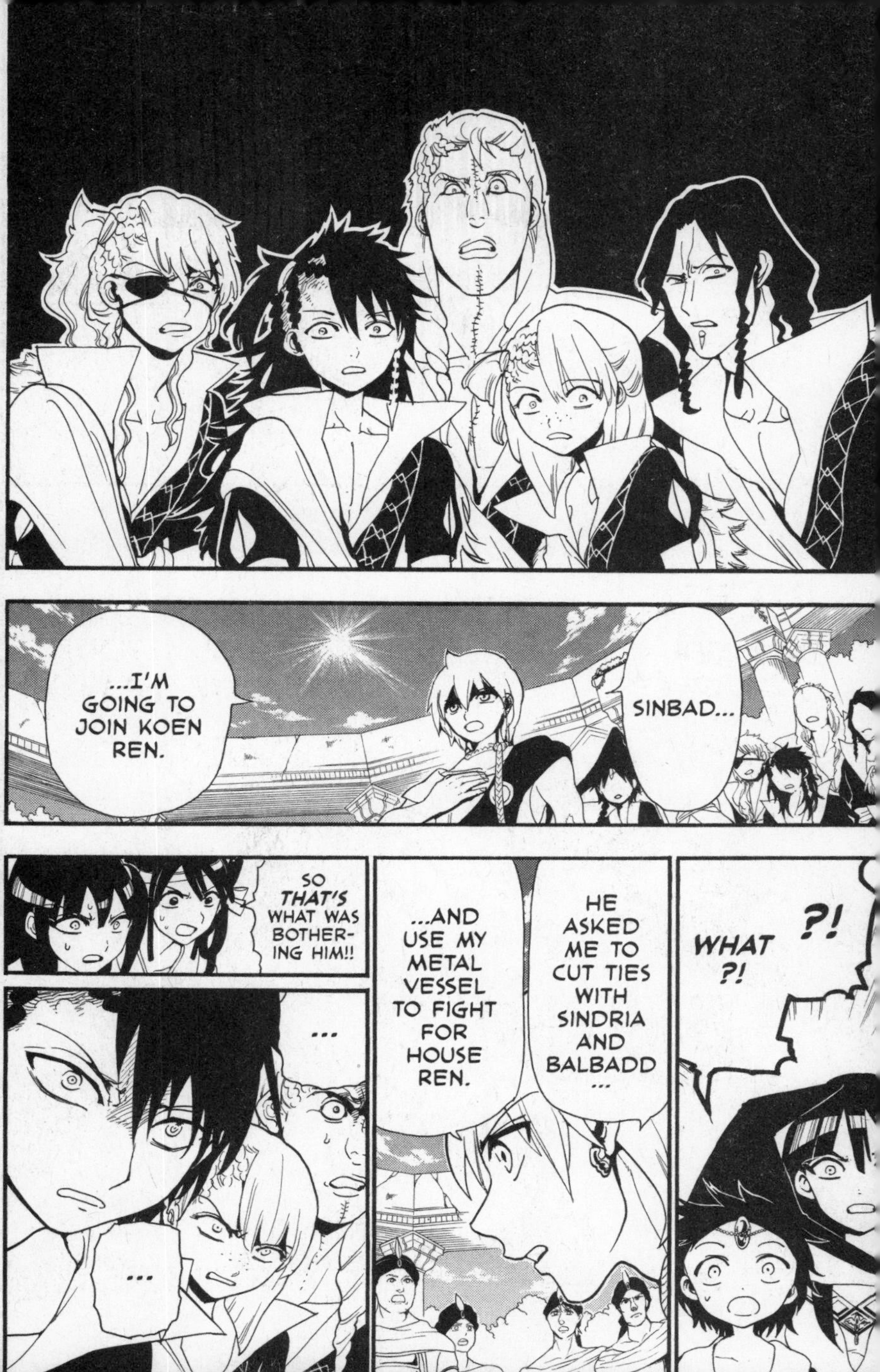
SINBAD...
...I'M GOING TO JOIN KOEN REN.
WHAT ?!
?!
HE ASKED ME TO CUT TIES WITH SINDRIA AND BALBADD ...
...AND USE MY METAL VESSEL TO FIGHT FOR HOUSE REN.
SO *THAT'S* WHAT WAS BOTHERING HIM!!
...
...

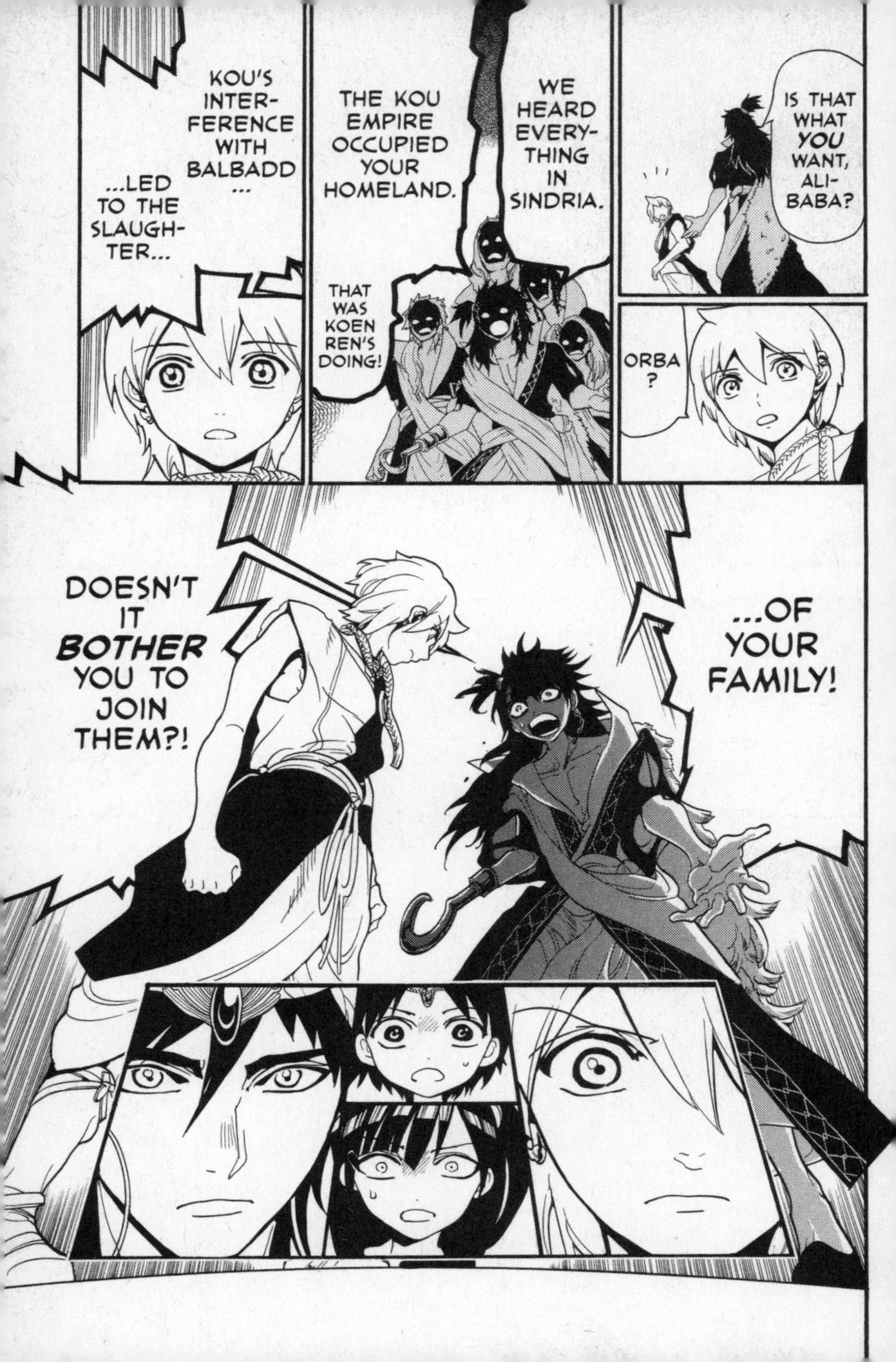
IS THAT WHAT YOU WANT, ALI-BABA?
ORBA?
WE HEARD EVERYTHING IN SINDRIA.
THE KOU EMPIRE OCCUPIED YOUR HOMELAND.
THAT WAS KOEN REN'S DOING!
KOU'S INTERFERENCE WITH BALBADD...
...LED TO THE SLAUGHTER...
...OF YOUR FAMILY!
DOESN'T IT BOTHER YOU TO JOIN THEM?!

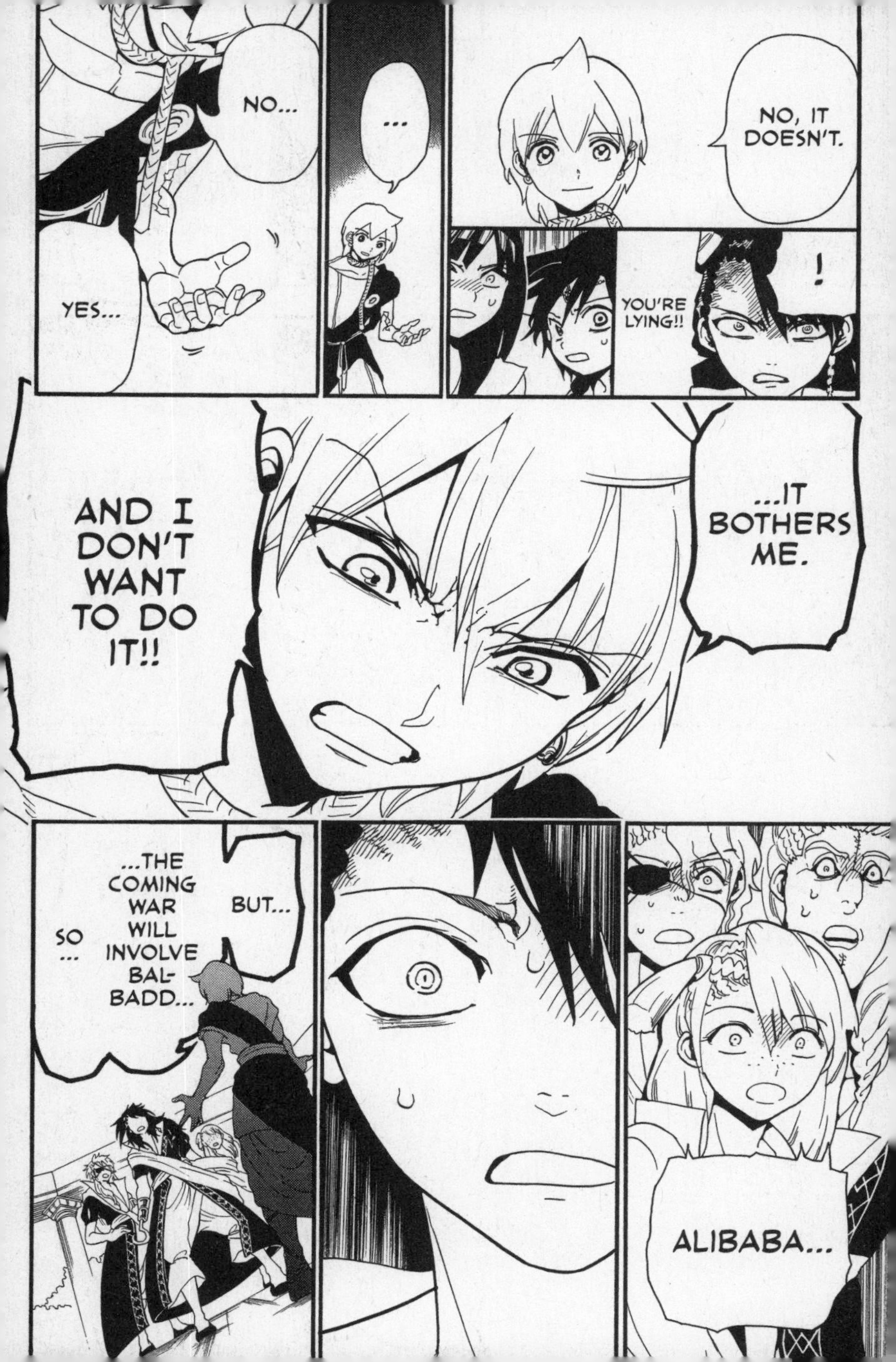
NO, IT DOESN'T.
!
YOU'RE LYING!!
...
NO...
YES...
...IT BOTHERS ME.
AND I DON'T WANT TO DO IT!!
ALIBABA...
BUT...
...THE COMING WAR WILL INVOLVE BAL-BADD...
SO ...

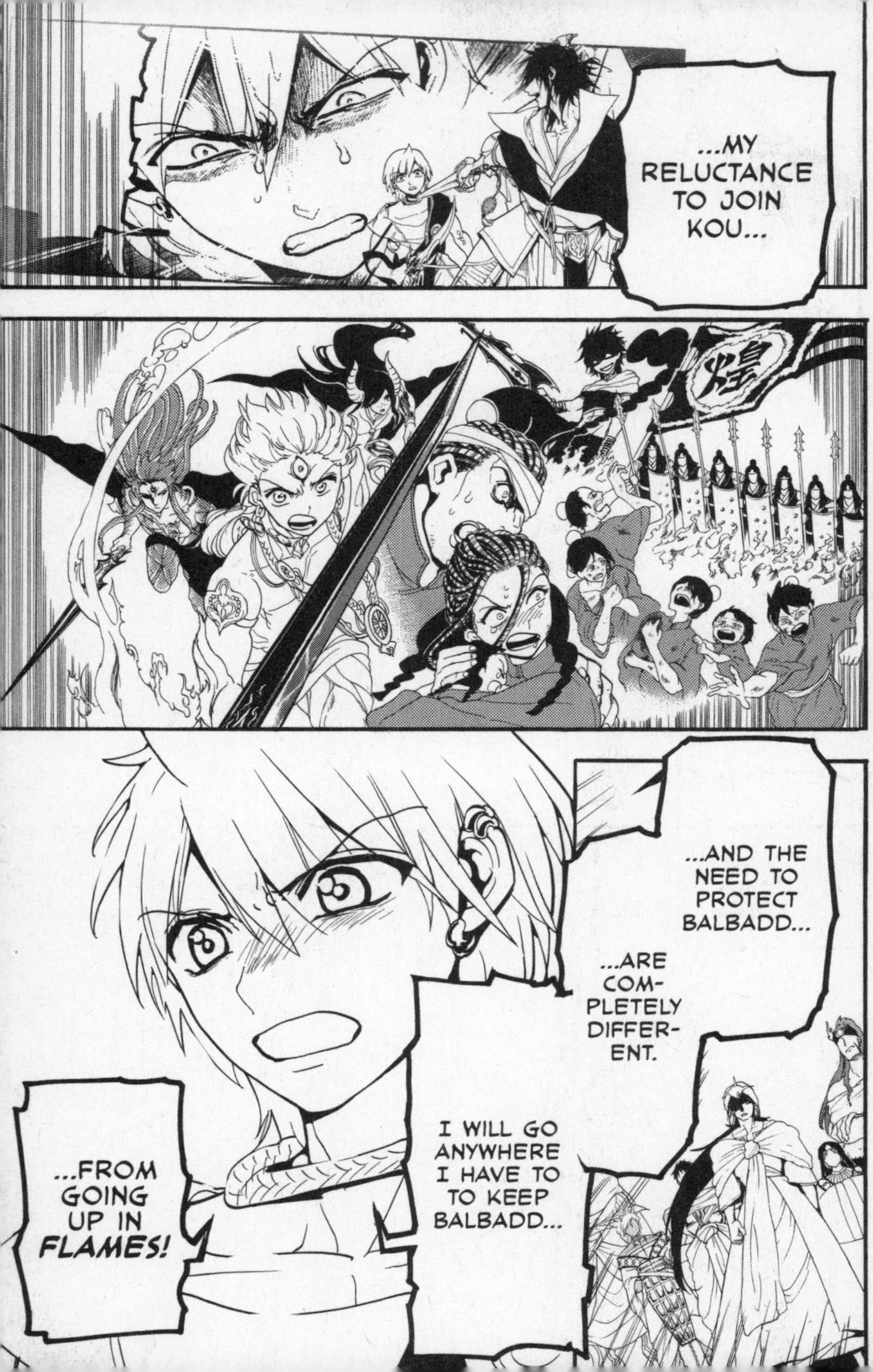
...MY RELUCTANCE TO JOIN KOU...
煌
...AND THE NEED TO PROTECT BALBADD...
...ARE COM-PLETELY DIFFER-ENT.
I WILL GO ANYWHERE I HAVE TO TO KEEP BALBADD...
...FROM GOING UP IN *FLAMES!*

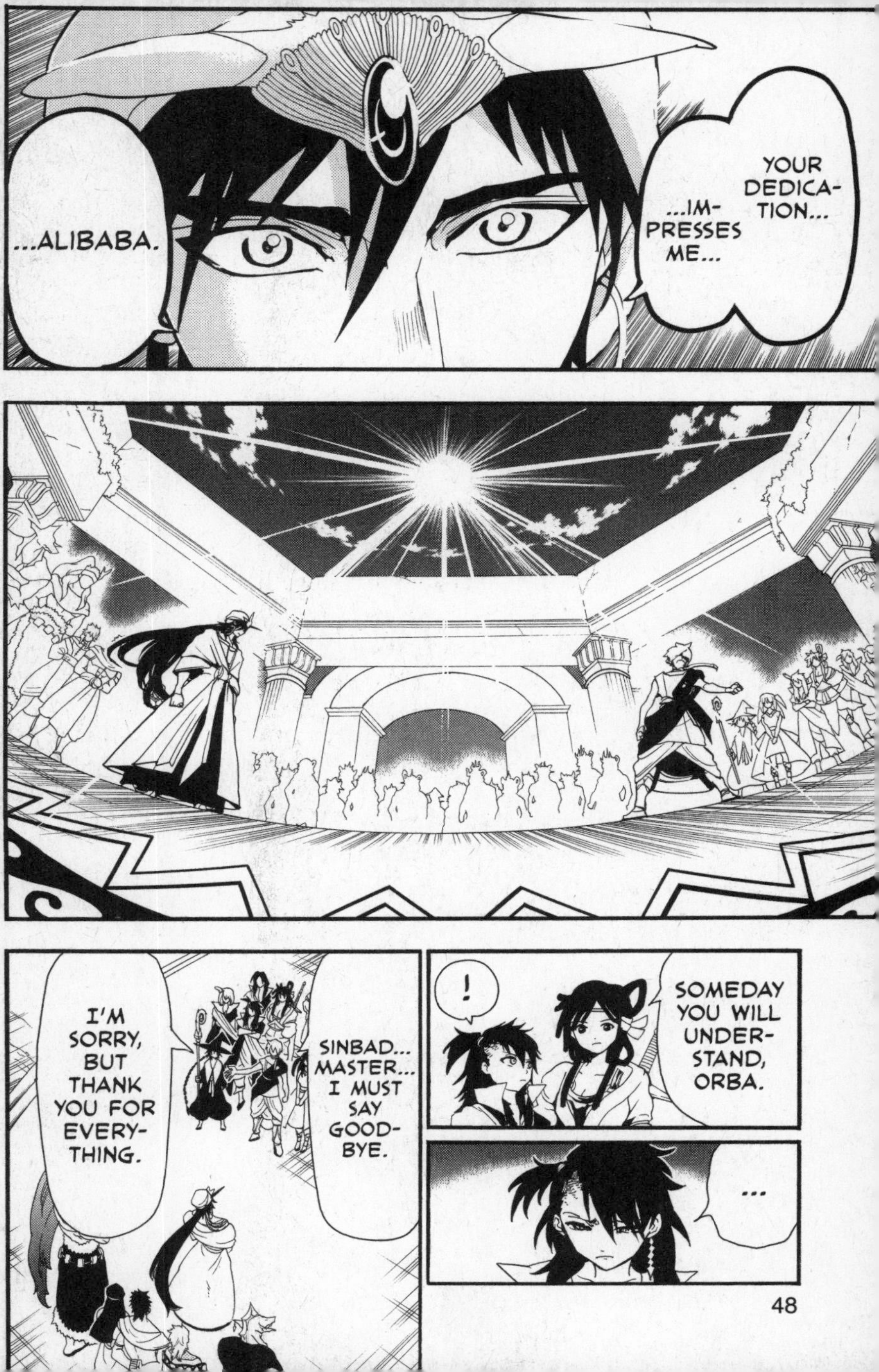
YOUR DEDICA-TION...
...IM-PRESSES ME...
...ALIBABA.
!
SOMEDAY YOU WILL UNDER-STAND, ORBA.
...
SINBAD... MASTER... I MUST SAY GOOD-BYE.
I'M SORRY, BUT THANK YOU FOR EVERY-THING.

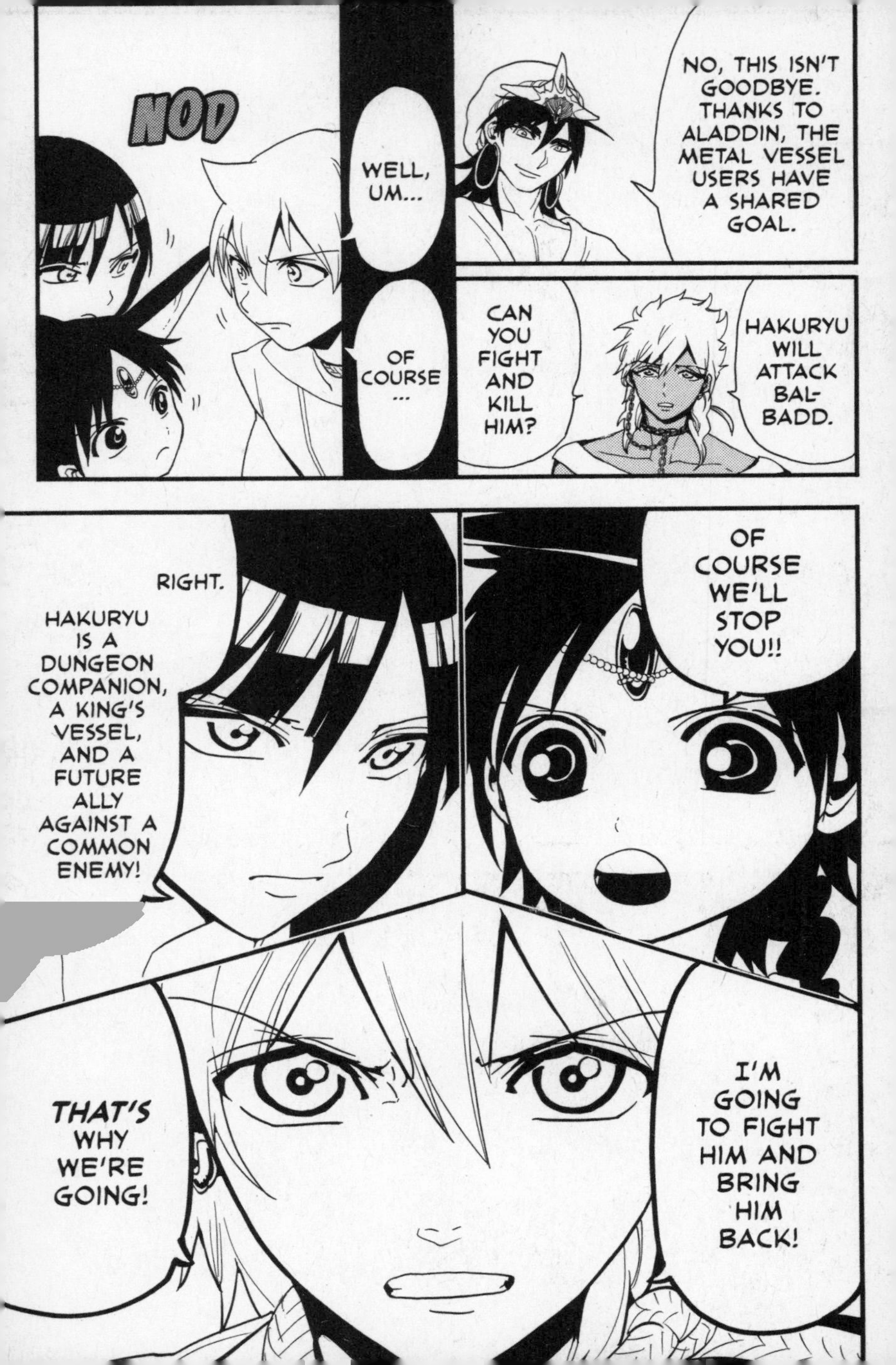
NO, THIS ISN'T GOODBYE. THANKS TO ALADDIN, THE METAL VESSEL USERS HAVE A SHARED GOAL.
HAKURYU WILL ATTACK BAL-BADD.
CAN YOU FIGHT AND KILL HIM?
WELL, UM...
OF COURSE...
NOD
OF COURSE WE'LL STOP YOU!!
RIGHT.
HAKURYU IS A DUNGEON COMPANION, A KING'S VESSEL, AND A FUTURE ALLY AGAINST A COMMON ENEMY!
I'M GOING TO FIGHT HIM AND BRING HIM BACK!
THAT'S WHY WE'RE GOING!

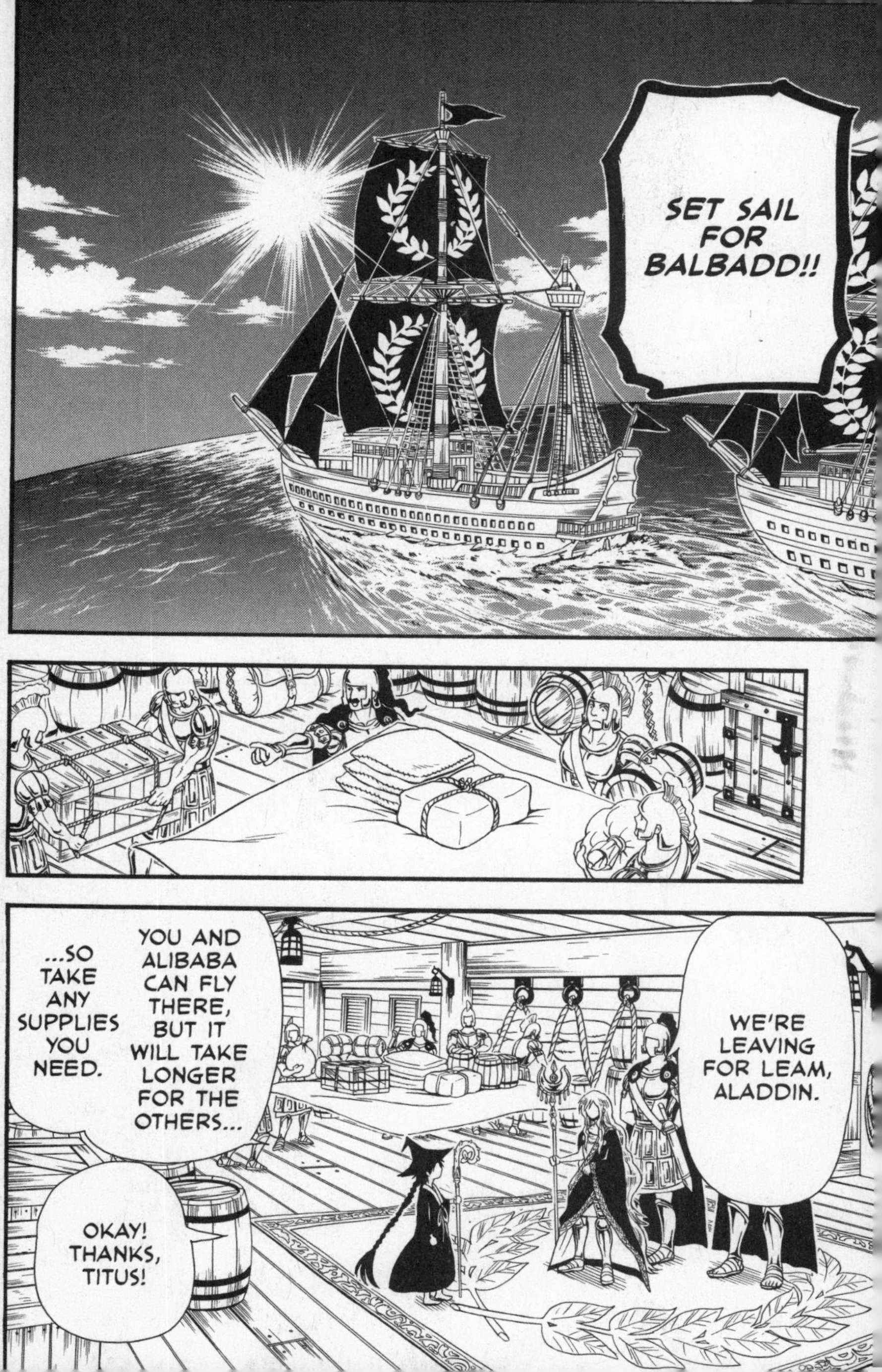
SET SAIL FOR BALBADD!!
WE'RE LEAVING FOR LEAM, ALADDIN.
YOU AND ALIBABA CAN FLY THERE, BUT IT WILL TAKE LONGER FOR THE OTHERS...
...SO TAKE ANY SUPPLIES YOU NEED.
OKAY! THANKS, TITUS!

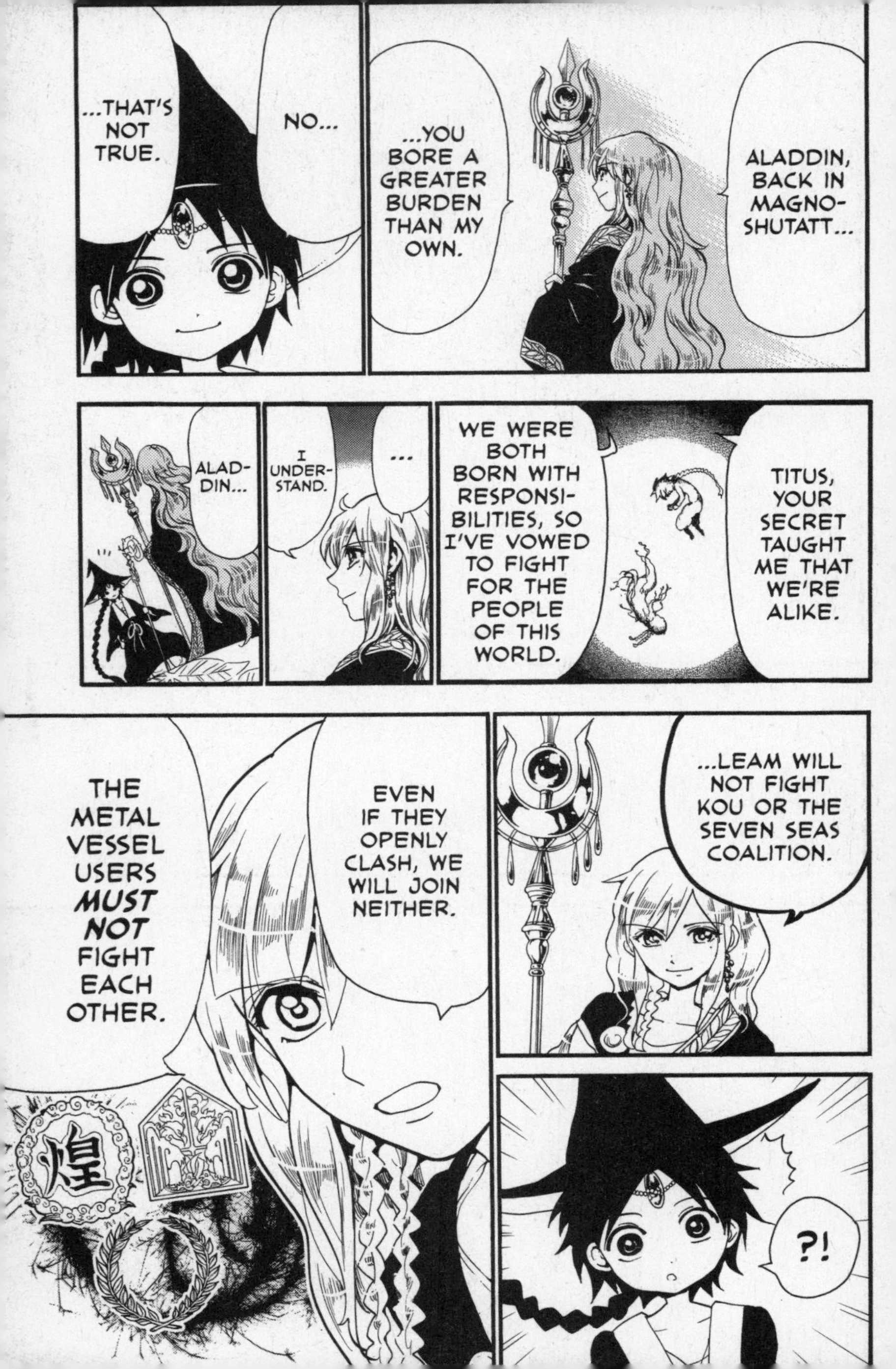
ALADDIN, BACK IN MAGNO-SHUTATT...
...YOU BORE A GREATER BURDEN THAN MY OWN.
NO...
...THAT'S NOT TRUE.
TITUS, YOUR SECRET TAUGHT ME THAT WE'RE ALIKE.
WE WERE BOTH BORN WITH RESPONSIBILITIES, SO I'VE VOWED TO FIGHT FOR THE PEOPLE OF THIS WORLD.
...
I UNDERSTAND.
ALADDIN...
...LEAM WILL NOT FIGHT KOU OR THE SEVEN SEAS COALITION.
?!
EVEN IF THEY OPENLY CLASH, WE WILL JOIN NEITHER.
THE METAL VESSEL USERS *MUST NOT* FIGHT EACH OTHER.

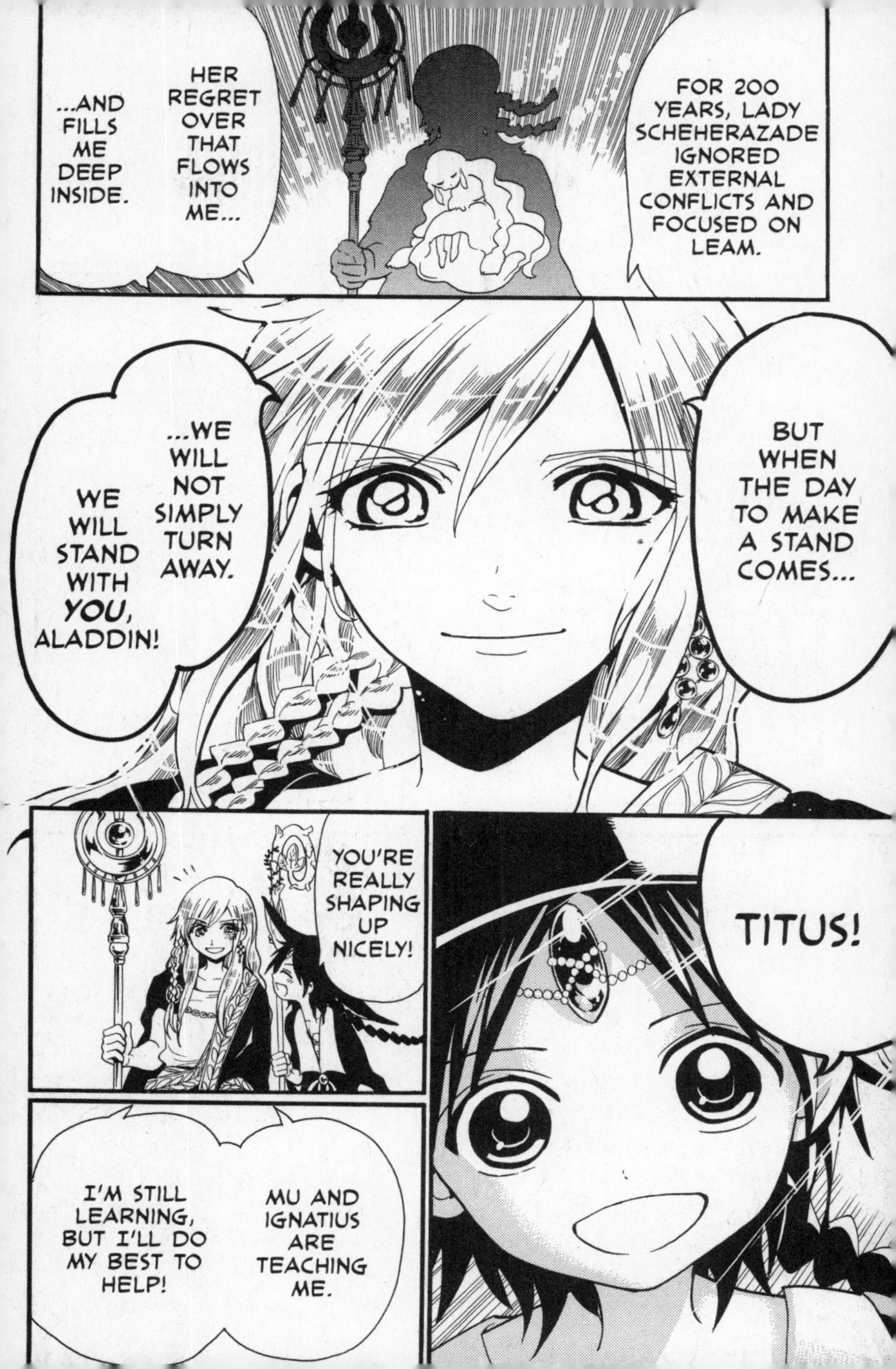
FOR 200 YEARS, LADY SCHEHERAZADE IGNORED EXTERNAL CONFLICTS AND FOCUSED ON LEAM.
HER REGRET OVER THAT FLOWS INTO ME...
...AND FILLS ME DEEP INSIDE.
BUT WHEN THE DAY TO MAKE A STAND COMES...
...WE WILL NOT SIMPLY TURN AWAY.
WE WILL STAND WITH *YOU*, ALADDIN!
TITUS!
YOU'RE REALLY SHAPING UP NICELY!
MU AND IGNATIUS ARE TEACHING ME.
I'M STILL LEARNING, BUT I'LL DO MY BEST TO HELP!

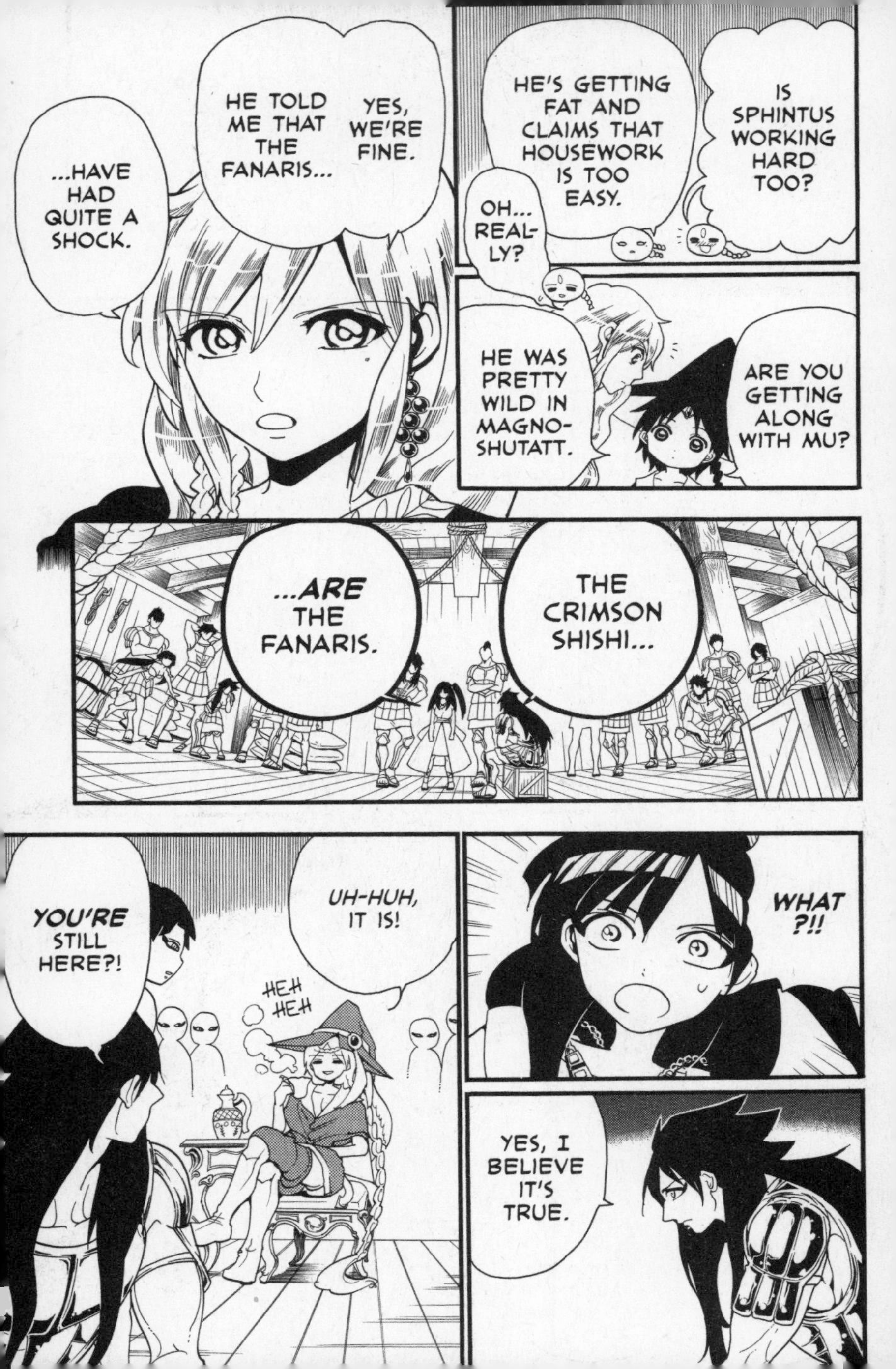

IS SPHINTUS WORKING HARD TOO?
HE'S GETTING FAT AND CLAIMS THAT HOUSEWORK IS TOO EASY.
OH... REAL-LY?
ARE YOU GETTING ALONG WITH MU?
HE WAS PRETTY WILD IN MAGNO-SHUTATT.
YES, WE'RE FINE.
HE TOLD ME THAT THE FANARIS...
...HAVE HAD QUITE A SHOCK.
THE CRIMSON SHISHI...
...ARE THE FANARIS.
WHAT?!!
YES, I BELIEVE IT'S TRUE.
UH-HUH, IT IS!
HEH HEH
YOU'RE STILL HERE?!

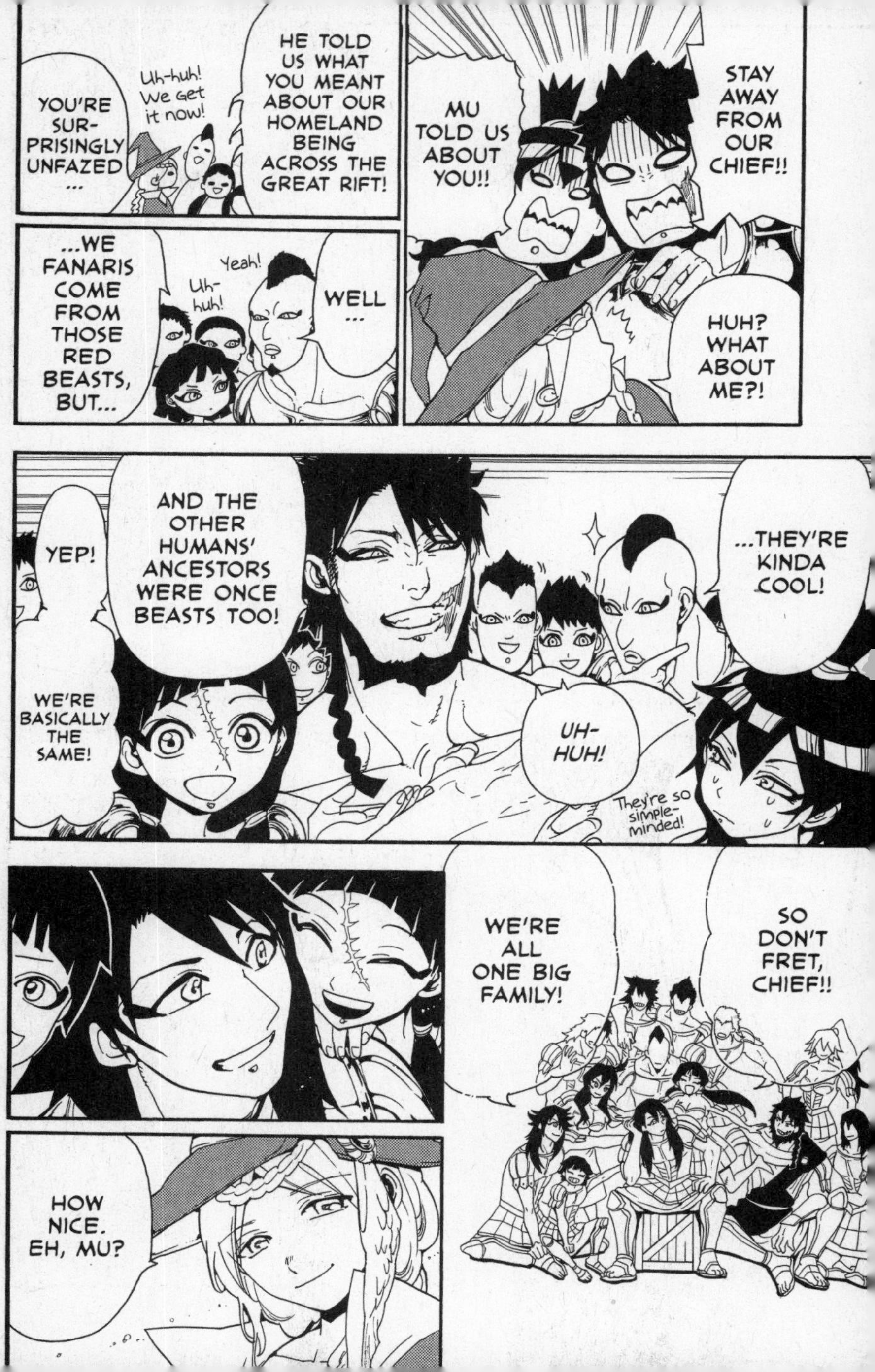
STAY AWAY FROM OUR CHIEF!!
MU TOLD US ABOUT YOU!!
HUH? WHAT ABOUT ME?!
HE TOLD US WHAT YOU MEANT ABOUT OUR HOMELAND BEING ACROSS THE GREAT RIFT!
Uh-huh! We get it now!
YOU'RE SUR-PRISINGLY UNFAZED...
WELL...
Yeah!
Uh-huh!
...WE FANARIS COME FROM THOSE RED BEASTS, BUT...
...THEY'RE KINDA COOL!
UH-HUH!
They're so simple-minded!
AND THE OTHER HUMANS' ANCESTORS WERE ONCE BEASTS TOO!
YEP!
WE'RE BASICALLY THE SAME!
SO DON'T FRET, CHIEF!!
WE'RE ALL ONE BIG FAMILY!
HOW NICE. EH, MU?

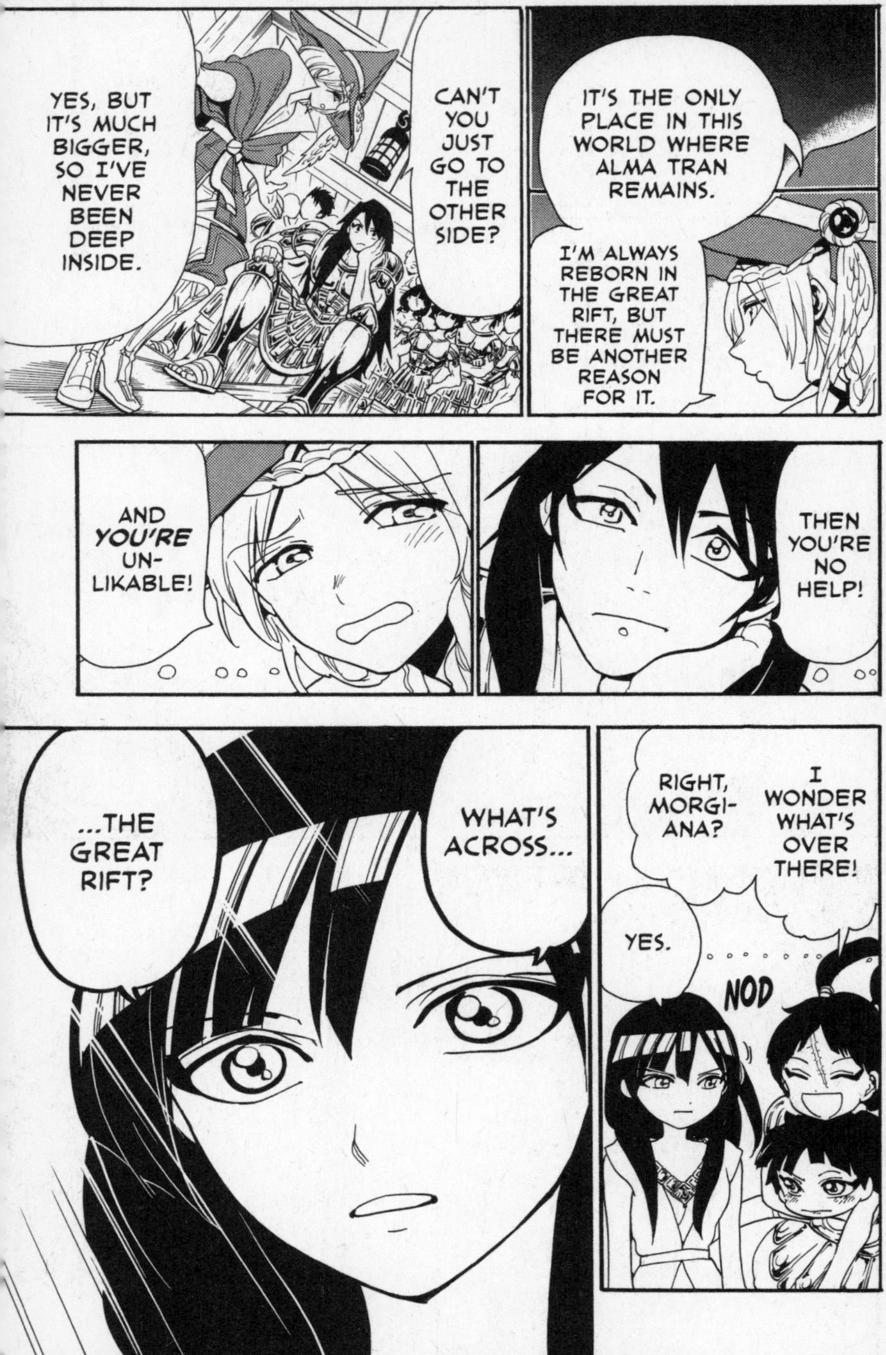
IT'S THE ONLY PLACE IN THIS WORLD WHERE ALMA TRAN REMAINS.
I'M ALWAYS REBORN IN THE GREAT RIFT, BUT THERE MUST BE ANOTHER REASON FOR IT.
CAN'T YOU JUST GO TO THE OTHER SIDE?
YES, BUT IT'S MUCH BIGGER, SO I'VE NEVER BEEN DEEP INSIDE.
THEN YOU'RE NO HELP!
AND *YOU'RE* UN-LIKABLE!
I WONDER WHAT'S OVER THERE!
RIGHT, MORGIANA?
YES.
NOD
WHAT'S ACROSS...
...THE GREAT RIFT?

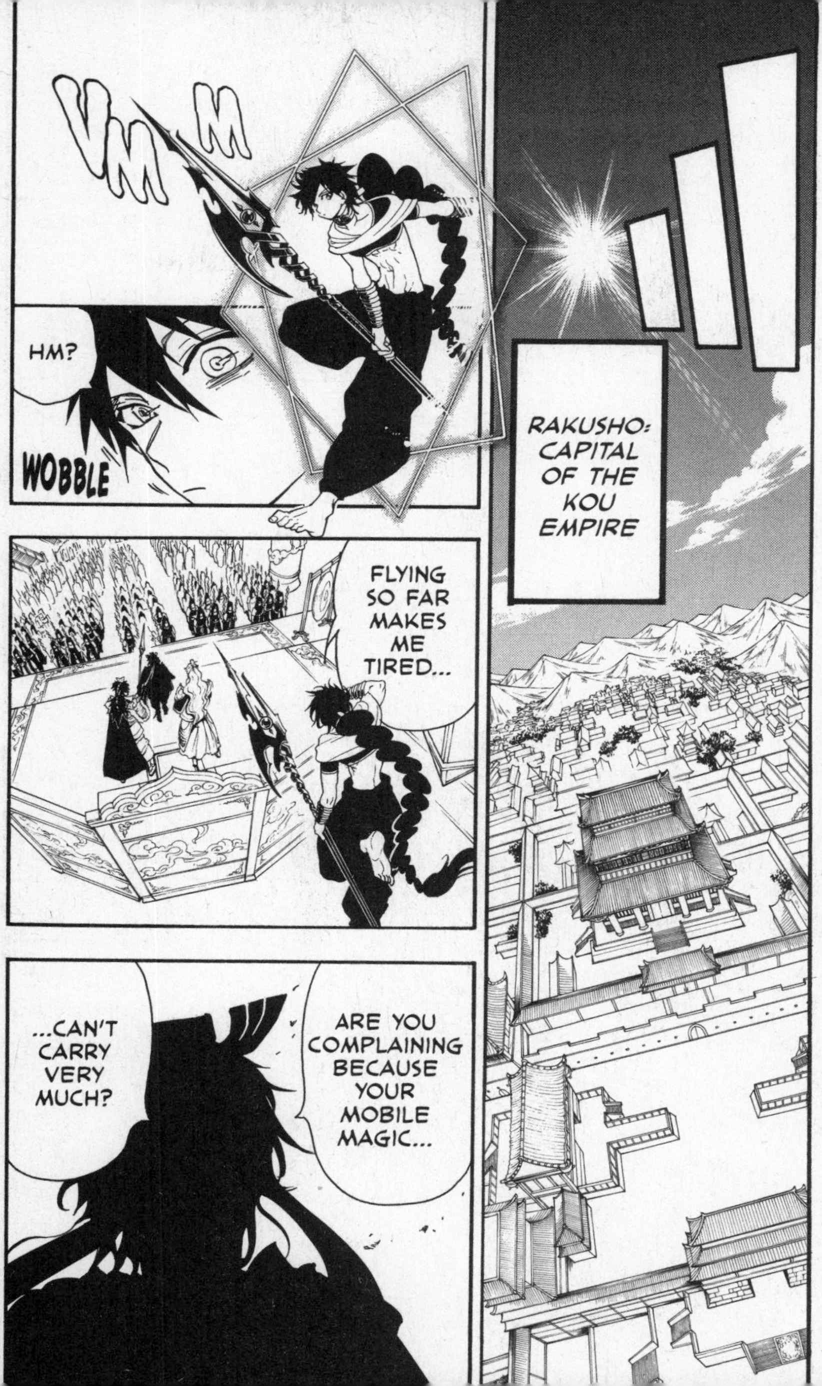
RAKUSHO: CAPITAL OF THE KOU EMPIRE
VMM
HM?
WOBBLE
FLYING SO FAR MAKES ME TIRED...
ARE YOU COMPLAINING BECAUSE YOUR MOBILE MAGIC...
...CAN'T CARRY VERY MUCH?

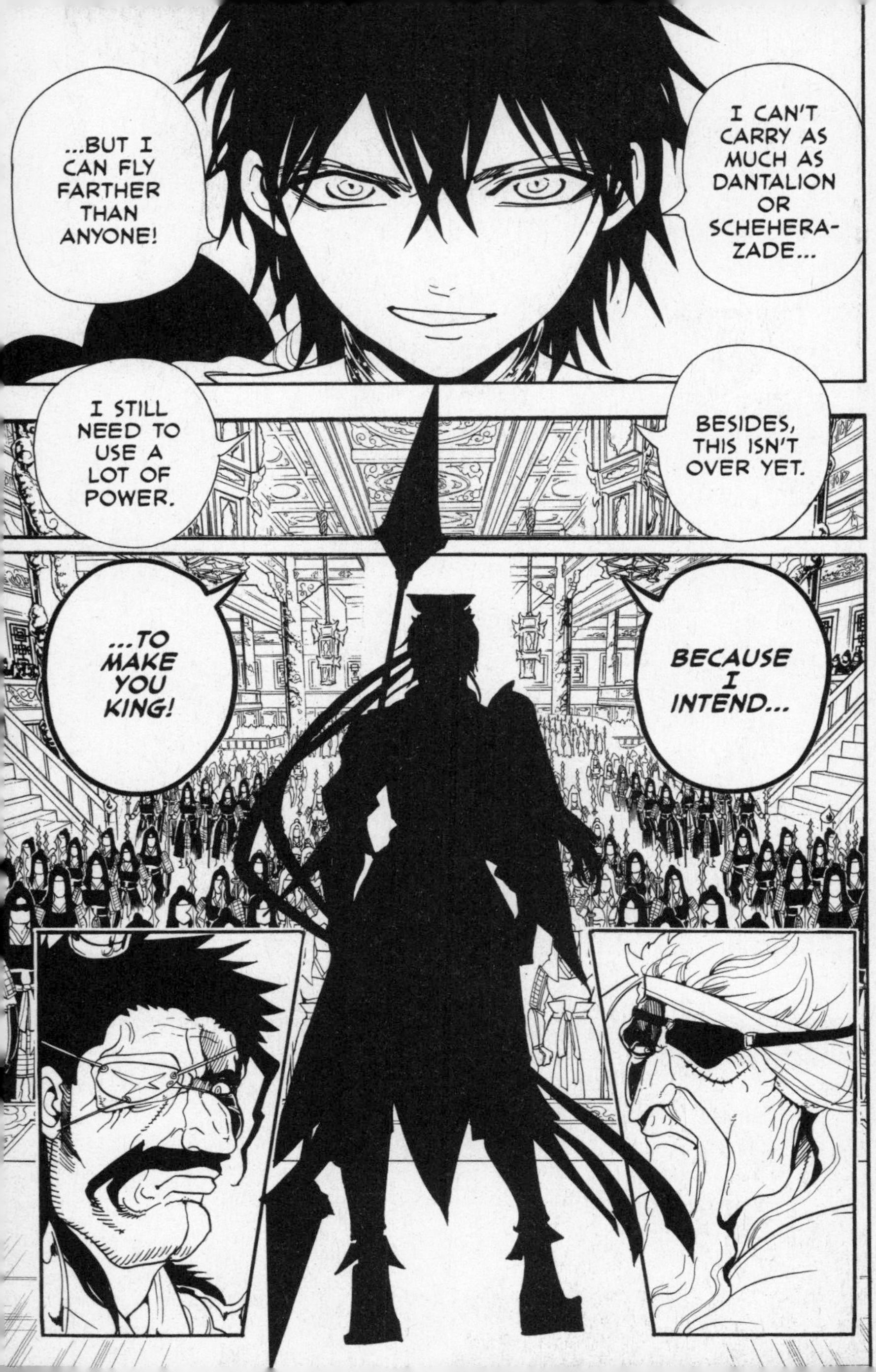
I CAN'T CARRY AS MUCH AS DANTALION OR SCHEHERA-ZADE...
...BUT I CAN FLY FARTHER THAN ANYONE!
BESIDES, THIS ISN'T OVER YET.
I STILL NEED TO USE A LOT OF POWER.
BECAUSE I INTEND...
...TO MAKE YOU KING!

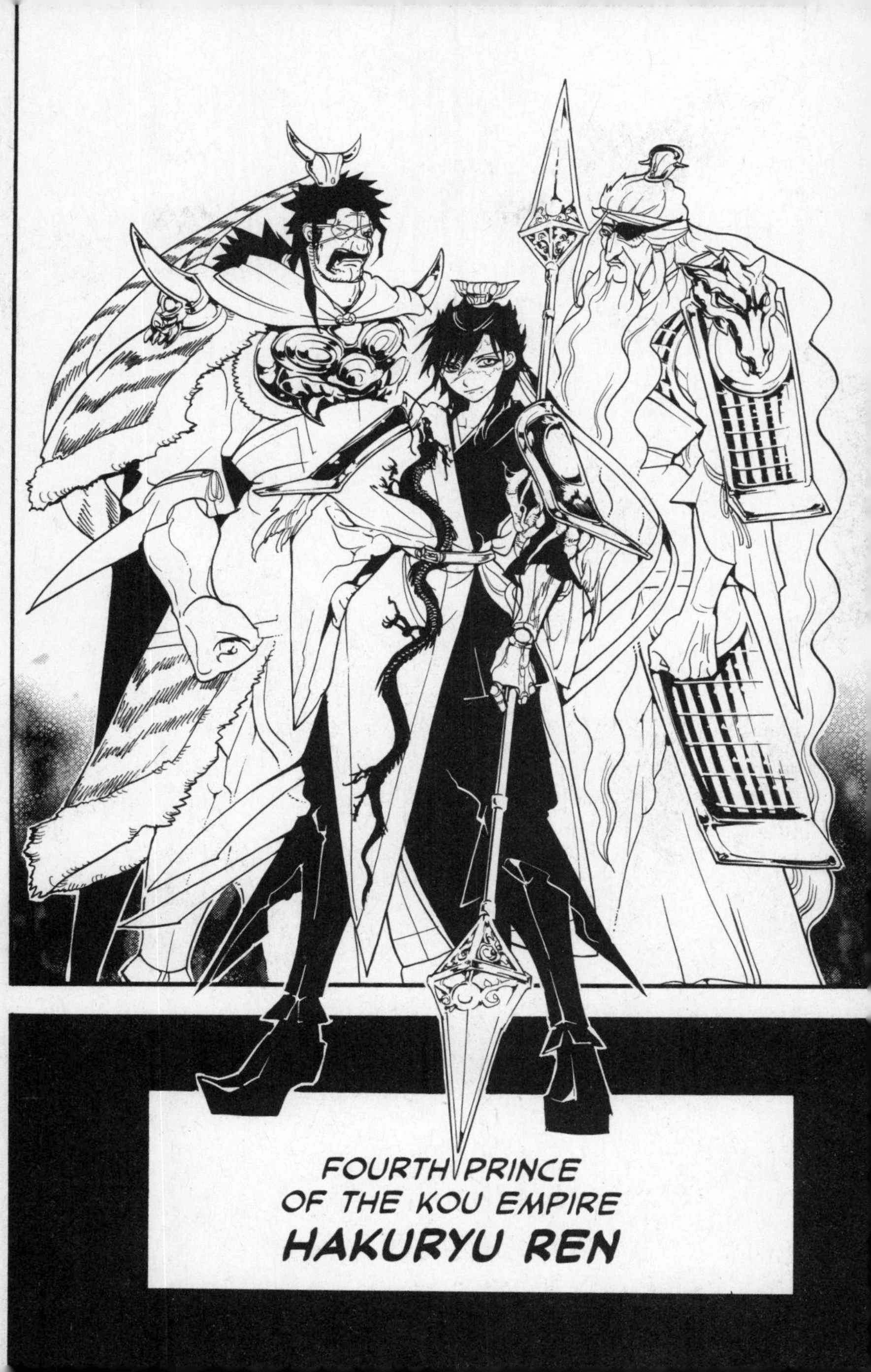
FOURTH PRINCE
OF THE KOU EMPIRE
HAKURYU REN

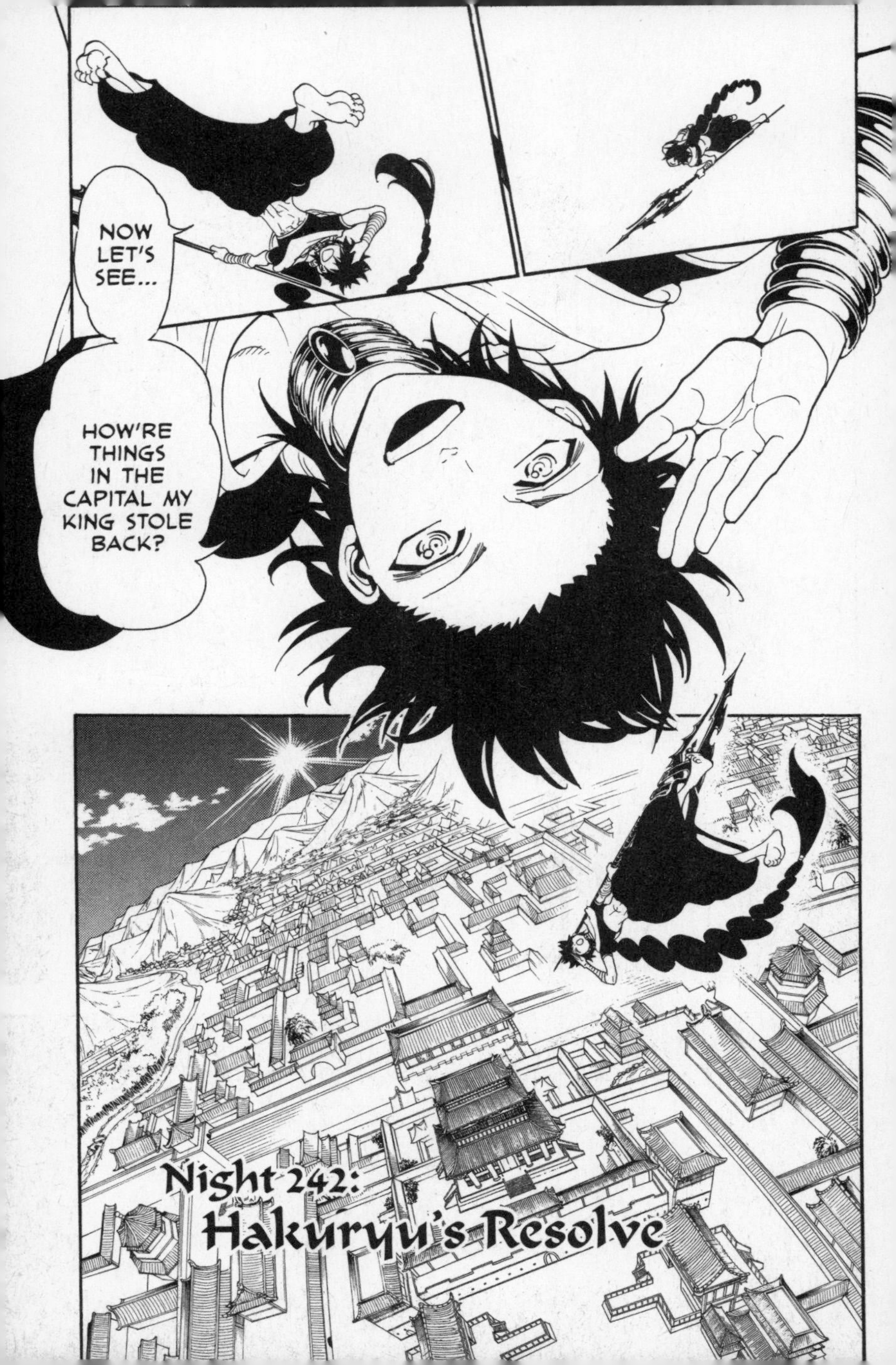
NOW LET'S SEE...
HOW'RE THINGS IN THE CAPITAL MY KING STOLE BACK?
Night 242:
Hakuryu's Resolve

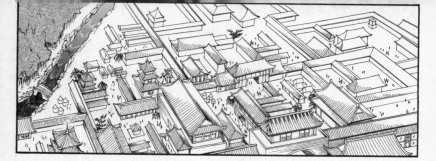

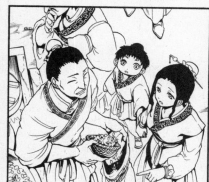

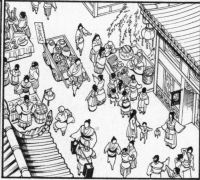

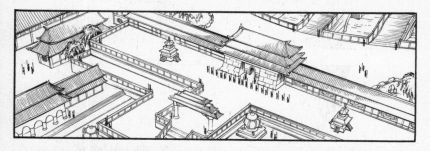

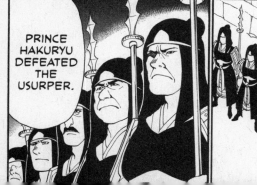

PRINCE HAKURYU DEFEATED THE USURPER.

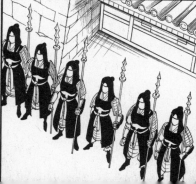

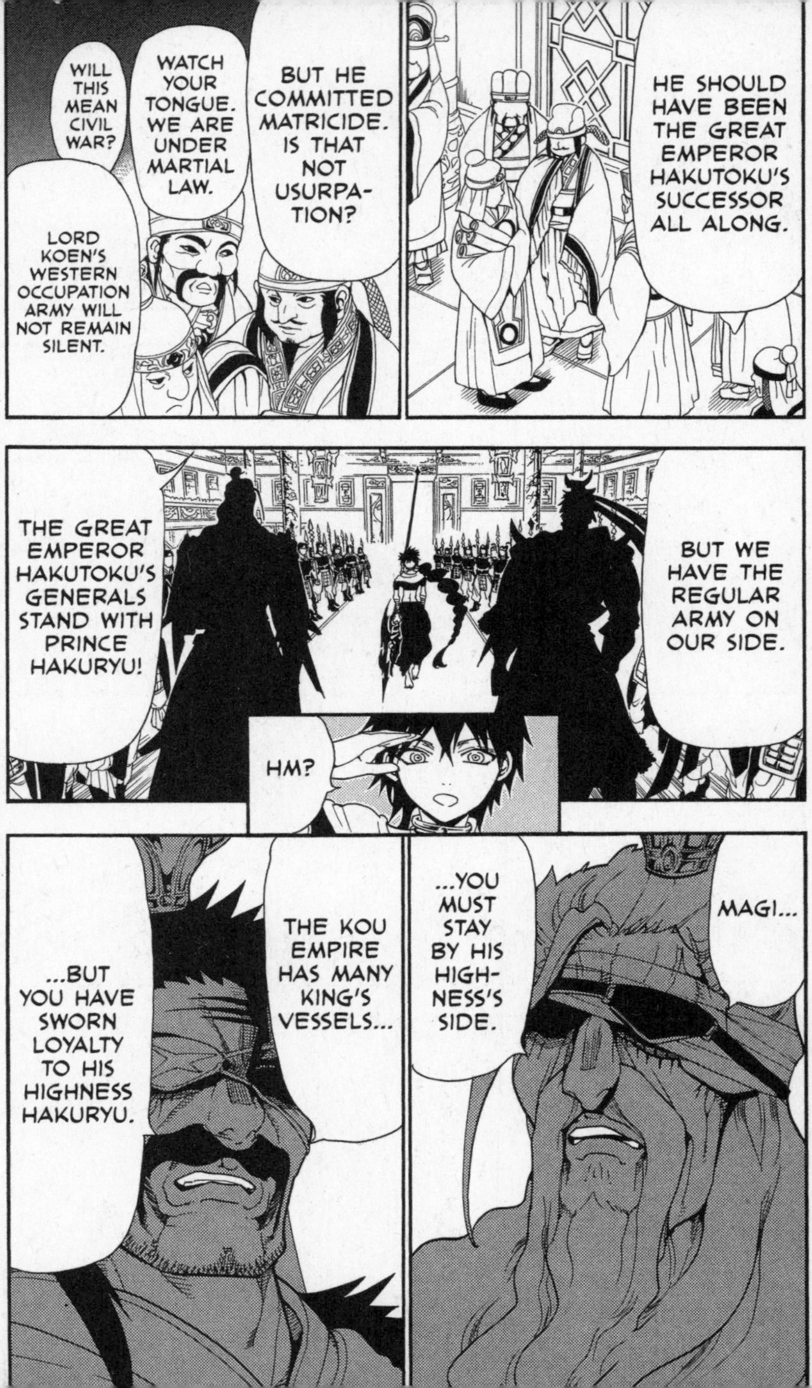
HE SHOULD HAVE BEEN THE GREAT EMPEROR HAKUTOKU'S SUCCESSOR ALL ALONG.
BUT HE COMMITTED MATRICIDE. IS THAT NOT USURPATION?
WATCH YOUR TONGUE. WE ARE UNDER MARTIAL LAW.
WILL THIS MEAN CIVIL WAR?
LORD KOEN'S WESTERN OCCUPATION ARMY WILL NOT REMAIN SILENT.
BUT WE HAVE THE REGULAR ARMY ON OUR SIDE.
THE GREAT EMPEROR HAKUTOKU'S GENERALS STAND WITH PRINCE HAKURYU!
HM?
MAGI...
...YOU MUST STAY BY HIS HIGHNESS'S SIDE.
THE KOU EMPIRE HAS MANY KING'S VESSELS...
...BUT YOU HAVE SWORN LOYALTY TO HIS HIGHNESS HAKURYU.

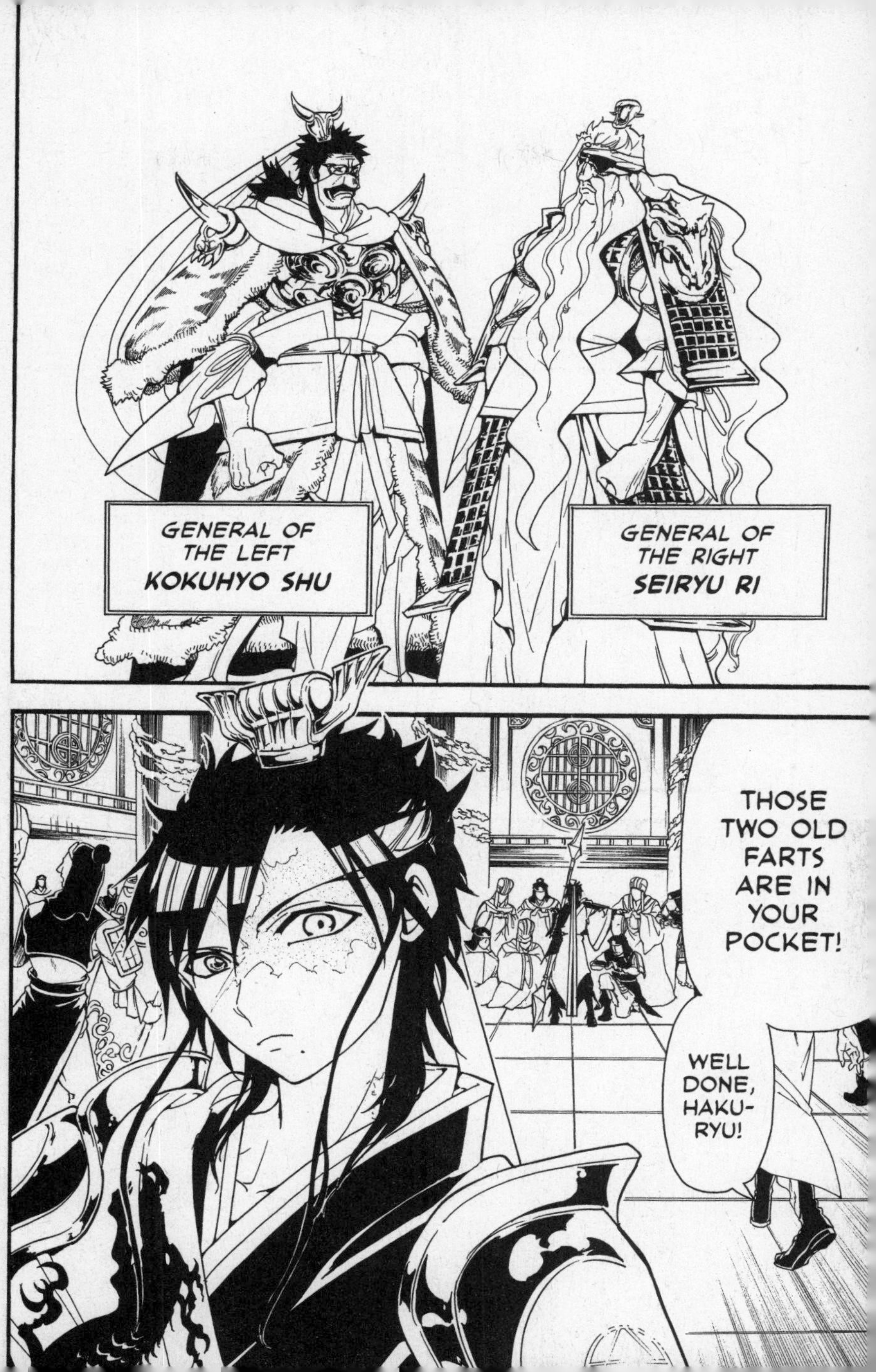
GENERAL OF THE RIGHT SEIRYU RI
GENERAL OF THE LEFT KOKUHYO SHU
THOSE TWO OLD FARTS ARE IN YOUR POCKET!
WELL DONE, HAKU-RYU!

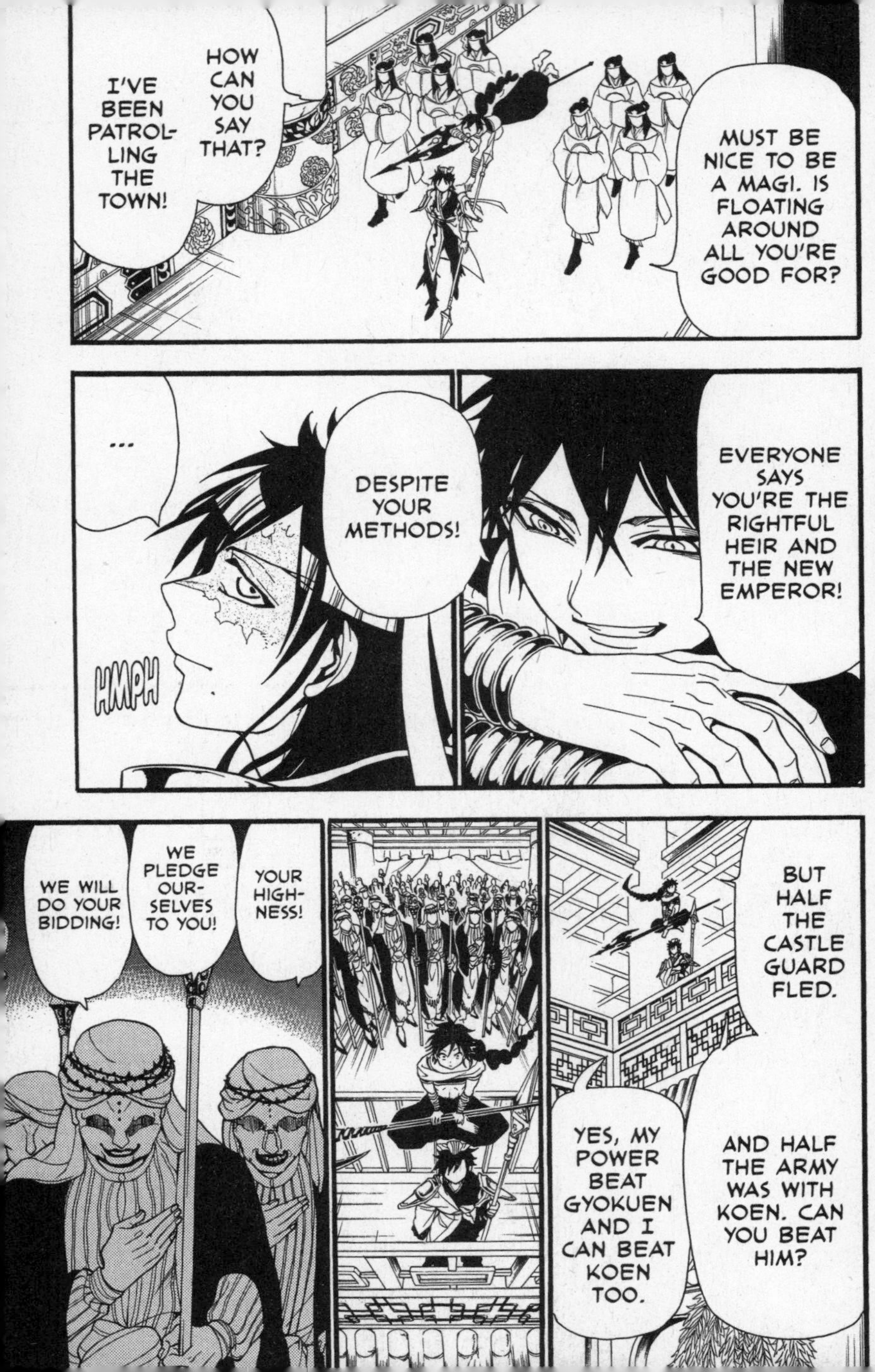
MUST BE NICE TO BE A MAGI. IS FLOATING AROUND ALL YOU'RE GOOD FOR?
HOW CAN YOU SAY THAT?
I'VE BEEN PATROLLING THE TOWN!
EVERYONE SAYS YOU'RE THE RIGHTFUL HEIR AND THE NEW EMPEROR!
DESPITE YOUR METHODS!
...
HMPH
BUT HALF THE CASTLE GUARD FLED.
AND HALF THE ARMY WAS WITH KOEN. CAN YOU BEAT HIM?
YES, MY POWER BEAT GYOKUEN AND I CAN BEAT KOEN TOO.
YOUR HIGHNESS!
WE PLEDGE OURSELVES TO YOU!
WE WILL DO YOUR BIDDING!

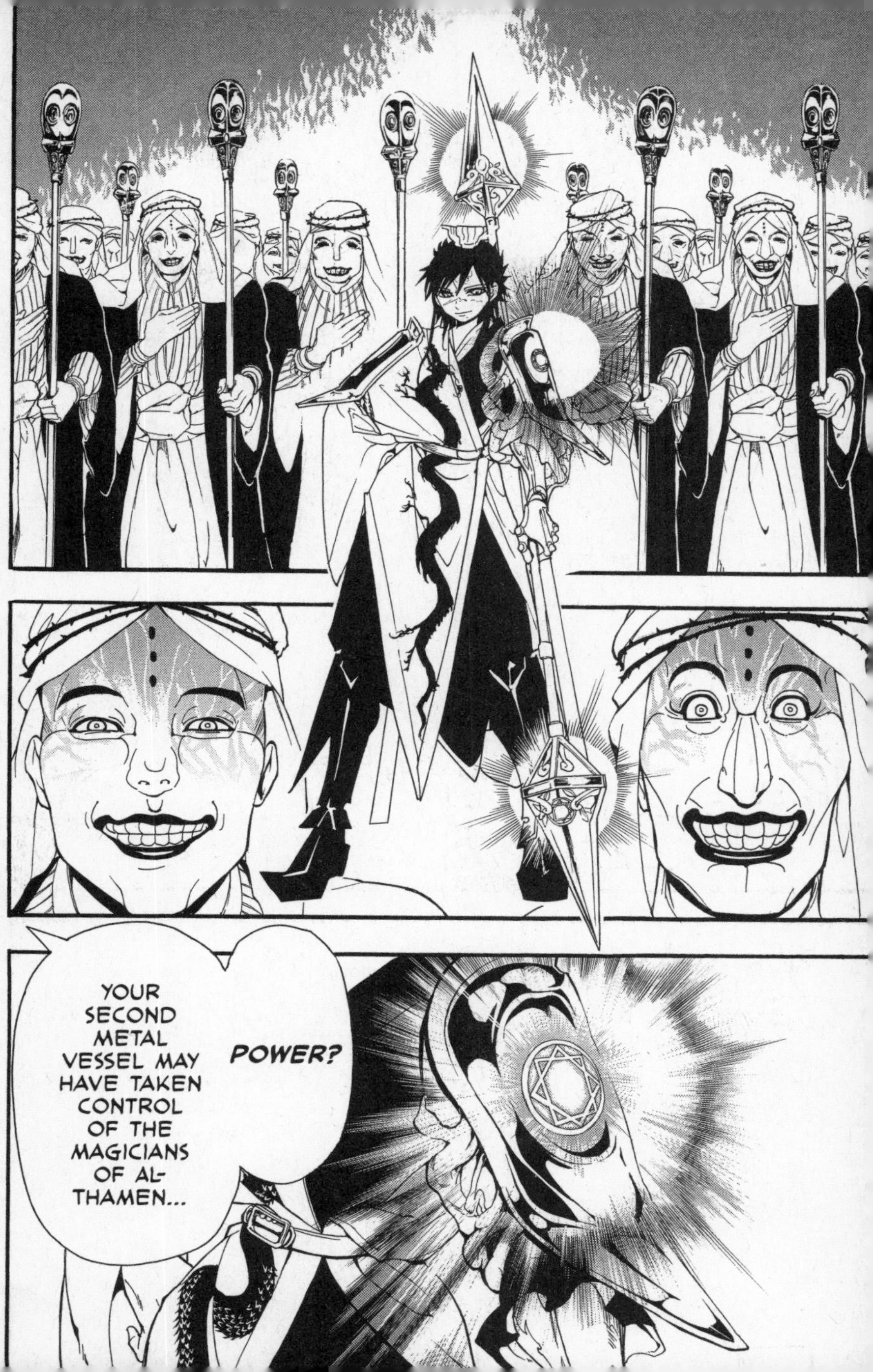
POWER?
YOUR SECOND METAL VESSEL MAY HAVE TAKEN CONTROL OF THE MAGICIANS OF AL-THAMEN...

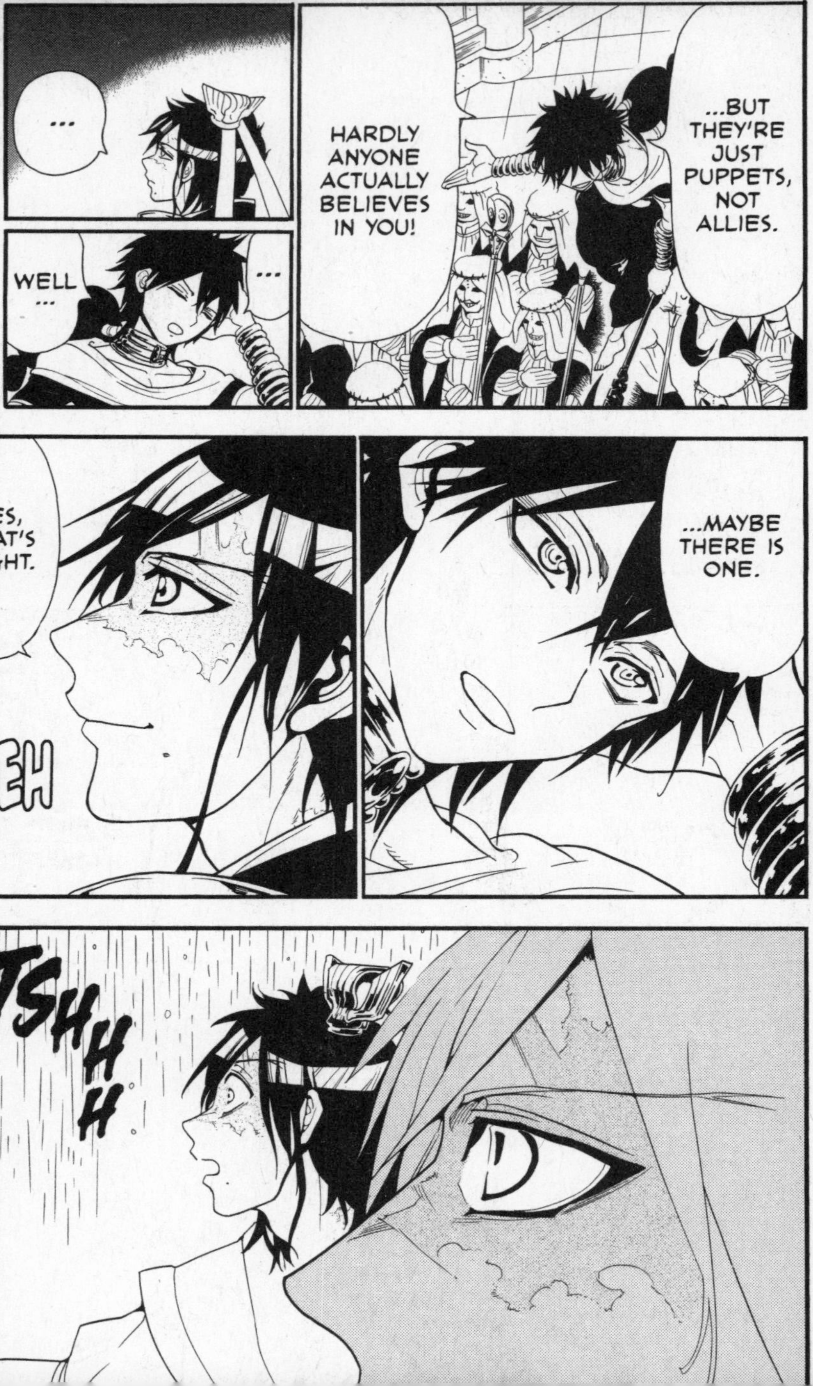
...BUT THEY'RE JUST PUPPETS, NOT ALLIES.
HARDLY ANYONE ACTUALLY BELIEVES IN YOU!
...
...
WELL ...
...MAYBE THERE IS ONE.
YES, THAT'S RIGHT.
HEH
TSHHHH

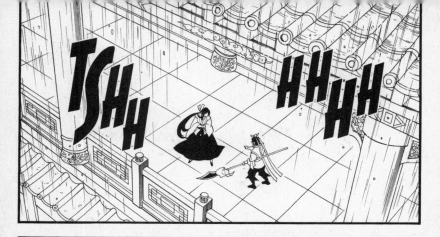

THE KOU EMPIRE IS ONE! I'M SORRY. I NEED TIME.

I CAN'T...

THIS IS WHAT I'VE LIVED FOR!!

YOU AND I MUST RESTORE THIS LAND!!!

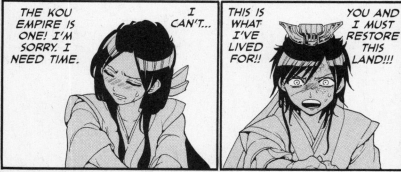

MY SISTER...

SISTER...

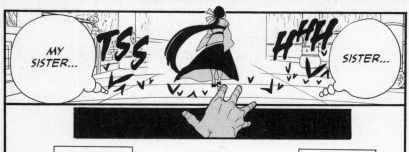

SHE WAS BORN WHEN KOU WAS STILL A MONARCHY FAR TO THE EAST.

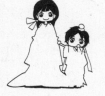

MY SISTER HAKUEI IS FIVE YEARS OLDER THAN ME.

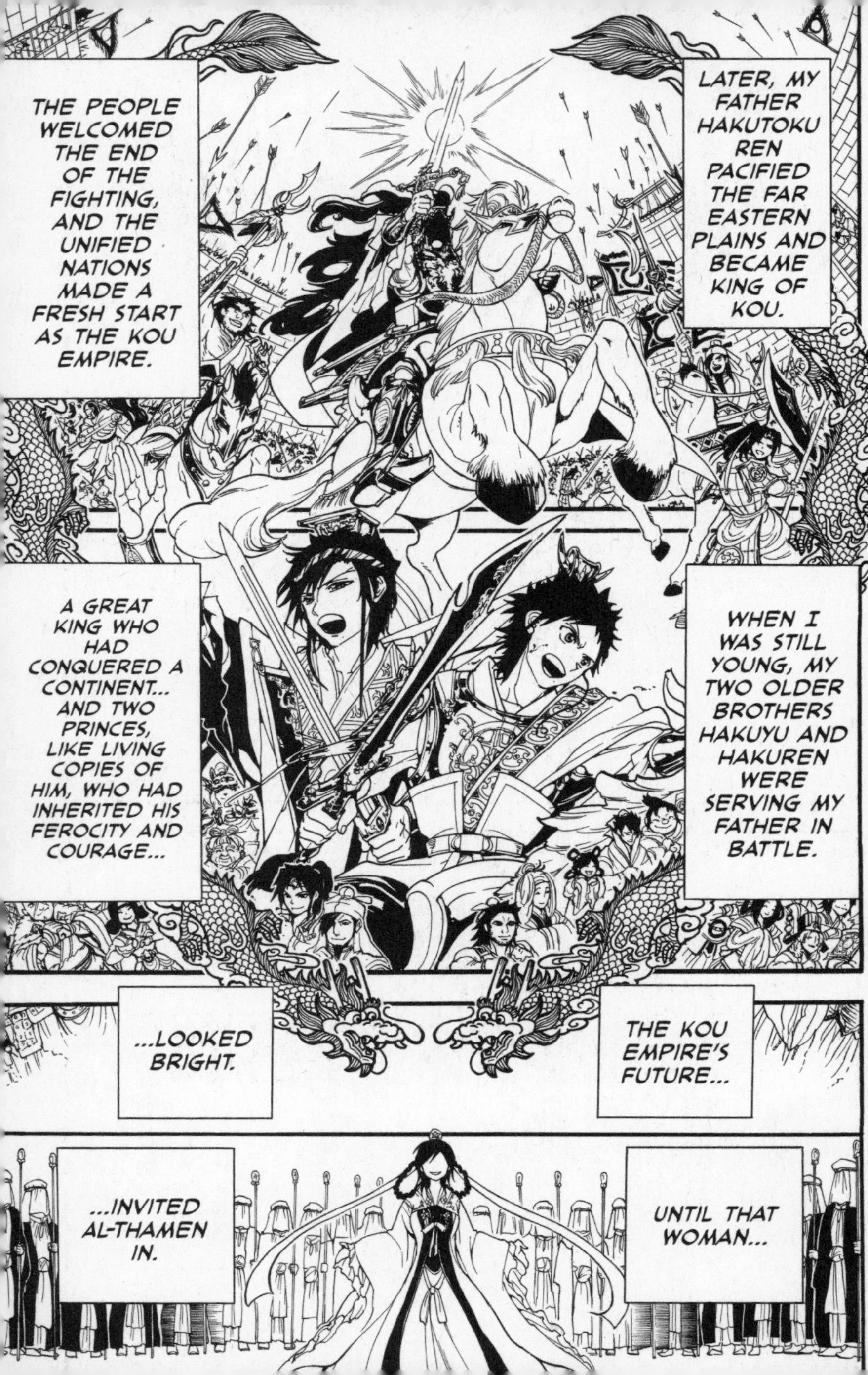
LATER, MY FATHER HAKUTOKU REN PACIFIED THE FAR EASTERN PLAINS AND BECAME KING OF KOU.
THE PEOPLE WELCOMED THE END OF THE FIGHTING, AND THE UNIFIED NATIONS MADE A FRESH START AS THE KOU EMPIRE.
WHEN I WAS STILL YOUNG, MY TWO OLDER BROTHERS HAKUYU AND HAKUREN WERE SERVING MY FATHER IN BATTLE.
A GREAT KING WHO HAD CONQUERED A CONTINENT... AND TWO PRINCES, LIKE LIVING COPIES OF HIM, WHO HAD INHERITED HIS FEROCITY AND COURAGE...
THE KOU EMPIRE'S FUTURE...
...LOOKED BRIGHT.
UNTIL THAT WOMAN...
...INVITED AL-THAMEN IN.

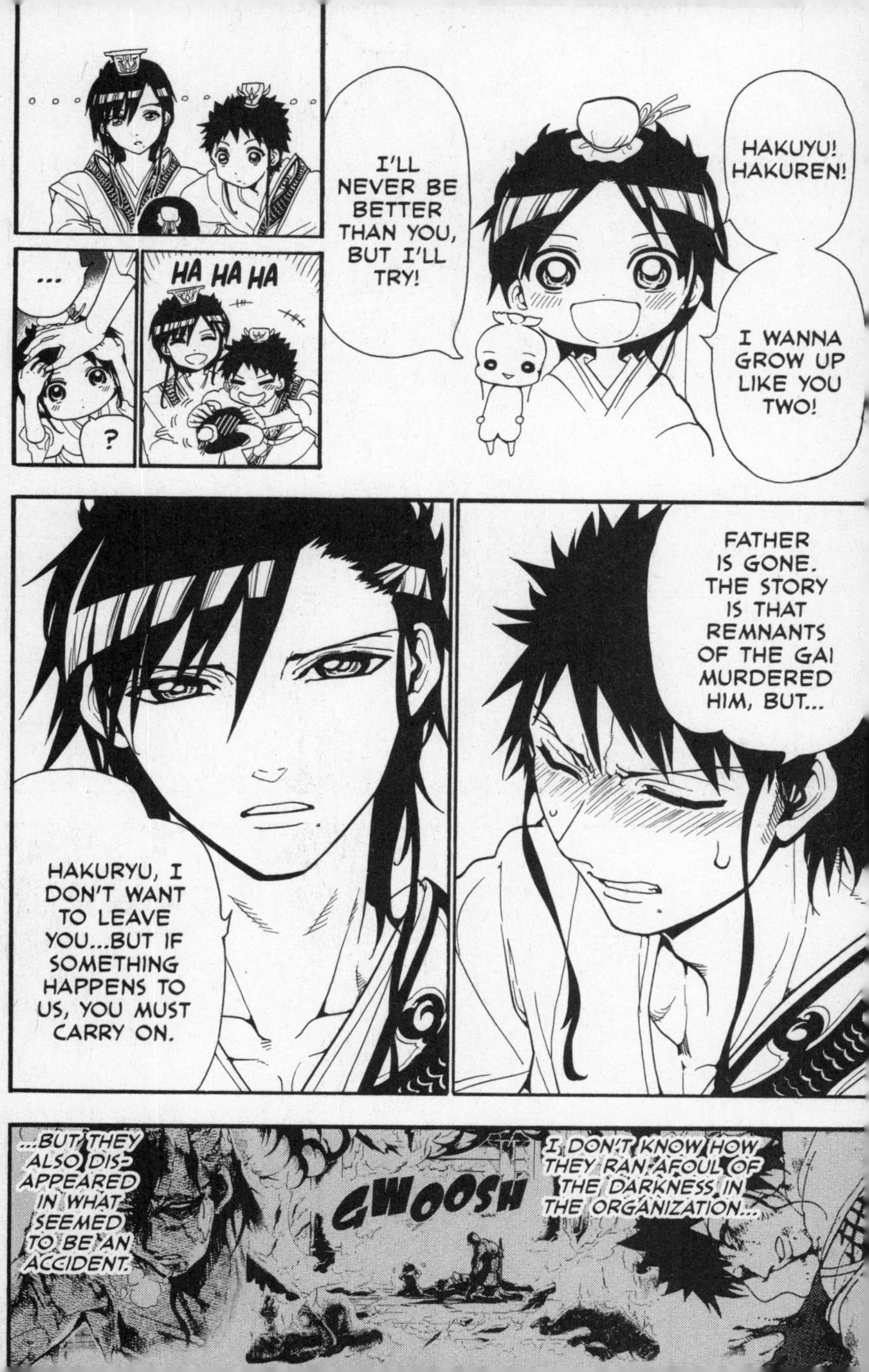
HAKUYU! HAKUREN!
I WANNA GROW UP LIKE YOU TWO!
I'LL NEVER BE BETTER THAN YOU, BUT I'LL TRY!
HA HA HA
...
?
FATHER IS GONE. THE STORY IS THAT REMNANTS OF THE GAI MURDERED HIM, BUT...
HAKURYU, I DON'T WANT TO LEAVE YOU...BUT IF SOMETHING HAPPENS TO US, YOU MUST CARRY ON.
I DON'T KNOW HOW THEY RAN AFOUL OF THE DARKNESS IN THE ORGANIZATION...
GWOOSH
...BUT THEY ALSO DIS-APPEARED IN WHAT SEEMED TO BE AN ACCIDENT.

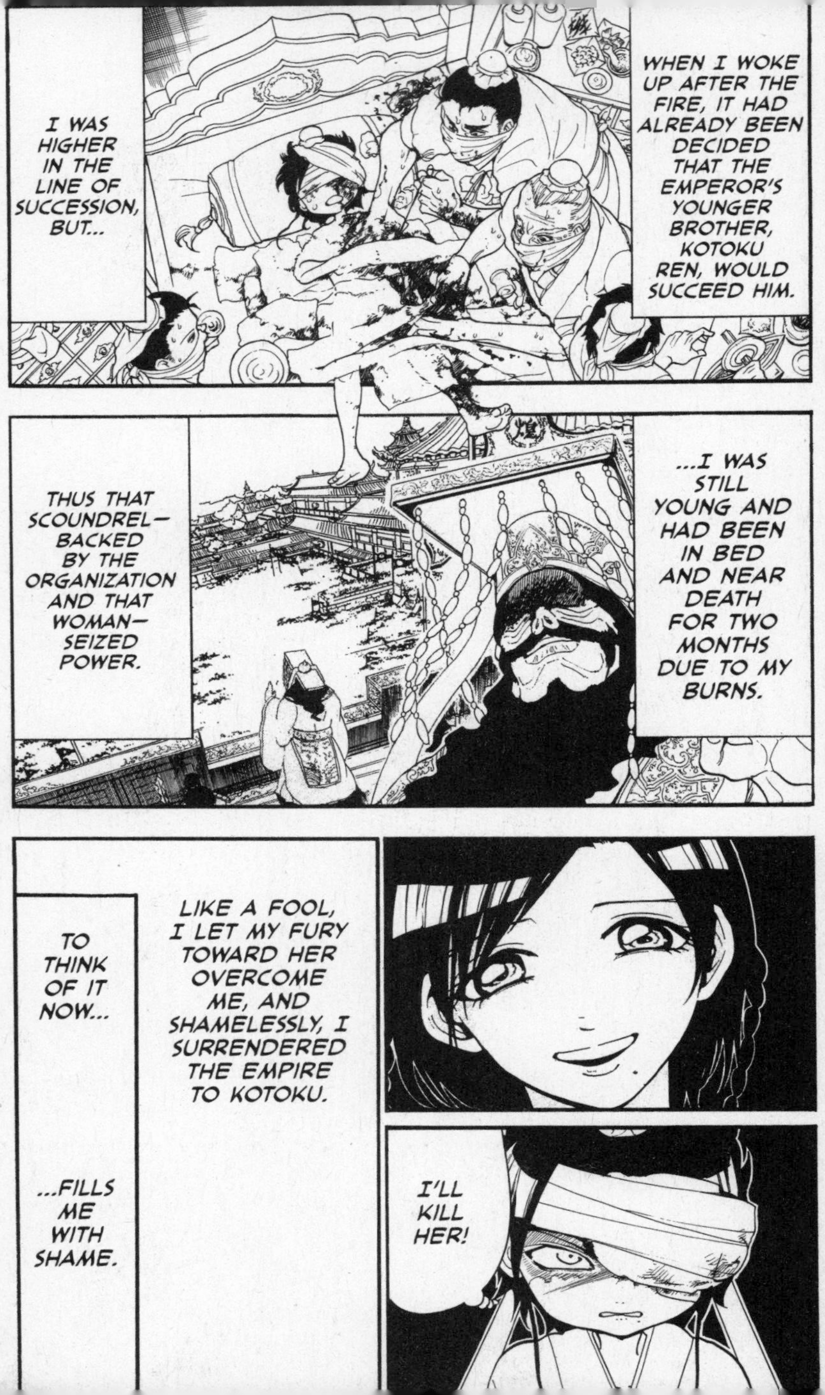

WHEN I WOKE UP AFTER THE FIRE, IT HAD ALREADY BEEN DECIDED THAT THE EMPEROR'S YOUNGER BROTHER, KOTOKU REN, WOULD SUCCEED HIM.
I WAS HIGHER IN THE LINE OF SUCCESSION, BUT...
...I WAS STILL YOUNG AND HAD BEEN IN BED AND NEAR DEATH FOR TWO MONTHS DUE TO MY BURNS.
THUS THAT SCOUNDREL—BACKED BY THE ORGANIZATION AND THAT WOMAN—SEIZED POWER.
I'LL KILL HER!
LIKE A FOOL, I LET MY FURY TOWARD HER OVERCOME ME, AND SHAMELESSLY, I SURRENDERED THE EMPIRE TO KOTOKU.
TO THINK OF IT NOW...
...FILLS ME WITH SHAME.

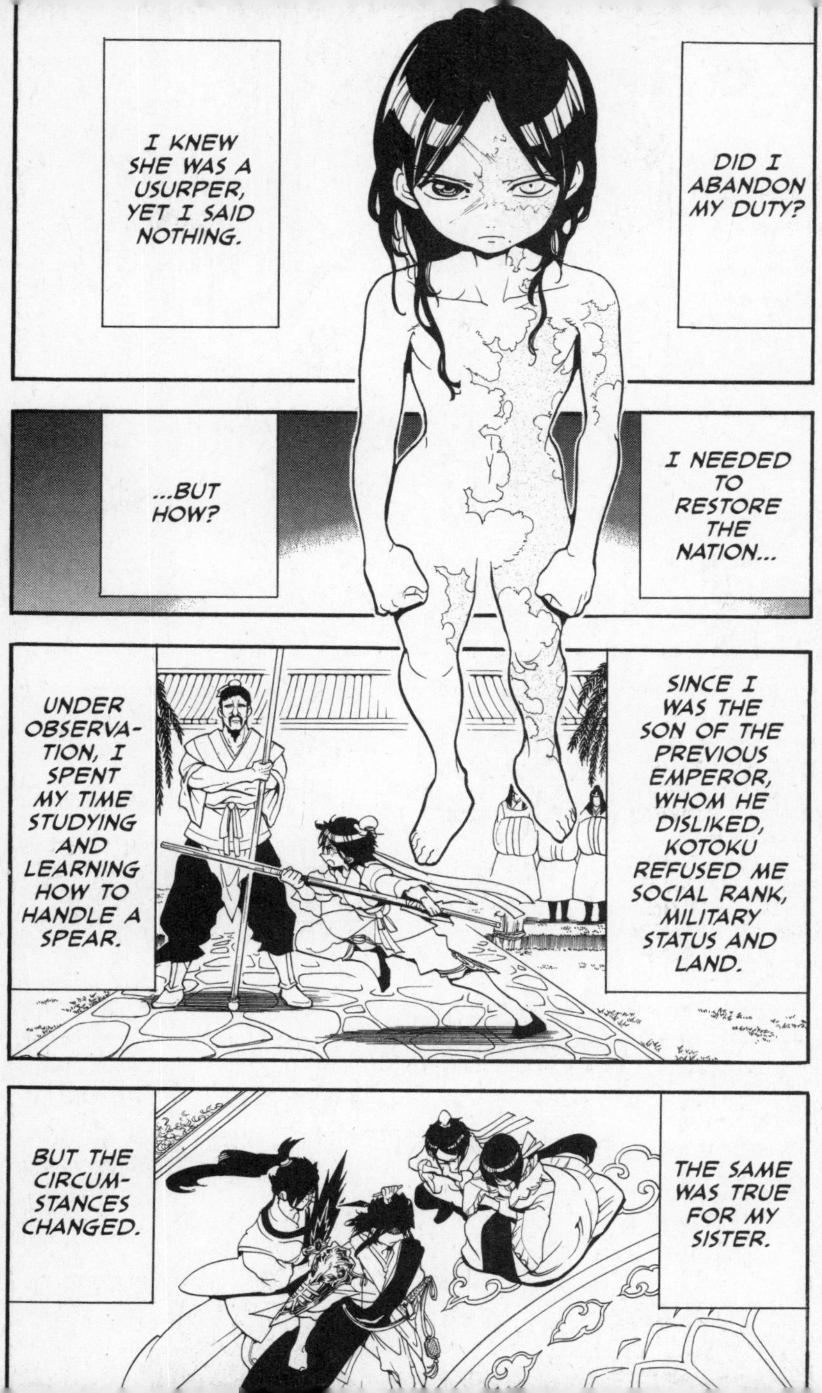
DID I ABANDON MY DUTY?
I KNEW SHE WAS A USURPER, YET I SAID NOTHING.
I NEEDED TO RESTORE THE NATION...
...BUT HOW?
SINCE I WAS THE SON OF THE PREVIOUS EMPEROR, WHOM HE DISLIKED, KOTOKU REFUSED ME SOCIAL RANK, MILITARY STATUS AND LAND.
UNDER OBSERVATION, I SPENT MY TIME STUDYING AND LEARNING HOW TO HANDLE A SPEAR.
THE SAME WAS TRUE FOR MY SISTER.
BUT THE CIRCUMSTANCES CHANGED.

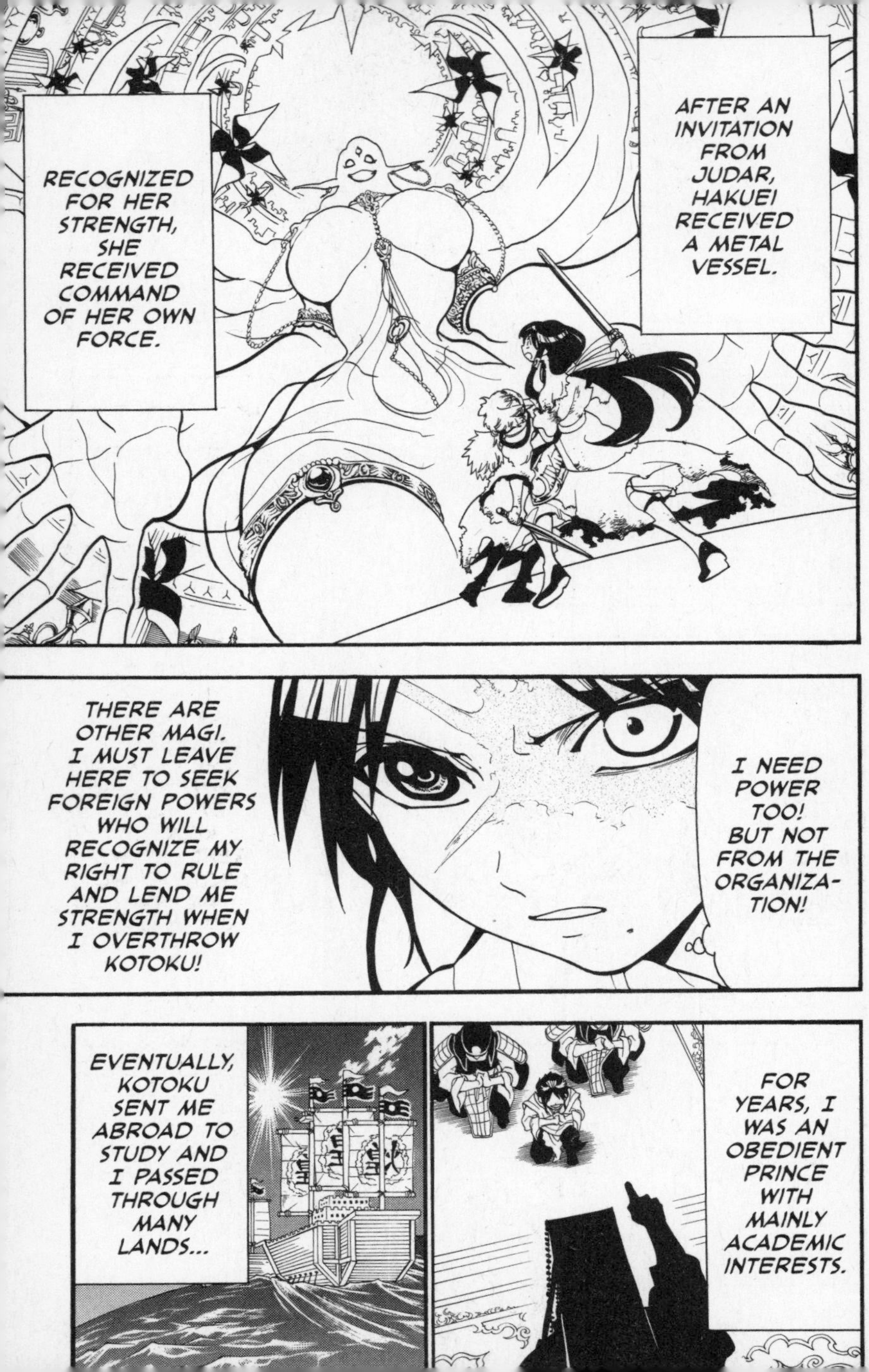
AFTER AN INVITATION FROM JUDAR, HAKUEI RECEIVED A METAL VESSEL.
RECOGNIZED FOR HER STRENGTH, SHE RECEIVED COMMAND OF HER OWN FORCE.
I NEED POWER TOO! BUT NOT FROM THE ORGANIZATION!
THERE ARE OTHER MAGI. I MUST LEAVE HERE TO SEEK FOREIGN POWERS WHO WILL RECOGNIZE MY RIGHT TO RULE AND LEND ME STRENGTH WHEN I OVERTHROW KOTOKU!
FOR YEARS, I WAS AN OBEDIENT PRINCE WITH MAINLY ACADEMIC INTERESTS.
EVENTUALLY, KOTOKU SENT ME ABROAD TO STUDY AND I PASSED THROUGH MANY LANDS...

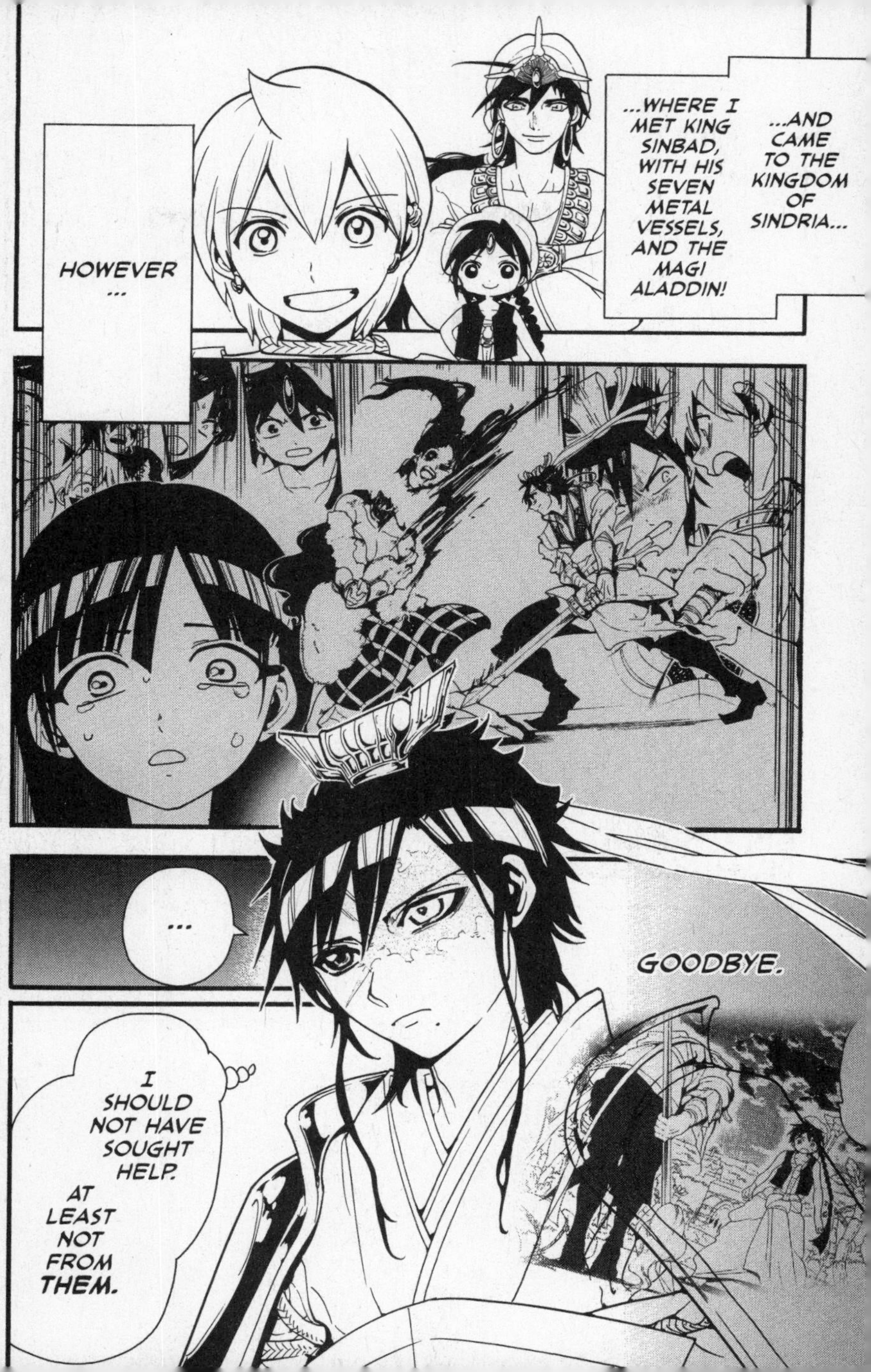
...AND CAME TO THE KINGDOM OF SINDRIA...
...WHERE I MET KING SINBAD, WITH HIS SEVEN METAL VESSELS, AND THE MAGI ALADDIN!
HOWEVER ...
GOODBYE.
...
I SHOULD NOT HAVE SOUGHT HELP.
AT LEAST NOT FROM THEM.

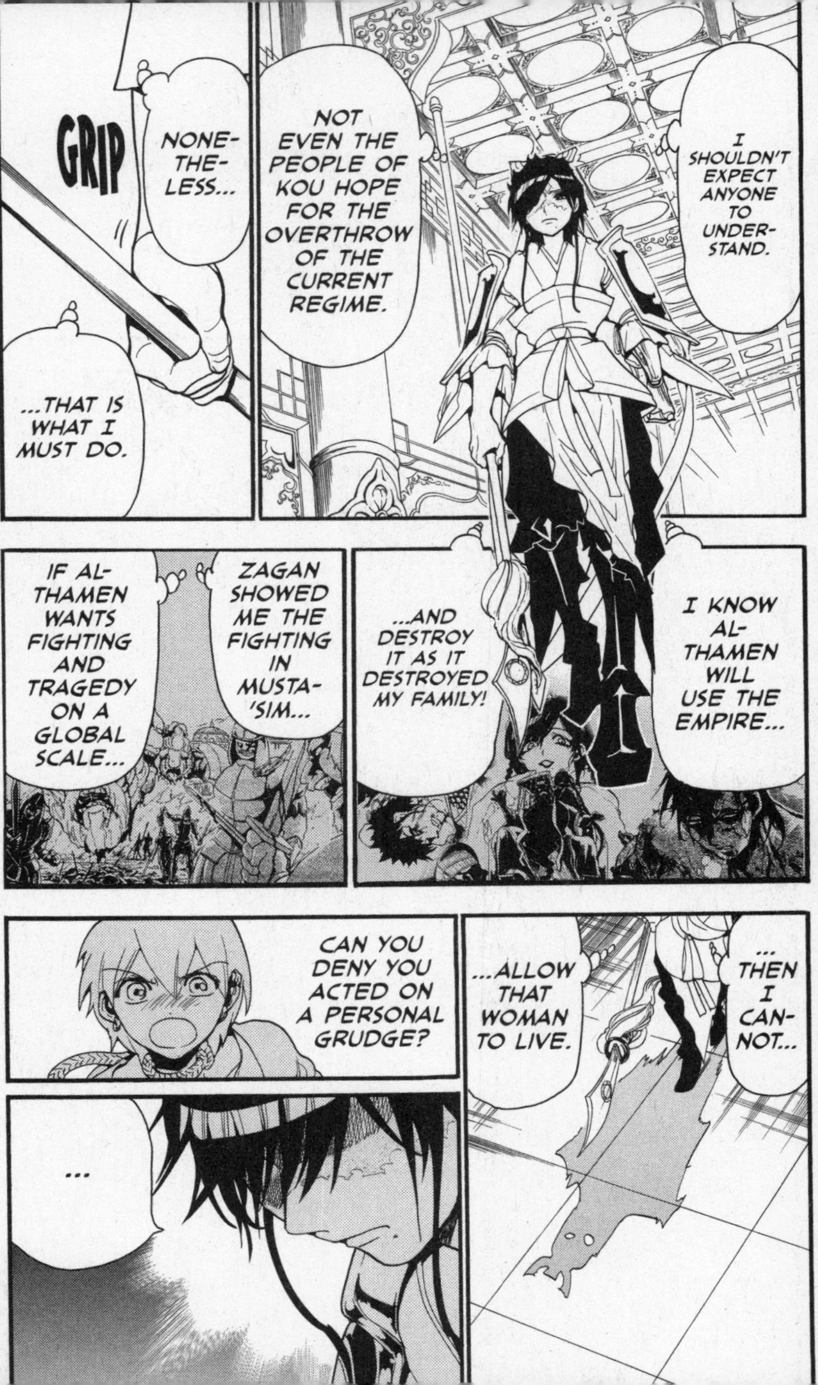
I SHOULDN'T EXPECT ANYONE TO UNDER-STAND.
NOT EVEN THE PEOPLE OF KOU HOPE FOR THE OVERTHROW OF THE CURRENT REGIME.
GRIP
NONE-THE-LESS...
...THAT IS WHAT I MUST DO.
I KNOW AL-THAMEN WILL USE THE EMPIRE...
...AND DESTROY IT AS IT DESTROYED MY FAMILY!
ZAGAN SHOWED ME THE FIGHTING IN MUSTA-'SIM...
IF AL-THAMEN WANTS FIGHTING AND TRAGEDY ON A GLOBAL SCALE...
...THEN I CAN-NOT...
...ALLOW THAT WOMAN TO LIVE.
CAN YOU DENY YOU ACTED ON A PERSONAL GRUDGE?
...

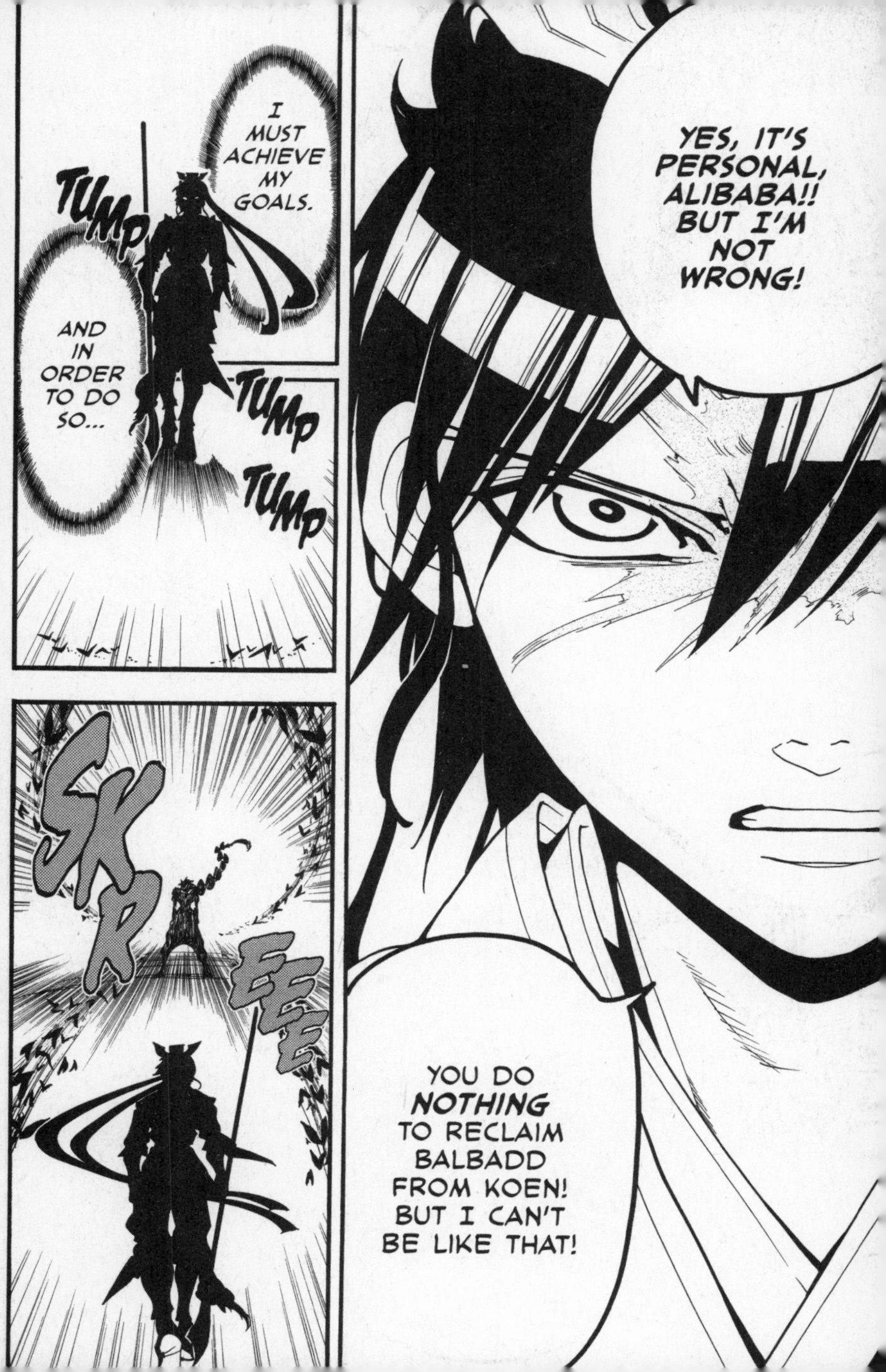
YES, IT'S PERSONAL, ALIBABA!! BUT I'M NOT WRONG!
YOU DO NOTHING TO RECLAIM BALBADD FROM KOEN! BUT I CAN'T BE LIKE THAT!
I MUST ACHIEVE MY GOALS.
TUMP
AND IN ORDER TO DO SO...
TUMP
TUMP
SKREEE

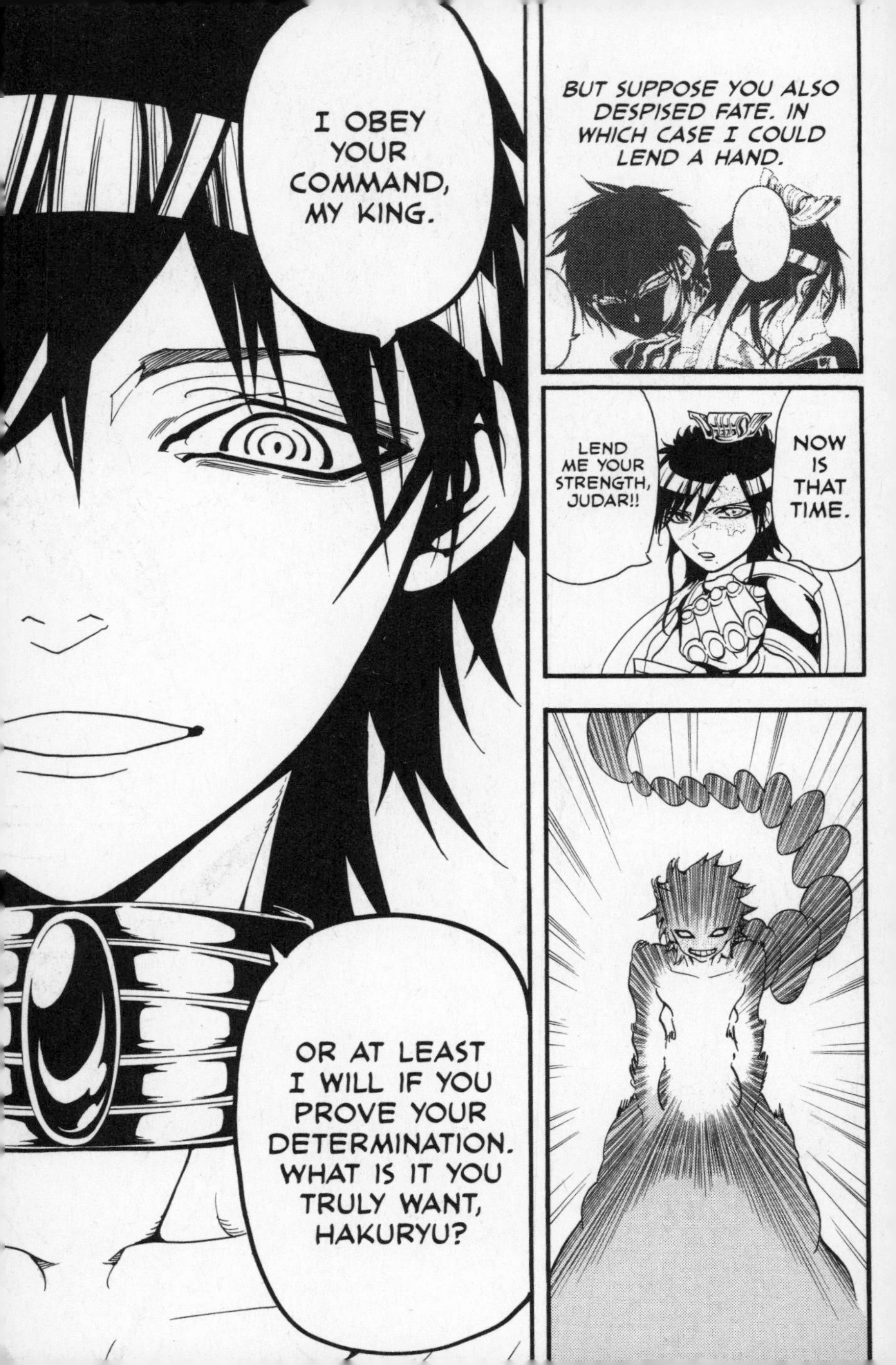
BUT SUPPOSE YOU ALSO DESPISED FATE. IN WHICH CASE I COULD LEND A HAND.
NOW IS THAT TIME.
LEND ME YOUR STRENGTH, JUDAR!!
I OBEY YOUR COMMAND, MY KING.
OR AT LEAST I WILL IF YOU PROVE YOUR DETERMINATION. WHAT IS IT YOU TRULY WANT, HAKURYU?

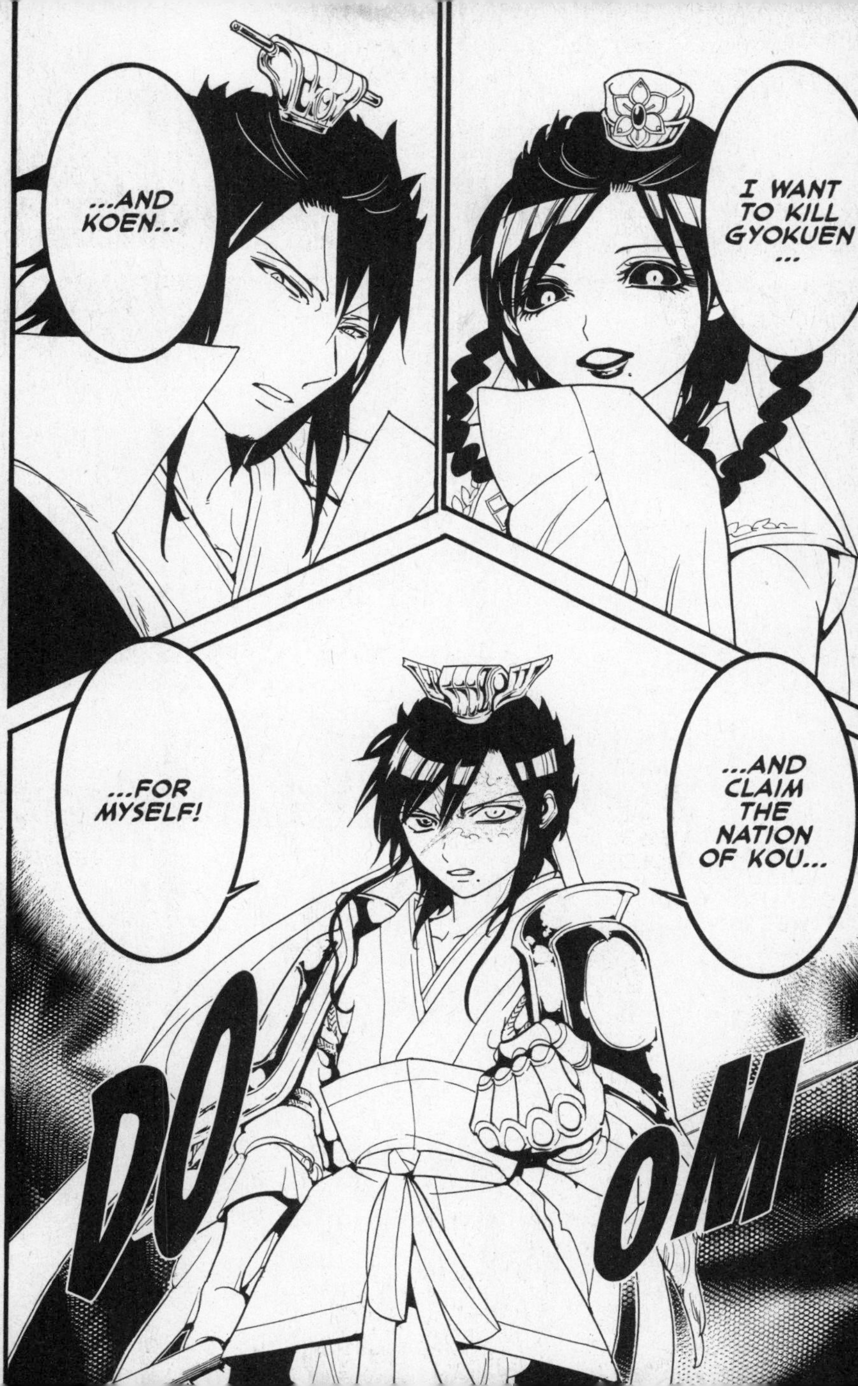
I WANT TO KILL GYOKUEN ...
...AND KOEN...
...AND CLAIM THE NATION OF KOU...
...FOR MYSELF!
DOOM

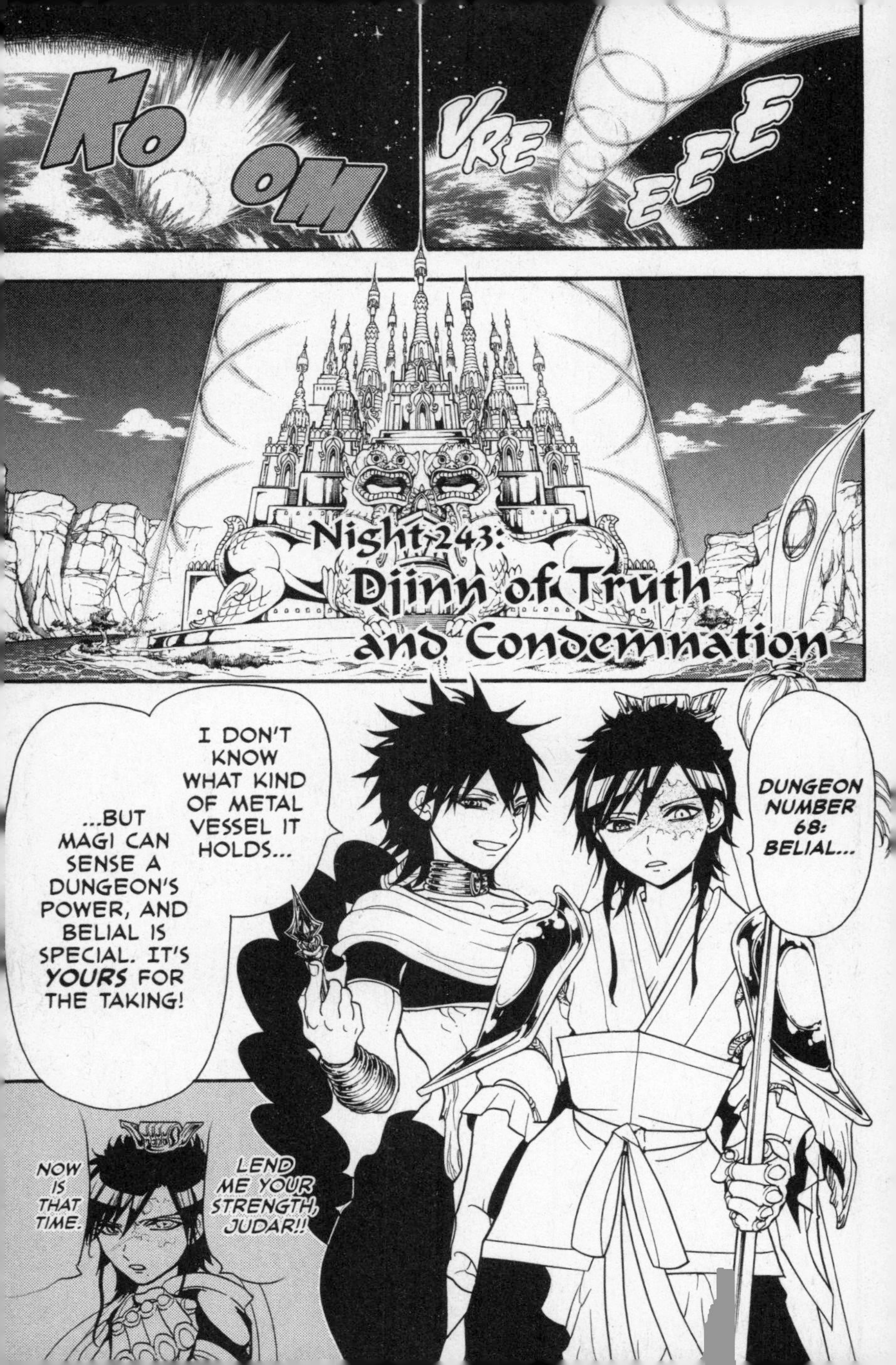
VREEEEE
KOOM
Night 243:
Djinn of Truth and Condemnation
DUNGEON NUMBER 68: BELIAL...
I DON'T KNOW WHAT KIND OF METAL VESSEL IT HOLDS...
...BUT MAGI CAN SENSE A DUNGEON'S POWER, AND BELIAL IS SPECIAL. IT'S *YOURS* FOR THE TAKING!
LEND ME YOUR STRENGTH, JUDAR!!
NOW IS THAT TIME.

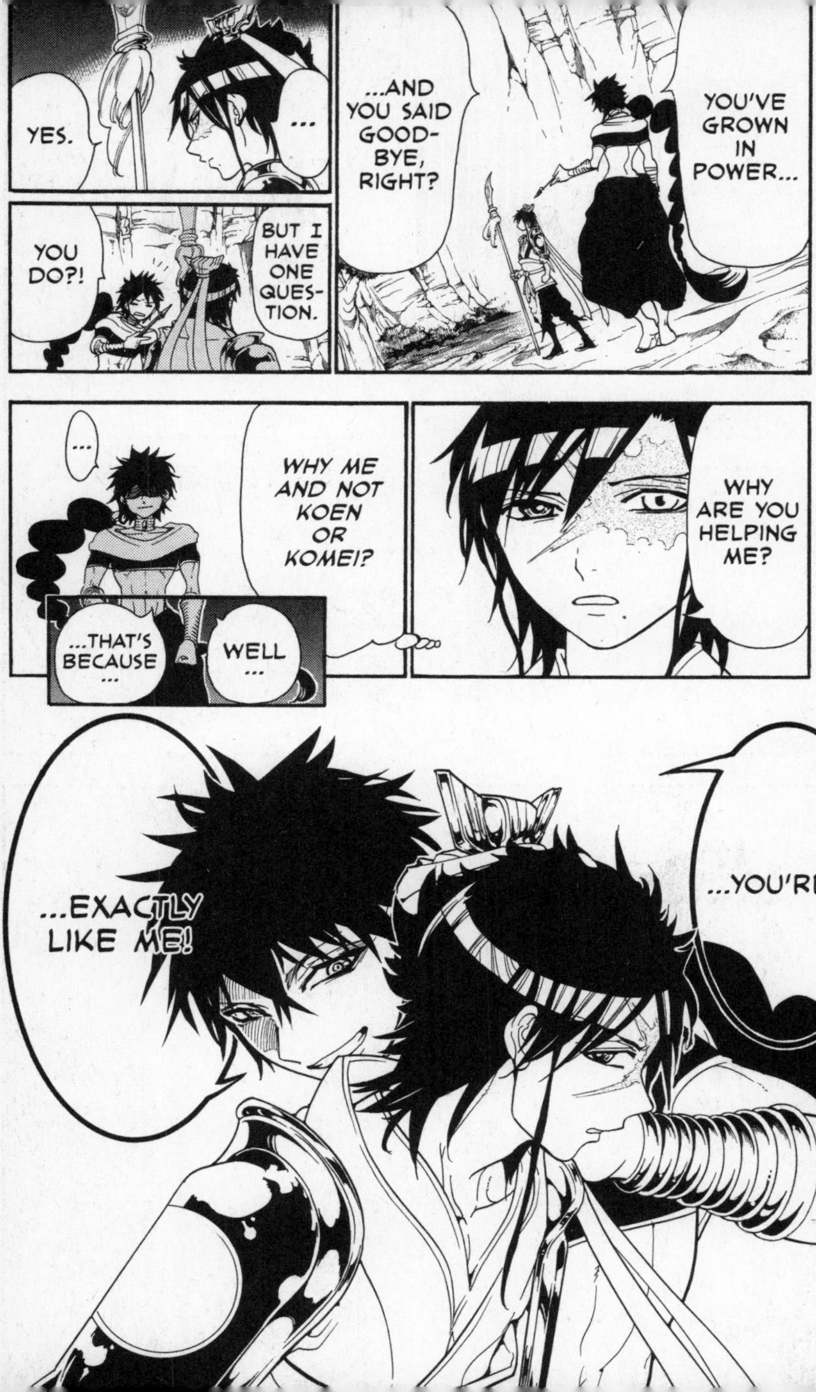
YOU'VE GROWN IN POWER...
...AND YOU SAID GOOD-BYE, RIGHT?
...
YES.
BUT I HAVE ONE QUES-TION.
YOU DO?!
WHY ARE YOU HELPING ME?
WHY ME AND NOT KOEN OR KOMEI?
...
WELL...
...THAT'S BECAUSE...
...YOU'RE...
...EXACTLY LIKE ME!

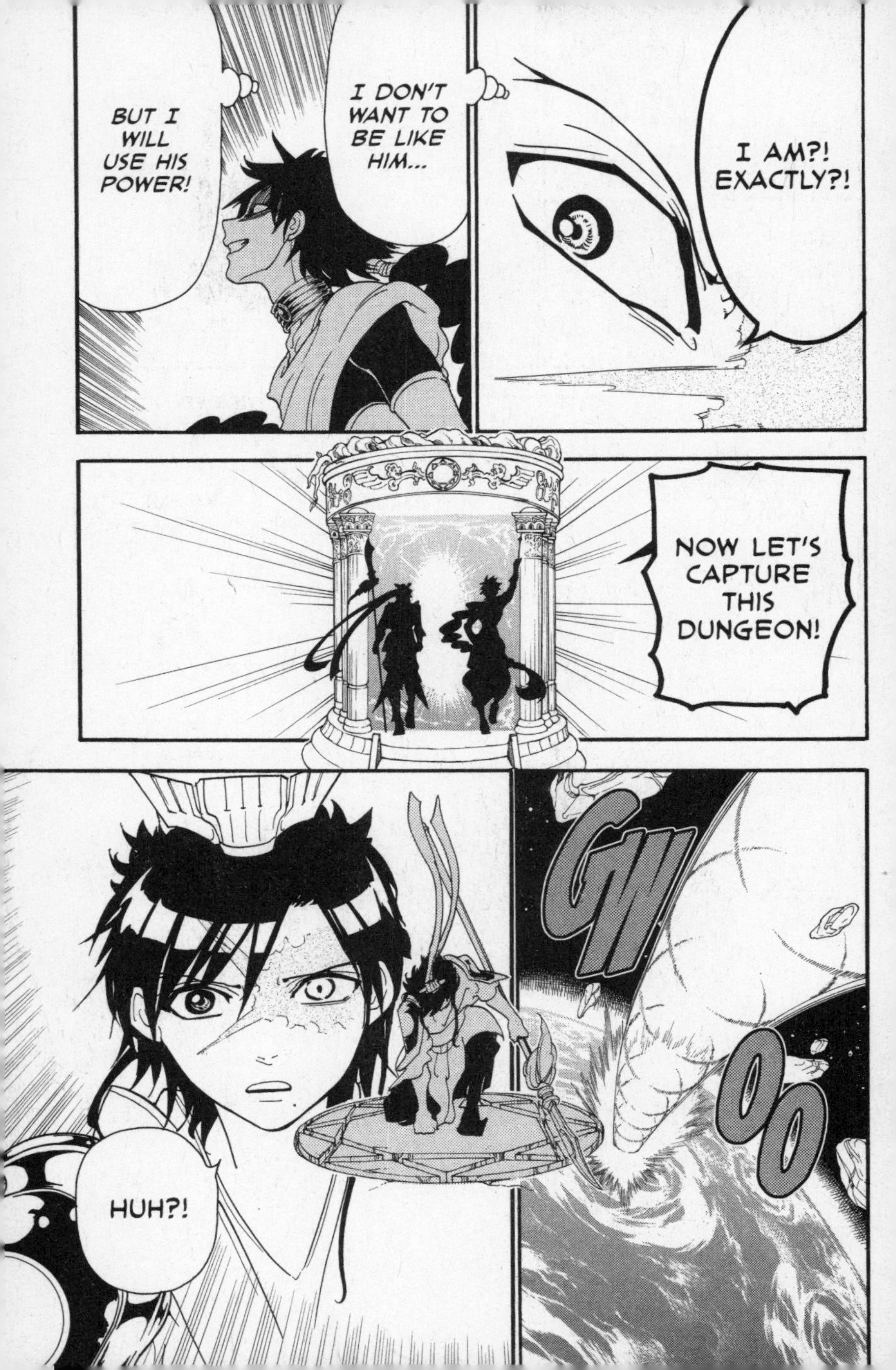
I AM?! EXACTLY?!
I DON'T WANT TO BE LIKE HIM...
BUT I WILL USE HIS POWER!
NOW LET'S CAPTURE THIS DUNGEON!
GWOO
HUH?!

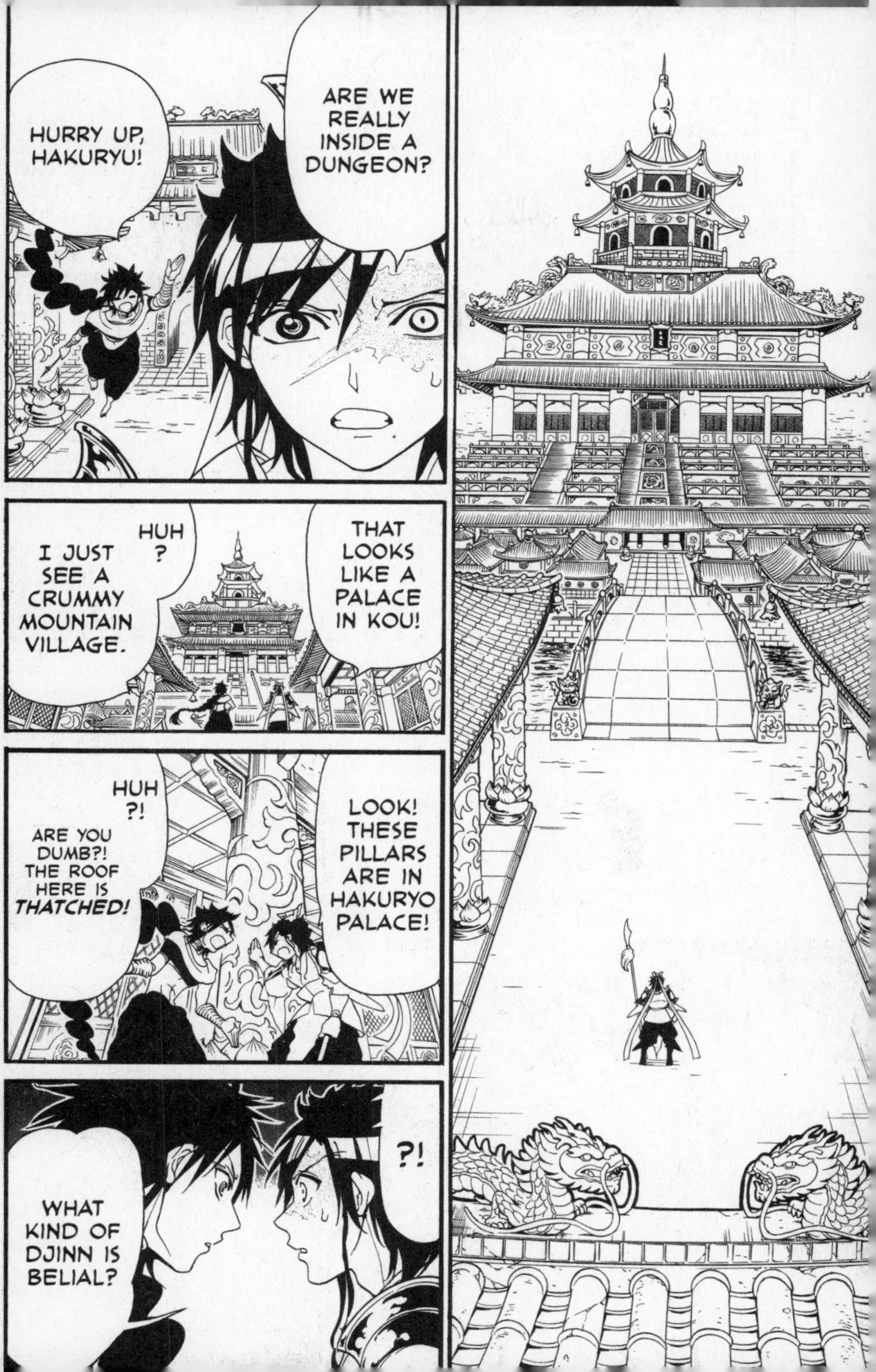
ARE WE REALLY INSIDE A DUNGEON?
HURRY UP, HAKURYU!
THAT LOOKS LIKE A PALACE IN KOU!
HUH ?
I JUST SEE A CRUMMY MOUNTAIN VILLAGE.
LOOK! THESE PILLARS ARE IN HAKURYO PALACE!
HUH ?!
ARE YOU DUMB?! THE ROOF HERE IS *THATCHED!*
?!
WHAT KIND OF DJINN IS BELIAL?

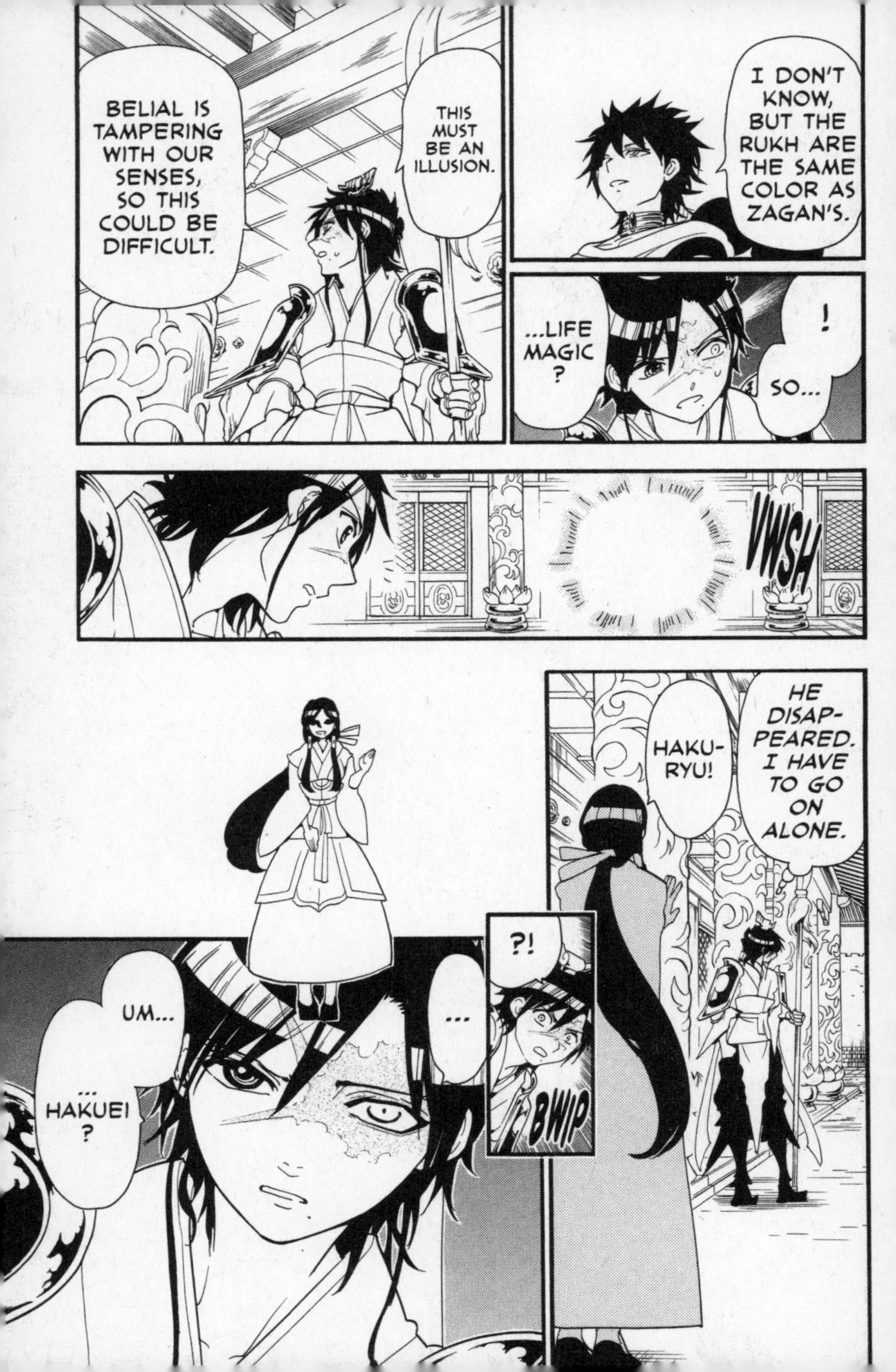
I DON'T KNOW, BUT THE RUKH ARE THE SAME COLOR AS ZAGAN'S.
!
SO...
...LIFE MAGIC?
THIS MUST BE AN ILLUSION.
BELIAL IS TAMPERING WITH OUR SENSES, SO THIS COULD BE DIFFICULT.
VWSH
HE DISAP-PEARED. I HAVE TO GO ON ALONE.
HAKU-RYU!
?!
BWIP
...
UM...
...HAKUEI?

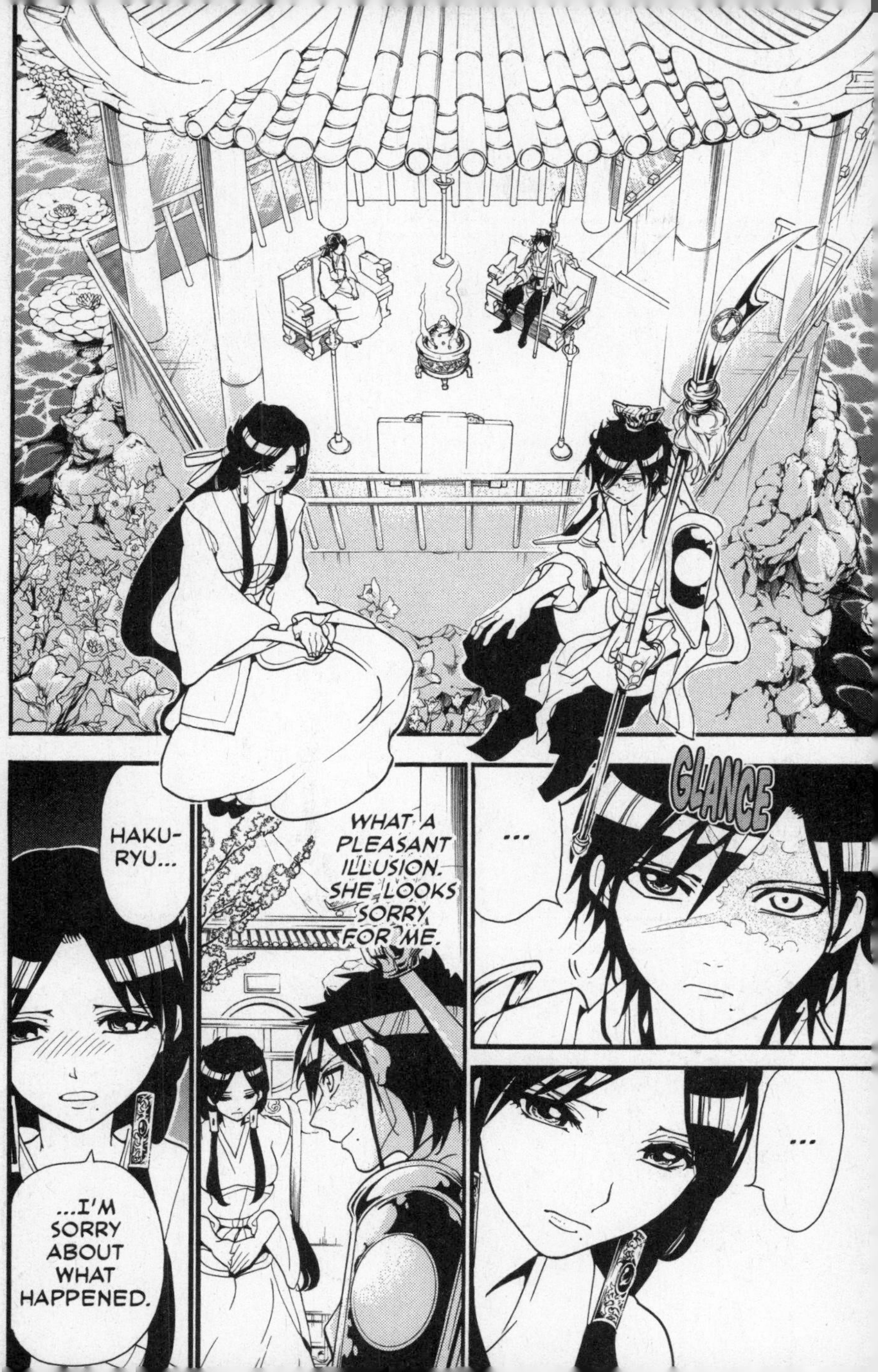
GLANCE
...
...
WHAT A PLEASANT ILLUSION. SHE LOOKS SORRY FOR ME.
HAKU-RYU...
...I'M SORRY ABOUT WHAT HAPPENED.

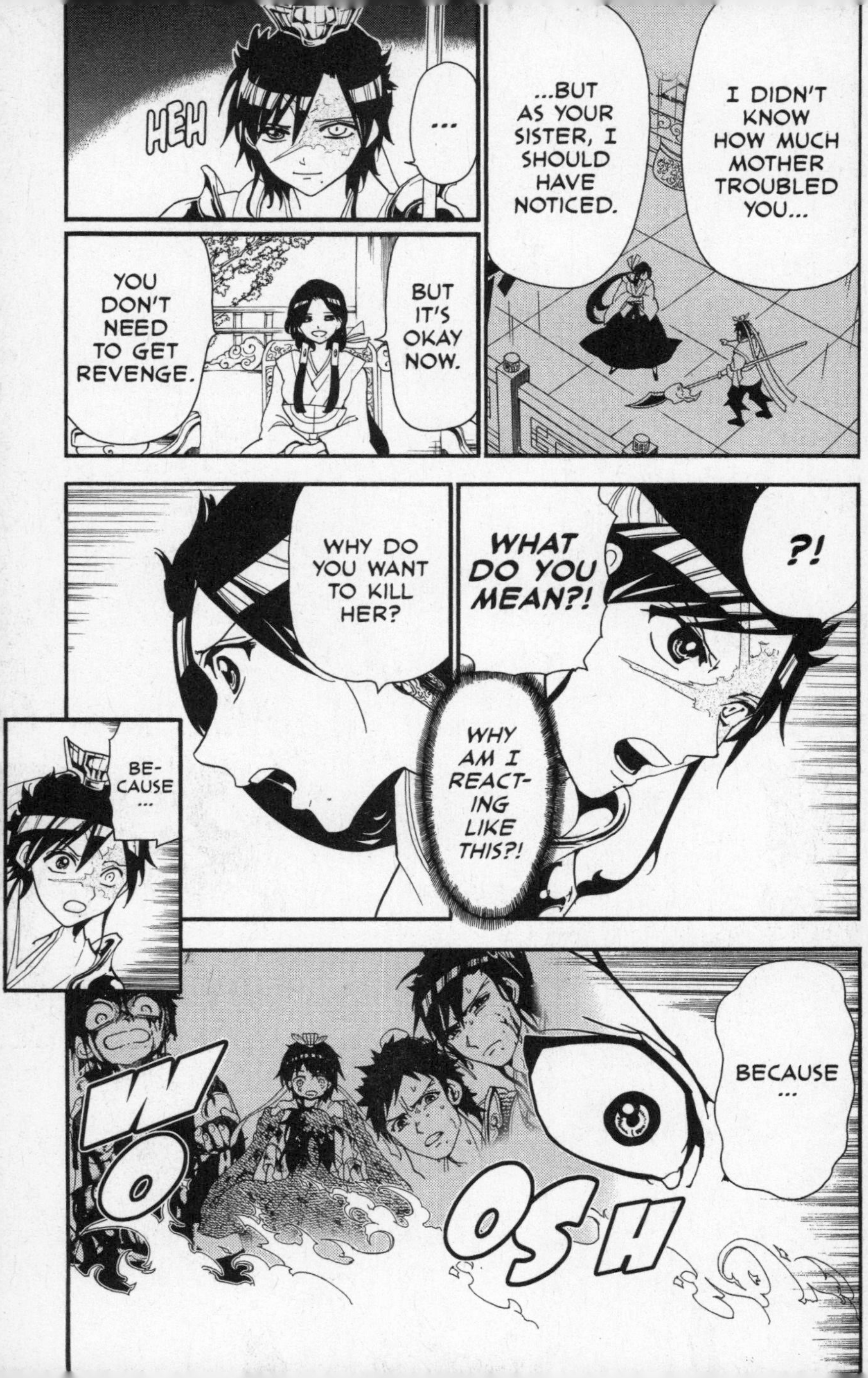
I DIDN'T KNOW HOW MUCH MOTHER TROUBLED YOU...
...BUT AS YOUR SISTER, I SHOULD HAVE NOTICED.
...
HEH
BUT IT'S OKAY NOW.
YOU DON'T NEED TO GET REVENGE.
?!
WHAT DO YOU MEAN?!
WHY DO YOU WANT TO KILL HER?
WHY AM I REACT-ING LIKE THIS?!
BE-CAUSE ...
BECAUSE ...
WHOOSH

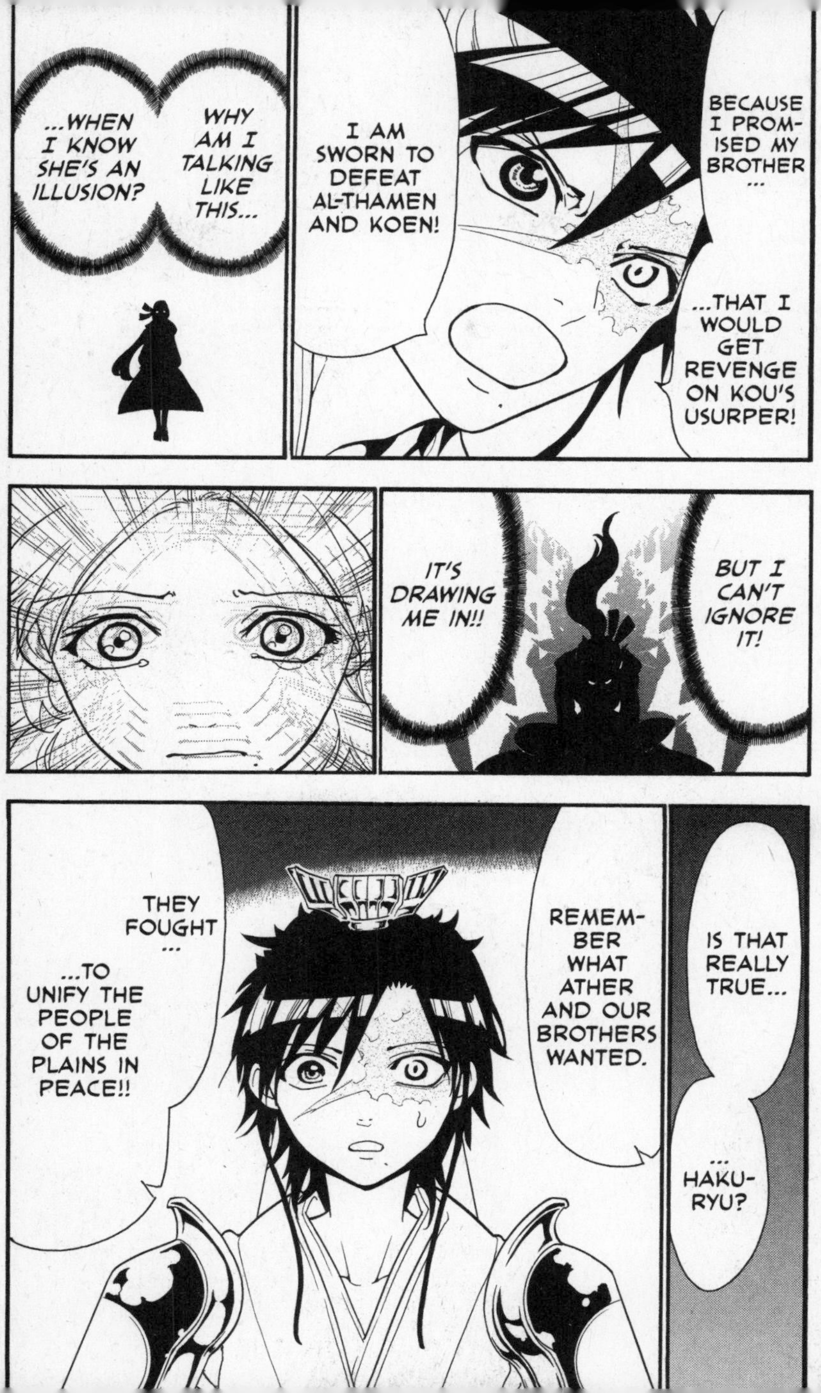
BECAUSE I PROMISED MY BROTHER ...
...THAT I WOULD GET REVENGE ON KOU'S USURPER!
I AM SWORN TO DEFEAT AL-THAMEN AND KOEN!
WHY AM I TALKING LIKE THIS...
...WHEN I KNOW SHE'S AN ILLUSION?
BUT I CAN'T IGNORE IT!
IT'S DRAWING ME IN!!
IS THAT REALLY TRUE...
... HAKU-RYU?
REMEM-BER WHAT ATHER AND OUR BROTHERS WANTED.
THEY FOUGHT ...
...TO UNIFY THE PEOPLE OF THE PLAINS IN PEACE!!

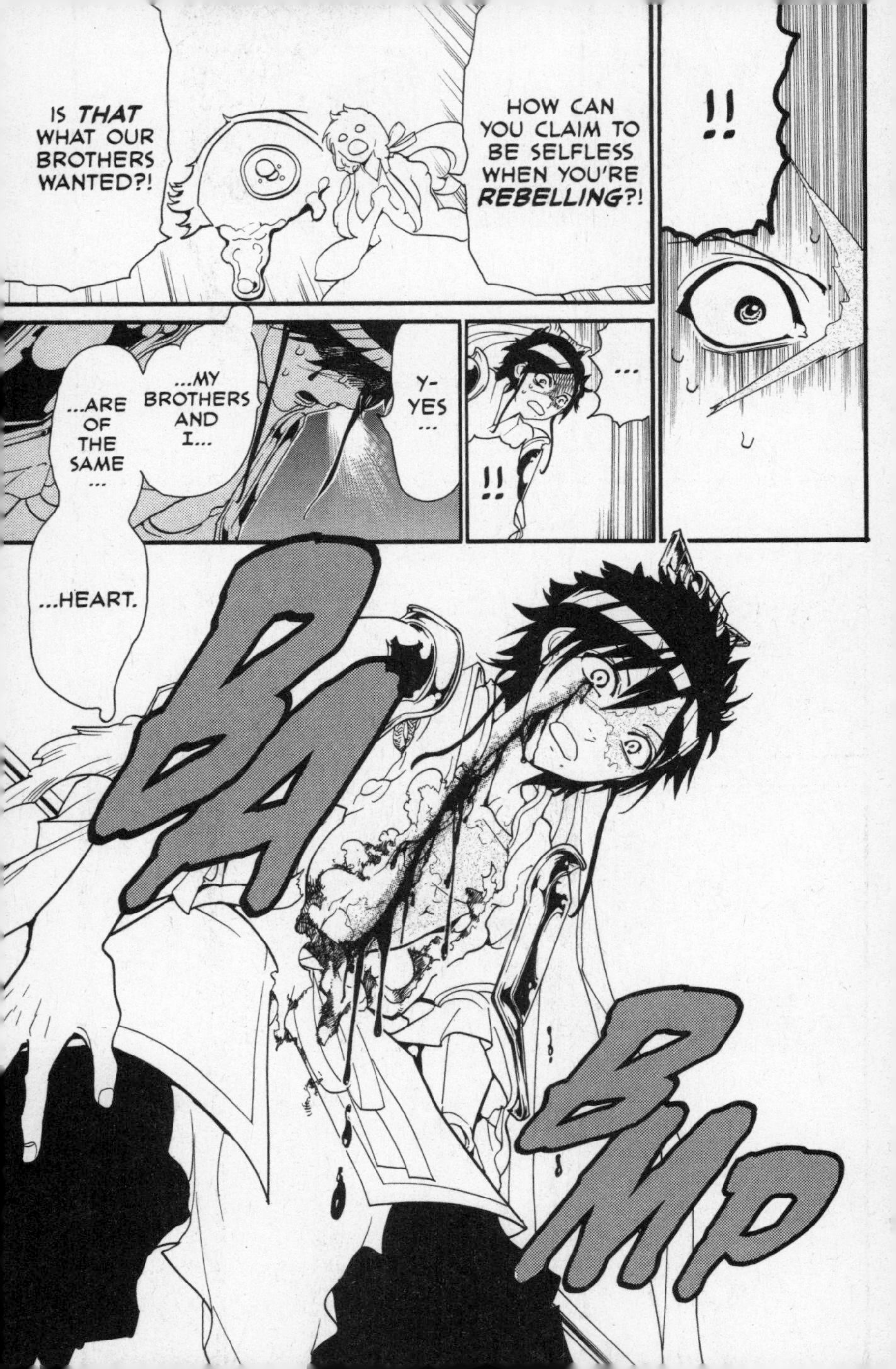
!!
HOW CAN YOU CLAIM TO BE SELFLESS WHEN YOU'RE *REBELLING*?!
IS *THAT* WHAT OUR BROTHERS WANTED?!
...
!!
Y- YES ...
...MY BROTHERS AND I...
...ARE OF THE SAME ...
...HEART.
BA
BMP

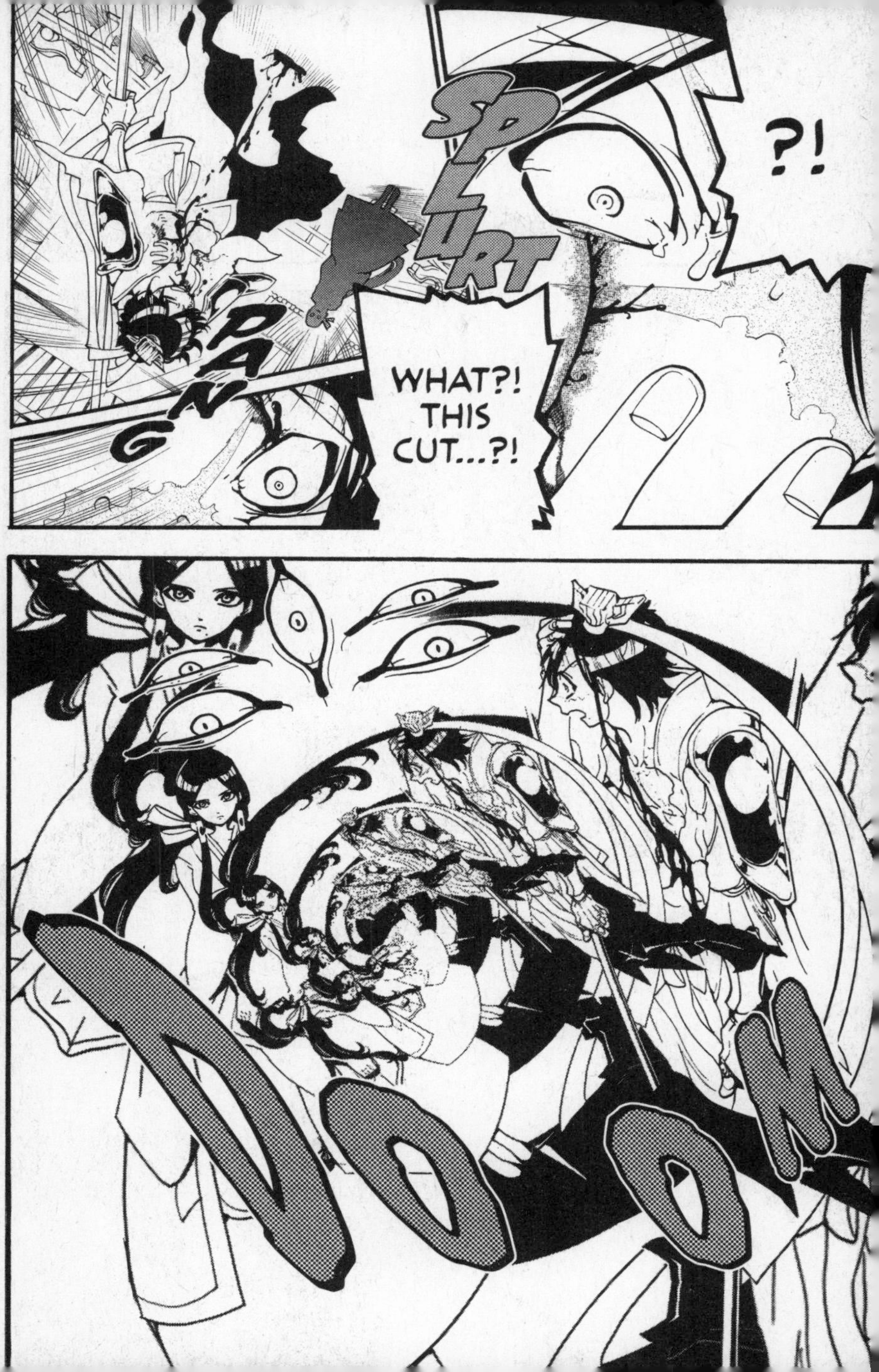
?!
SPLURT
WHAT?! THIS CUT...?!
CLANG
DOOOM

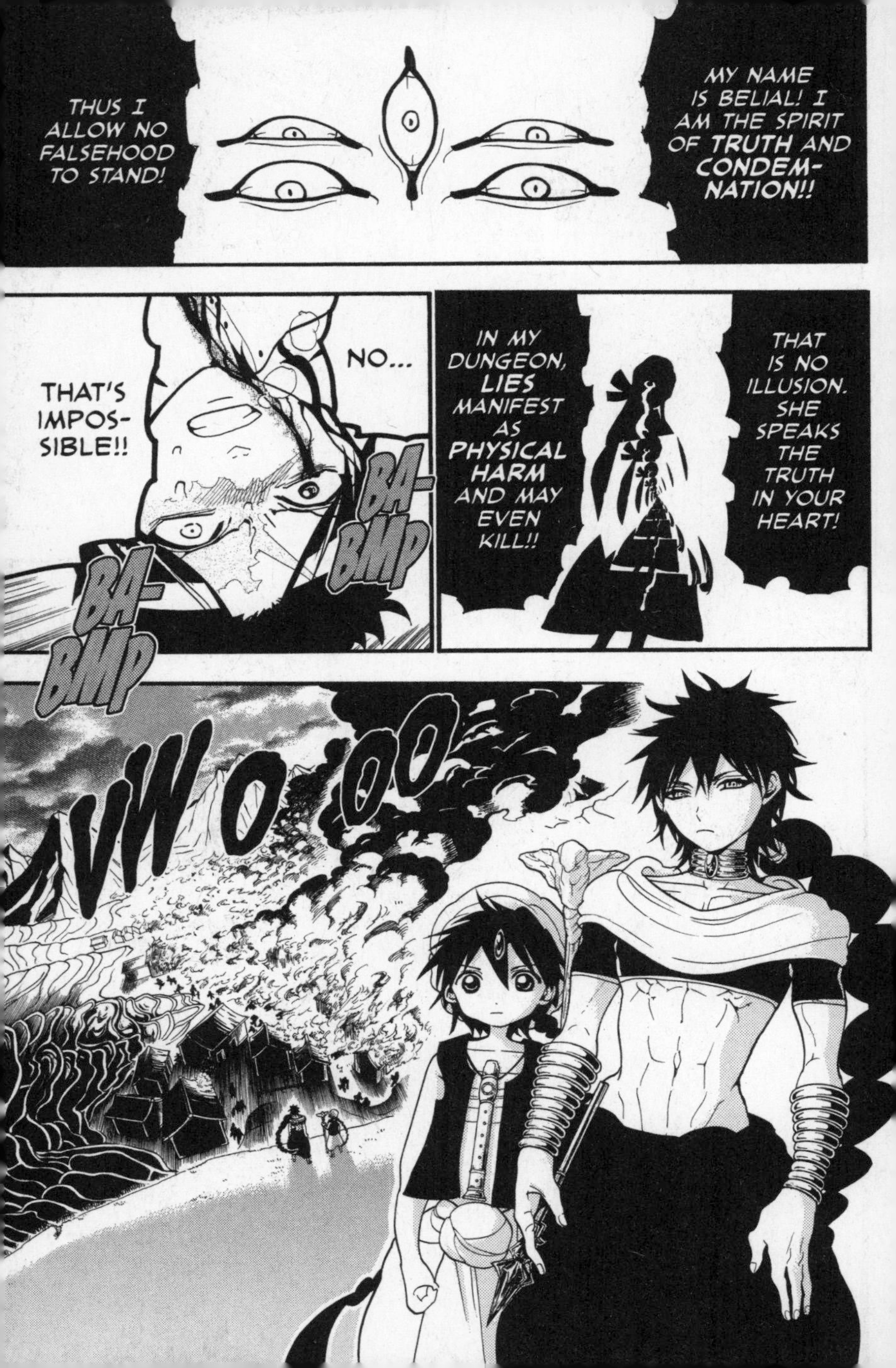
MY NAME IS BELIAL! I AM THE SPIRIT OF TRUTH AND CONDEMNATION!!
THUS I ALLOW NO FALSEHOOD TO STAND!
THAT IS NO ILLUSION. SHE SPEAKS THE TRUTH IN YOUR HEART!
IN MY DUNGEON, LIES MANIFEST AS PHYSICAL HARM AND MAY EVEN KILL!!
NO...
THAT'S IMPOSSIBLE!!
BA-BMP
BA-BMP
VWOOOO

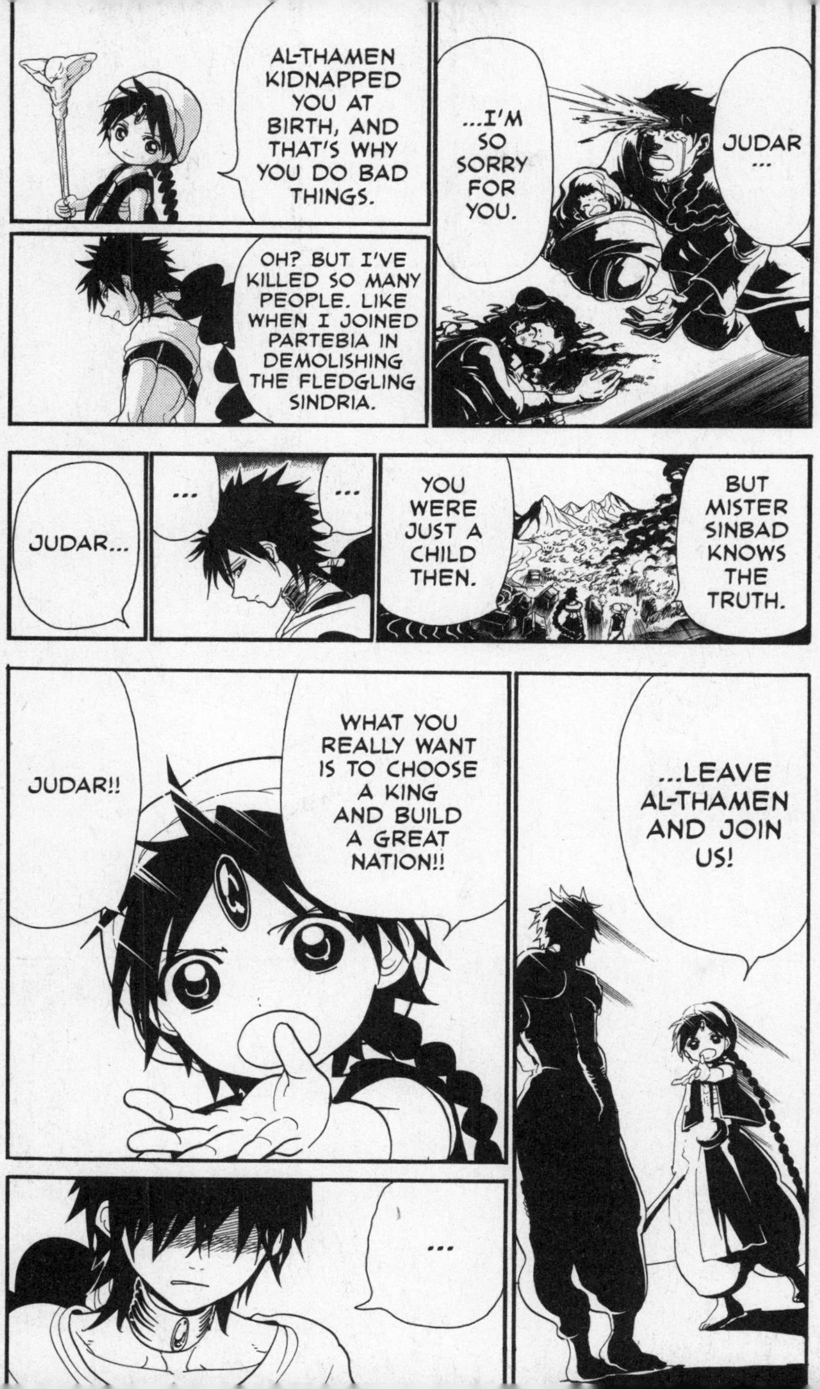
JUDAR ...
...I'M SO SORRY FOR YOU.
AL-THAMEN KIDNAPPED YOU AT BIRTH, AND THAT'S WHY YOU DO BAD THINGS.
OH? BUT I'VE KILLED SO MANY PEOPLE. LIKE WHEN I JOINED PARTEBIA IN DEMOLISHING THE FLEDGLING SINDRIA.
BUT MISTER SINBAD KNOWS THE TRUTH.
YOU WERE JUST A CHILD THEN.
...
...
JUDAR...
...LEAVE AL-THAMEN AND JOIN US!
WHAT YOU REALLY WANT IS TO CHOOSE A KING AND BUILD A GREAT NATION!!
JUDAR!!
...

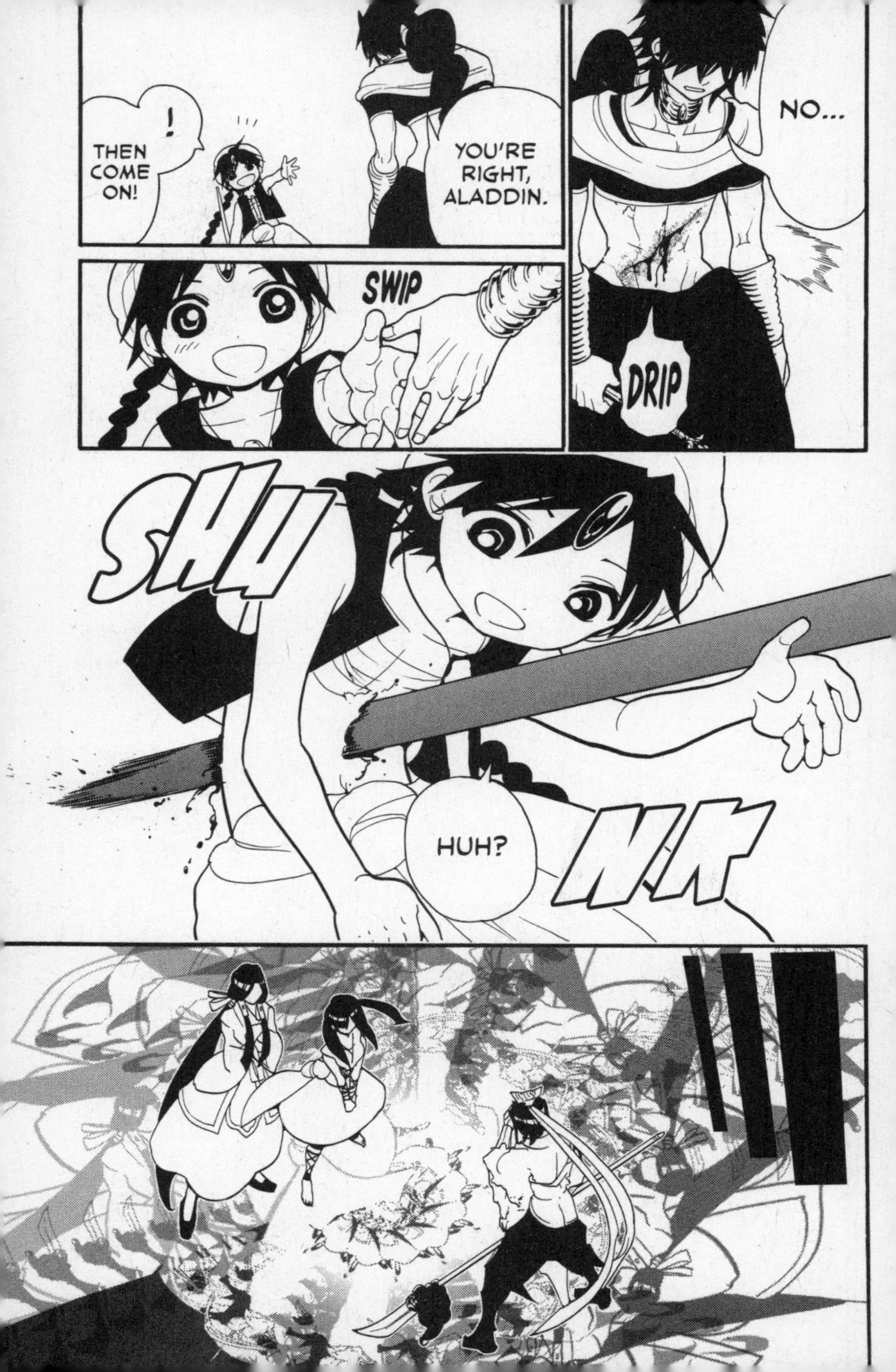
NO...
DRIP
YOU'RE RIGHT, ALADDIN.
!
THEN COME ON!
SWIP
SHU
NK
HUH?

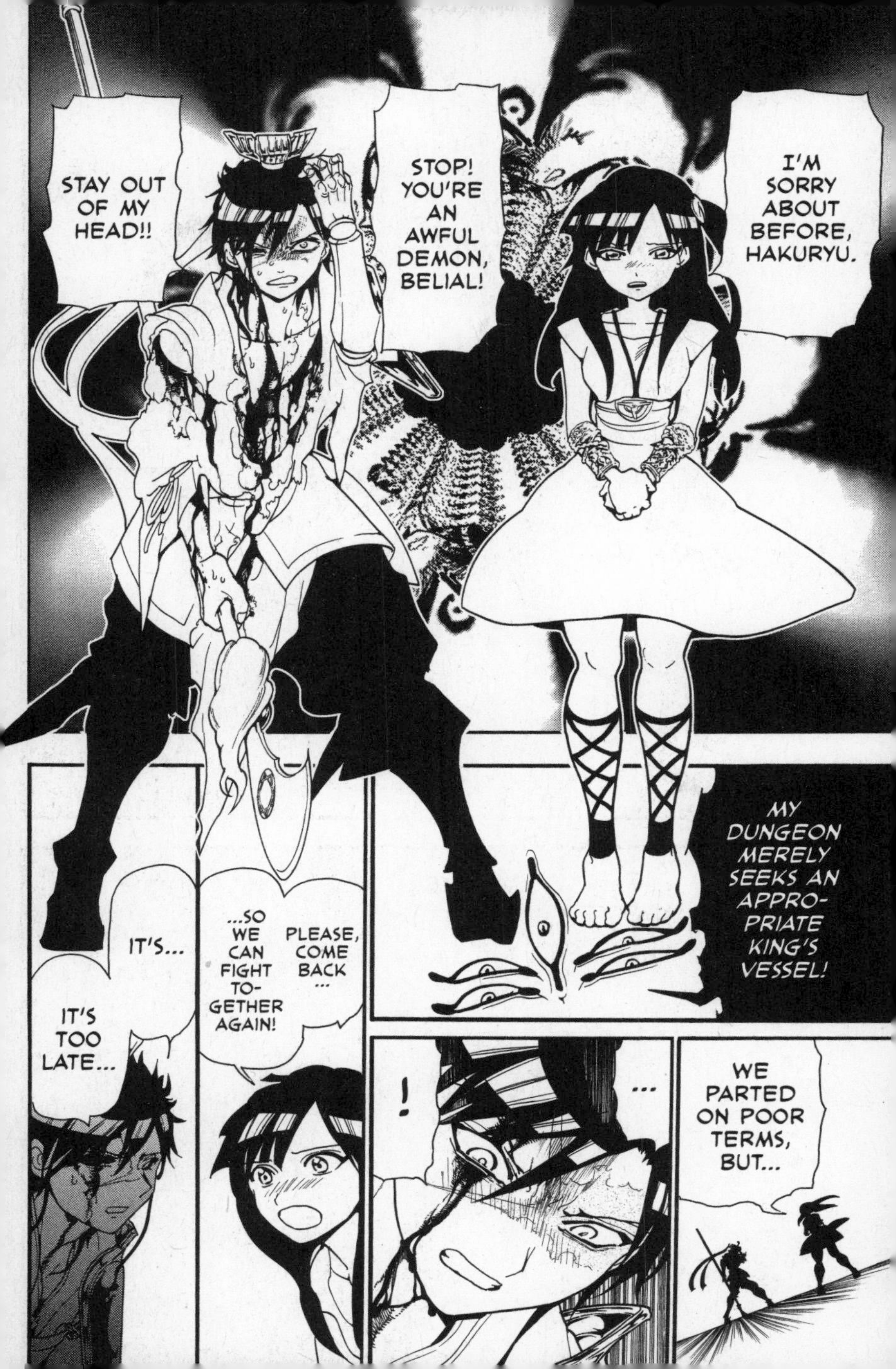
I'M SORRY ABOUT BEFORE, HAKURYU.
STOP! YOU'RE AN AWFUL DEMON, BELIAL!
STAY OUT OF MY HEAD!!
MY DUNGEON MERELY SEEKS AN APPRO-PRIATE KING'S VESSEL!
WE PARTED ON POOR TERMS, BUT...
...
!
PLEASE, COME BACK...
...SO WE CAN FIGHT TO-GETHER AGAIN!
IT'S...
IT'S TOO LATE...

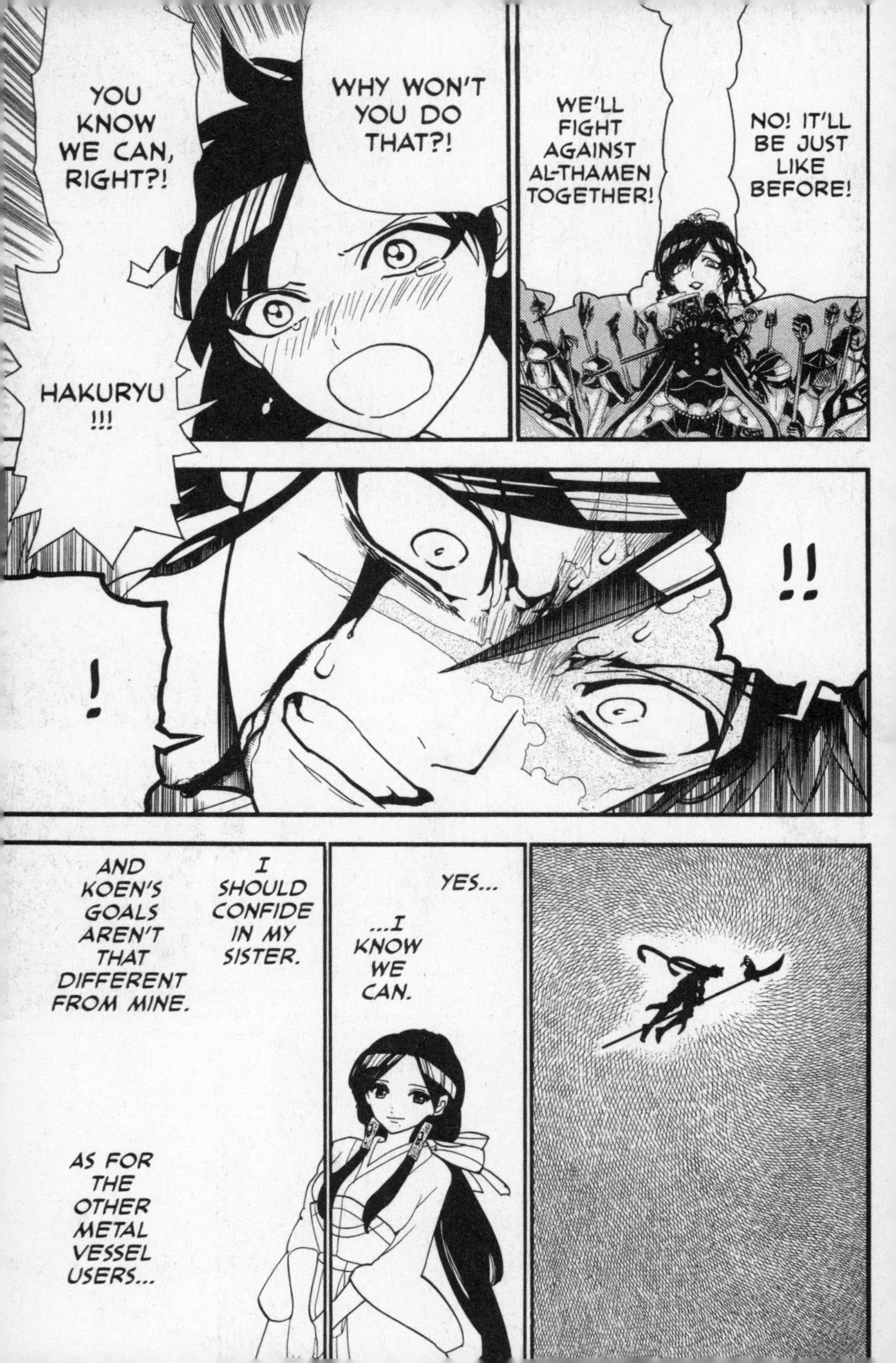
NO! IT'LL BE JUST LIKE BEFORE!
WE'LL FIGHT AGAINST AL-THAMEN TOGETHER!
WHY WON'T YOU DO THAT?!
YOU KNOW WE CAN, RIGHT?!
HAKURYU!!!
!!
!
YES...
...I KNOW WE CAN.
I SHOULD CONFIDE IN MY SISTER.
AND KOEN'S GOALS AREN'T THAT DIFFERENT FROM MINE.
AS FOR THE OTHER METAL VESSEL USERS...

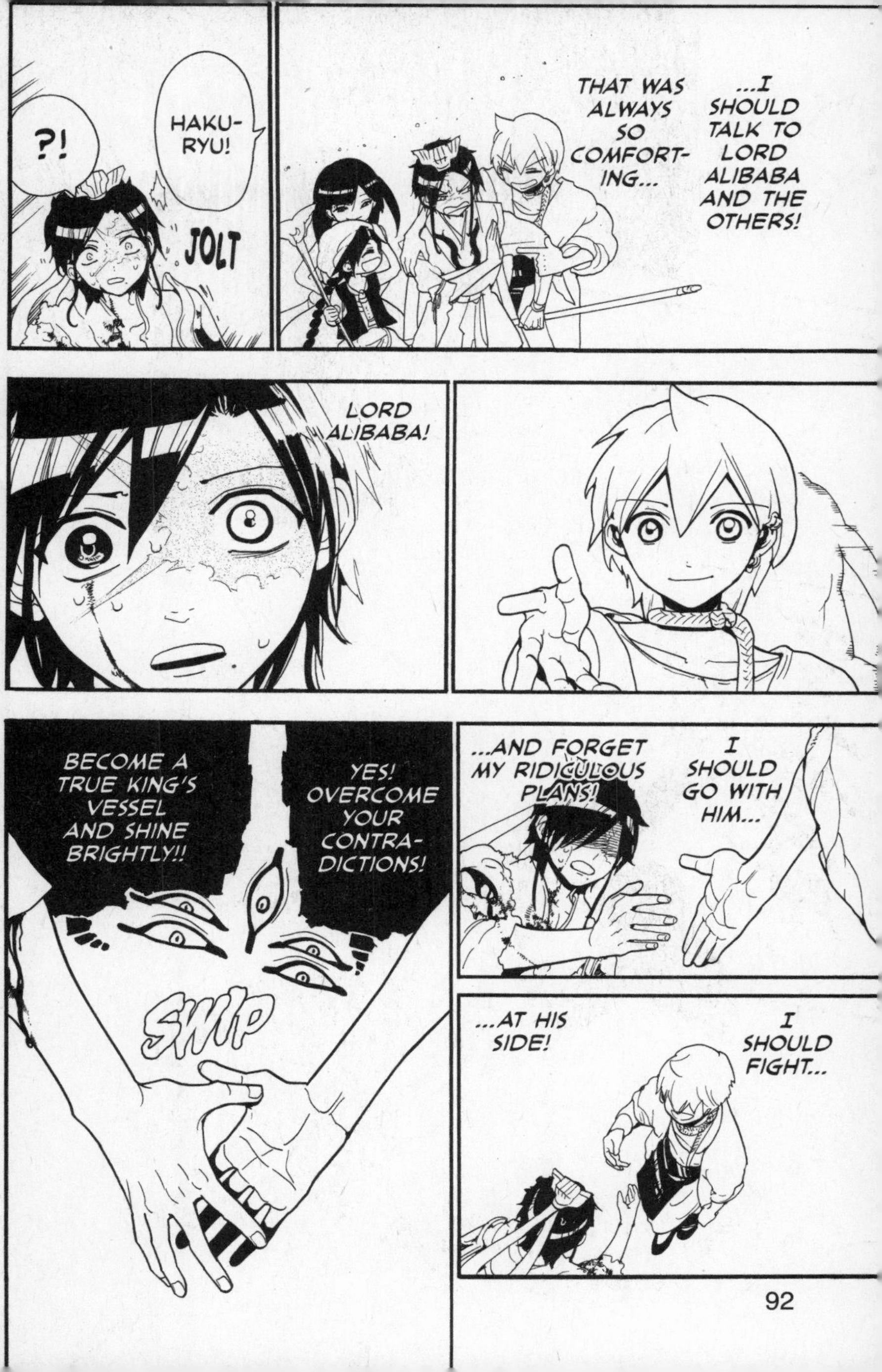
...I SHOULD TALK TO LORD ALIBABA AND THE OTHERS!
THAT WAS ALWAYS SO COMFORTING...
HAKU-RYU!
?!
JOLT
LORD ALIBABA!
I SHOULD GO WITH HIM...
...AND FORGET MY RIDICULOUS PLANS!
I SHOULD FIGHT...
...AT HIS SIDE!
YES! OVERCOME YOUR CONTRADICTIONS!
BECOME A TRUE KING'S VESSEL AND SHINE BRIGHTLY!!
SWIP

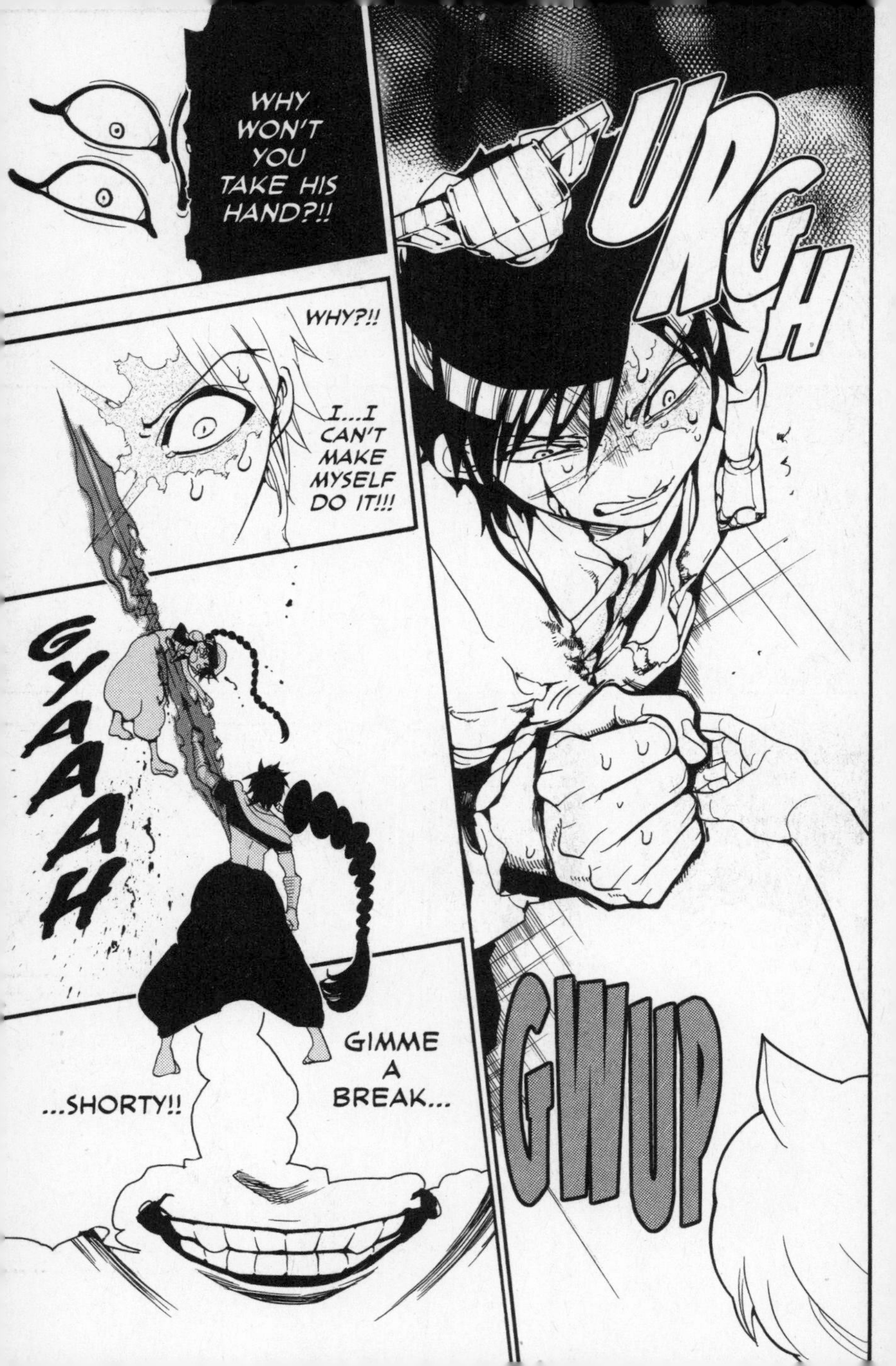
UNGH
GWUP
WHY WON'T YOU TAKE HIS HAND?!!
WHY?!!
I...I CAN'T MAKE MYSELF DO IT!!!
GYAAAH
GIMME A BREAK...
...SHORTY!!

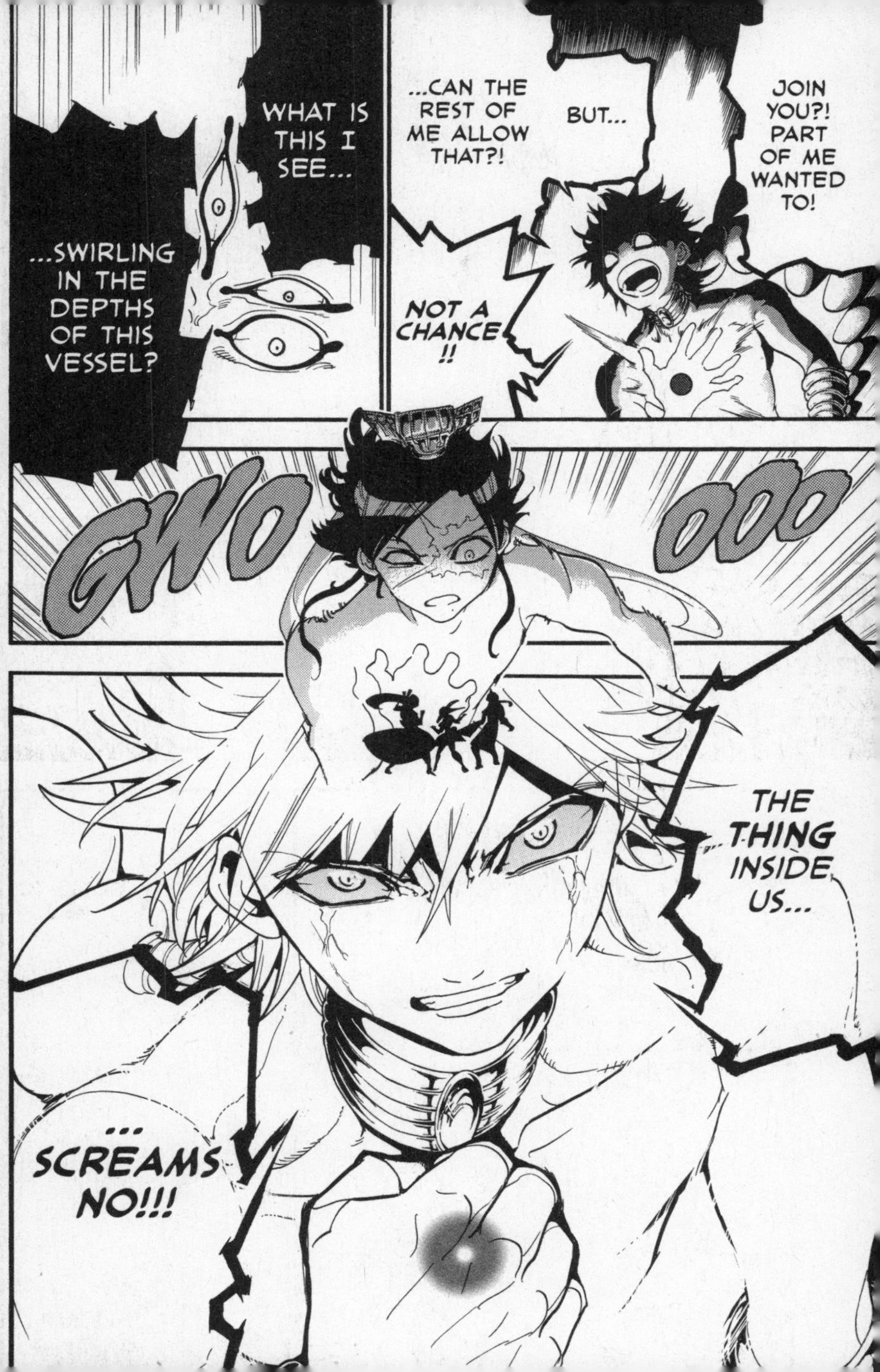
JOIN YOU?! PART OF ME WANTED TO!
BUT...
...CAN THE REST OF ME ALLOW THAT?!
NOT A CHANCE!!
WHAT IS THIS I SEE...
...SWIRLING IN THE DEPTHS OF THIS VESSEL?
GWOOOO
THE THING INSIDE US...
...SCREAMS NO!!!

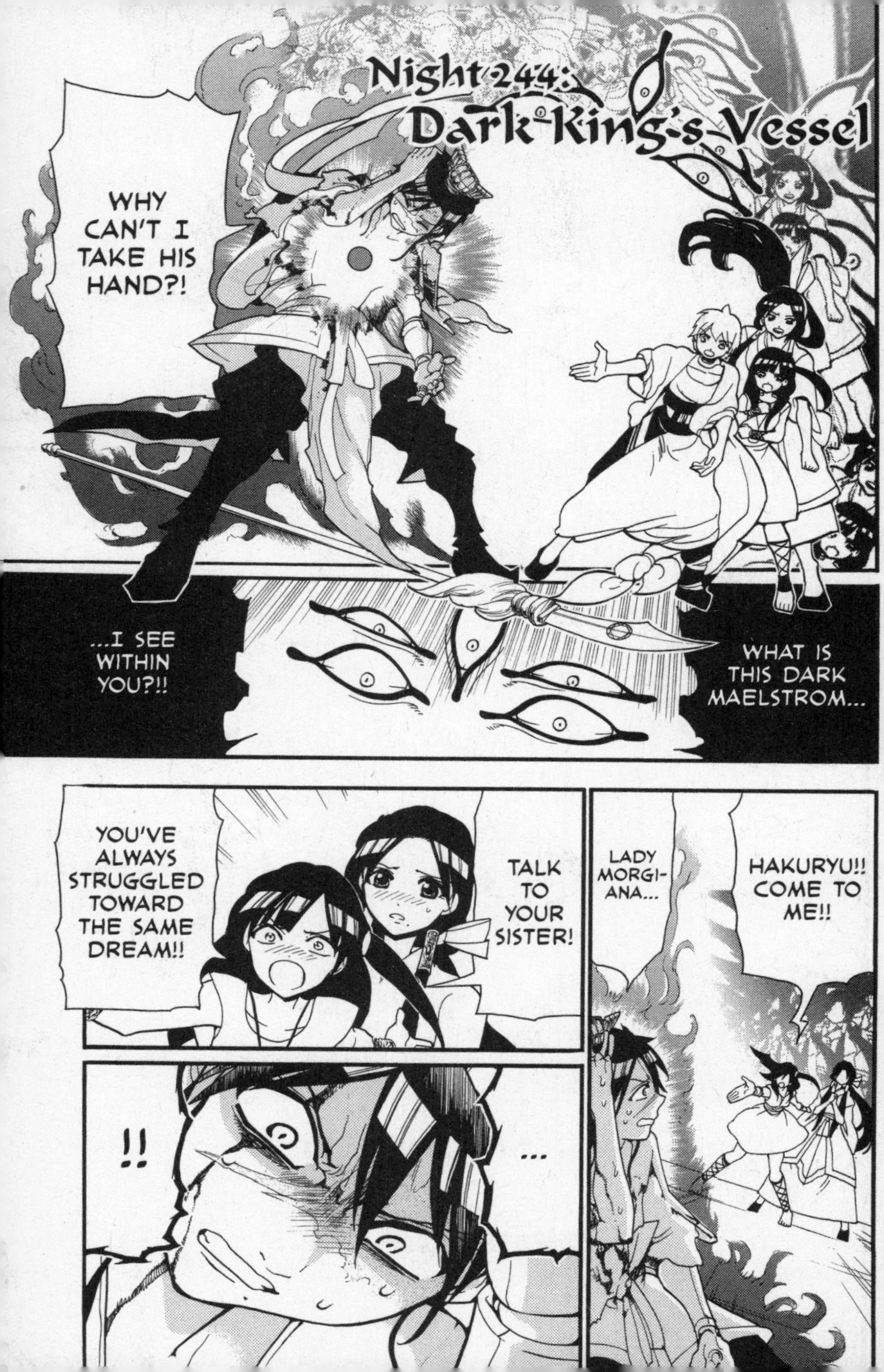
Night 244: Dark King's Vessel
WHY CAN'T I TAKE HIS HAND?!
WHAT IS THIS DARK MAELSTROM...
...I SEE WITHIN YOU?!!
HAKURYU!! COME TO ME!!
LADY MORGIANA...
TALK TO YOUR SISTER!
YOU'VE ALWAYS STRUGGLED TOWARD THE SAME DREAM!!
...
!!

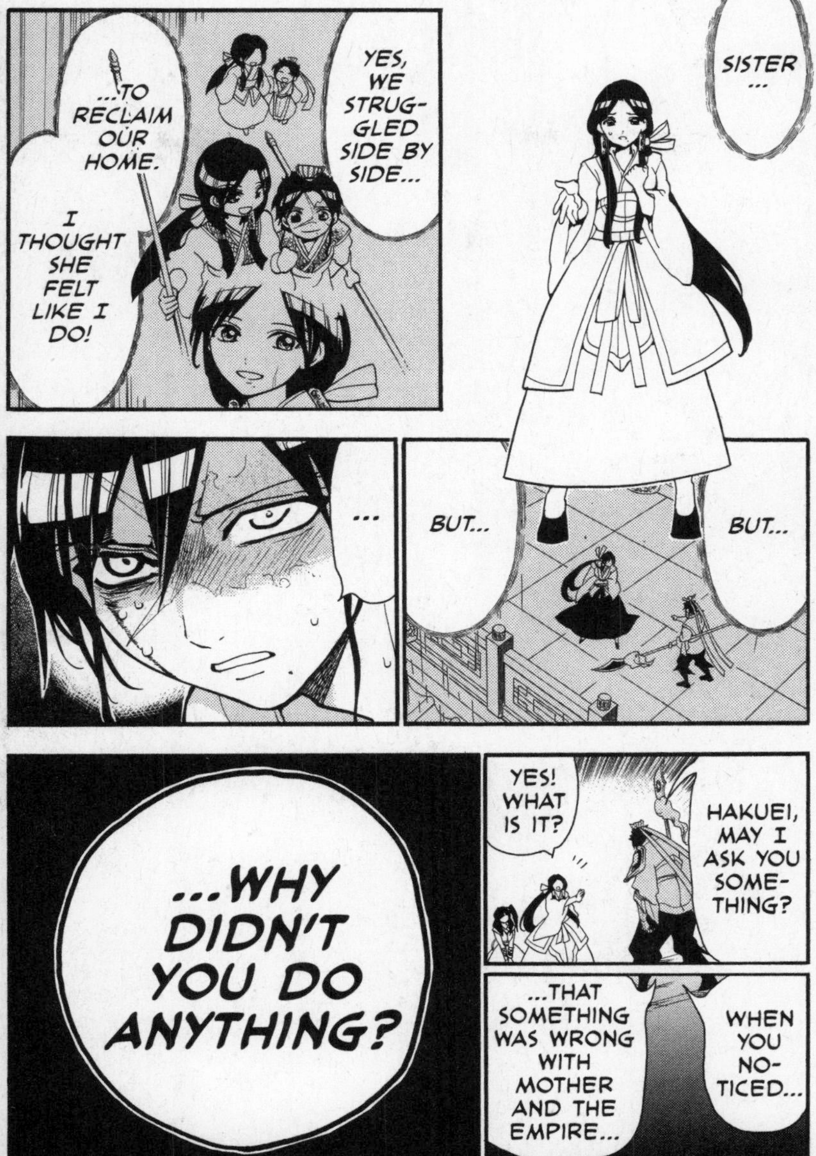
SISTER ...
YES, WE STRUG-GLED SIDE BY SIDE...
...TO RECLAIM OUR HOME.
I THOUGHT SHE FELT LIKE I DO!
BUT...
BUT...
...
HAKUEI, MAY I ASK YOU SOME-THING?
YES! WHAT IS IT?
WHEN YOU NO-TICED...
...THAT SOMETHING WAS WRONG WITH MOTHER AND THE EMPIRE...
...WHY DIDN'T YOU DO ANYTHING?

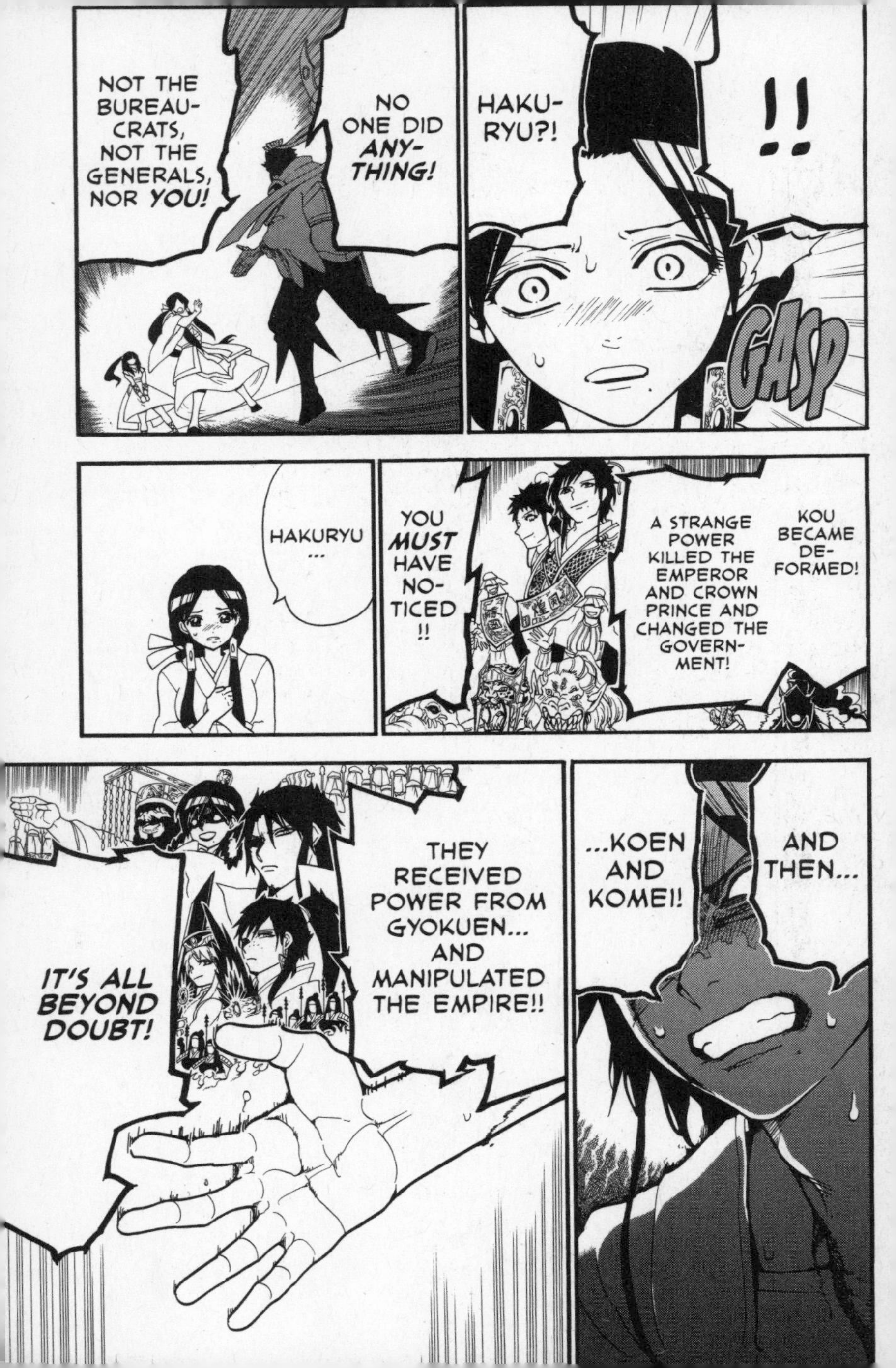
!!
HAKU-RYU?!
GASP
NO ONE DID ANYTHING!
NOT THE BUREAUCRATS, NOT THE GENERALS, NOR YOU!
KOU BECAME DEFORMED!
A STRANGE POWER KILLED THE EMPEROR AND CROWN PRINCE AND CHANGED THE GOVERNMENT!
YOU MUST HAVE NOTICED!!
HAKURYU...
AND THEN...
...KOEN AND KOMEI!!
THEY RECEIVED POWER FROM GYOKUEN... AND MANIPULATED THE EMPIRE!!
IT'S ALL BEYOND DOUBT!

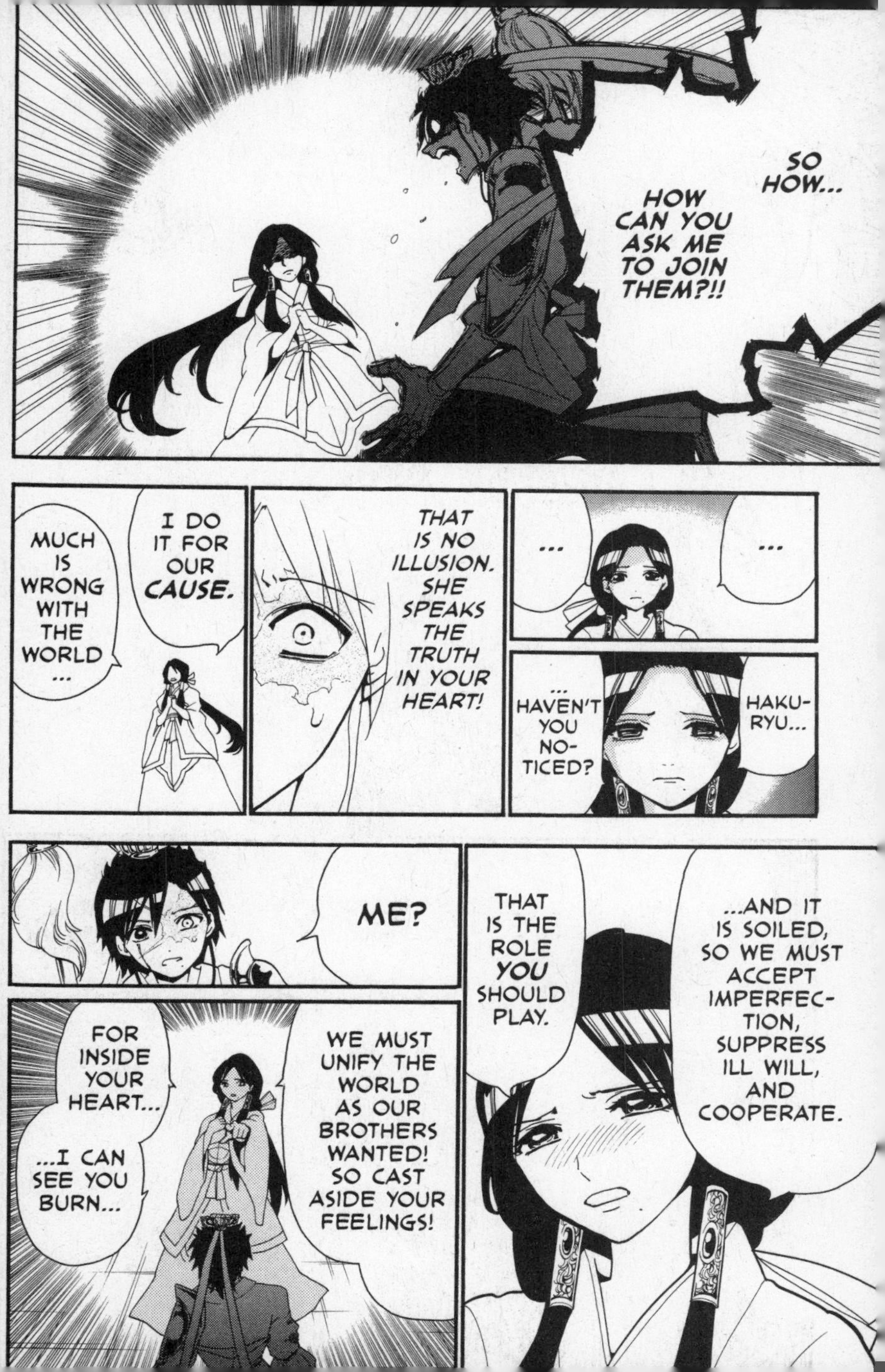
SO HOW...
HOW CAN YOU ASK ME TO JOIN THEM?!!
...
...
HAKU-RYU...
...HAVEN'T YOU NO-TICED?
THAT IS NO ILLUSION. SHE SPEAKS THE TRUTH IN YOUR HEART!
I DO IT FOR OUR CAUSE.
MUCH IS WRONG WITH THE WORLD...
...AND IT IS SOILED, SO WE MUST ACCEPT IMPERFEC-TION, SUPPRESS ILL WILL, AND COOPERATE.
THAT IS THE ROLE YOU SHOULD PLAY.
ME?
WE MUST UNIFY THE WORLD AS OUR BROTHERS WANTED! SO CAST ASIDE YOUR FEELINGS!
FOR INSIDE YOUR HEART...
...I CAN SEE YOU BURN...

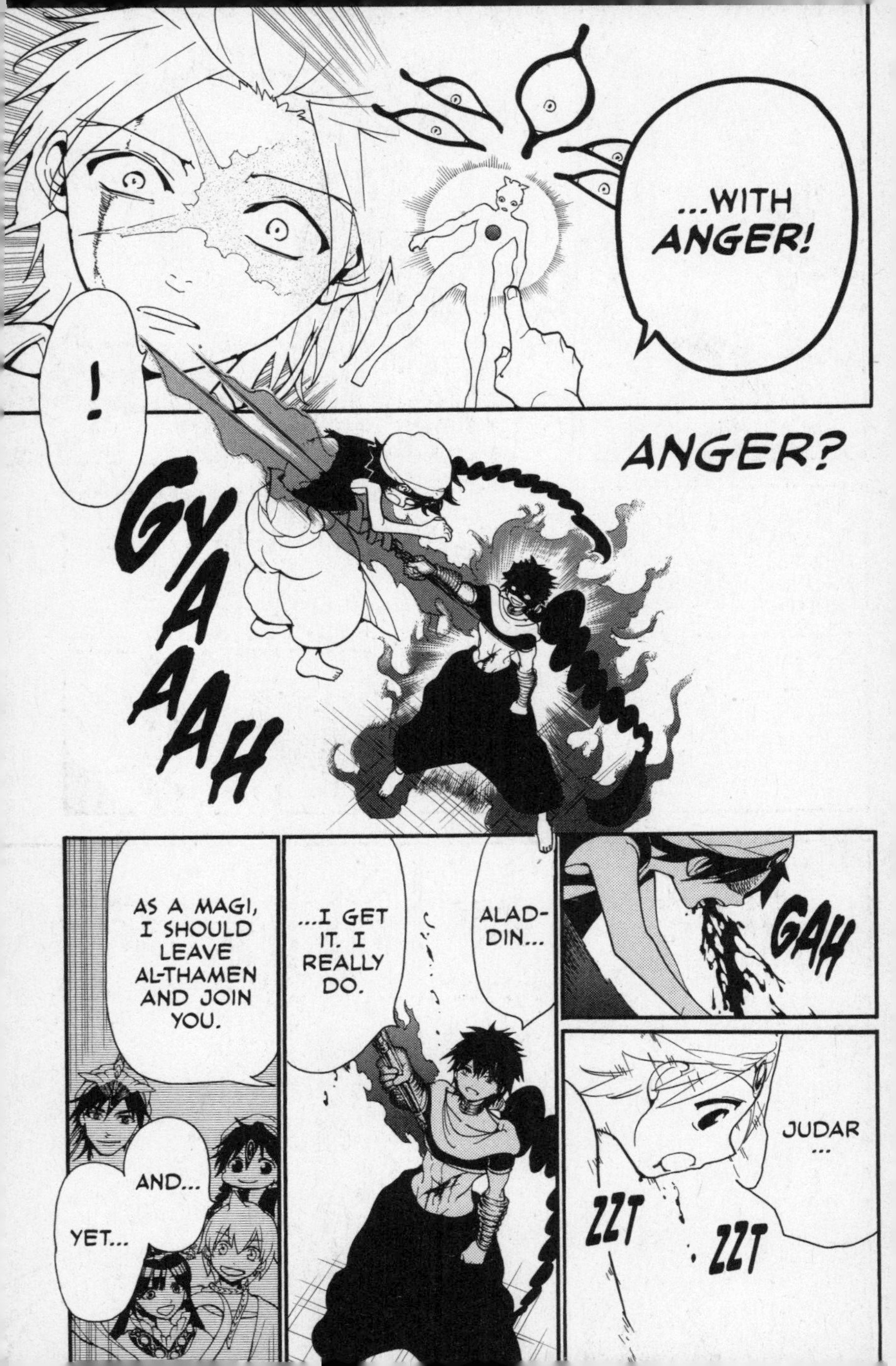
...WITH ANGER!
!
ANGER?
GYAAAH
GAH
JUDAR...
ZZT
ZZT
ALAD-DIN...
...I GET IT. I REALLY DO.
AS A MAGI, I SHOULD LEAVE AL-THAMEN AND JOIN YOU.
AND...
YET...

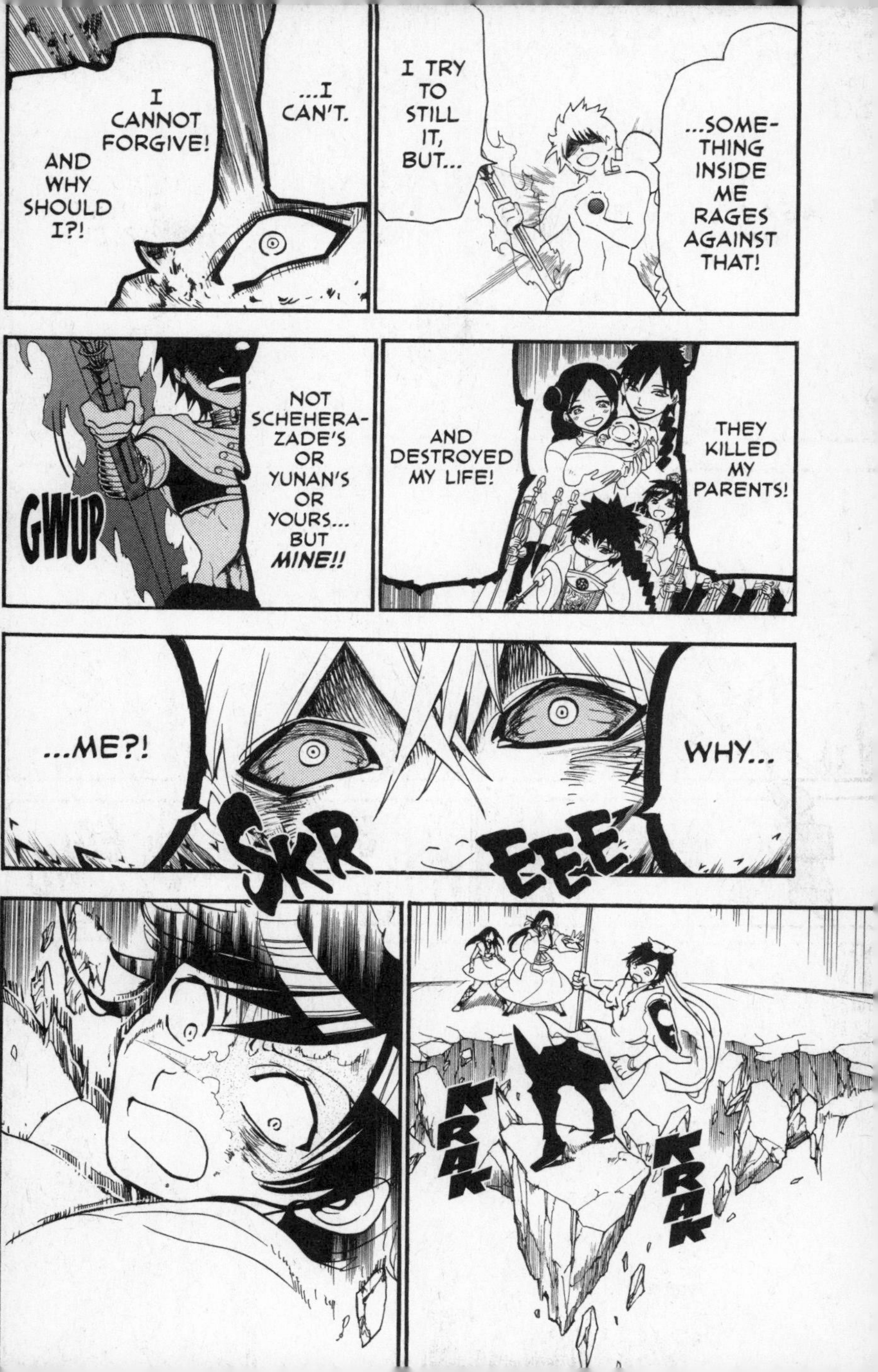
I TRY TO STILL IT, BUT...
...SOME-THING INSIDE ME RAGES AGAINST THAT!
...I CAN'T.
I CANNOT FORGIVE!
AND WHY SHOULD I?!
THEY KILLED MY PARENTS!
AND DESTROYED MY LIFE!
NOT SCHEHERA-ZADE'S OR YUNAN'S OR YOURS... BUT *MINE!!*
GWUP
WHY...
...ME?!
SKREEE
KRAK
KRAK

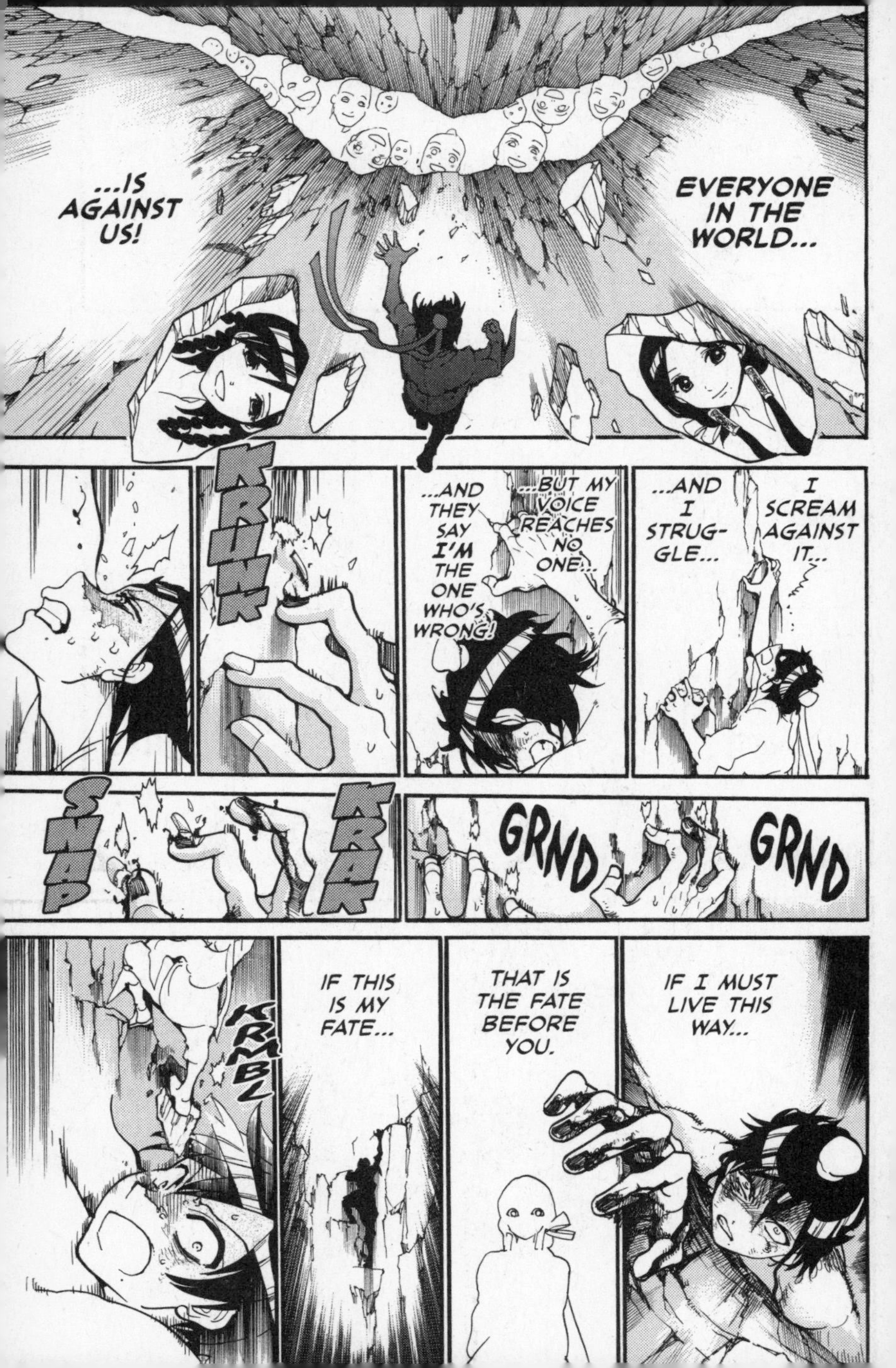
EVERYONE IN THE WORLD...
...IS AGAINST US!
I SCREAM AGAINST IT...
...AND I STRUGGLE...
...BUT MY VOICE REACHES NO ONE...
...AND THEY SAY I'M THE ONE WHO'S WRONG!
KRUNK
GRND
GRND
KRAK
SNAP
IF I MUST LIVE THIS WAY...
THAT IS THE FATE BEFORE YOU.
IF THIS IS MY FATE...
KRMBL

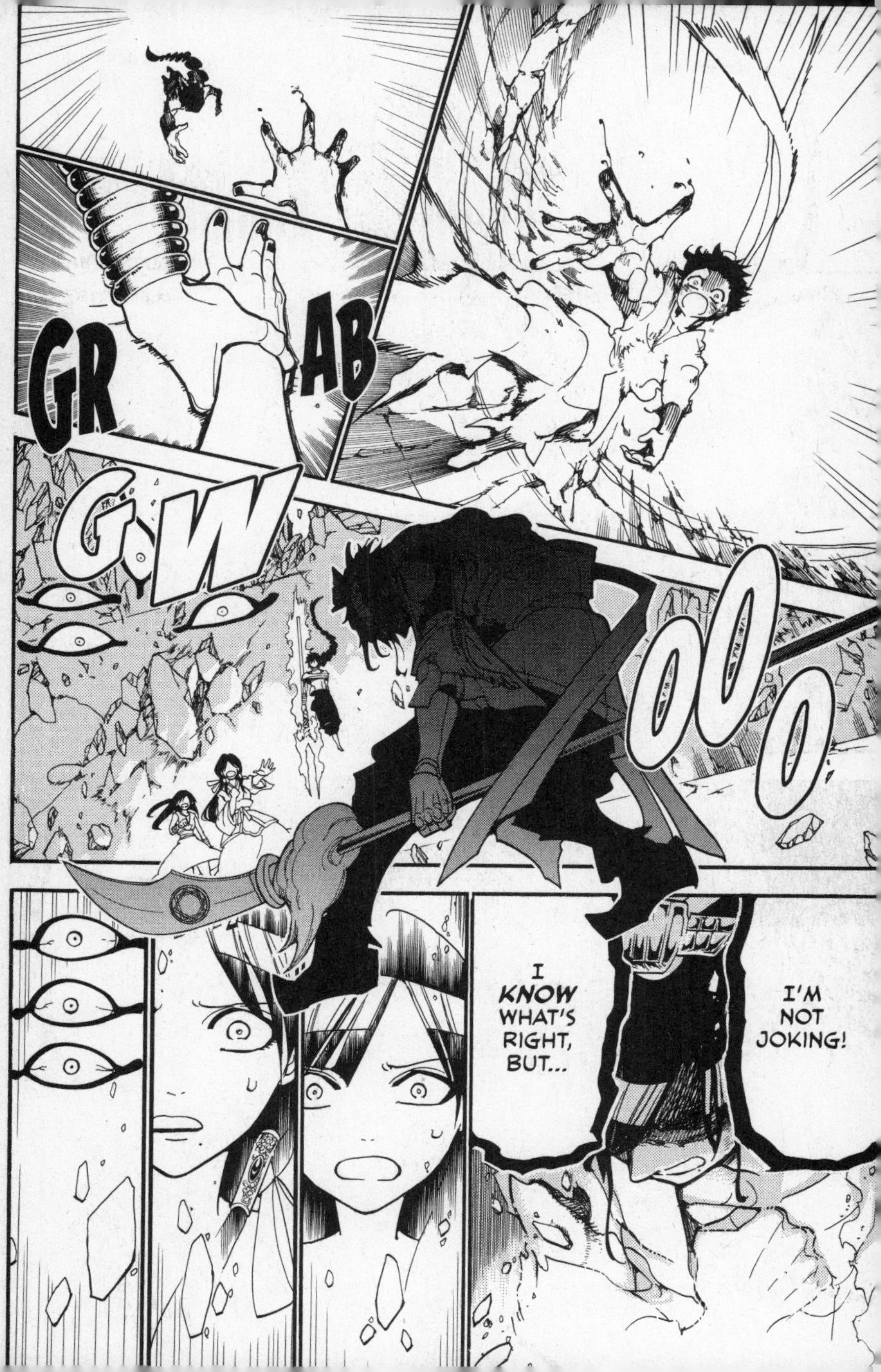
GRAB
GWOOOO
I'M NOT JOKING!
I KNOW WHAT'S RIGHT, BUT...

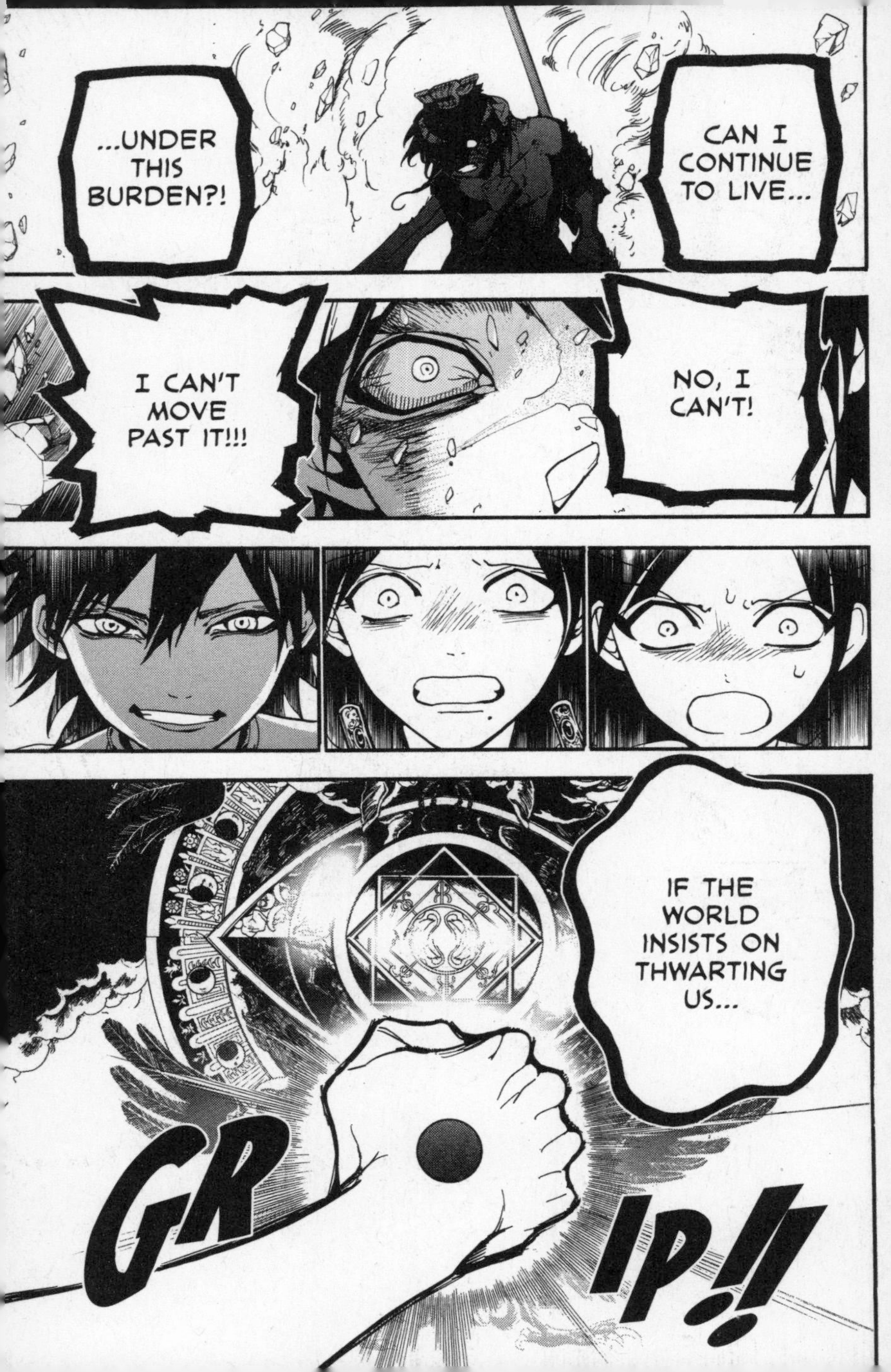
CAN I CONTINUE TO LIVE...
...UNDER THIS BURDEN?!
NO, I CAN'T!
I CAN'T MOVE PAST IT!!!
IF THE WORLD INSISTS ON THWARTING US...
GRIP!!

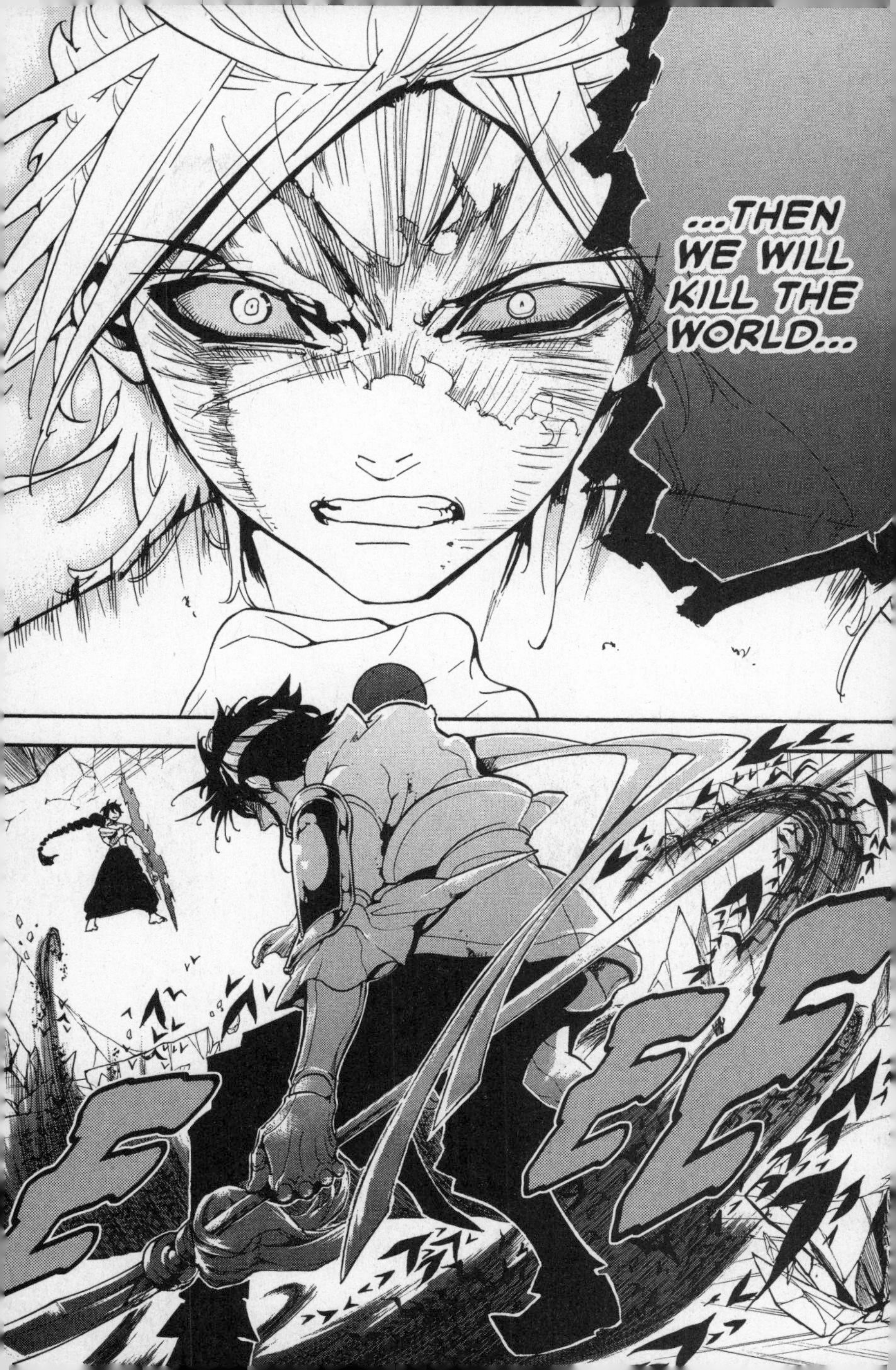
...THEN WE WILL KILL THE WORLD...

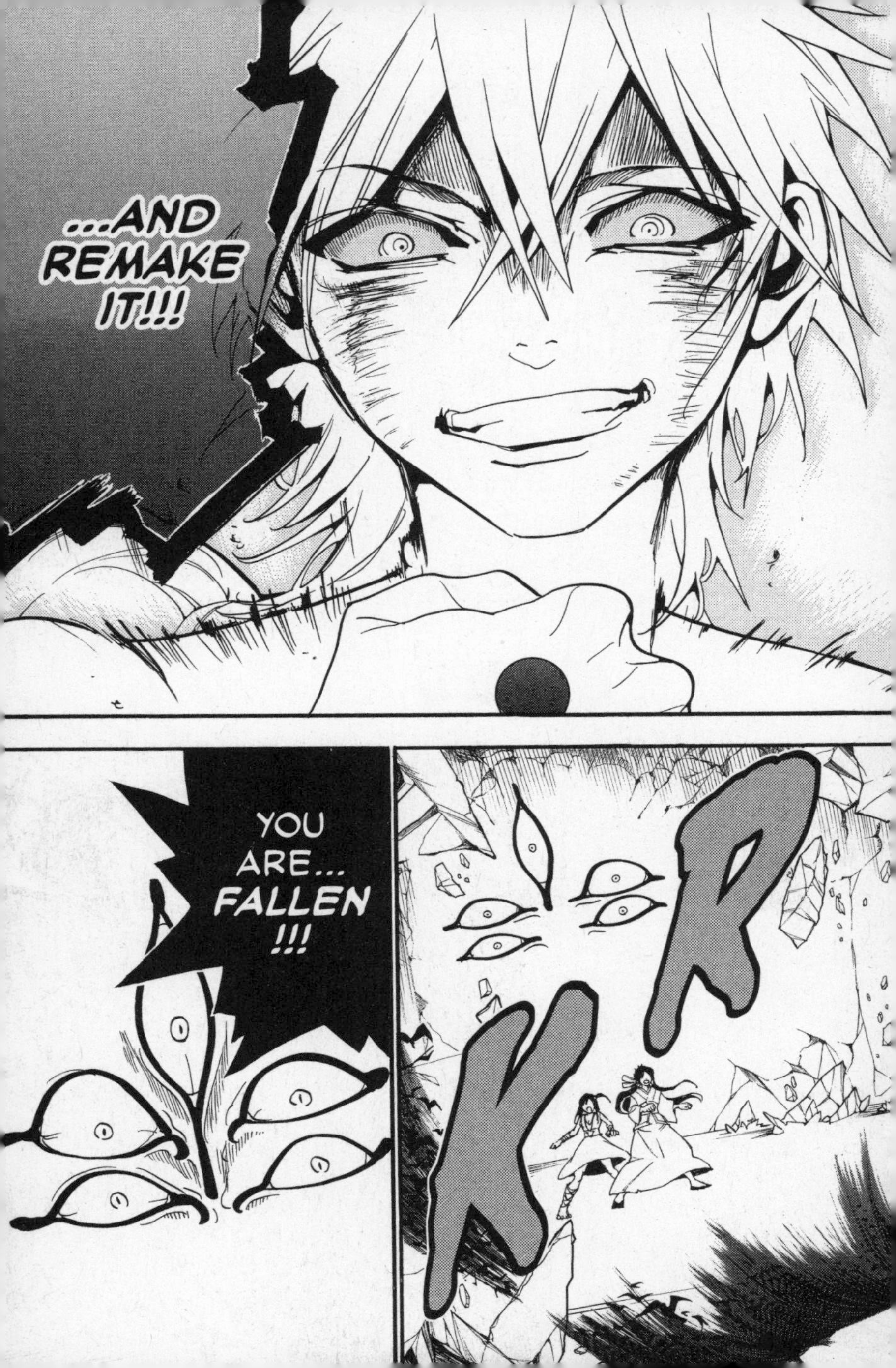
...AND REMAKE IT!!!
KR
YOU ARE... FALLEN!!!

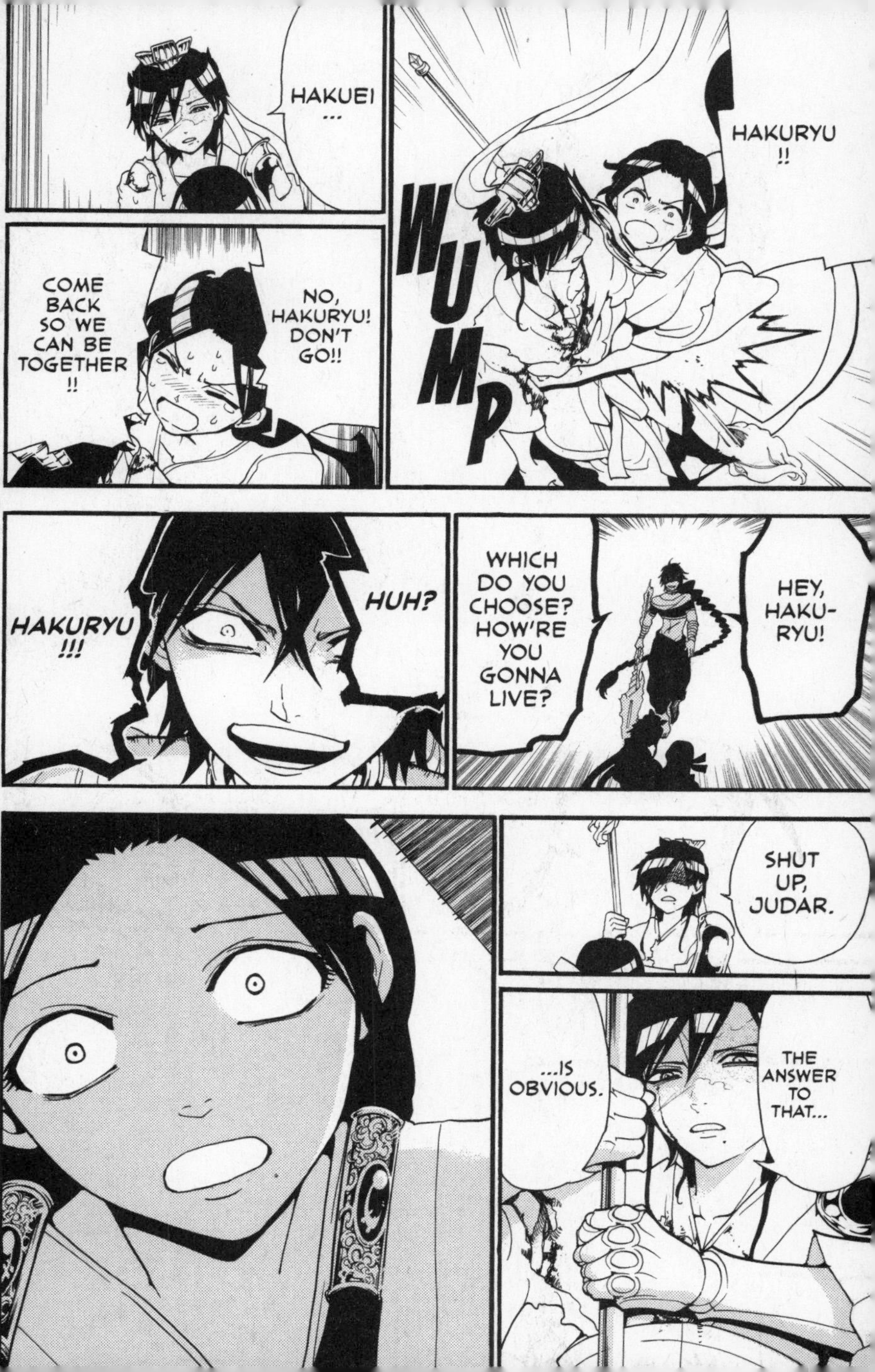
HAKURYU !!
WUMP
HAKUEI ...
NO, HAKURYU! DON'T GO!!
COME BACK SO WE CAN BE TOGETHER !!
HEY, HAKU-RYU!
WHICH DO YOU CHOOSE? HOW'RE YOU GONNA LIVE?
HUH?
HAKURYU !!!
SHUT UP, JUDAR.
THE ANSWER TO THAT...
...IS OBVIOUS.

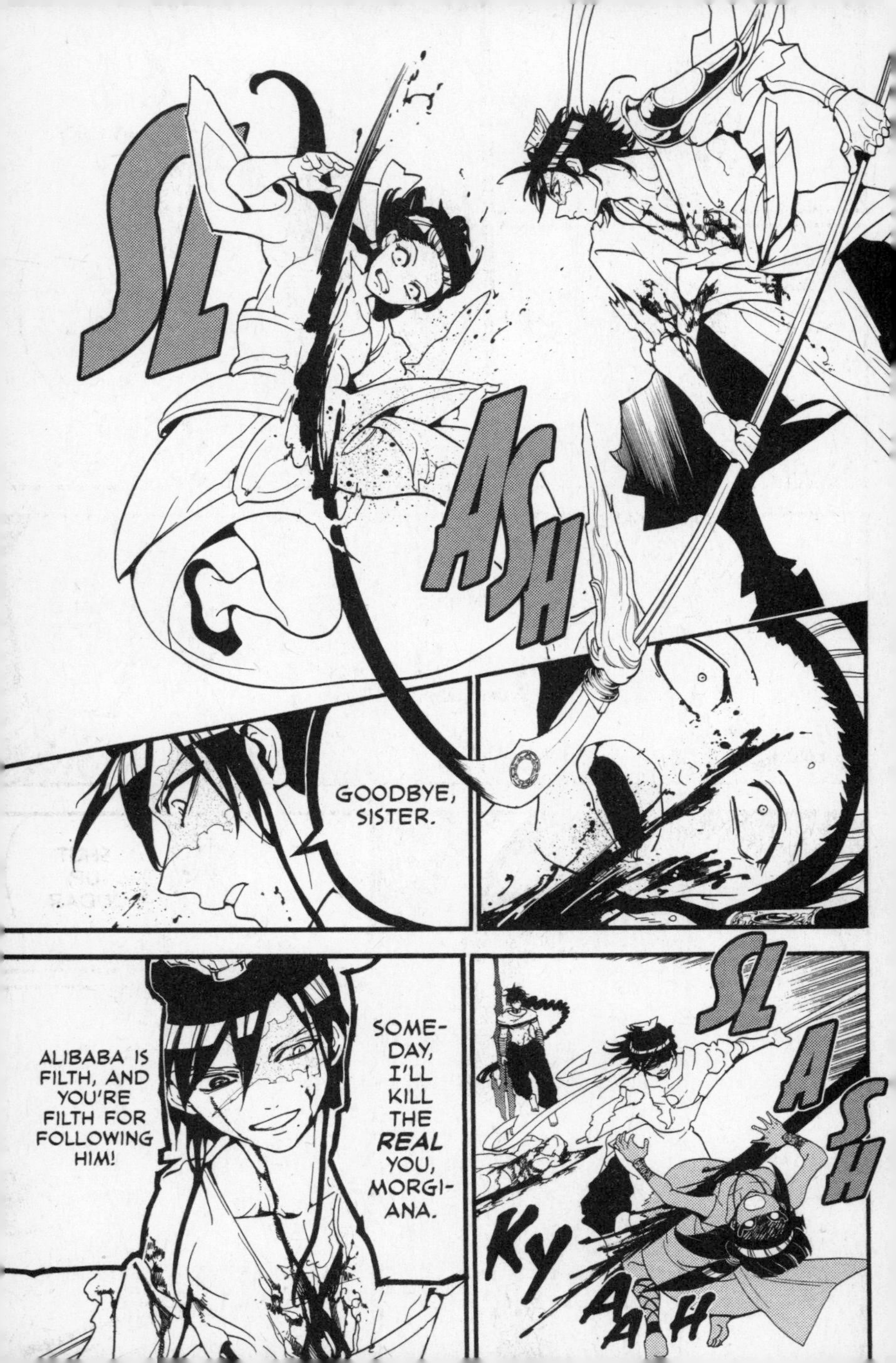
SLASH
GOODBYE, SISTER.
SLASH
KyAAH
SOMEDAY, I'LL KILL THE *REAL* YOU, MORGIANA.
ALIBABA IS FILTH, AND YOU'RE FILTH FOR FOLLOWING HIM!

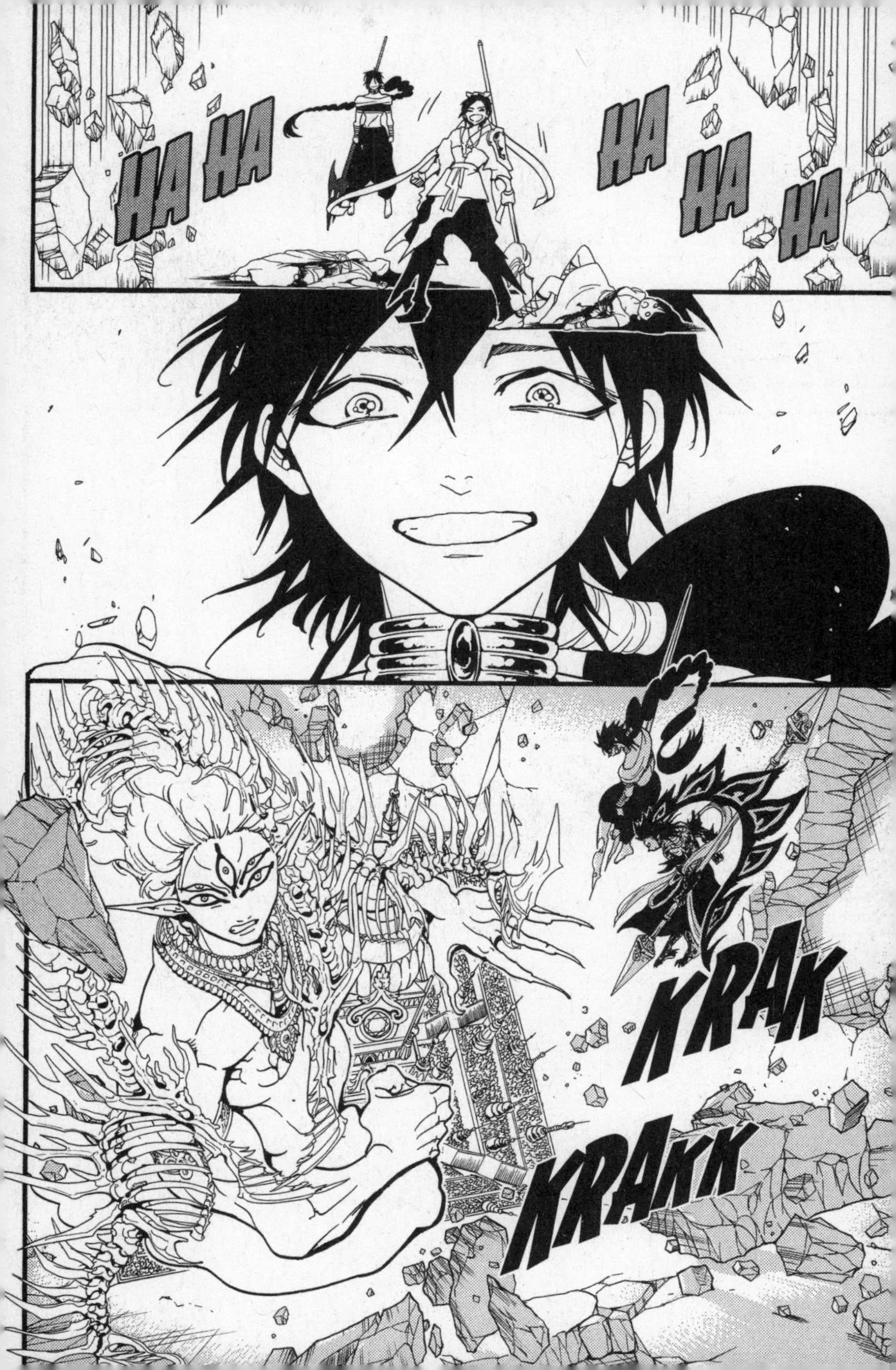
HA HA HA
HA HA
KRAK
KRAKK

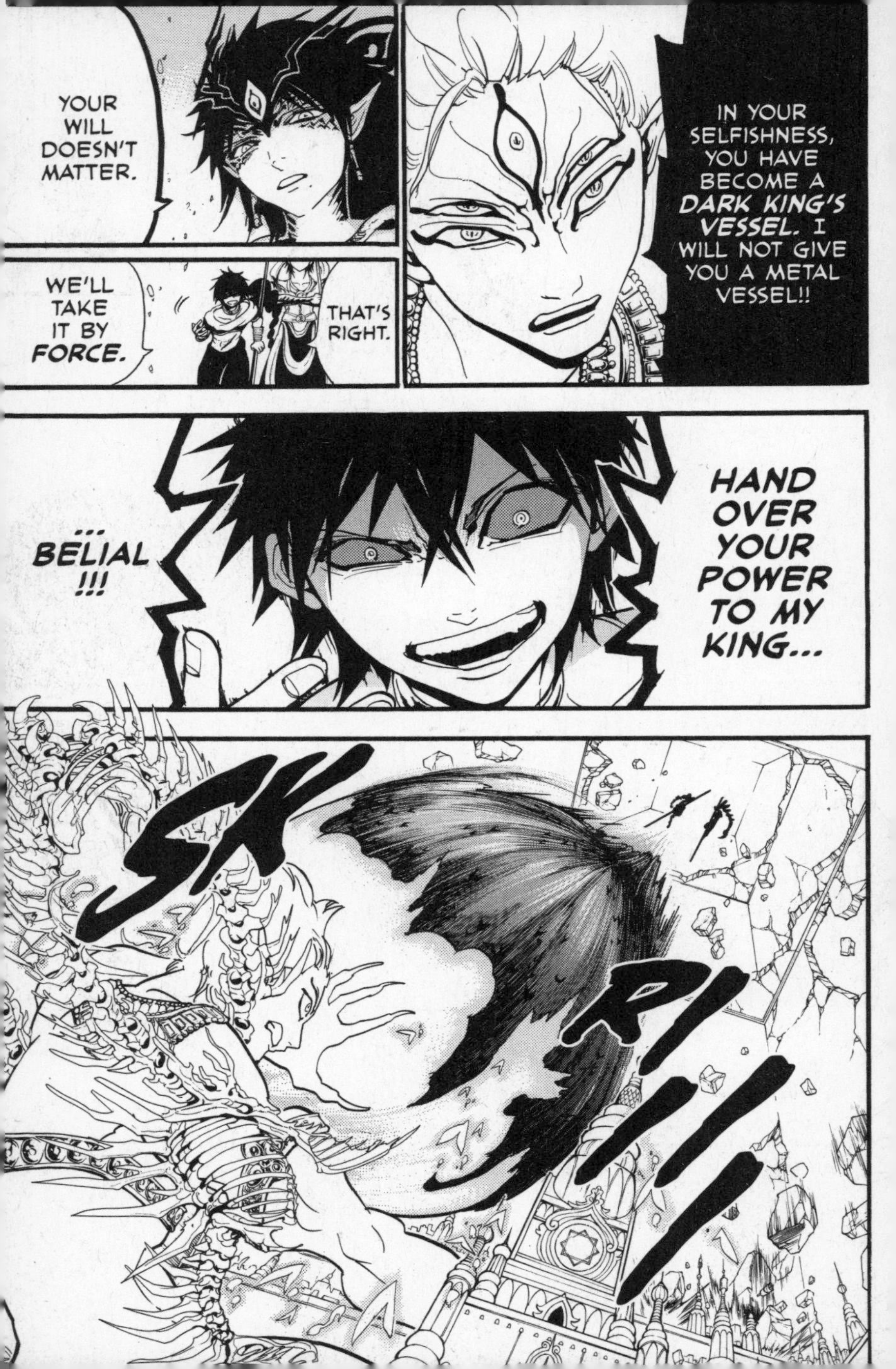
IN YOUR SELFISHNESS, YOU HAVE BECOME A *DARK KING'S VESSEL*. I WILL NOT GIVE YOU A METAL VESSEL!!
YOUR WILL DOESN'T MATTER.
THAT'S RIGHT.
WE'LL TAKE IT BY *FORCE*.
HAND OVER YOUR POWER TO MY KING...
...BELIAL!!!

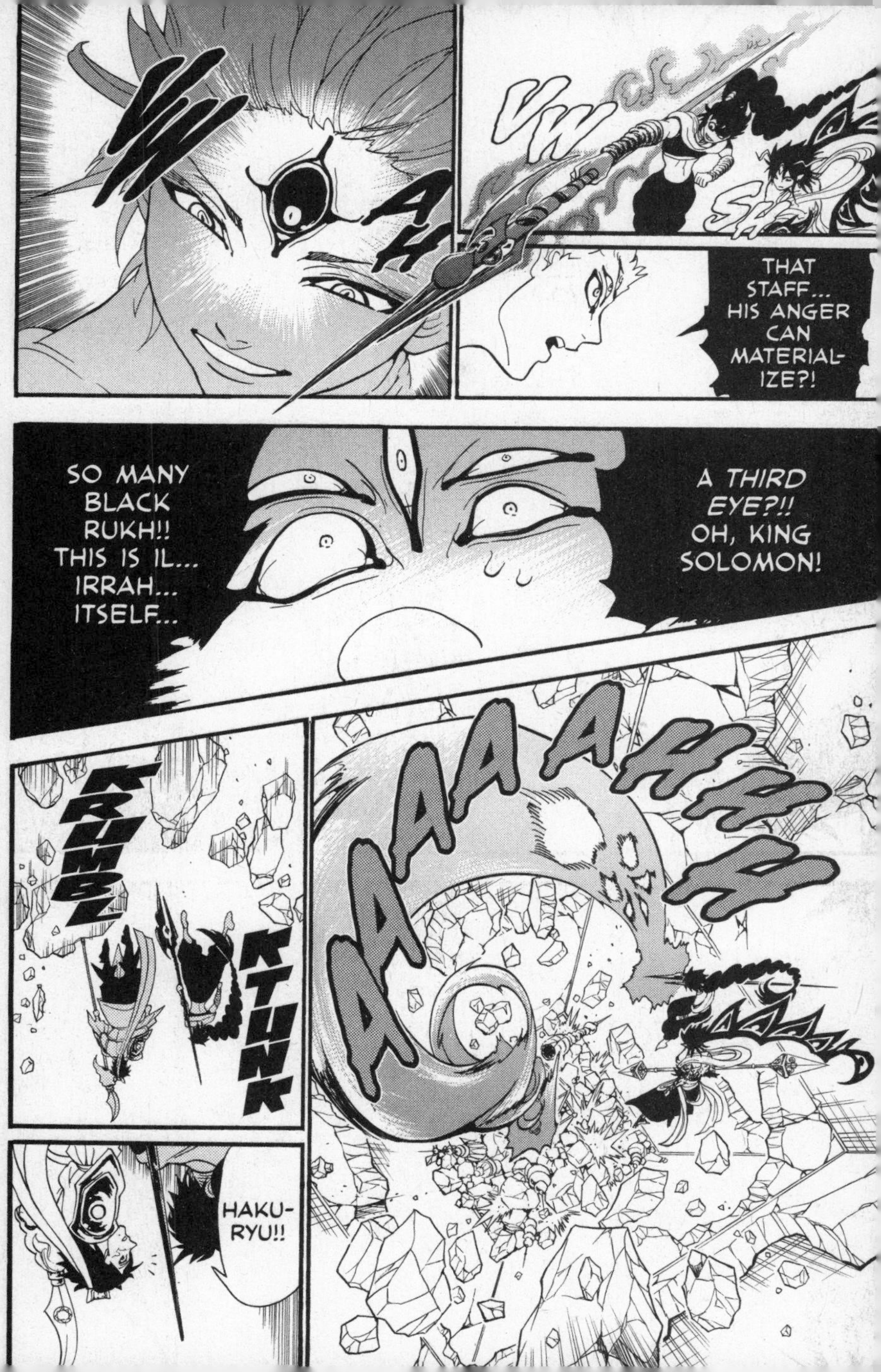
VW
SH
THAT STAFF... HIS ANGER CAN MATERIAL-IZE?!
WAH
A THIRD EYE?!! OH, KING SOLOMON!
SO MANY BLACK RUKH!! THIS IS IL... IRRAH... ITSELF...
AAAAAAHHHH
KRUMBL
KTUNK
HAKU-RYU!!

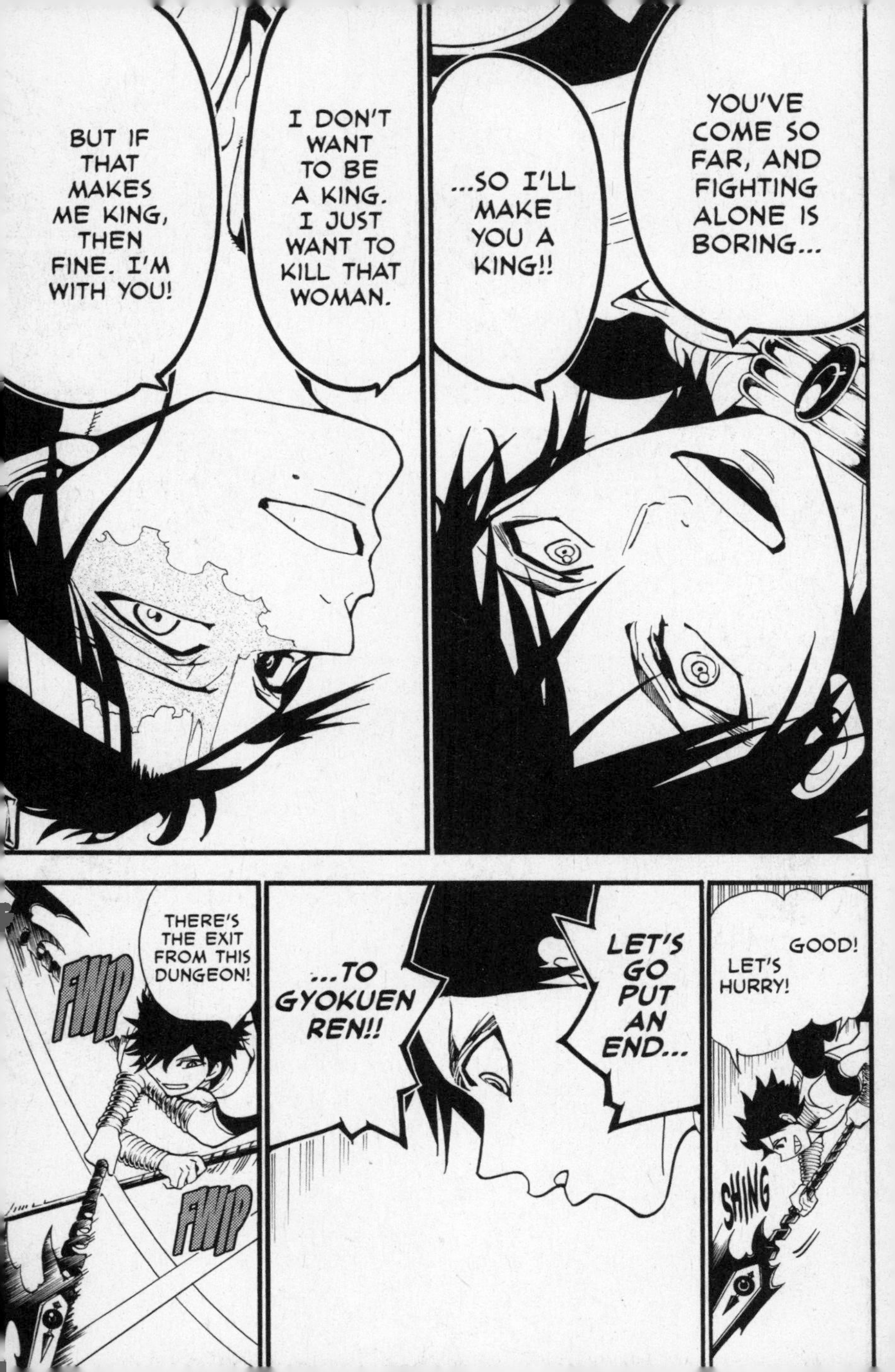
YOU'VE COME SO FAR, AND FIGHTING ALONE IS BORING...
...SO I'LL MAKE YOU A KING!!
I DON'T WANT TO BE A KING. I JUST WANT TO KILL THAT WOMAN.
BUT IF THAT MAKES ME KING, THEN FINE. I'M WITH YOU!
GOOD!
LET'S HURRY!
SHING
LET'S GO PUT AN END...
...TO GYOKUEN REN!!
THERE'S THE EXIT FROM THIS DUNGEON!
FWIP
FWIP

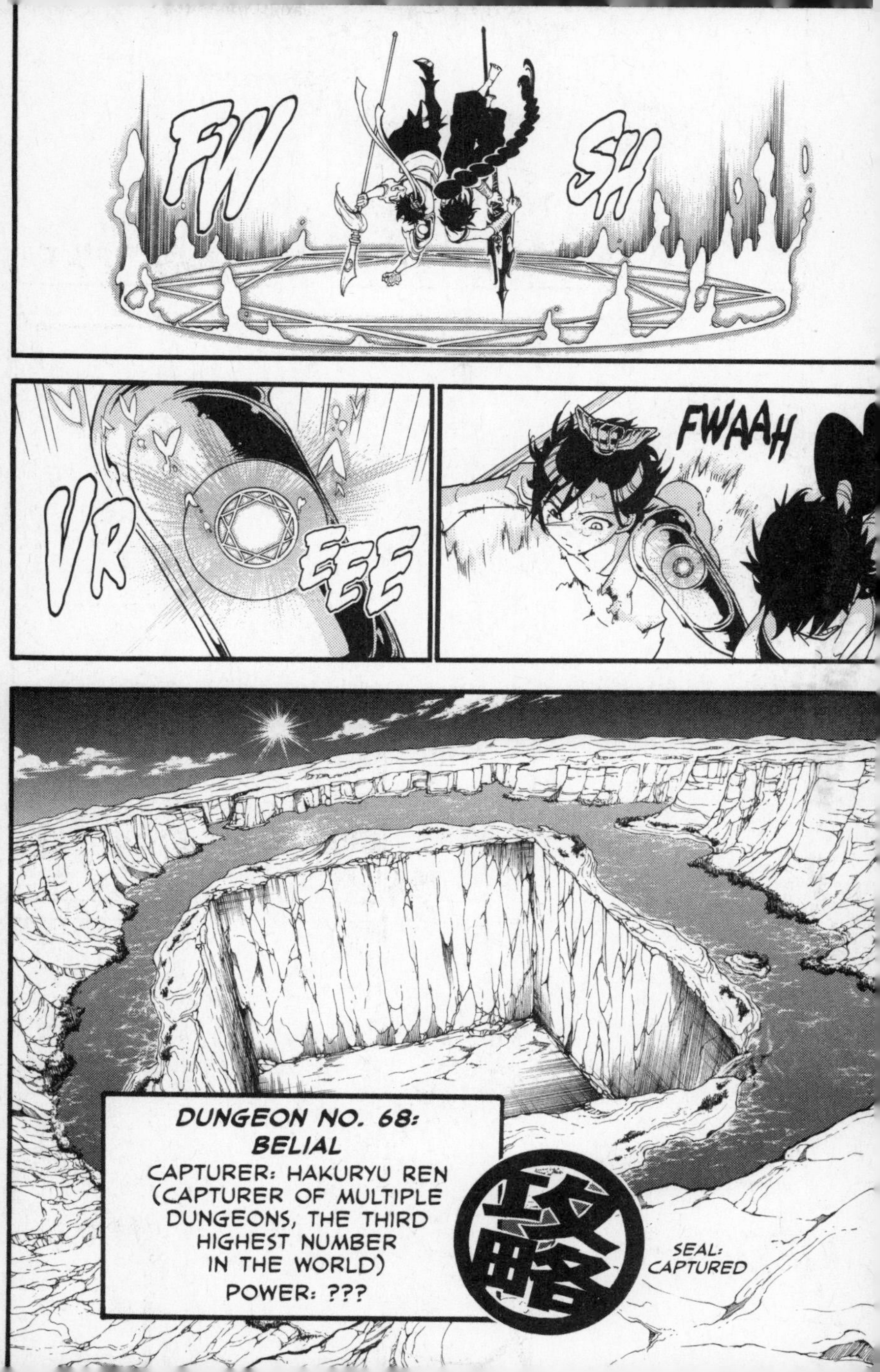
FW
SH
FWAAH
VR
EEE
DUNGEON NO. 68: BELIAL
CAPTURER: HAKURYU REN (CAPTURER OF MULTIPLE DUNGEONS, THE THIRD HIGHEST NUMBER IN THE WORLD)
POWER: ???
攻略
SEAL: CAPTURED

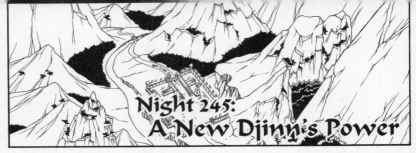

Night 245:
A New Djinn's Power

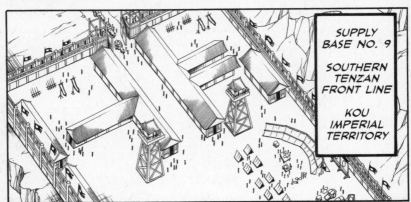

SUPPLY BASE NO. 9

SOUTHERN TENZAN FRONT LINE

KOU IMPERIAL TERRITORY

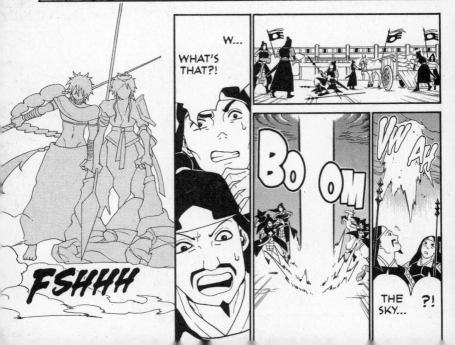

W...

WHAT'S THAT?!

BO OM

VW AH

FSHHH

THE SKY... ?!

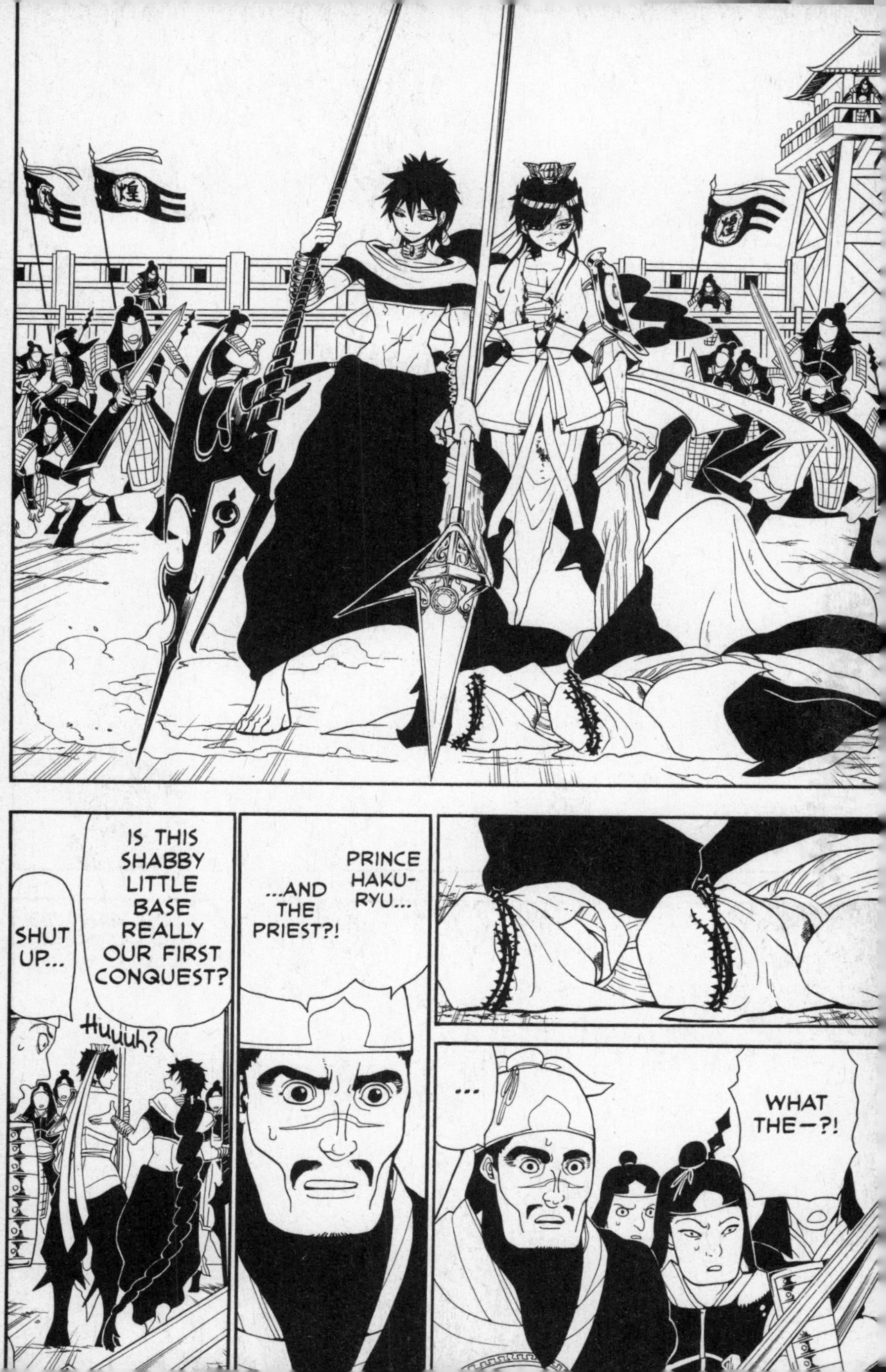
WHAT THE—?!
...
PRINCE HAKU-RYU...
...AND THE PRIEST?!
IS THIS SHABBY LITTLE BASE REALLY OUR FIRST CONQUEST?
SHUT UP...
Huuuh?

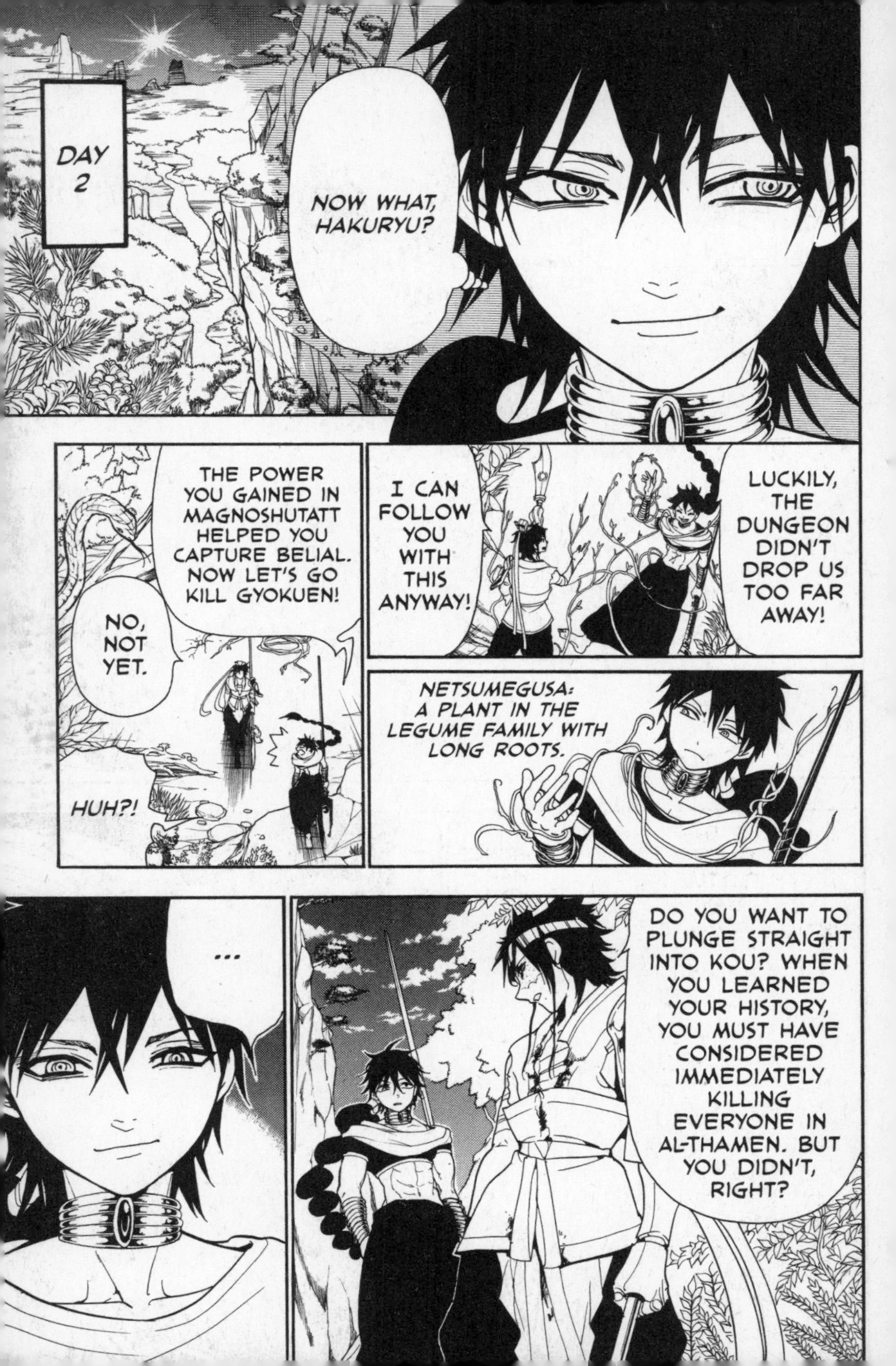
NOW WHAT, HAKURYU?
DAY 2
LUCKILY, THE DUNGEON DIDN'T DROP US TOO FAR AWAY!
I CAN FOLLOW YOU WITH THIS ANYWAY!
NETSUMEGUSA: A PLANT IN THE LEGUME FAMILY WITH LONG ROOTS.
THE POWER YOU GAINED IN MAGNOSHUTATT HELPED YOU CAPTURE BELIAL. NOW LET'S GO KILL GYOKUEN!
NO, NOT YET.
HUH?!
DO YOU WANT TO PLUNGE STRAIGHT INTO KOU? WHEN YOU LEARNED YOUR HISTORY, YOU MUST HAVE CONSIDERED IMMEDIATELY KILLING EVERYONE IN AL-THAMEN. BUT YOU DIDN'T, RIGHT?
...

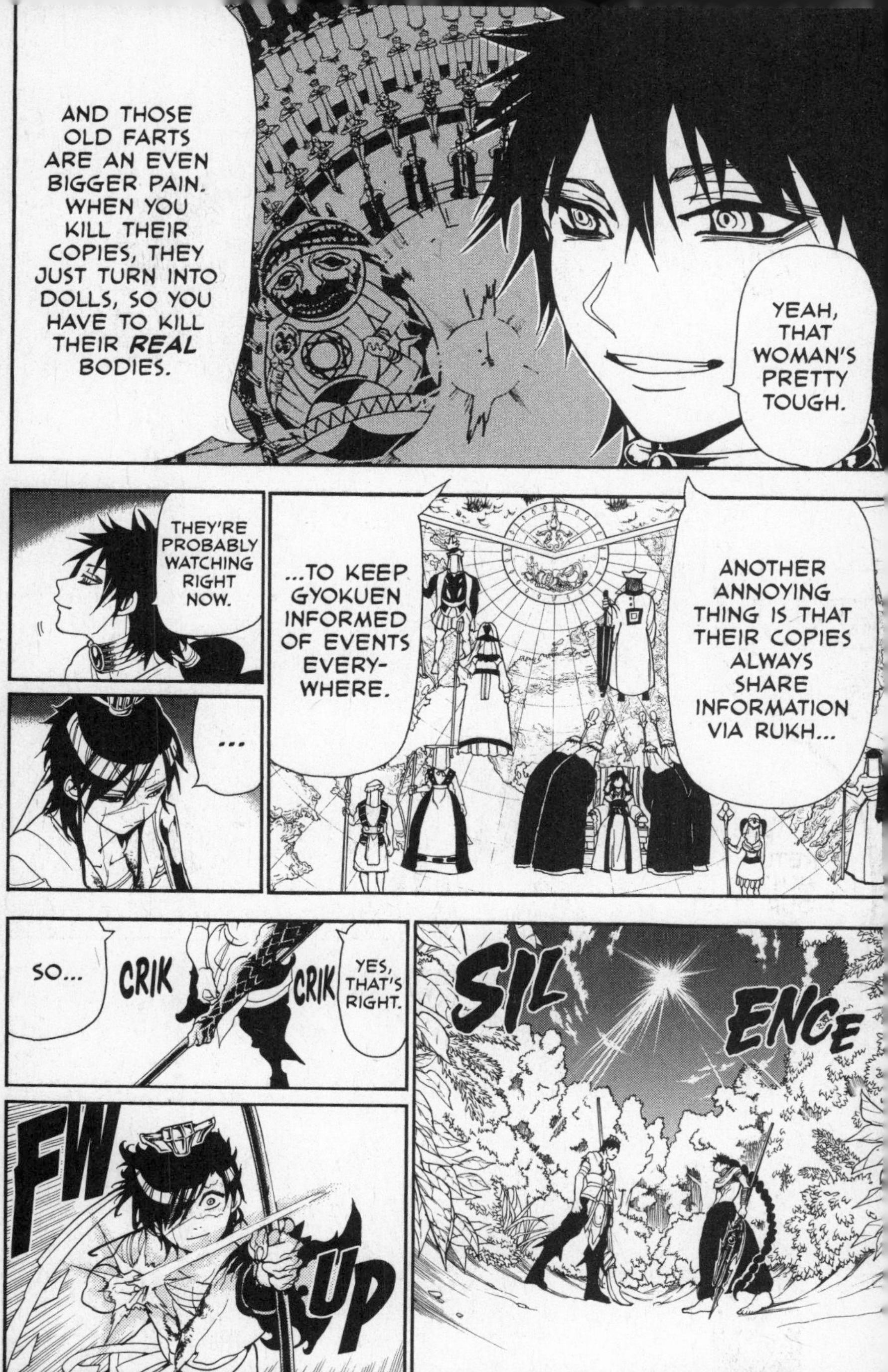
YEAH, THAT WOMAN'S PRETTY TOUGH.
AND THOSE OLD FARTS ARE AN EVEN BIGGER PAIN. WHEN YOU KILL THEIR COPIES, THEY JUST TURN INTO DOLLS, SO YOU HAVE TO KILL THEIR *REAL* BODIES.
ANOTHER ANNOYING THING IS THAT THEIR COPIES ALWAYS SHARE INFORMATION VIA RUKH...
...TO KEEP GYOKUEN INFORMED OF EVENTS EVERY-WHERE.
THEY'RE PROBABLY WATCHING RIGHT NOW.
...
SIL
ENCE
YES, THAT'S RIGHT.
CRIK
CRIK
SO...
FW
UP

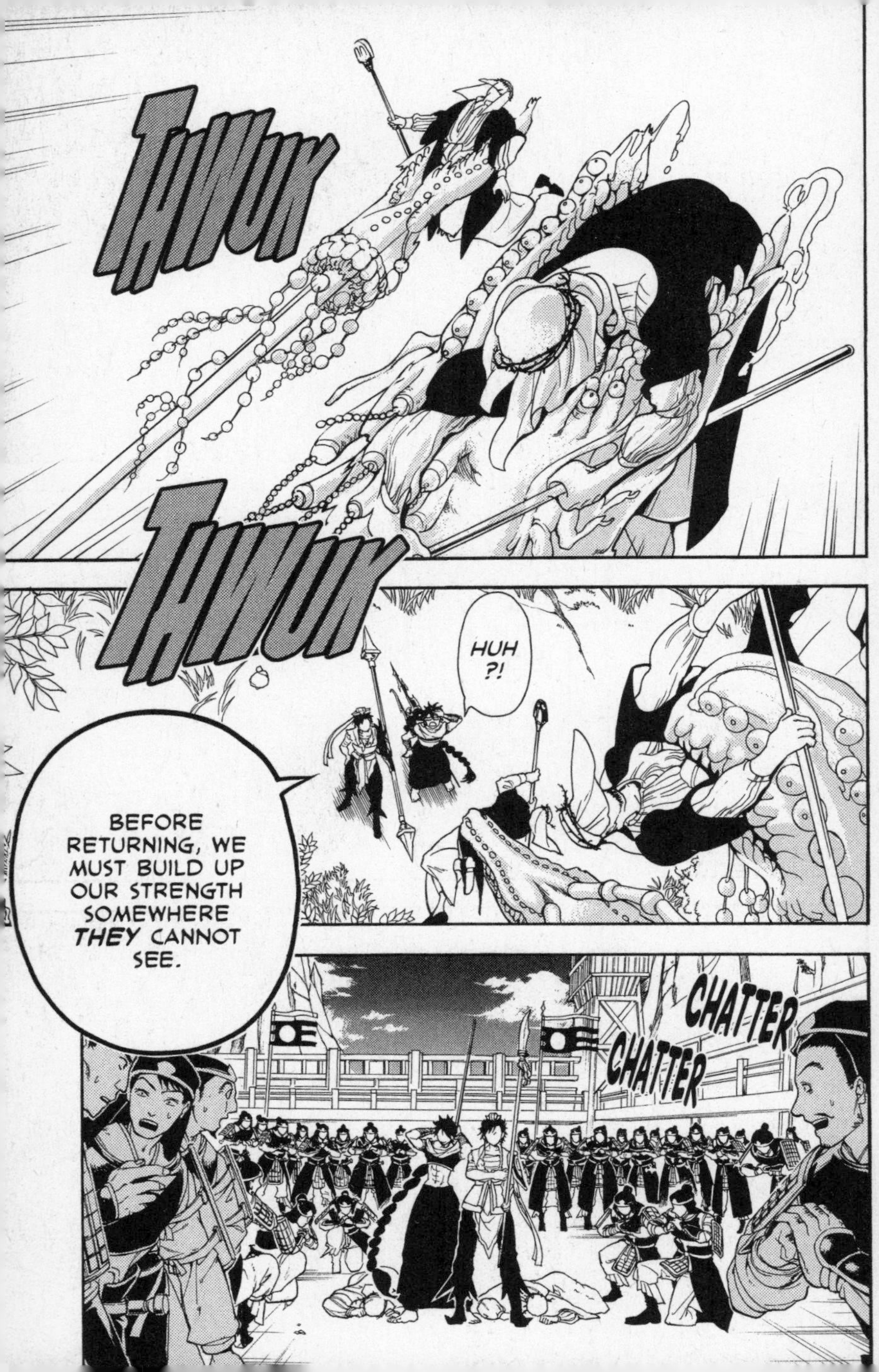
THWUK
THWUK
HUH ?!
BEFORE RETURNING, WE MUST BUILD UP OUR STRENGTH SOMEWHERE *THEY* CANNOT SEE.
CHATTER
CHATTER

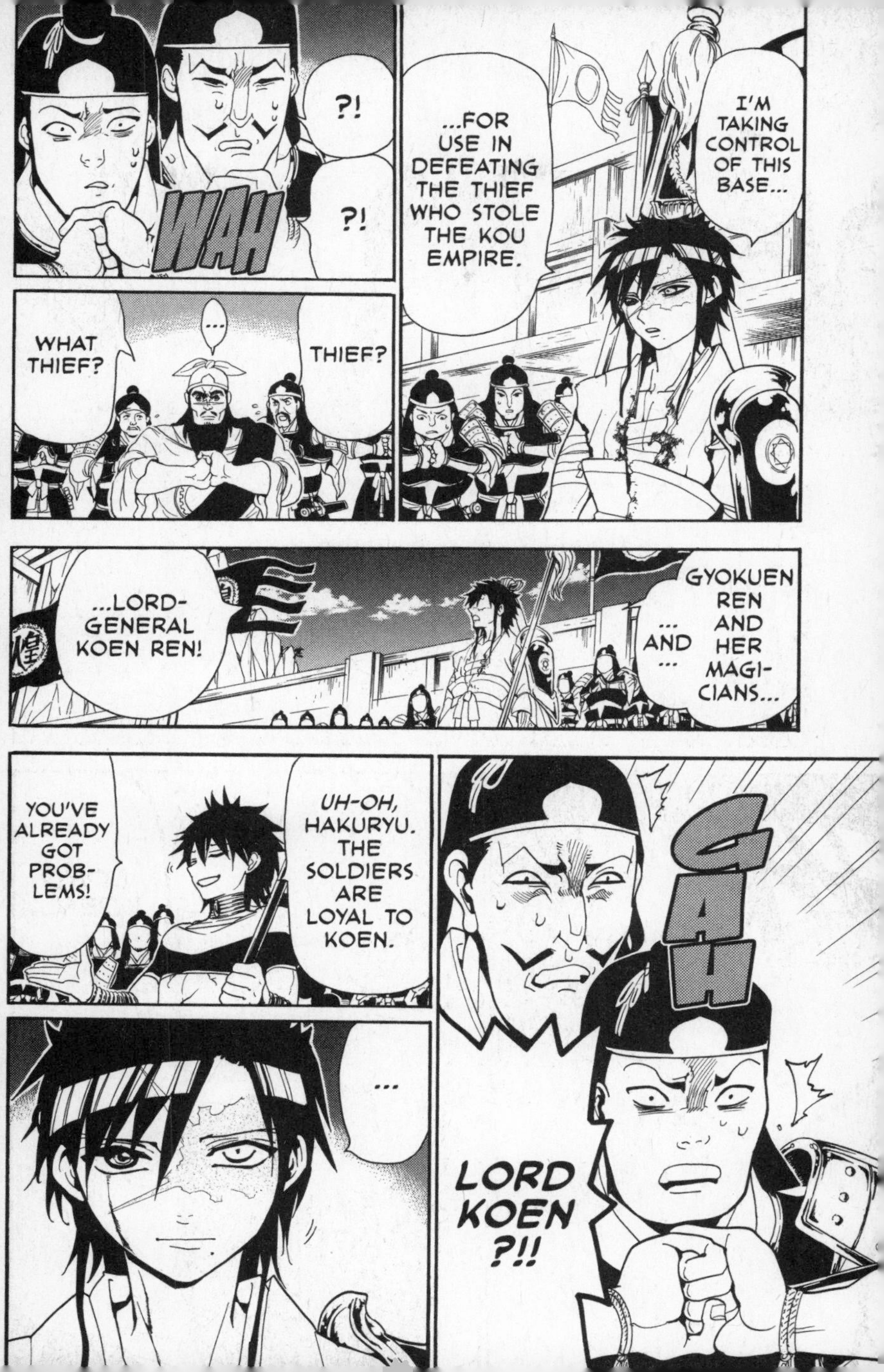
I'M TAKING CONTROL OF THIS BASE...
...FOR USE IN DEFEATING THE THIEF WHO STOLE THE KOU EMPIRE.
?!
?!
WAH
THIEF?
...
WHAT THIEF?
GYOKUEN REN AND HER MAGICIANS...
... AND ...
...LORD-GENERAL KOEN REN!
GAH
LORD KOEN ?!!
UH-OH, HAKURYU. THE SOLDIERS ARE LOYAL TO KOEN.
YOU'VE ALREADY GOT PROBLEMS!
...

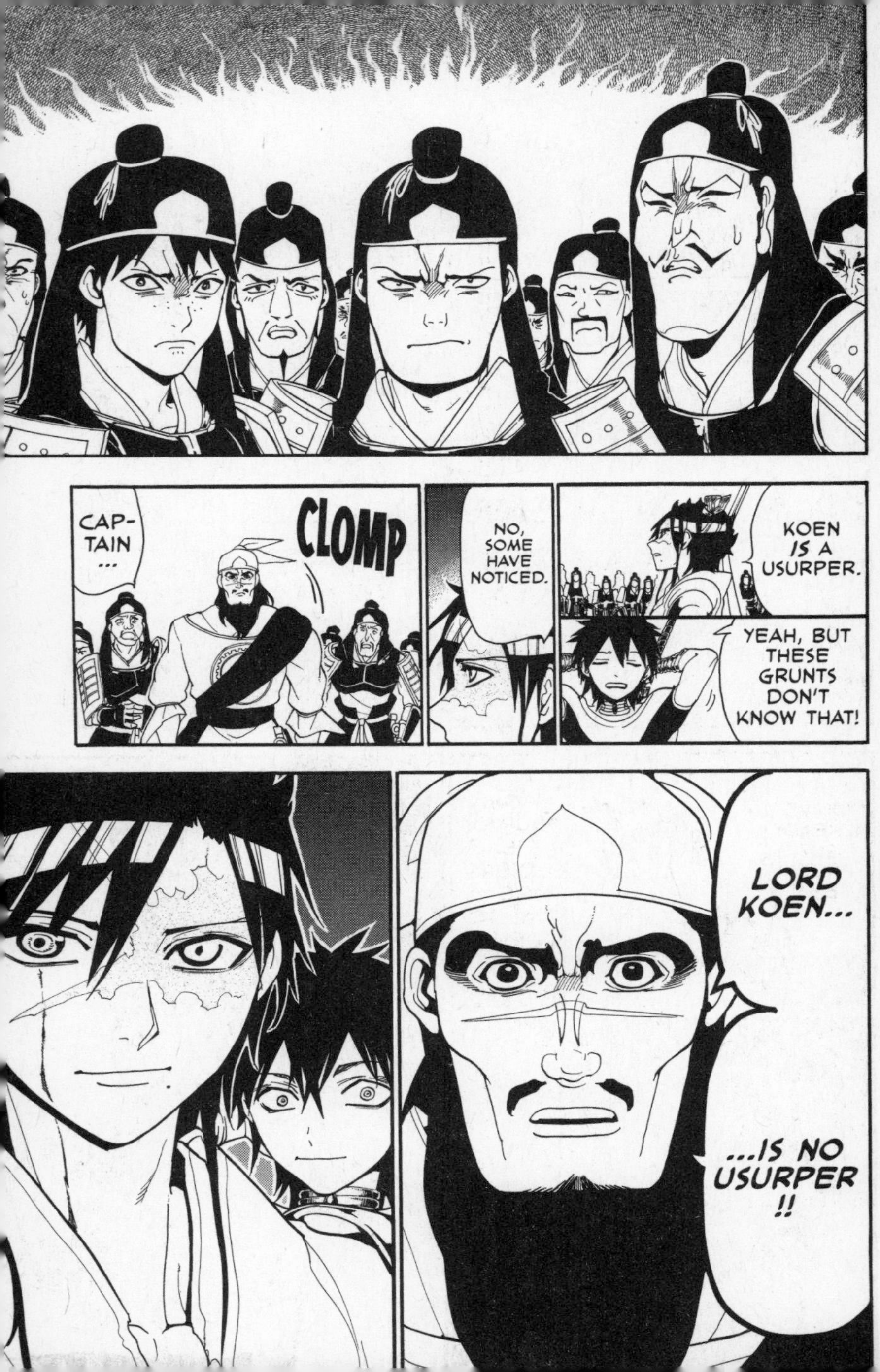
KOEN IS A USURPER.
YEAH, BUT THESE GRUNTS DON'T KNOW THAT!
NO, SOME HAVE NOTICED.
CLOMP
CAP-TAIN ...
LORD KOEN...
...IS NO USURPER !!

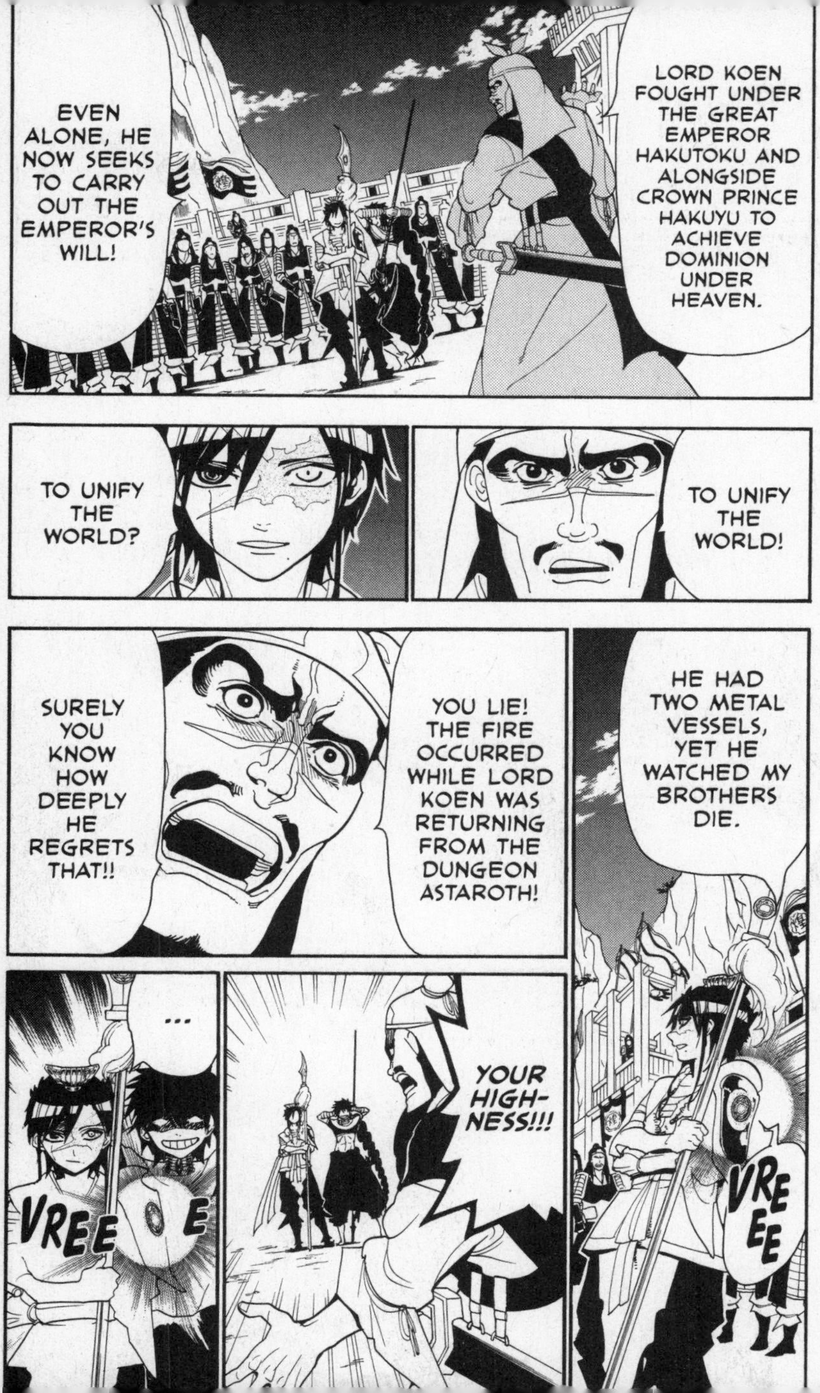
LORD KOEN FOUGHT UNDER THE GREAT EMPEROR HAKUTOKU AND ALONGSIDE CROWN PRINCE HAKUYU TO ACHIEVE DOMINION UNDER HEAVEN.
EVEN ALONE, HE NOW SEEKS TO CARRY OUT THE EMPEROR'S WILL!
TO UNIFY THE WORLD!
TO UNIFY THE WORLD?
HE HAD TWO METAL VESSELS, YET HE WATCHED MY BROTHERS DIE.
VREEE
YOU LIE! THE FIRE OCCURRED WHILE LORD KOEN WAS RETURNING FROM THE DUNGEON ASTAROTH!
SURELY YOU KNOW HOW DEEPLY HE REGRETS THAT!!
YOUR HIGHNESS!!!
...
VREEE

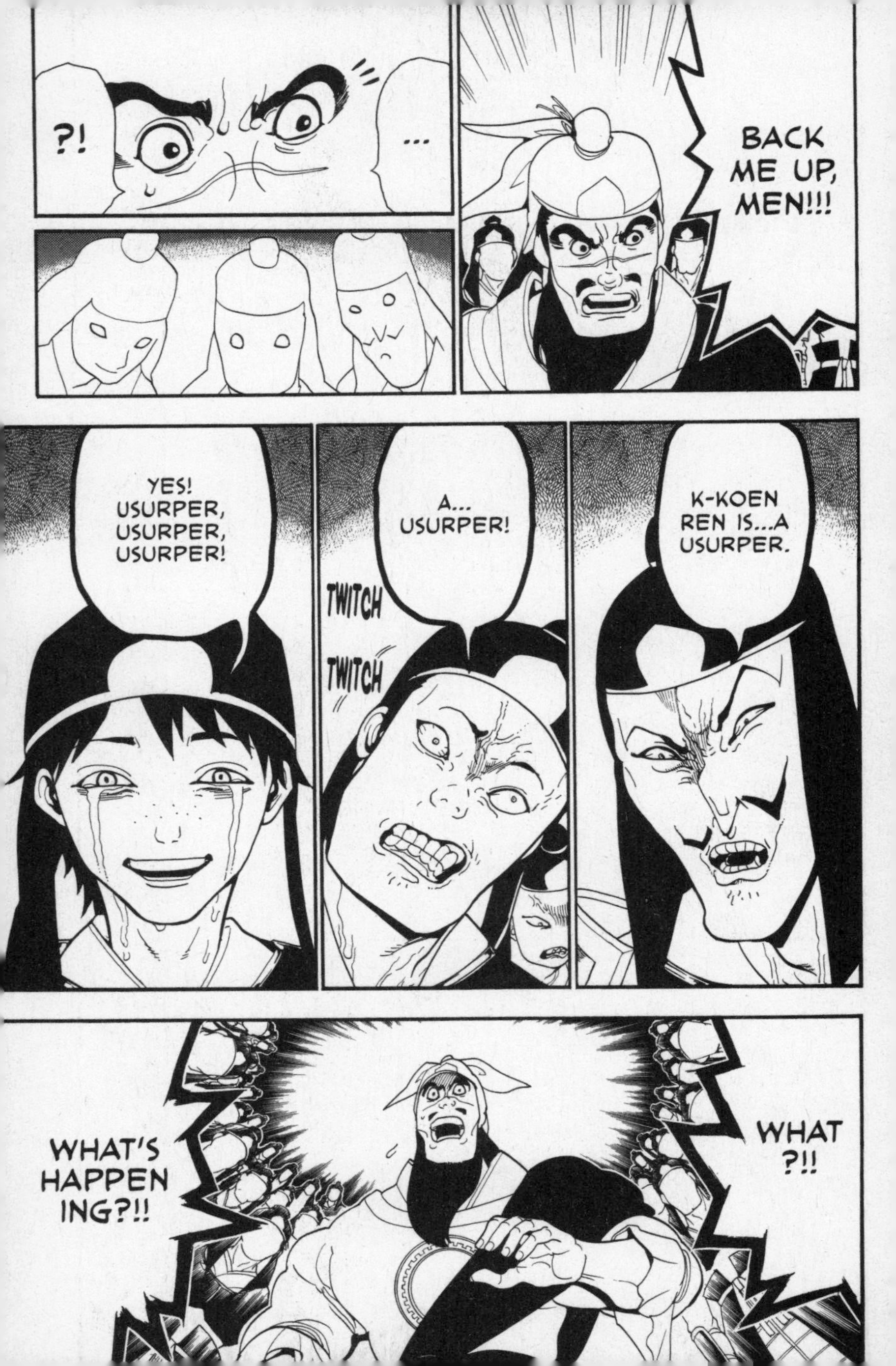
BACK ME UP, MEN!!!
...
?!
K-KOEN REN IS...A USURPER.
A... USURPER!
TWITCH
TWITCH
YES! USURPER, USURPER, USURPER!
WHAT ?!!
WHAT'S HAPPEN ING?!!

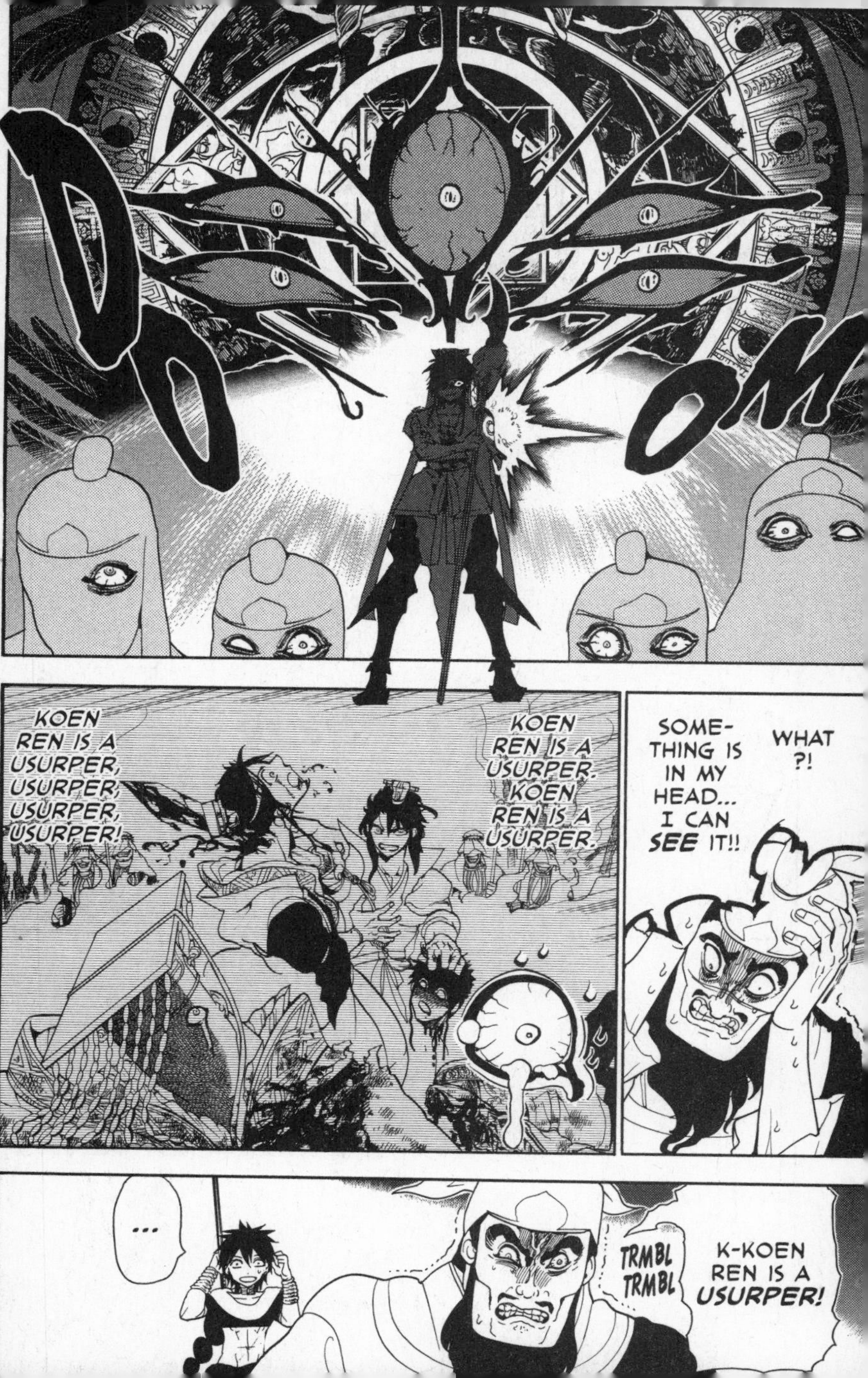
DOOOM
WHAT ?!
SOMETHING IS IN MY HEAD... I CAN SEE IT!!
KOEN REN IS A USURPER. KOEN REN IS A USURPER.
KOEN REN IS A USURPER, USURPER, USURPER, USURPER!
K-KOEN REN IS A USURPER!
TRMBL TRMBL
...

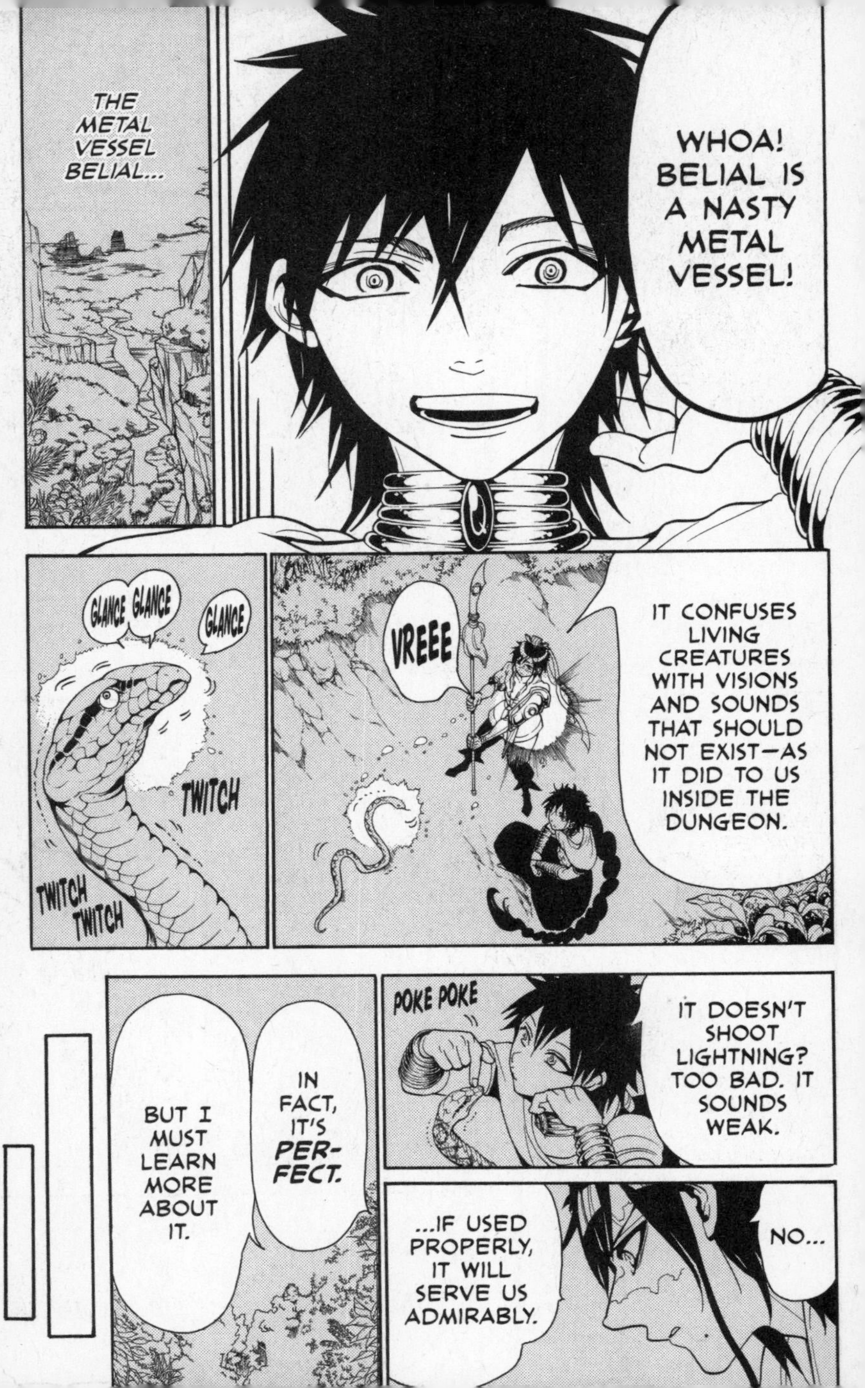
WHOA! BELIAL IS A NASTY METAL VESSEL!
THE METAL VESSEL BELIAL...
IT CONFUSES LIVING CREATURES WITH VISIONS AND SOUNDS THAT SHOULD NOT EXIST—AS IT DID TO US INSIDE THE DUNGEON.
VREEE
GLANCE
GLANCE GLANCE
TWITCH
TWITCH TWITCH
IT DOESN'T SHOOT LIGHTNING? TOO BAD. IT SOUNDS WEAK.
POKE POKE
NO...
...IF USED PROPERLY, IT WILL SERVE US ADMIRABLY.
IN FACT, IT'S *PERFECT.*
BUT I MUST LEARN MORE ABOUT IT.

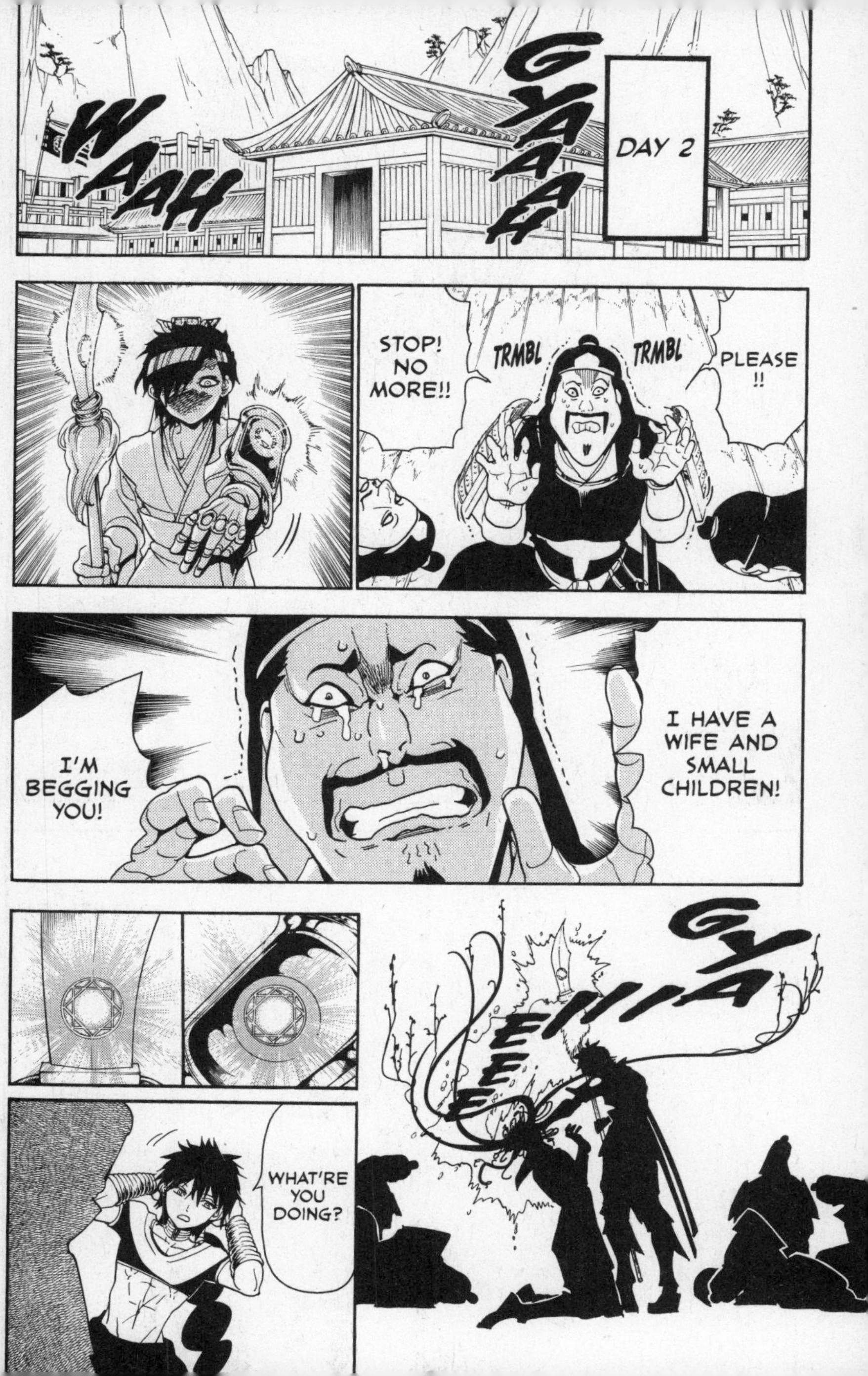
DAY 2
GYAAAA
WAAH
PLEASE !!
TRMBL
TRMBL
STOP! NO MORE!!
I HAVE A WIFE AND SMALL CHILDREN!
I'M BEGGING YOU!
WHAT'RE YOU DOING?

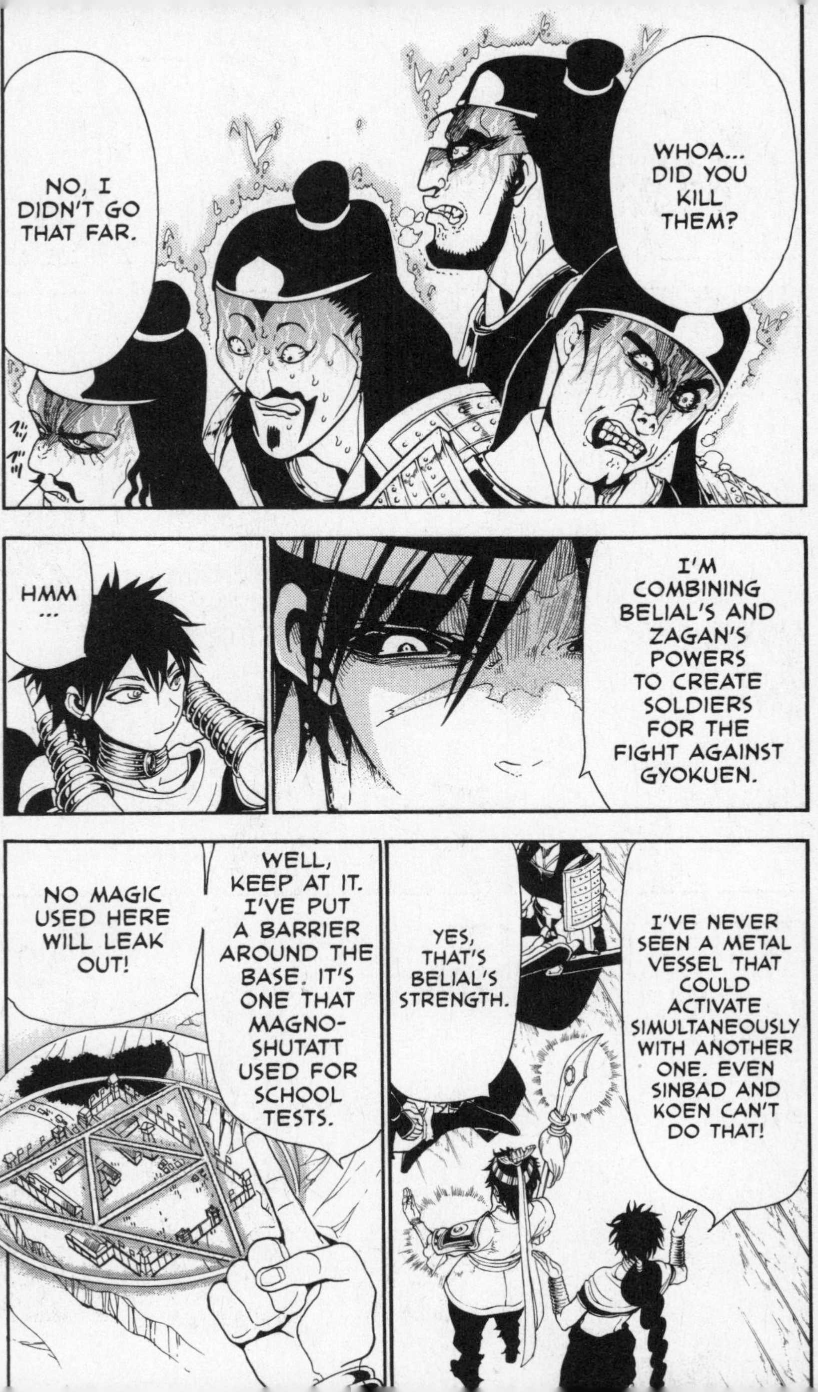
WHOA... DID YOU KILL THEM?
NO, I DIDN'T GO THAT FAR.
I'M COMBINING BELIAL'S AND ZAGAN'S POWERS TO CREATE SOLDIERS FOR THE FIGHT AGAINST GYOKUEN.
HMM ...
I'VE NEVER SEEN A METAL VESSEL THAT COULD ACTIVATE SIMULTANEOUSLY WITH ANOTHER ONE. EVEN SINBAD AND KOEN CAN'T DO THAT!
YES, THAT'S BELIAL'S STRENGTH.
WELL, KEEP AT IT. I'VE PUT A BARRIER AROUND THE BASE. IT'S ONE THAT MAGNO-SHUTATT USED FOR SCHOOL TESTS.
NO MAGIC USED HERE WILL LEAK OUT!

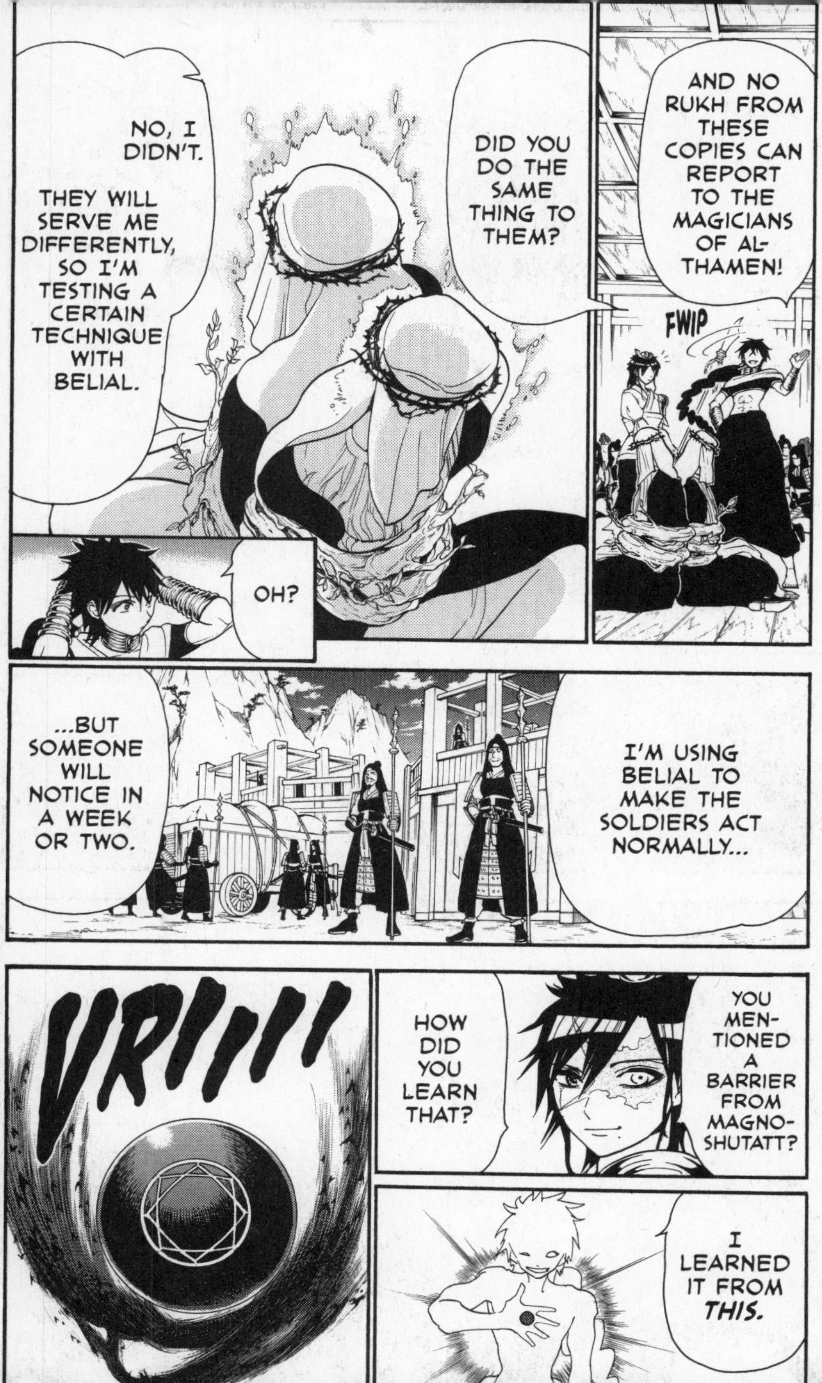
AND NO RUKH FROM THESE COPIES CAN REPORT TO THE MAGICIANS OF AL-THAMEN!
FWIP
DID YOU DO THE SAME THING TO THEM?
NO, I DIDN'T.
THEY WILL SERVE ME DIFFERENTLY, SO I'M TESTING A CERTAIN TECHNIQUE WITH BELIAL.
OH?
I'M USING BELIAL TO MAKE THE SOLDIERS ACT NORMALLY...
...BUT SOMEONE WILL NOTICE IN A WEEK OR TWO.
YOU MEN-TIONED A BARRIER FROM MAGNO-SHUTATT?
HOW DID YOU LEARN THAT?
I LEARNED IT FROM *THIS.*
VRIIII

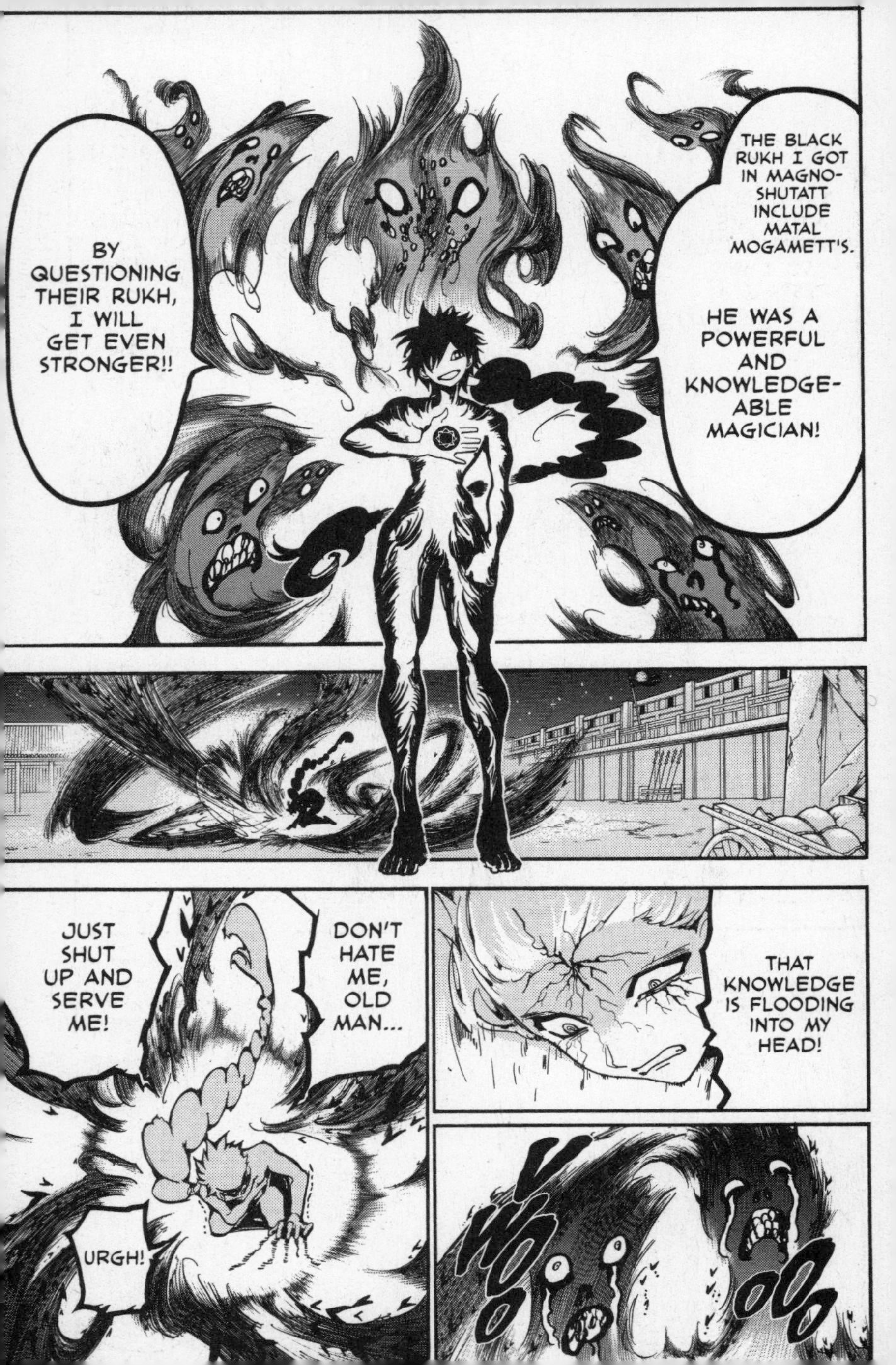
THE BLACK RUKH I GOT IN MAGNO-SHUTATT INCLUDE MATAL MOGAMETT'S.
HE WAS A POWERFUL AND KNOWLEDGE-ABLE MAGICIAN!
BY QUESTIONING THEIR RUKH, I WILL GET EVEN STRONGER!!
THAT KNOWLEDGE IS FLOODING INTO MY HEAD!
DON'T HATE ME, OLD MAN...
JUST SHUT UP AND SERVE ME!
URGH!

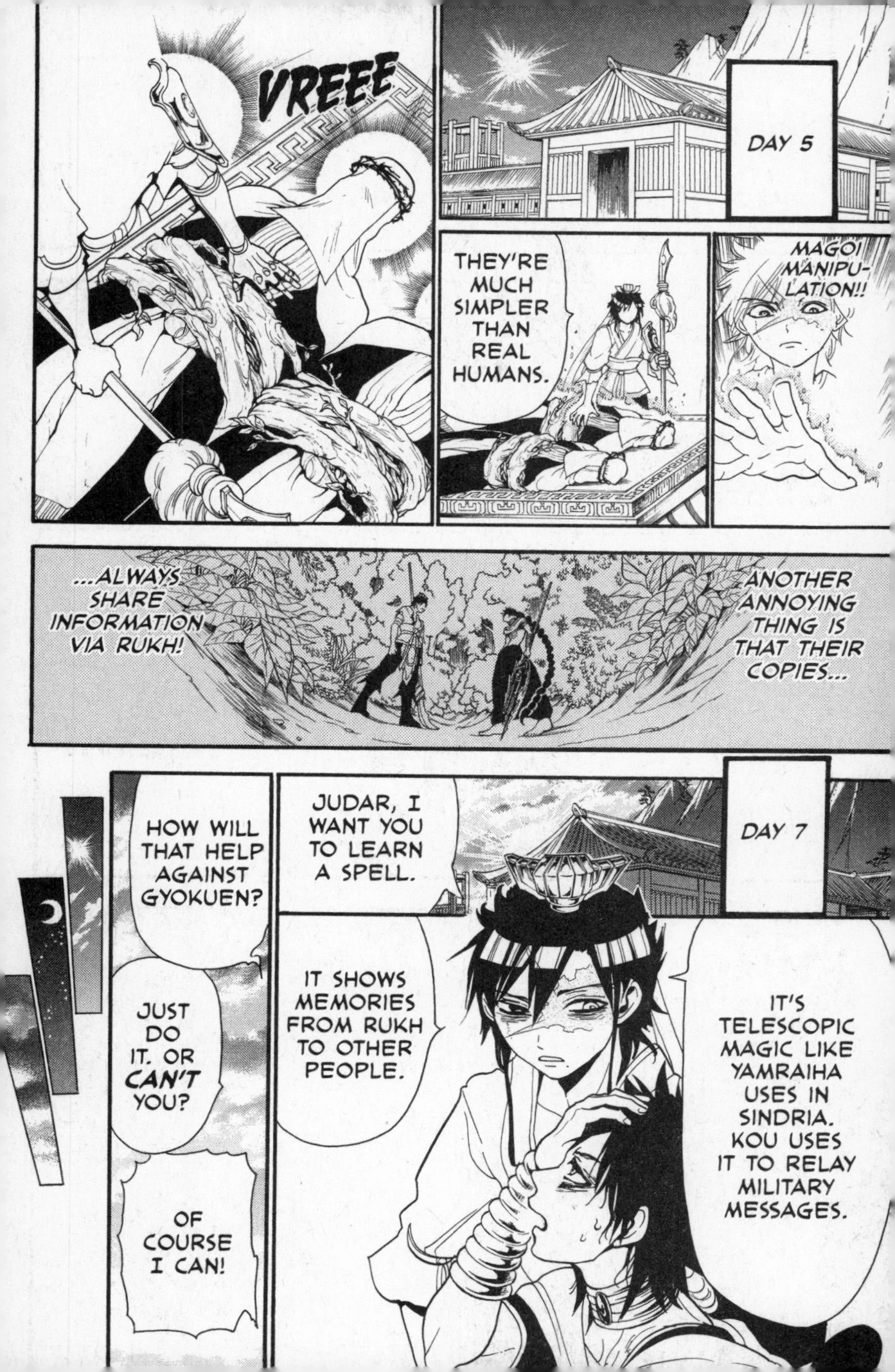
DAY 5
MAGOI MANIPULATION!!
THEY'RE MUCH SIMPLER THAN REAL HUMANS.
VREEE
ANOTHER ANNOYING THING IS THAT THEIR COPIES...
...ALWAYS SHARE INFORMATION VIA RUKH!
DAY 7
JUDAR, I WANT YOU TO LEARN A SPELL.
HOW WILL THAT HELP AGAINST GYOKUEN?
IT'S TELESCOPIC MAGIC LIKE YAMRAIHA USES IN SINDRIA. KOU USES IT TO RELAY MILITARY MESSAGES.
IT SHOWS MEMORIES FROM RUKH TO OTHER PEOPLE.
JUST DO IT. OR *CAN'T* YOU?
OF COURSE I CAN!

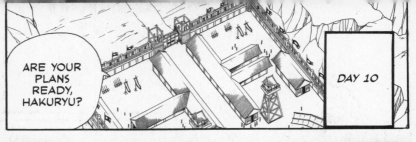

ARE YOUR PLANS READY, HAKURYU?

DAY 10

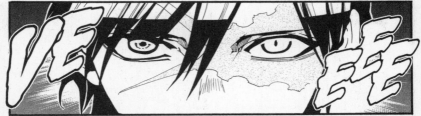

VE EEE

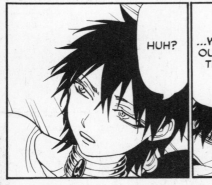

HUH?

...WE'RE OUT OF TIME.

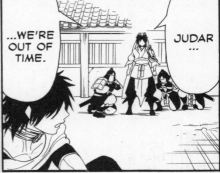

JUDAR...

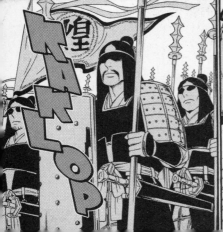

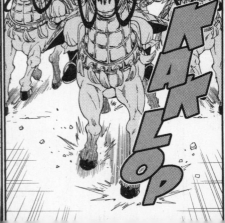

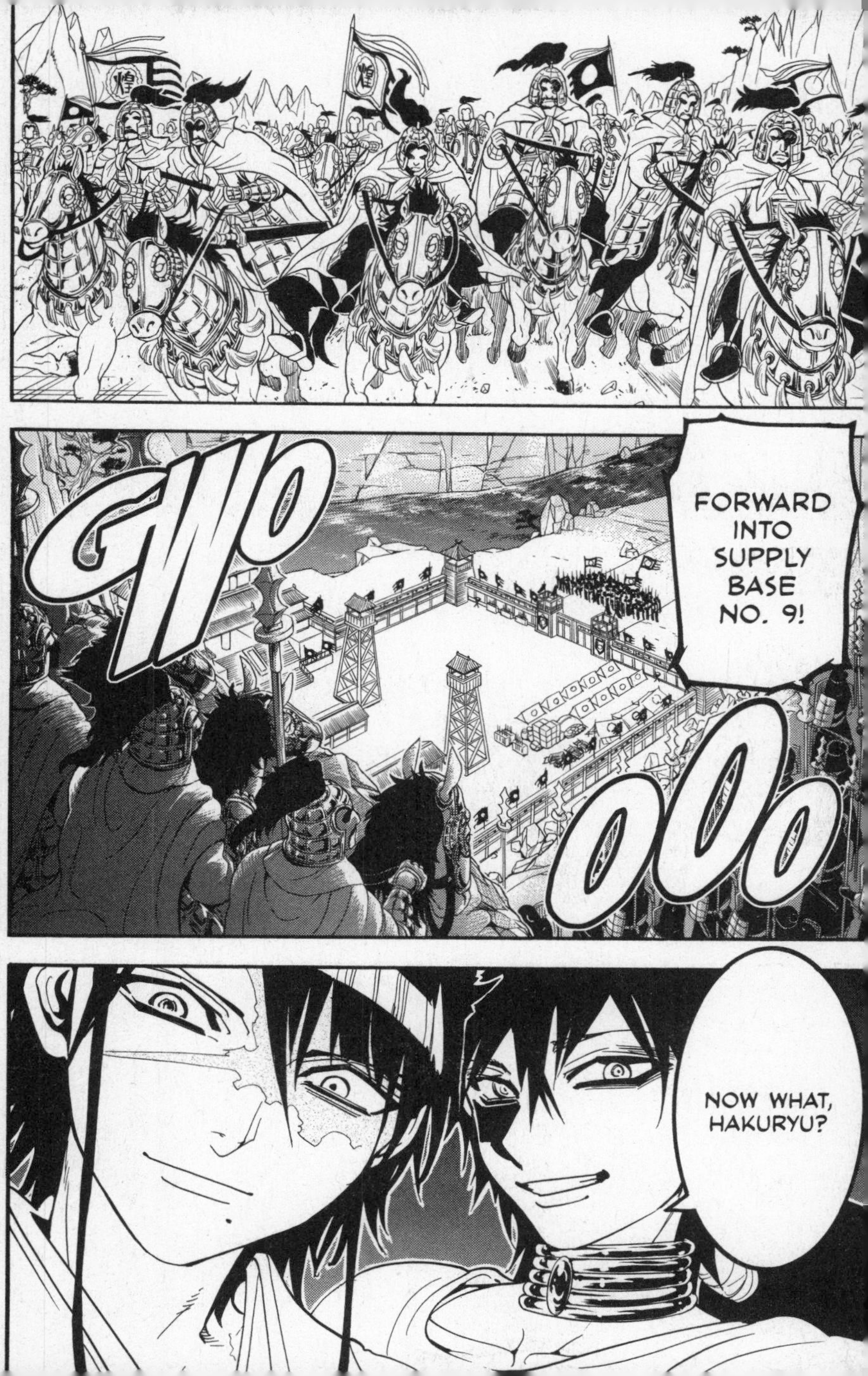
FORWARD INTO SUPPLY BASE NO. 9!
GWOOO
NOW WHAT, HAKURYU?

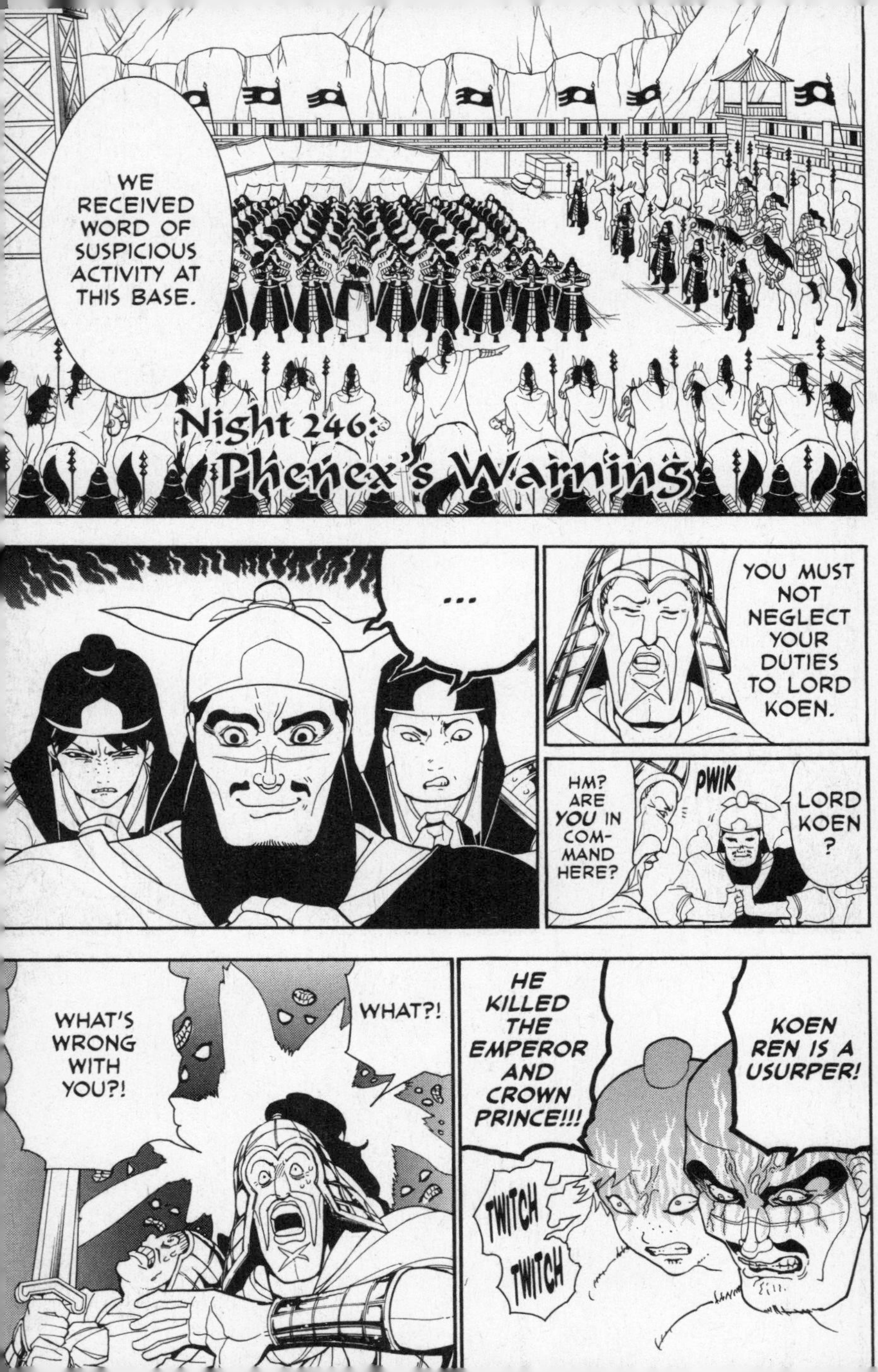
WE RECEIVED WORD OF SUSPICIOUS ACTIVITY AT THIS BASE.
Night 246: Phenex's Warning
YOU MUST NOT NEGLECT YOUR DUTIES TO LORD KOEN.
LORD KOEN?
PWIK
HM? ARE YOU IN COM-MAND HERE?
...
KOEN REN IS A USURPER!
HE KILLED THE EMPEROR AND CROWN PRINCE!!!
TWITCH
TWITCH
WHAT?!
WHAT'S WRONG WITH YOU?!

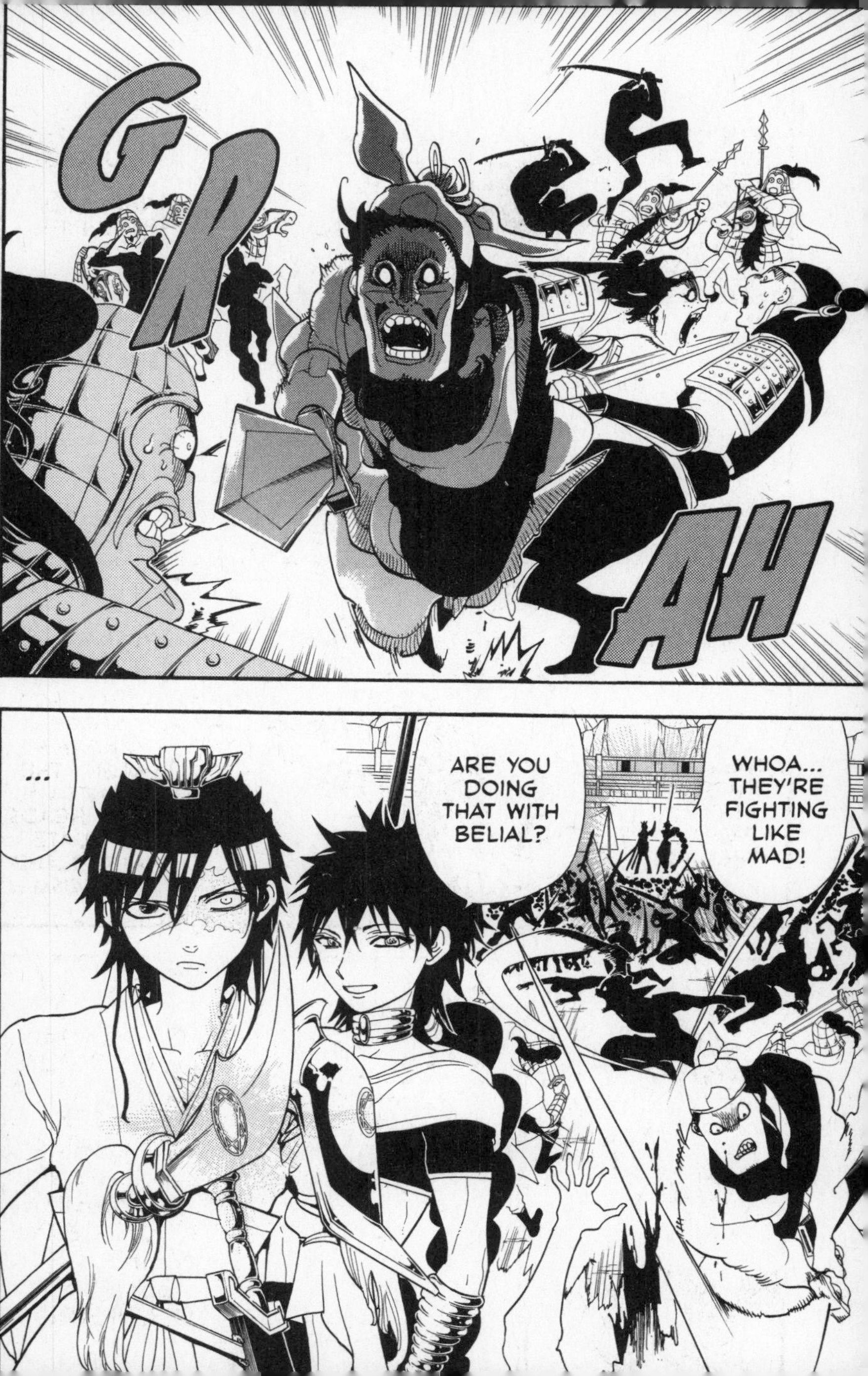
GRAH
WHOA... THEY'RE FIGHTING LIKE MAD!
ARE YOU DOING THAT WITH BELIAL?
...

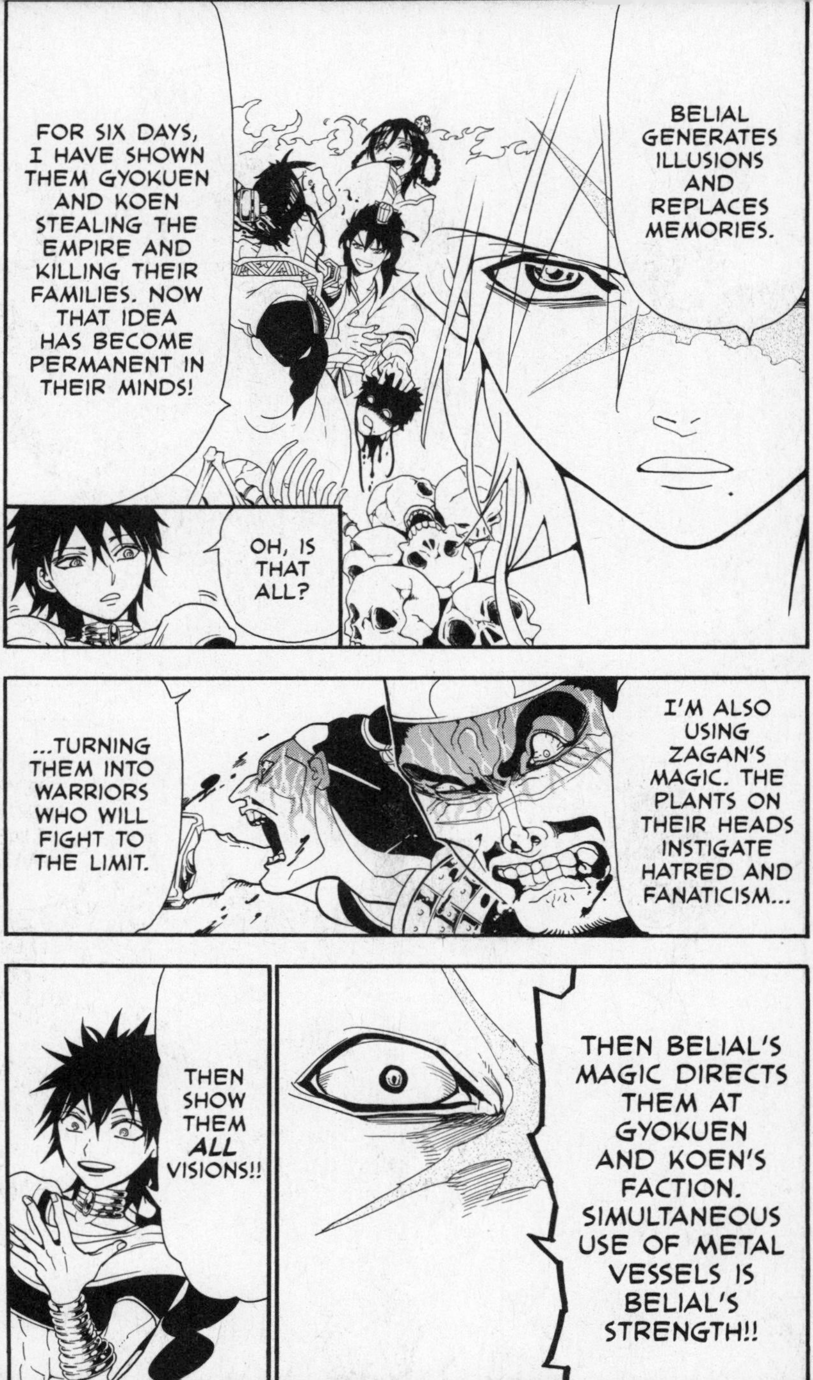
BELIAL GENERATES ILLUSIONS AND REPLACES MEMORIES.
FOR SIX DAYS, I HAVE SHOWN THEM GYOKUEN AND KOEN STEALING THE EMPIRE AND KILLING THEIR FAMILIES. NOW THAT IDEA HAS BECOME PERMANENT IN THEIR MINDS!
OH, IS THAT ALL?
I'M ALSO USING ZAGAN'S MAGIC. THE PLANTS ON THEIR HEADS INSTIGATE HATRED AND FANATICISM...
...TURNING THEM INTO WARRIORS WHO WILL FIGHT TO THE LIMIT.
THEN BELIAL'S MAGIC DIRECTS THEM AT GYOKUEN AND KOEN'S FACTION. SIMULTANEOUS USE OF METAL VESSELS IS BELIAL'S STRENGTH!!
THEN SHOW THEM *ALL* VISIONS!!

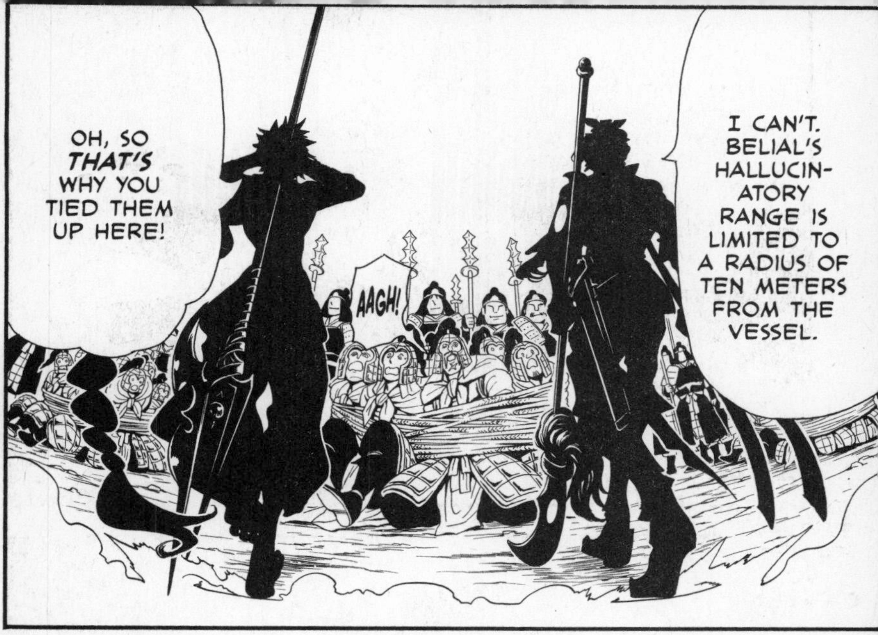
I CAN'T. BELIAL'S HALLUCIN-ATORY RANGE IS LIMITED TO A RADIUS OF TEN METERS FROM THE VESSEL.
AAGH!
OH, SO *THAT'S* WHY YOU TIED THEM UP HERE!

HAKURYU TOOK OVER 100 PRISONERS AND SPENT SIX DAYS INSTILLING OBEDIENCE.

DURING THAT TIME, ANOTHER FORCE ARRIVED, WHICH HE SEIZED IN THE SAME WAY, INCREASING HIS NUMBERS BY ANOTHER 200.

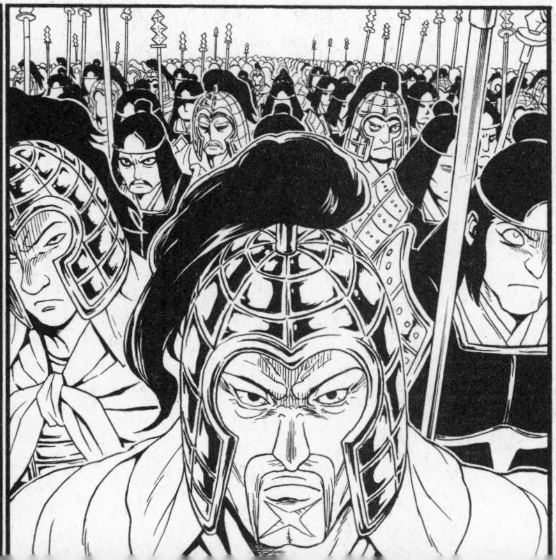

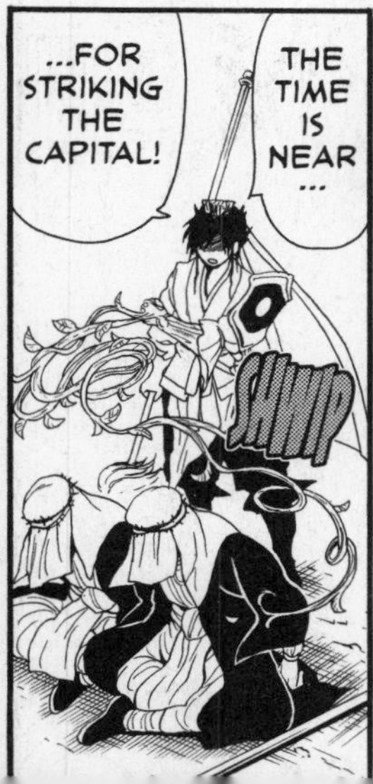
THE TIME IS NEAR ...
...FOR STRIKING THE CAPITAL!
SHWIP

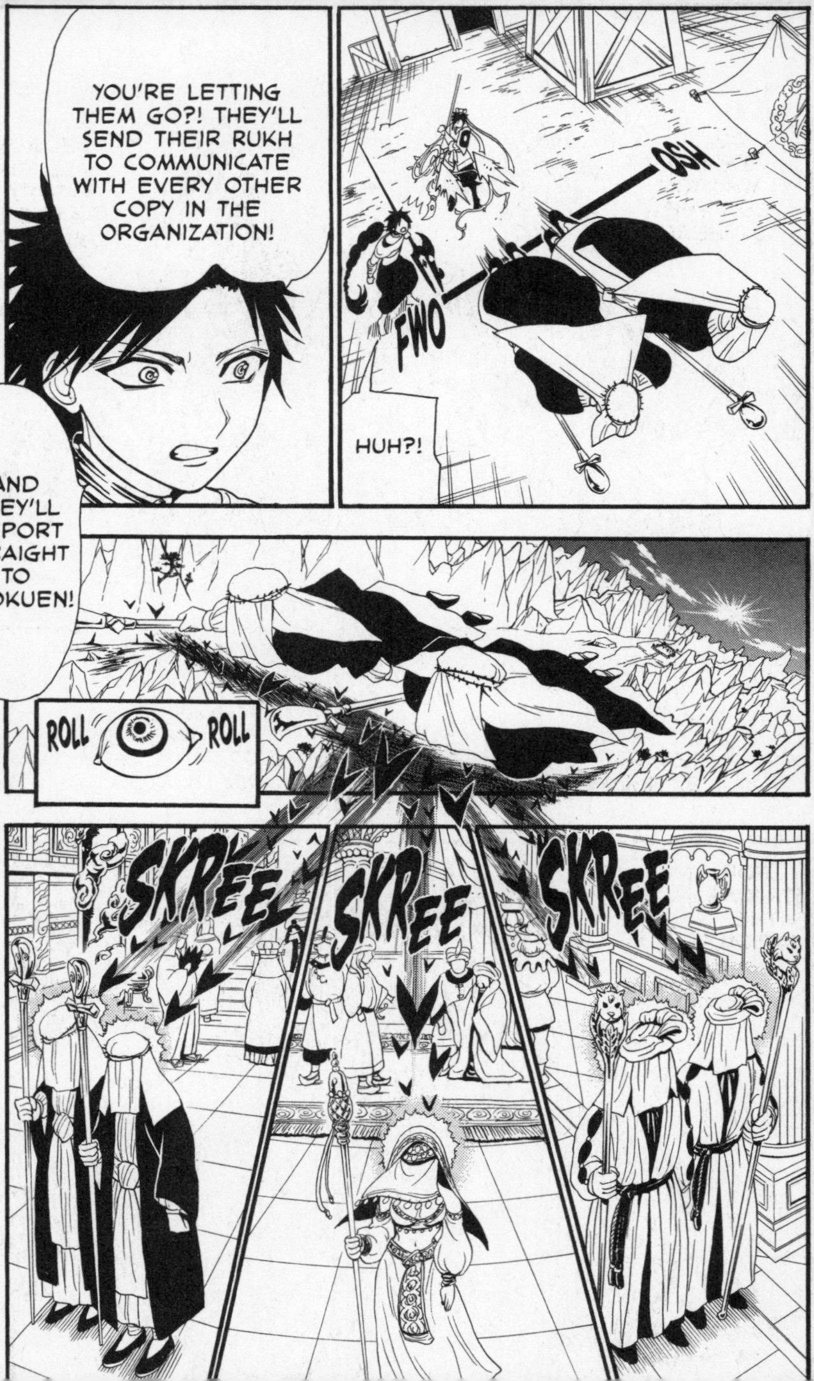
OSH
FWO
HUH?!
YOU'RE LETTING THEM GO?! THEY'LL SEND THEIR RUKH TO COMMUNICATE WITH EVERY OTHER COPY IN THE ORGANIZATION!
AND THEY'LL REPORT STRAIGHT TO GYOKUEN!
ROLL ROLL
SKREE
SKREE
SKREE

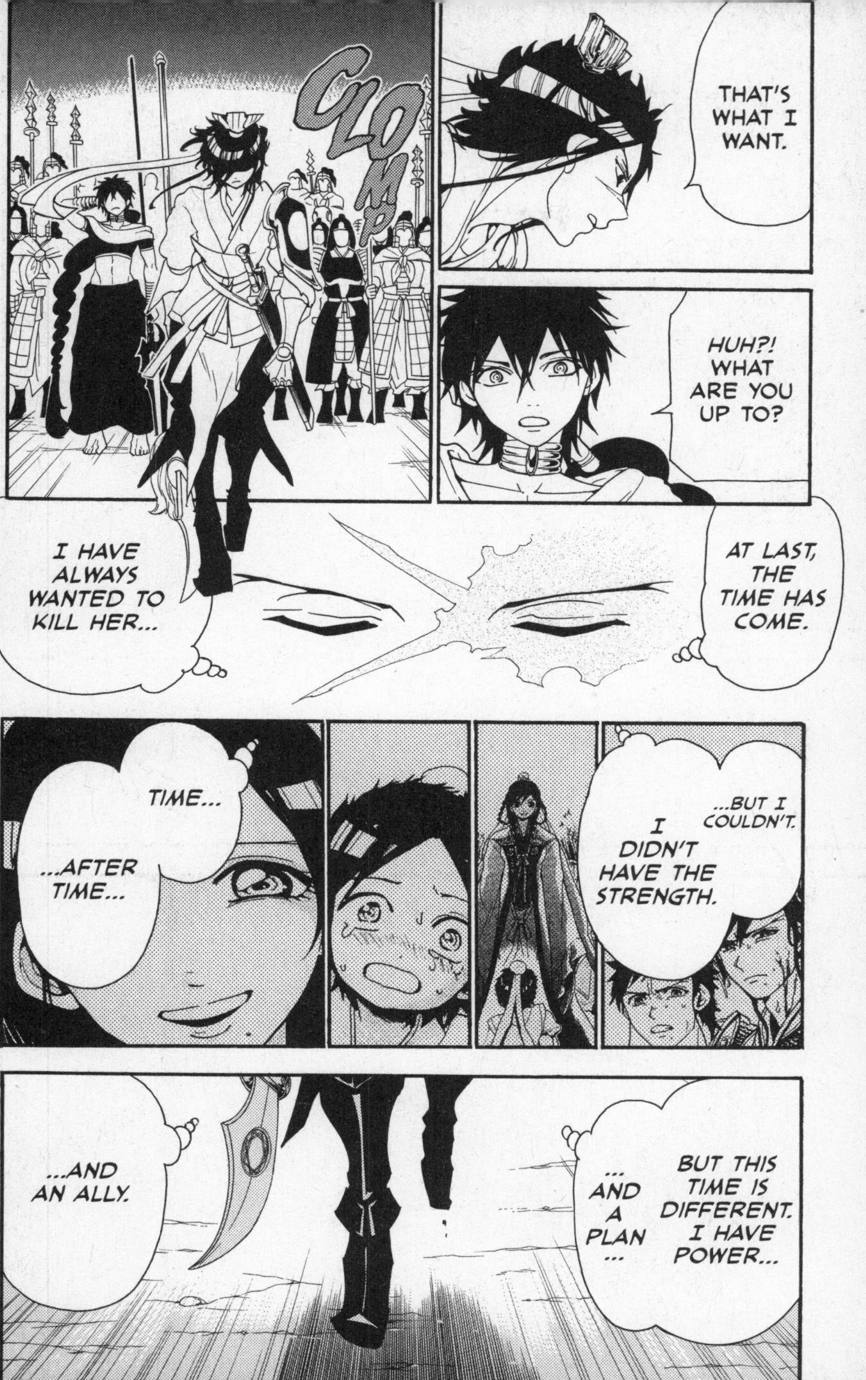
THAT'S WHAT I WANT.
HUH?! WHAT ARE YOU UP TO?
CLOMP
AT LAST, THE TIME HAS COME.
I HAVE ALWAYS WANTED TO KILL HER...
...BUT I COULDN'T.
I DIDN'T HAVE THE STRENGTH.
TIME...
...AFTER TIME...
BUT THIS TIME IS DIFFERENT. I HAVE POWER...
... AND A PLAN ...
...AND AN ALLY.

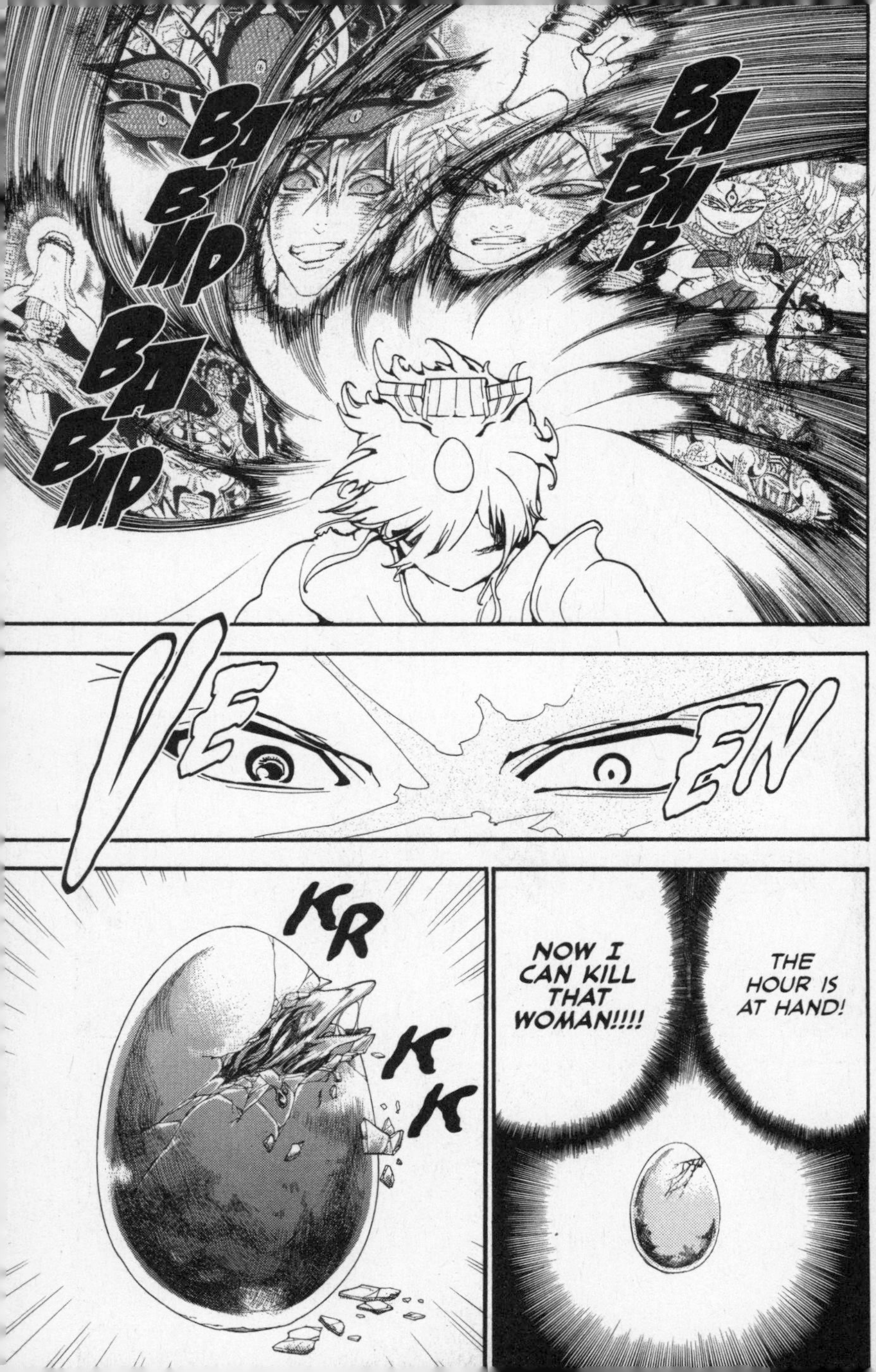
BA BA BMP
BA BA BMP BA BA BMP
VEEN
THE HOUR IS AT HAND!
NOW I CAN KILL THAT WOMAN!!!!
KR K K

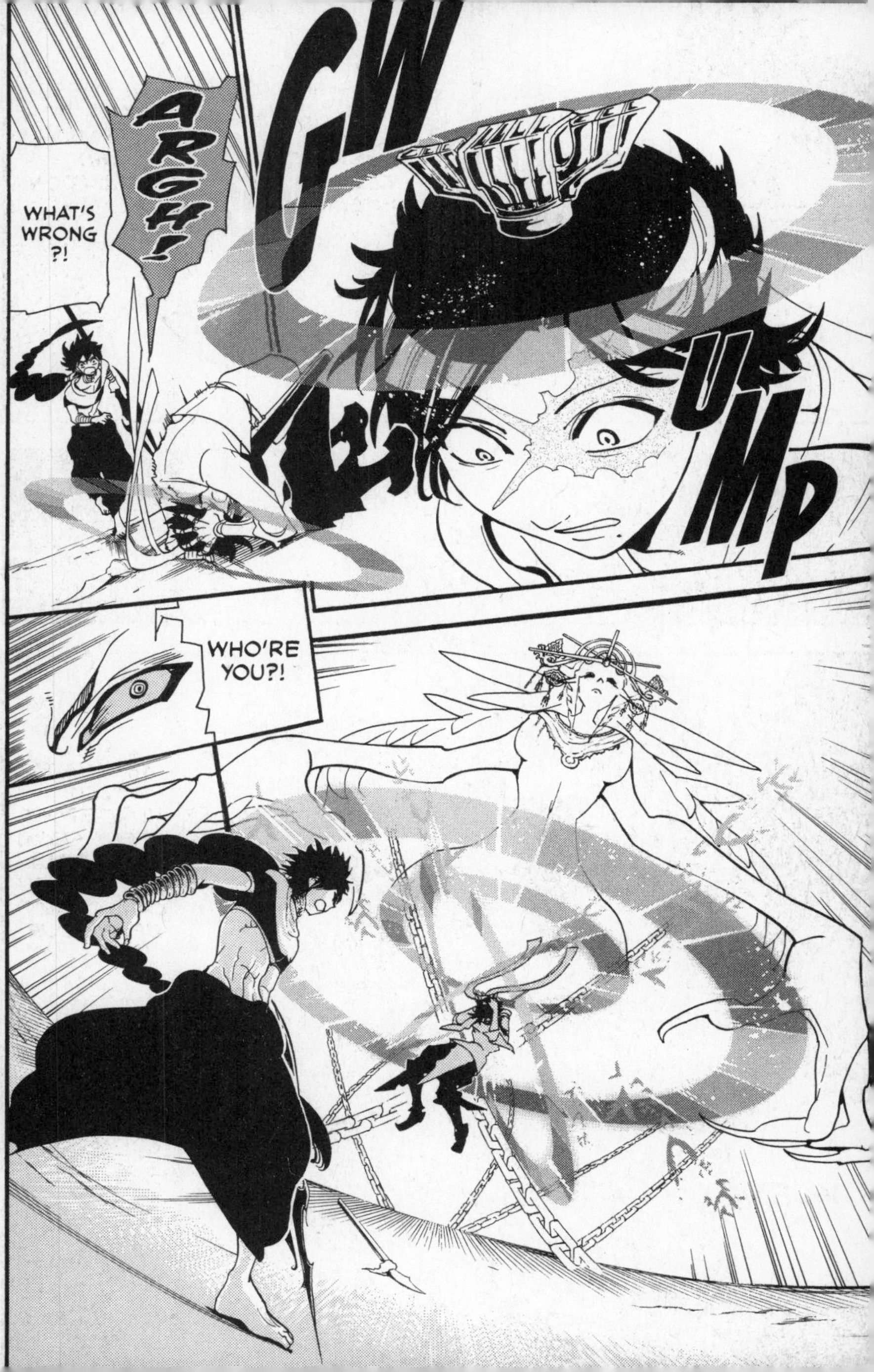
GWUMP
ARGH!
WHAT'S WRONG?!
WHO'RE YOU?!

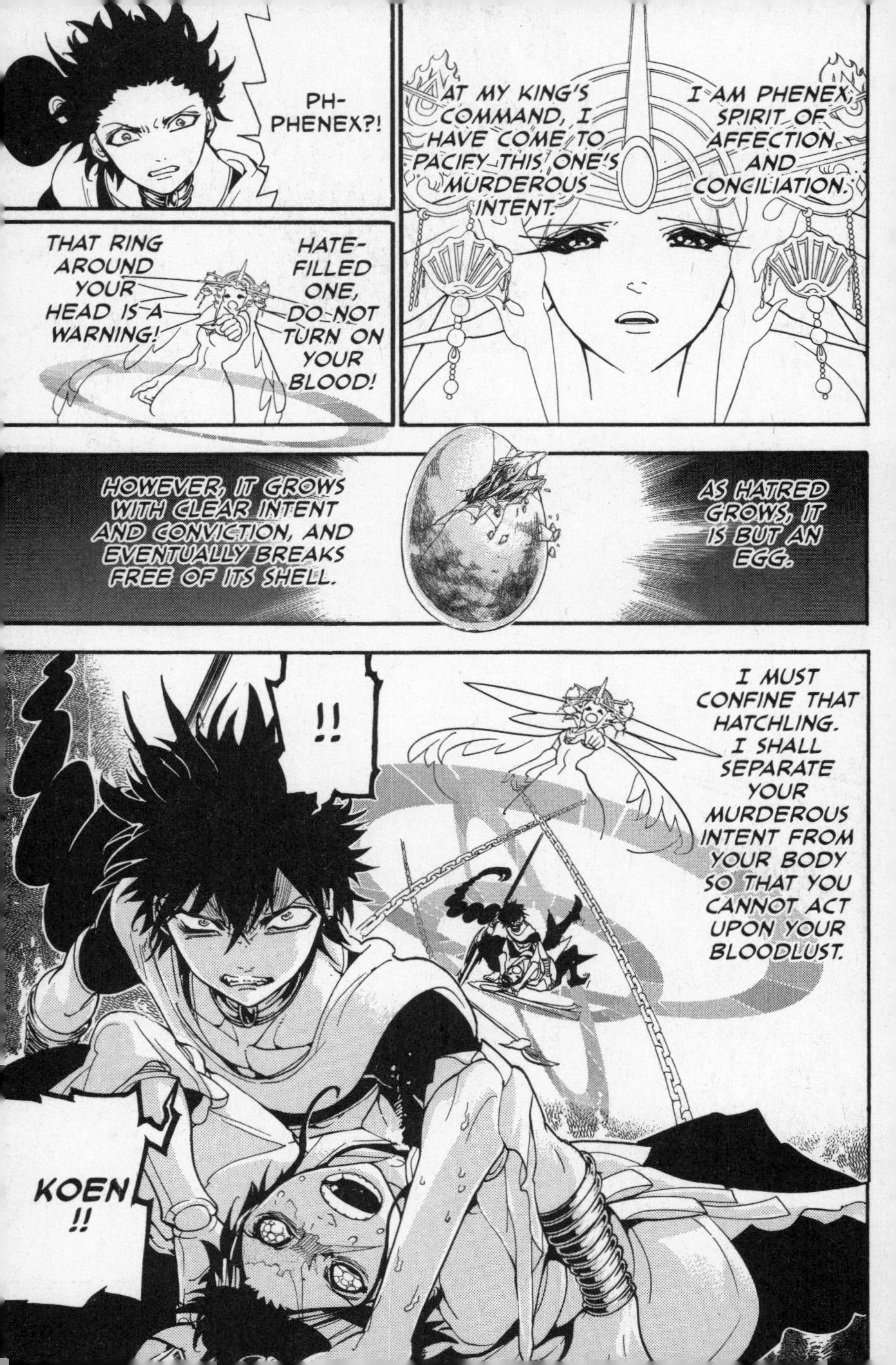
I AM PHENEX, SPIRIT OF AFFECTION AND CONCILIATION.
AT MY KING'S COMMAND, I HAVE COME TO PACIFY THIS ONE'S MURDEROUS INTENT.
PH-PHENEX?!
HATE-FILLED ONE, DO NOT TURN ON YOUR BLOOD!
THAT RING AROUND YOUR HEAD IS A WARNING!
AS HATRED GROWS, IT IS BUT AN EGG.
HOWEVER, IT GROWS WITH CLEAR INTENT AND CONVICTION, AND EVENTUALLY BREAKS FREE OF ITS SHELL.
I MUST CONFINE THAT HATCHLING. I SHALL SEPARATE YOUR MURDEROUS INTENT FROM YOUR BODY SO THAT YOU CANNOT ACT UPON YOUR BLOODLUST.
!!
KOEN !!

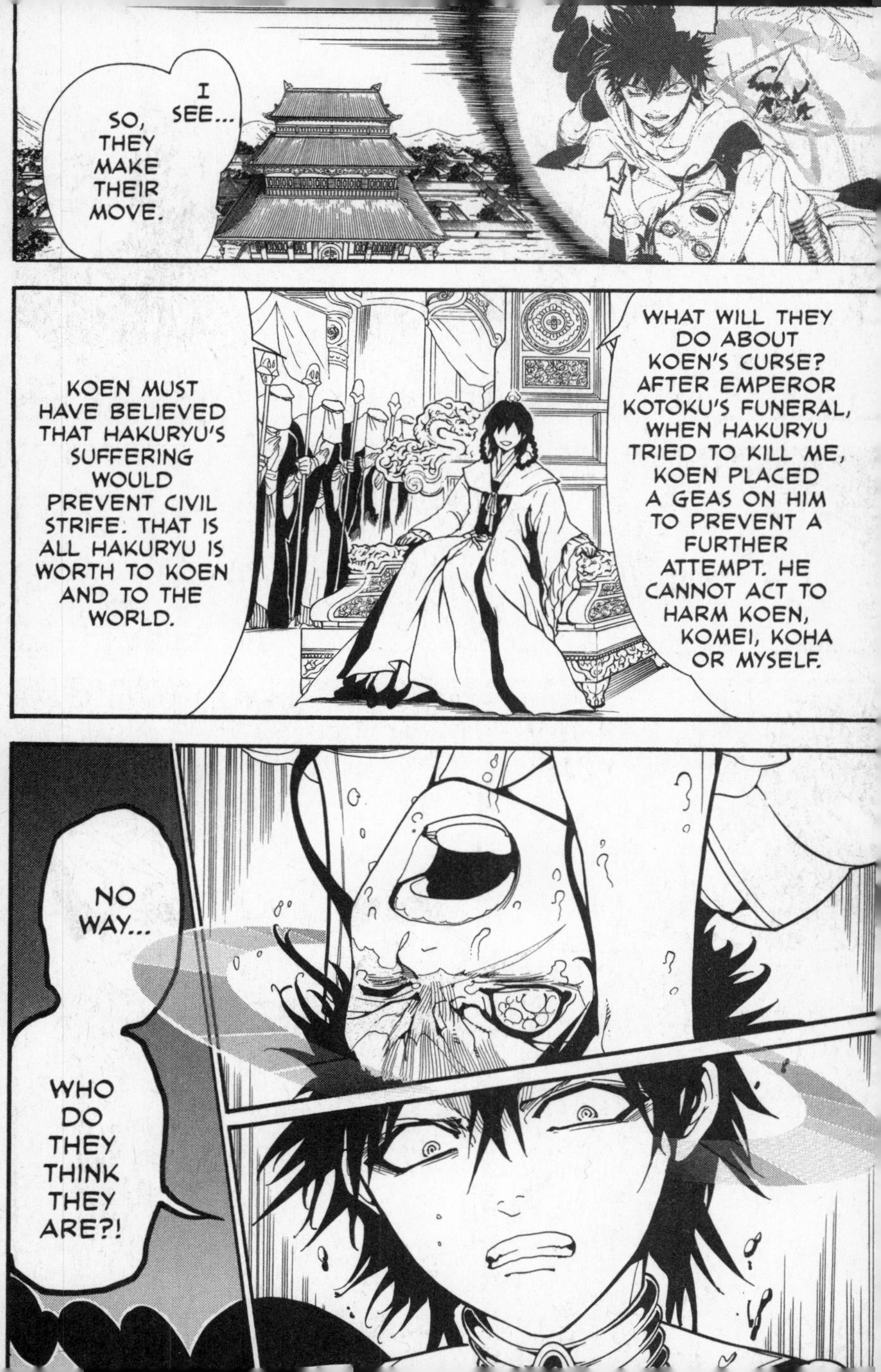
I SEE...
SO, THEY MAKE THEIR MOVE.
WHAT WILL THEY DO ABOUT KOEN'S CURSE? AFTER EMPEROR KOTOKU'S FUNERAL, WHEN HAKURYU TRIED TO KILL ME, KOEN PLACED A GEAS ON HIM TO PREVENT A FURTHER ATTEMPT. HE CANNOT ACT TO HARM KOEN, KOMEI, KOHA OR MYSELF.
KOEN MUST HAVE BELIEVED THAT HAKURYU'S SUFFERING WOULD PREVENT CIVIL STRIFE. THAT IS ALL HAKURYU IS WORTH TO KOEN AND TO THE WORLD.
NO WAY...
WHO DO THEY THINK THEY ARE?!

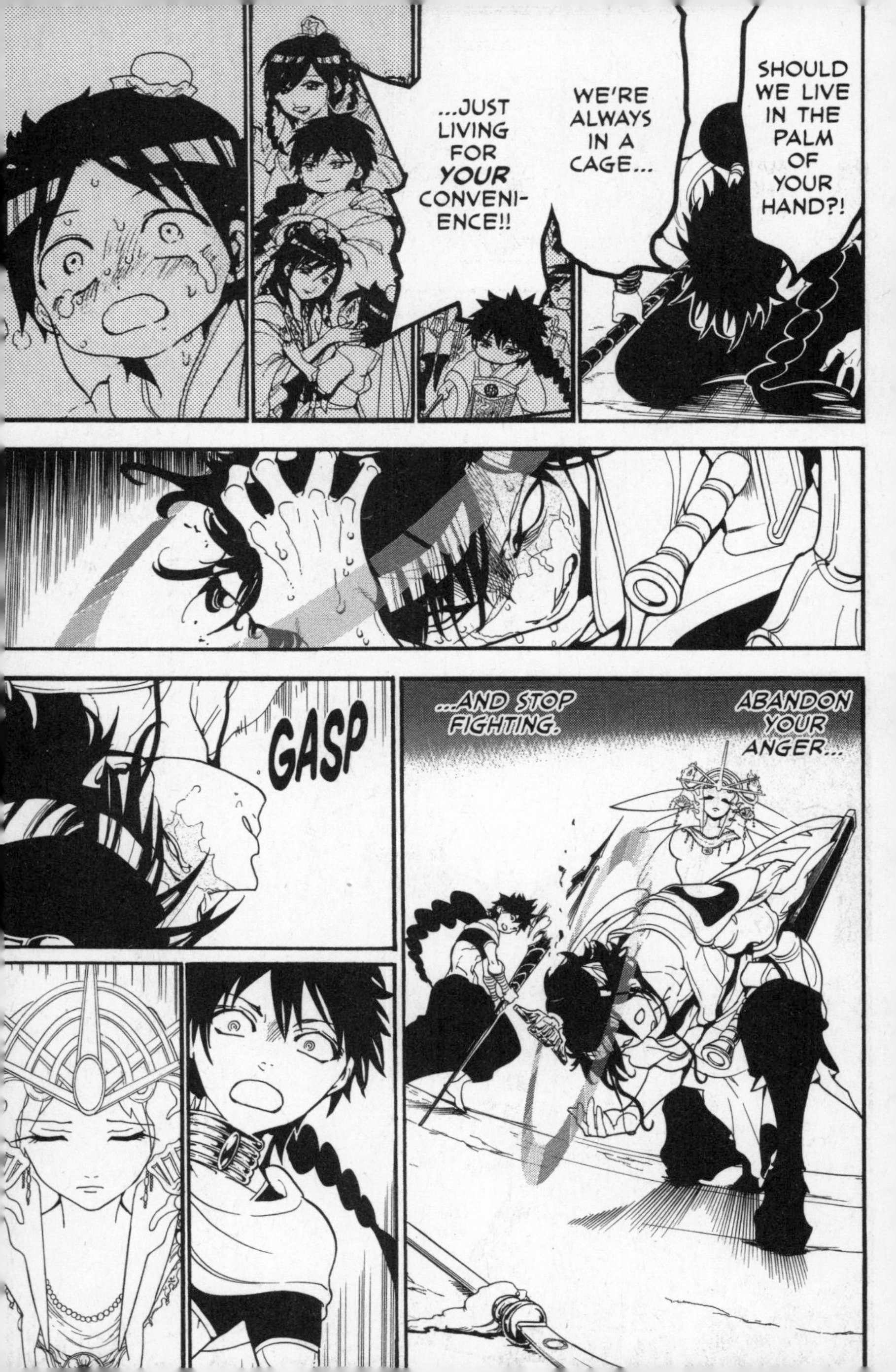
SHOULD WE LIVE IN THE PALM OF YOUR HAND?!
WE'RE ALWAYS IN A CAGE...
...JUST LIVING FOR YOUR CONVENIENCE!!
ABANDON YOUR ANGER...
...AND STOP FIGHTING.
GASP

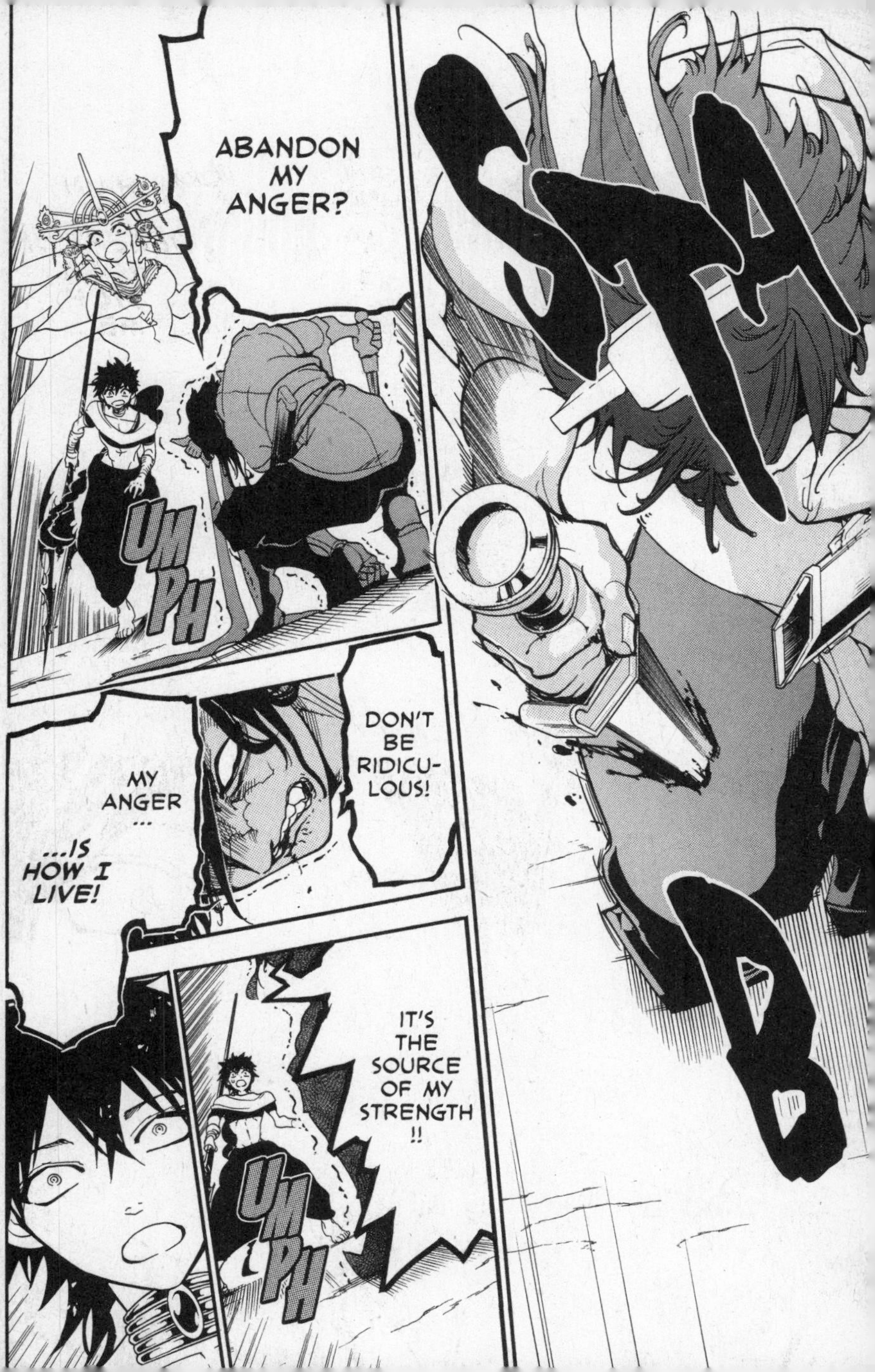

STAB
ABANDON MY ANGER?
UMPH
DON'T BE RIDICULOUS!
MY ANGER...
...IS HOW I LIVE!
IT'S THE SOURCE OF MY STRENGTH!!
UMPH

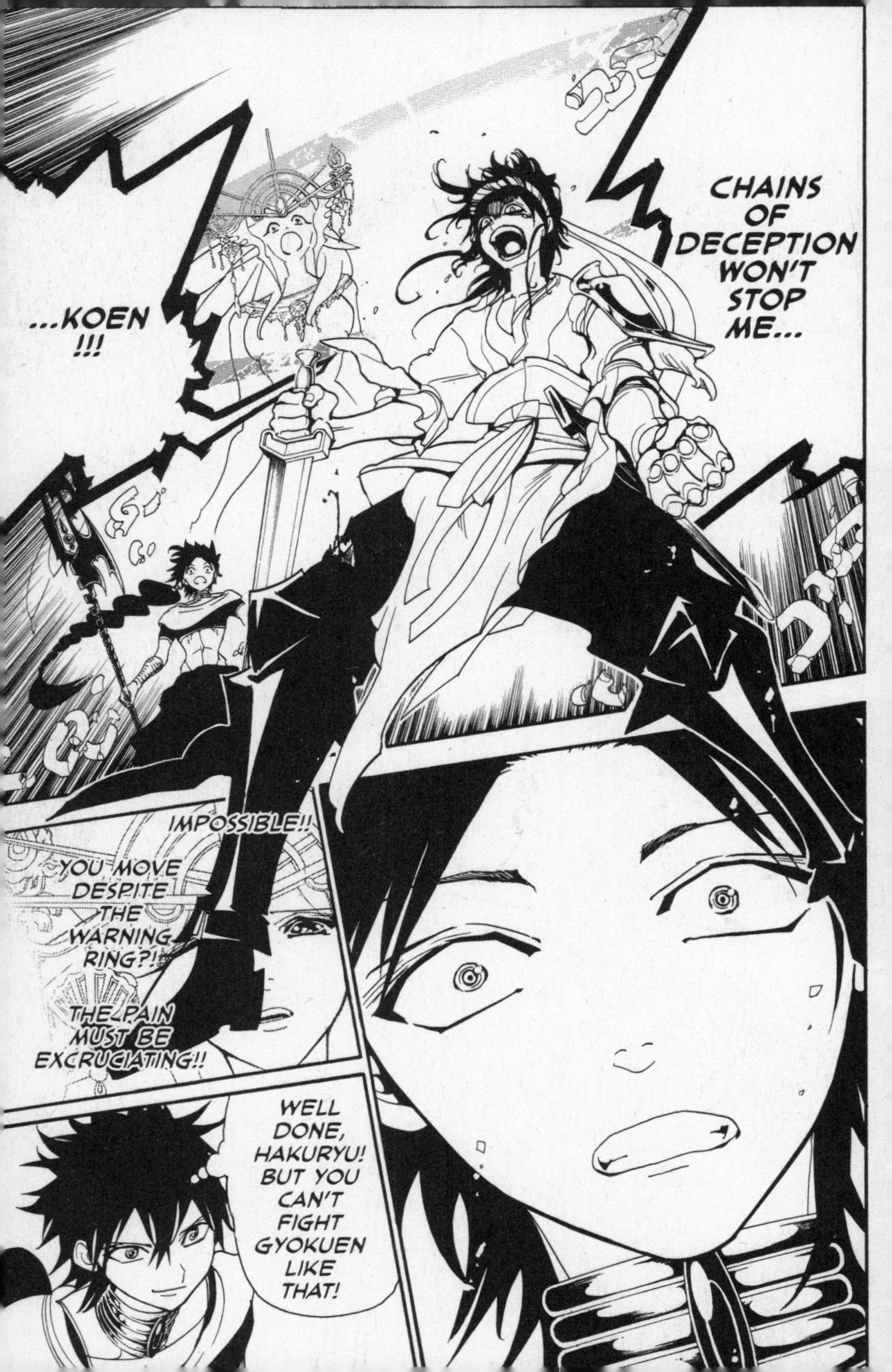
CHAINS OF DECEPTION WON'T STOP ME...
...KOEN!!!
IMPOSSIBLE!!
YOU MOVE DESPITE THE WARNING RING?!
THE PAIN MUST BE EXCRUCIATING!!
WELL DONE, HAKURYU! BUT YOU CAN'T FIGHT GYOKUEN LIKE THAT!

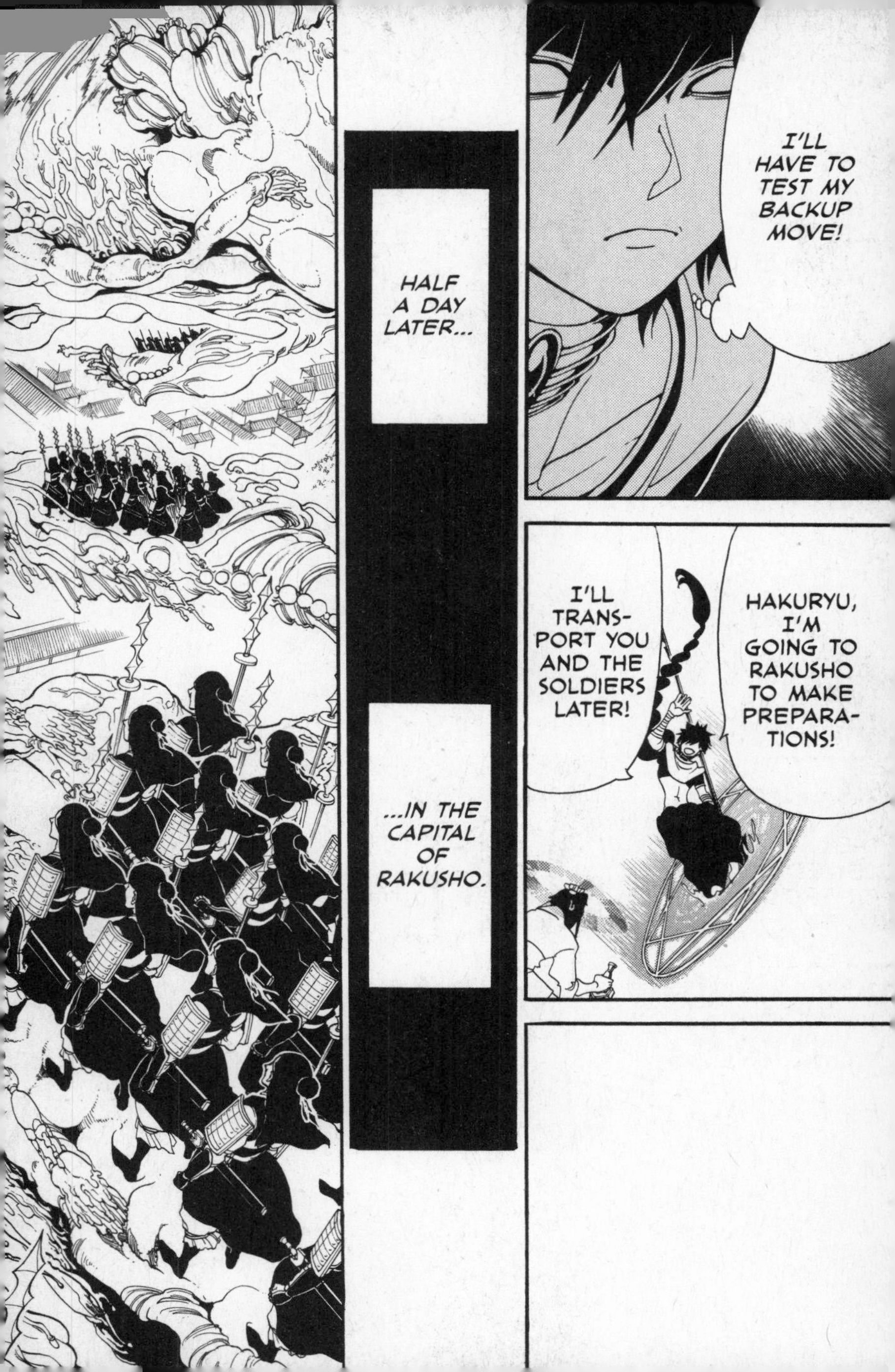
I'LL HAVE TO TEST MY BACKUP MOVE!
HAKURYU, I'M GOING TO RAKUSHO TO MAKE PREPARATIONS!
I'LL TRANSPORT YOU AND THE SOLDIERS LATER!
HALF A DAY LATER...
...IN THE CAPITAL OF RAKUSHO.

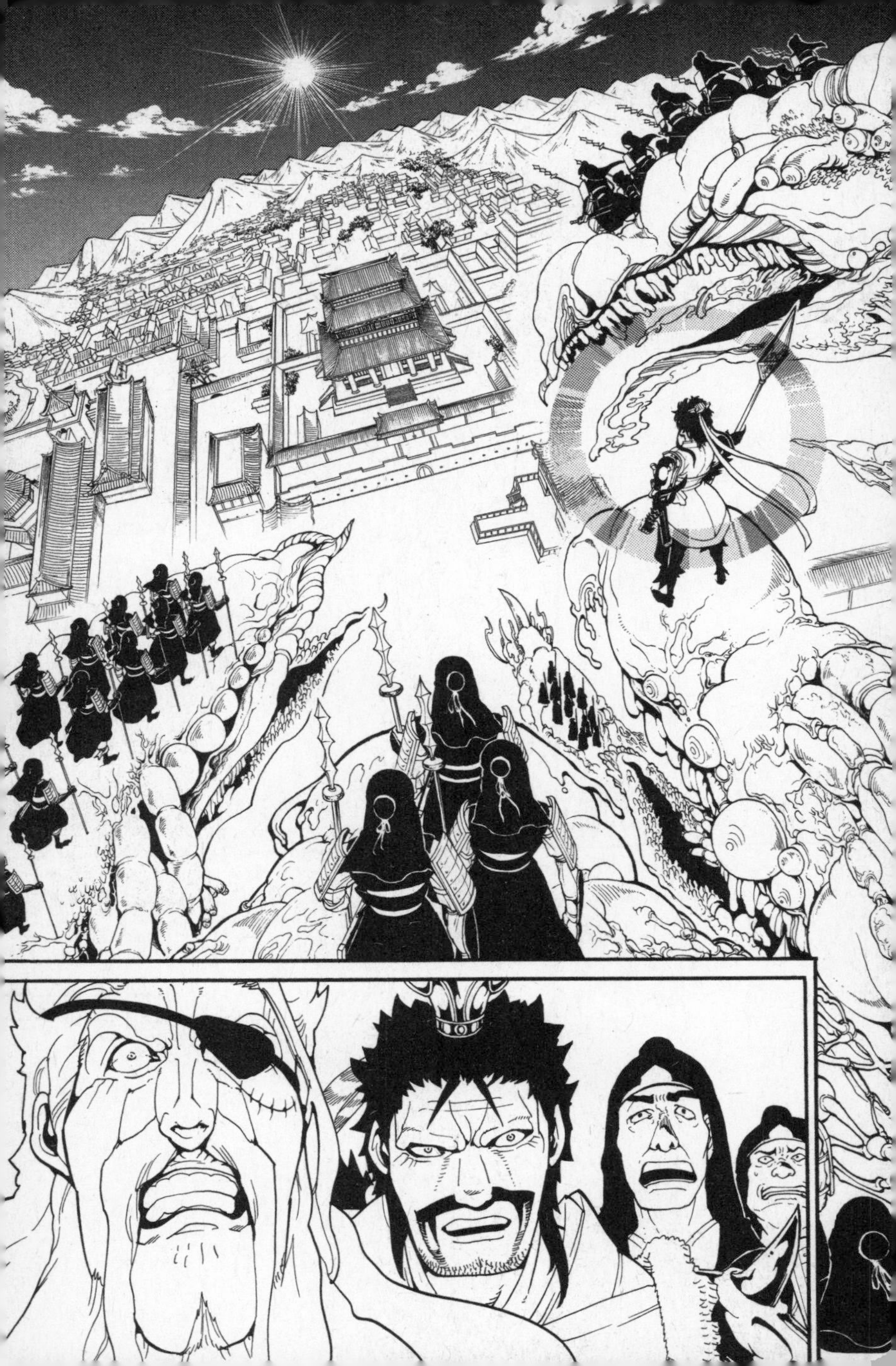

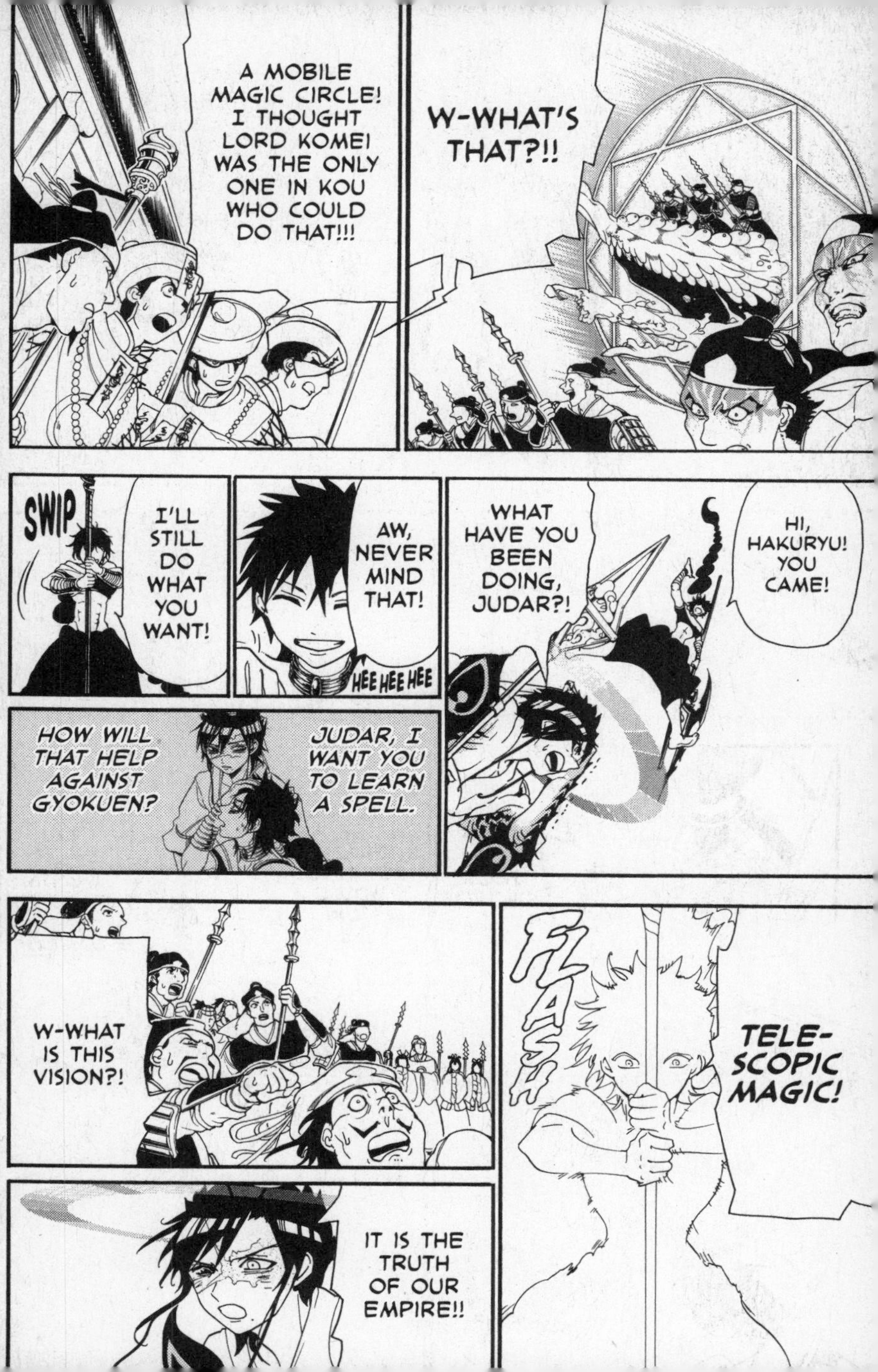
W-WHAT'S THAT?!!
A MOBILE MAGIC CIRCLE! I THOUGHT LORD KOMEI WAS THE ONLY ONE IN KOU WHO COULD DO THAT!!!
HI, HAKURYU! YOU CAME!
WHAT HAVE YOU BEEN DOING, JUDAR?!
AW, NEVER MIND THAT!
HEE HEE HEE
SWIP
I'LL STILL DO WHAT YOU WANT!
JUDAR, I WANT YOU TO LEARN A SPELL.
HOW WILL THAT HELP AGAINST GYOKUEN?
FLASH
TELE-SCOPIC MAGIC!
W-WHAT IS THIS VISION?!
IT IS THE TRUTH OF OUR EMPIRE!!

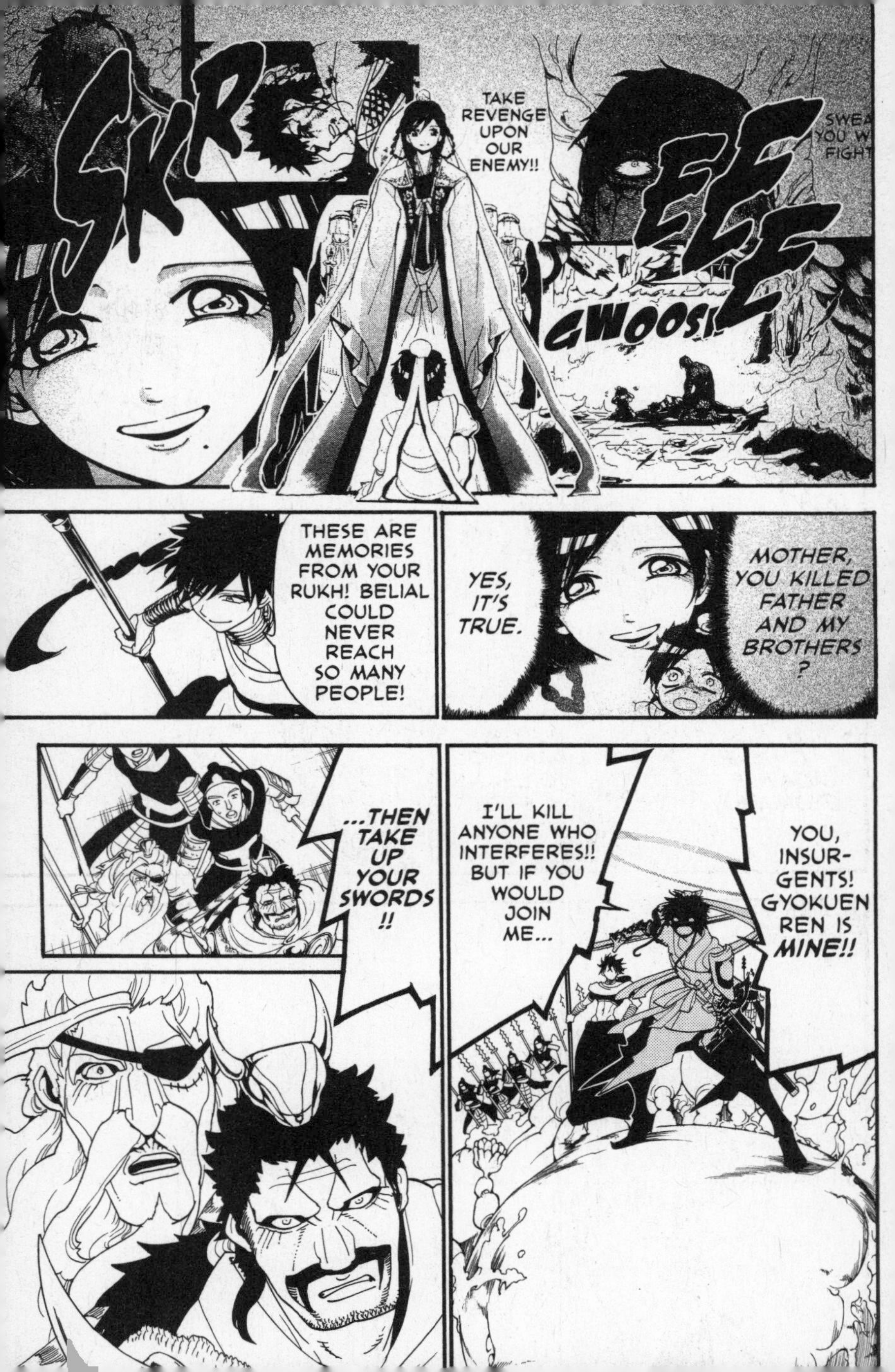
SWEA
YOU W
FIGHT
SKREEEE
TAKE REVENGE UPON OUR ENEMY!!
GWOOSH
MOTHER, YOU KILLED FATHER AND MY BROTHERS?
YES, IT'S TRUE.
THESE ARE MEMORIES FROM YOUR RUKH! BELIAL COULD NEVER REACH SO MANY PEOPLE!
YOU, INSURGENTS! GYOKUEN REN IS MINE!!
I'LL KILL ANYONE WHO INTERFERES!! BUT IF YOU WOULD JOIN ME...
...THEN TAKE UP YOUR SWORDS!!

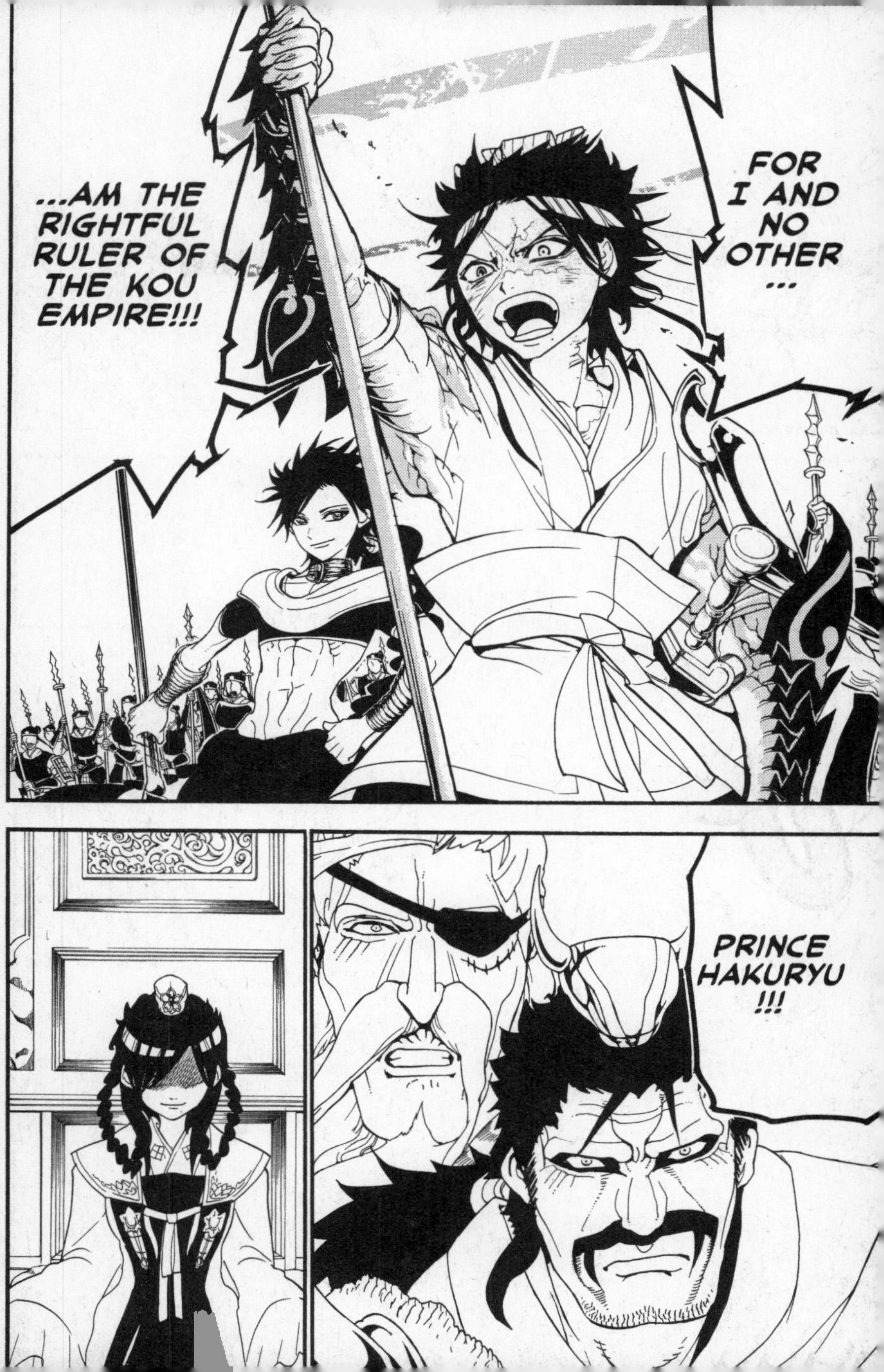
FOR I AND NO OTHER ...
...AM THE RIGHTFUL RULER OF THE KOU EMPIRE!!!
PRINCE HAKURYU !!!

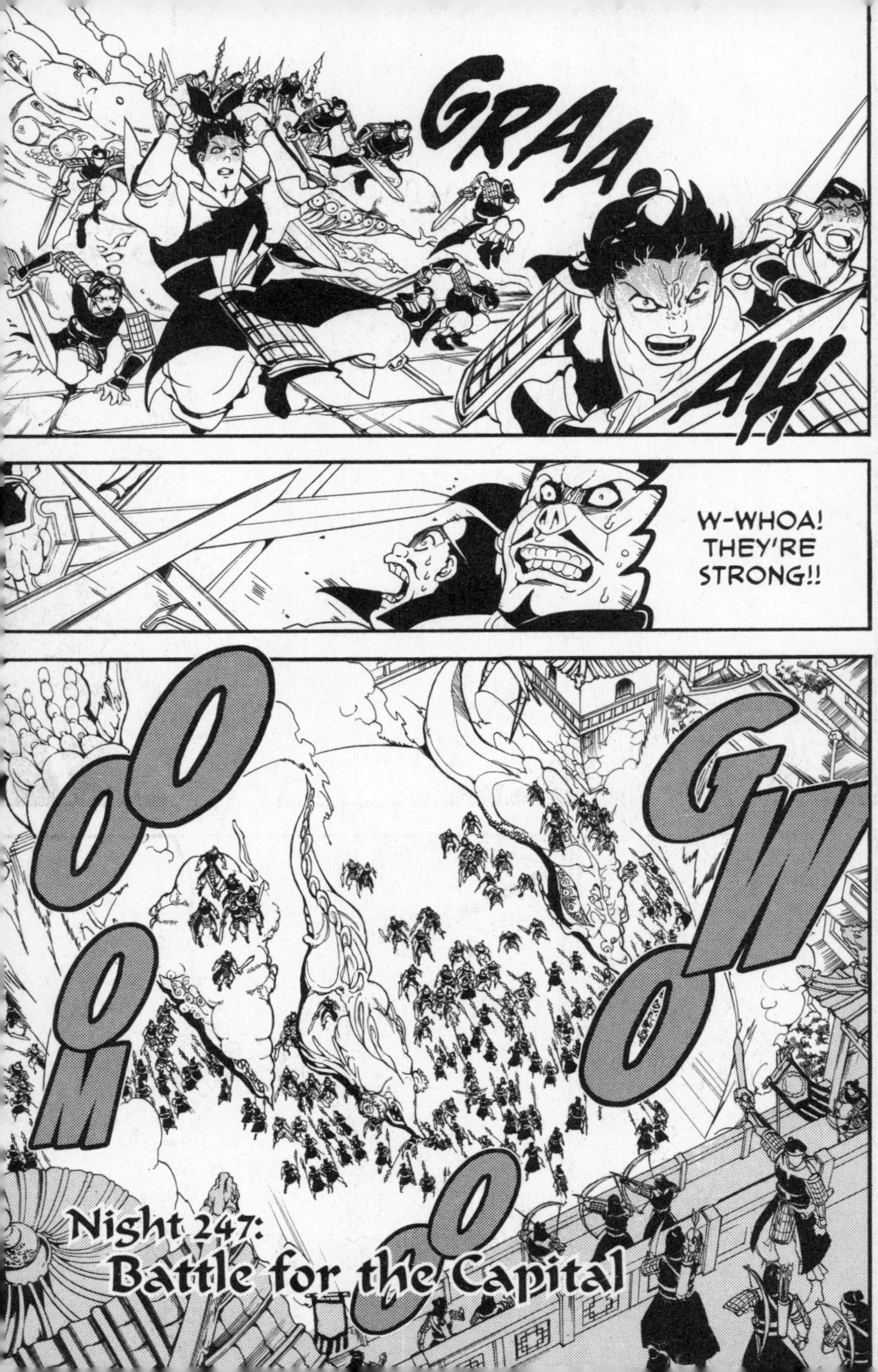
GRAAAH
W-WHOA! THEY'RE STRONG!!
GWOOOOOOM
Night 247:
Battle for the Capital

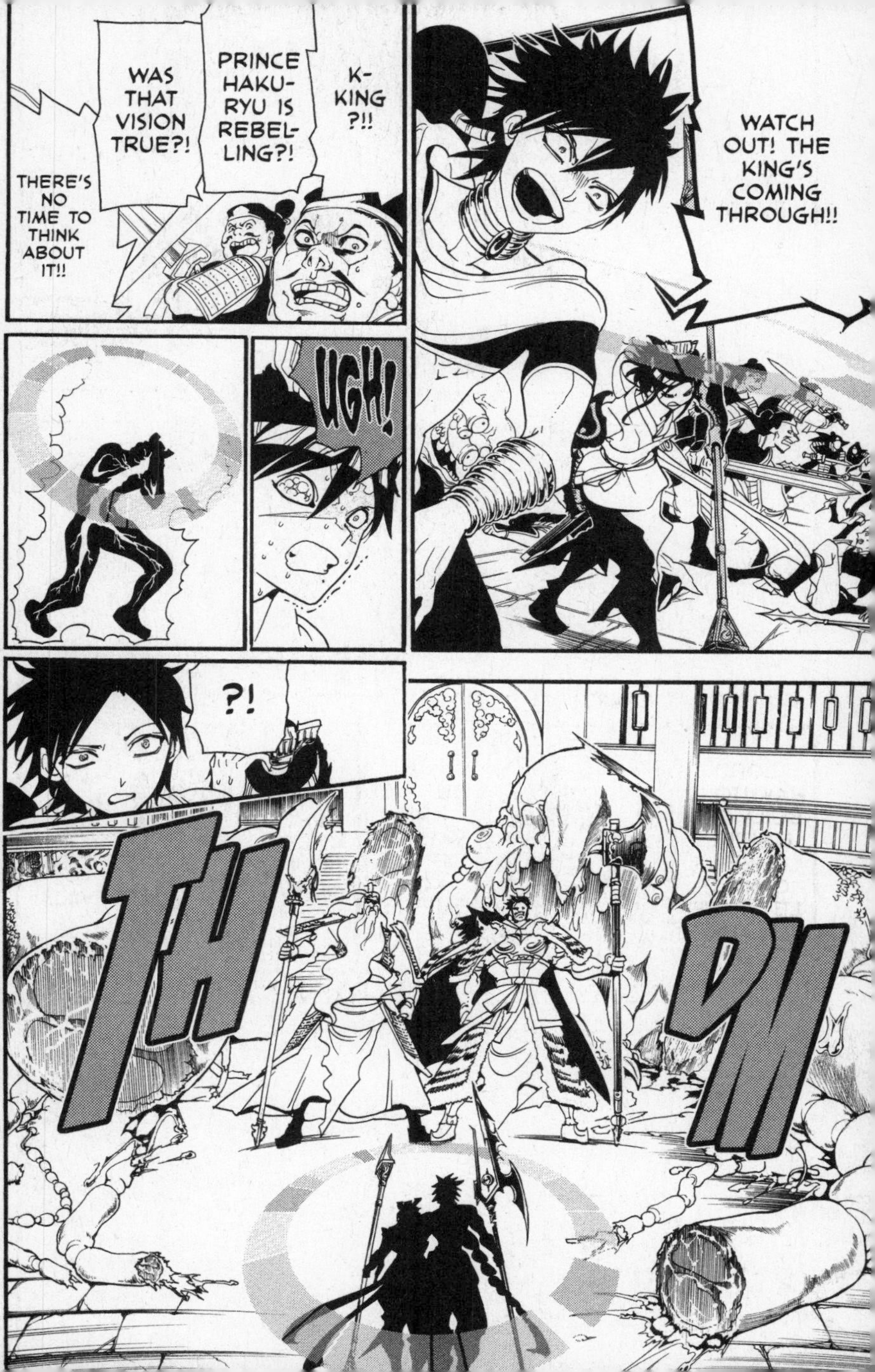
WATCH OUT! THE KING'S COMING THROUGH!!
K-KING?!!
PRINCE HAKU-RYU IS REBEL-LING?!
WAS THAT VISION TRUE?!
THERE'S NO TIME TO THINK ABOUT IT!!
UGH!
?!
THDN

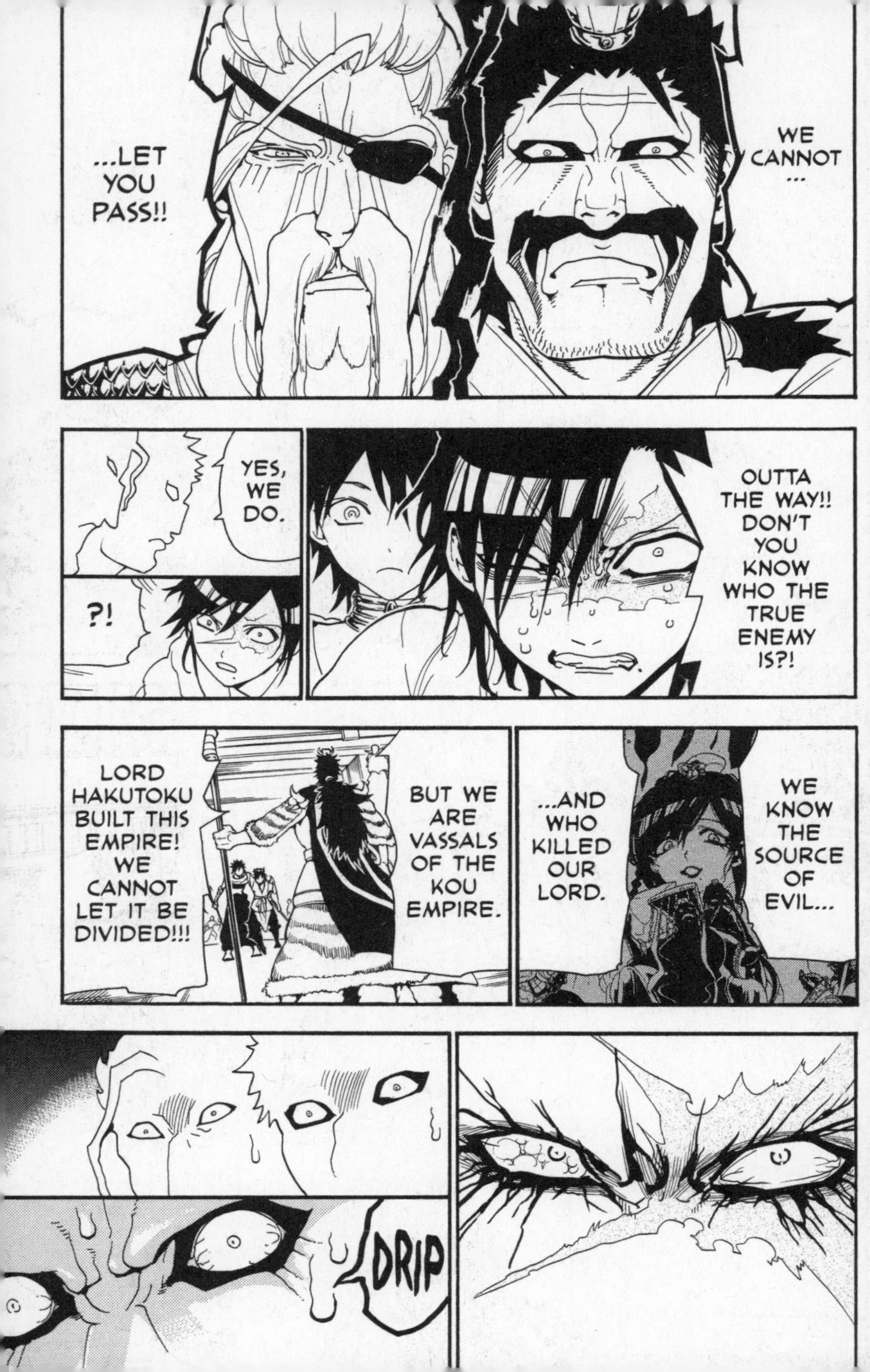

WE CANNOT ...
...LET YOU PASS!!
OUTTA THE WAY!! DON'T YOU KNOW WHO THE TRUE ENEMY IS?!
YES, WE DO.
?!
WE KNOW THE SOURCE OF EVIL...
...AND WHO KILLED OUR LORD.
BUT WE ARE VASSALS OF THE KOU EMPIRE.
LORD HAKUTOKU BUILT THIS EMPIRE! WE CANNOT LET IT BE DIVIDED!!!
DRIP

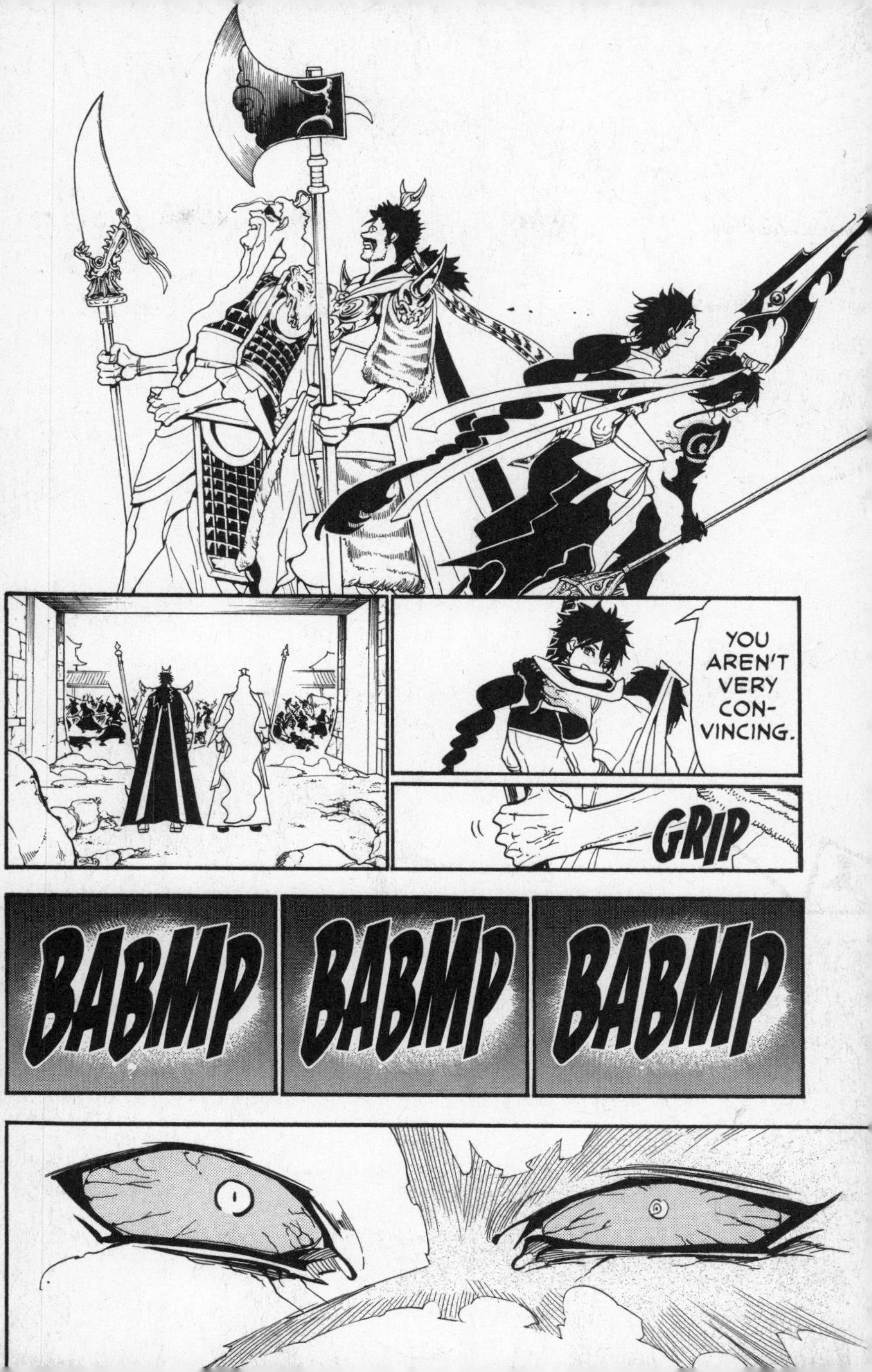
YOU AREN'T VERY CON-VINCING.
GRIP
BABMP
BABMP
BABMP

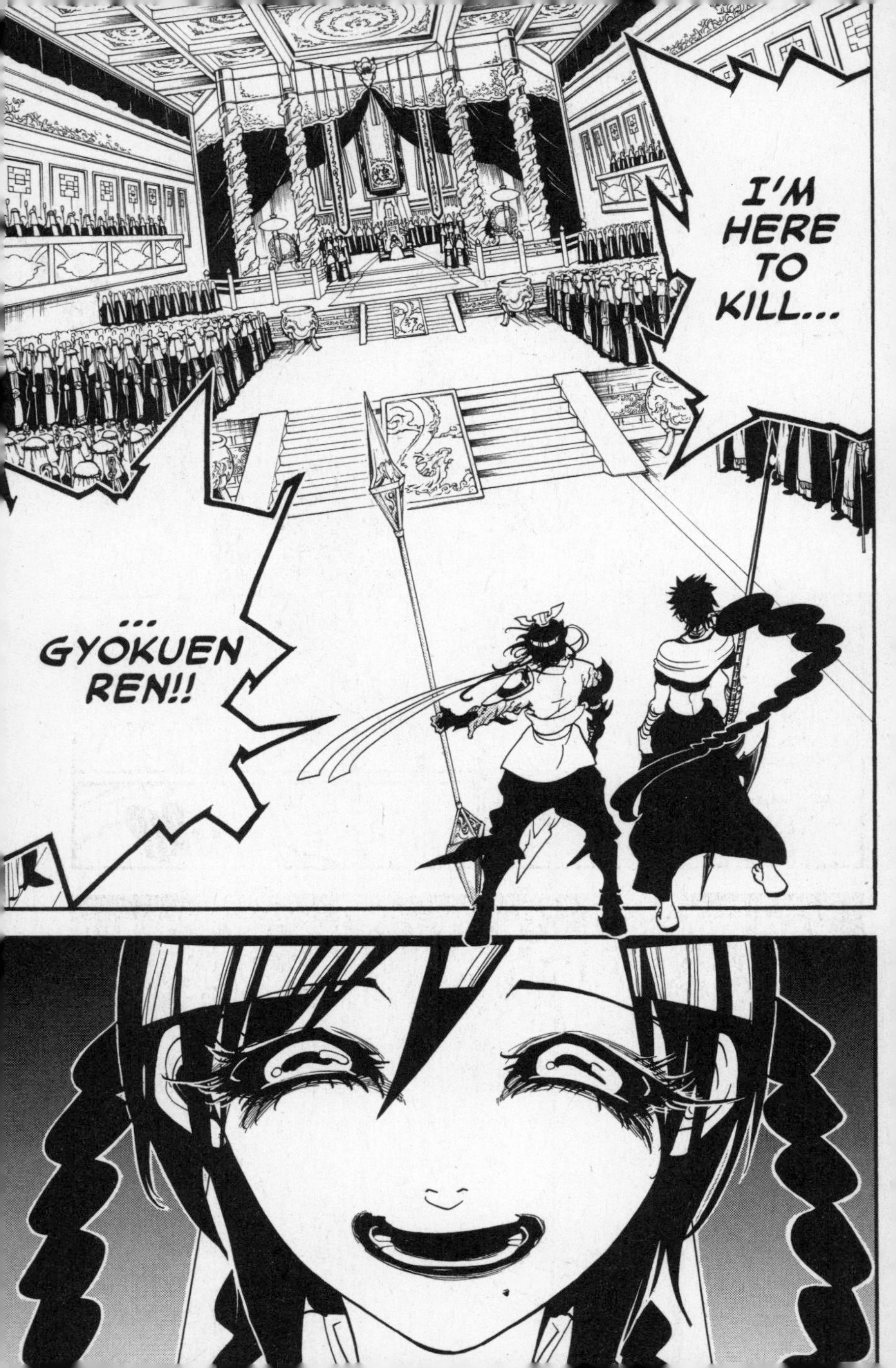
I'M HERE TO KILL...
... GYŌKUEN REN!!

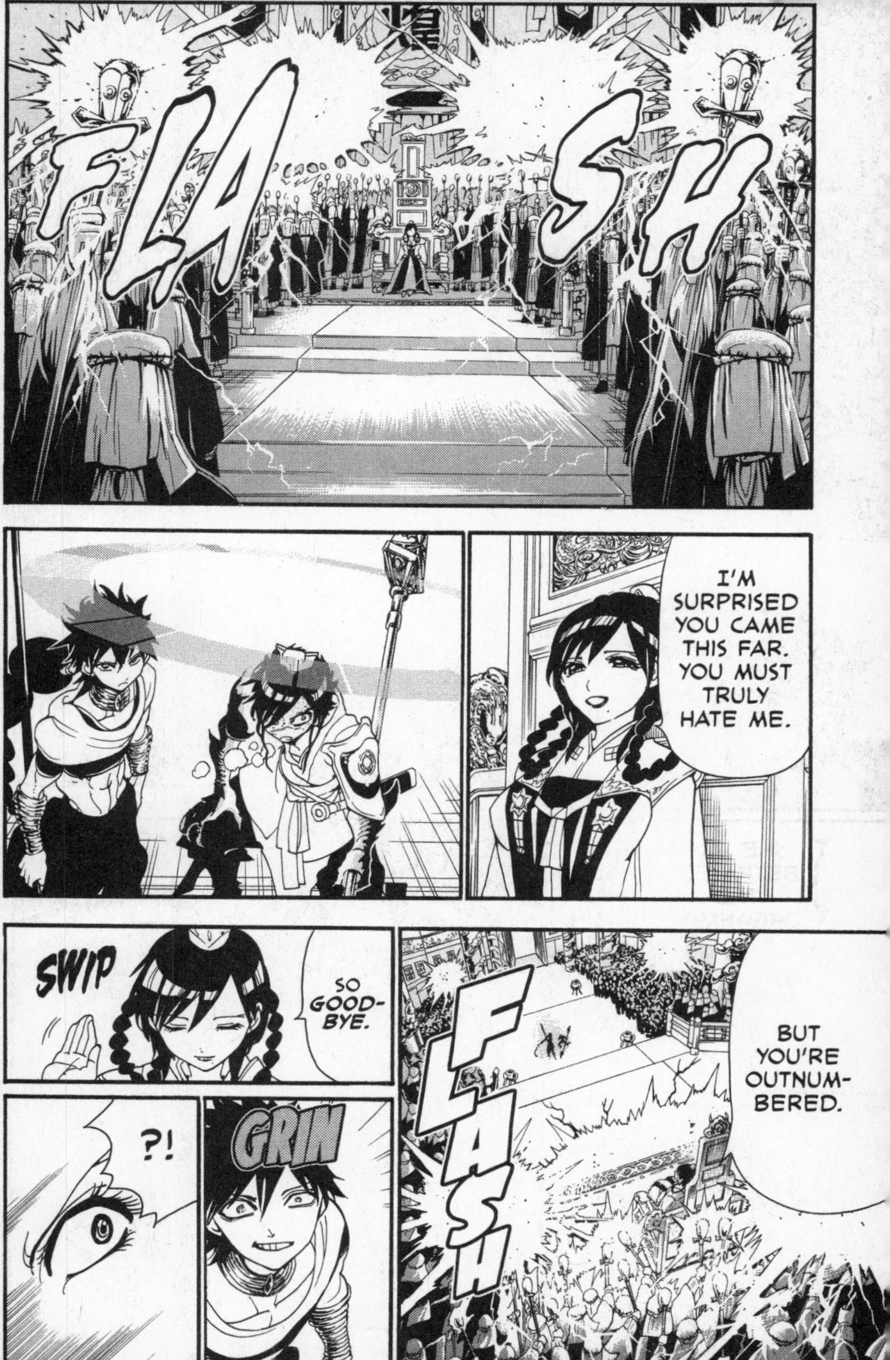
FLASH
I'M SURPRISED YOU CAME THIS FAR. YOU MUST TRULY HATE ME.
BUT YOU'RE OUTNUM-BERED.
FLASH
SO GOOD-BYE.
SWIP
GRIN
?!

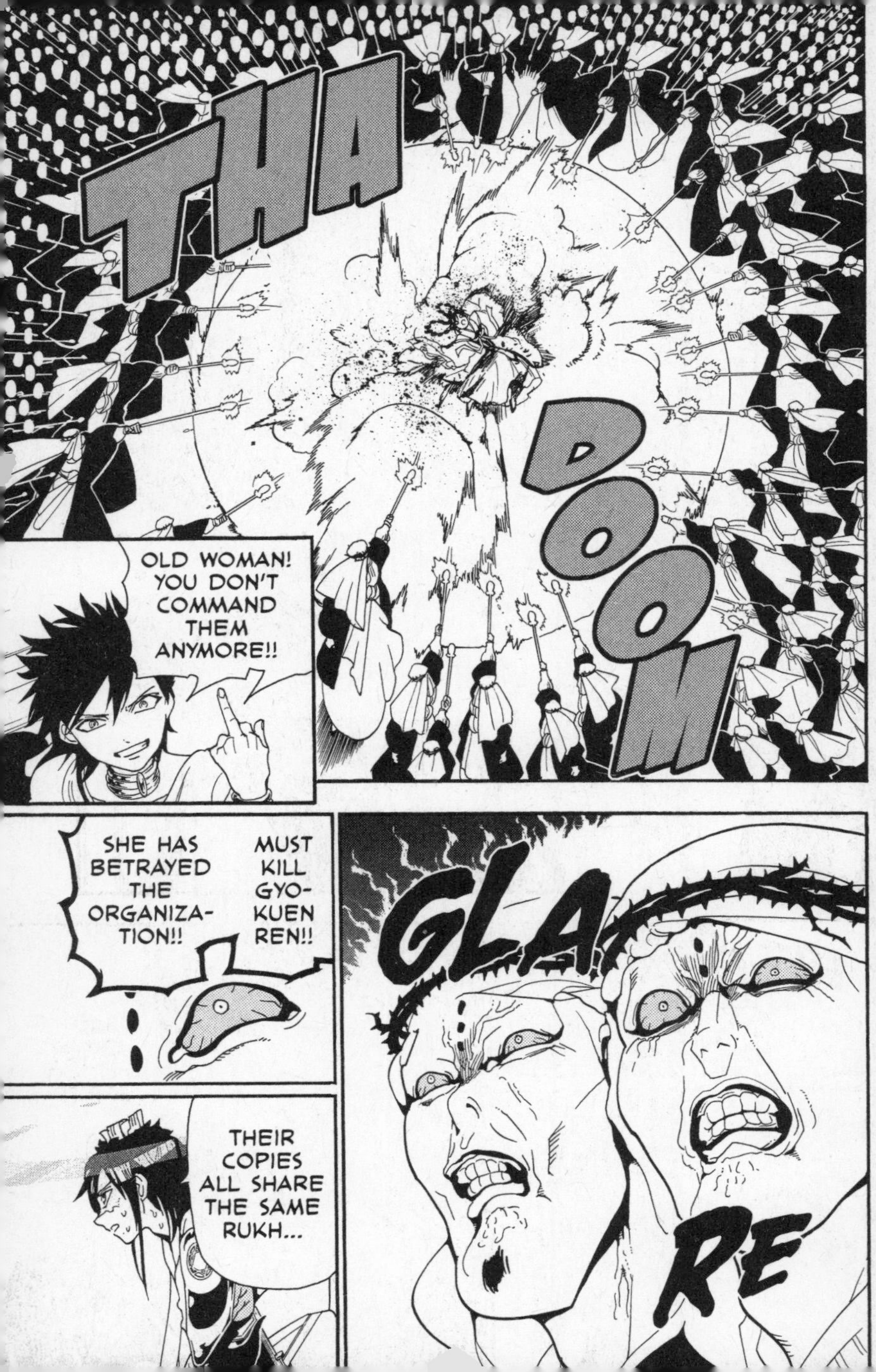

THA
DOOOM
OLD WOMAN! YOU DON'T COMMAND THEM ANYMORE!!
GLARE
MUST KILL GYO-KUEN REN!!
SHE HAS BETRAYED THE ORGANIZA-TION!!
...
THEIR COPIES ALL SHARE THE SAME RUKH...

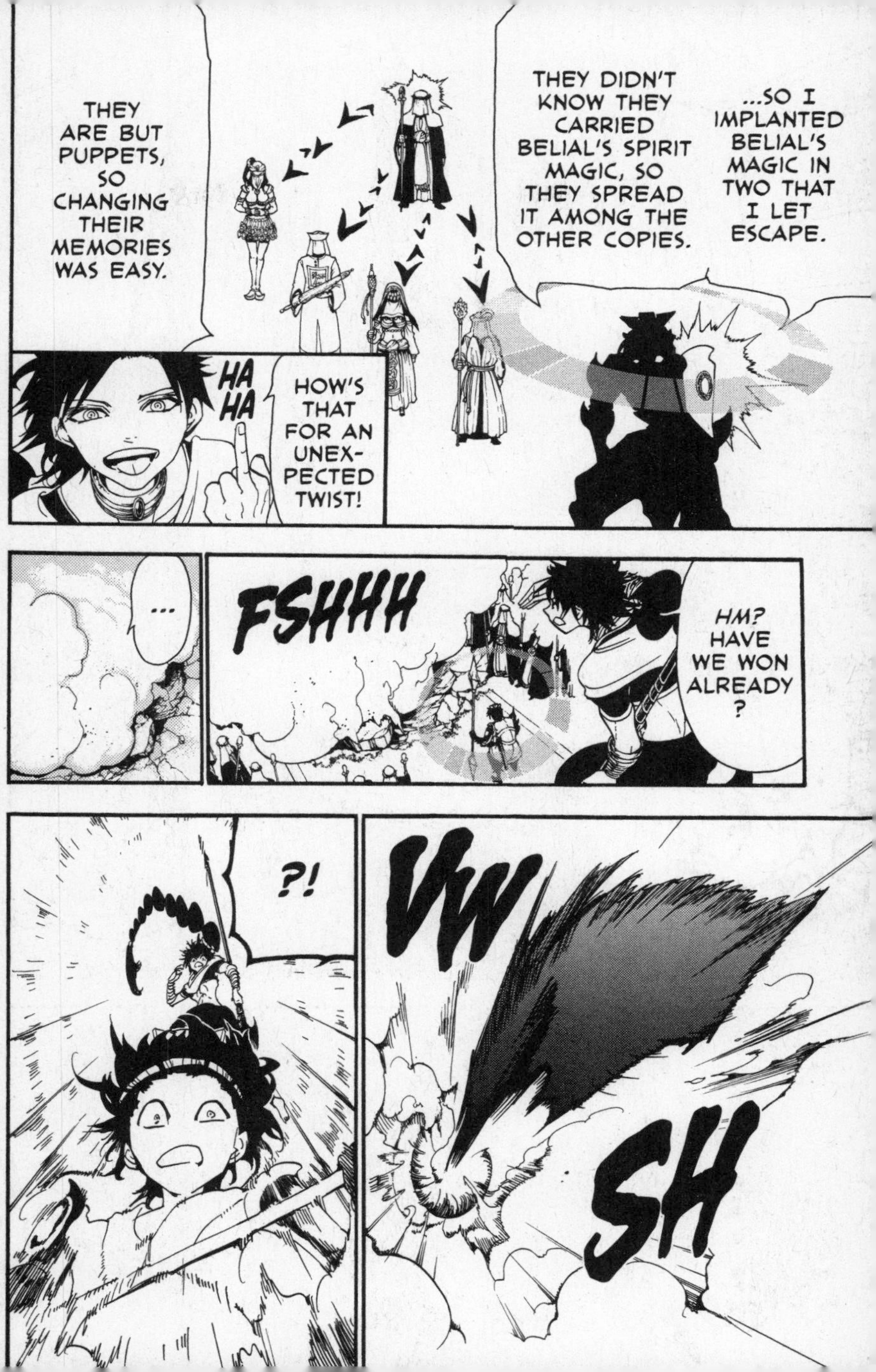

...SO I IMPLANTED BELIAL'S MAGIC IN TWO THAT I LET ESCAPE.
THEY DIDN'T KNOW THEY CARRIED BELIAL'S SPIRIT MAGIC, SO THEY SPREAD IT AMONG THE OTHER COPIES.
THEY ARE BUT PUPPETS, SO CHANGING THEIR MEMORIES WAS EASY.
HOW'S THAT FOR AN UNEXPECTED TWIST!
HA HA
HM? HAVE WE WON ALREADY?
FSHHH
...
VWSH
?!

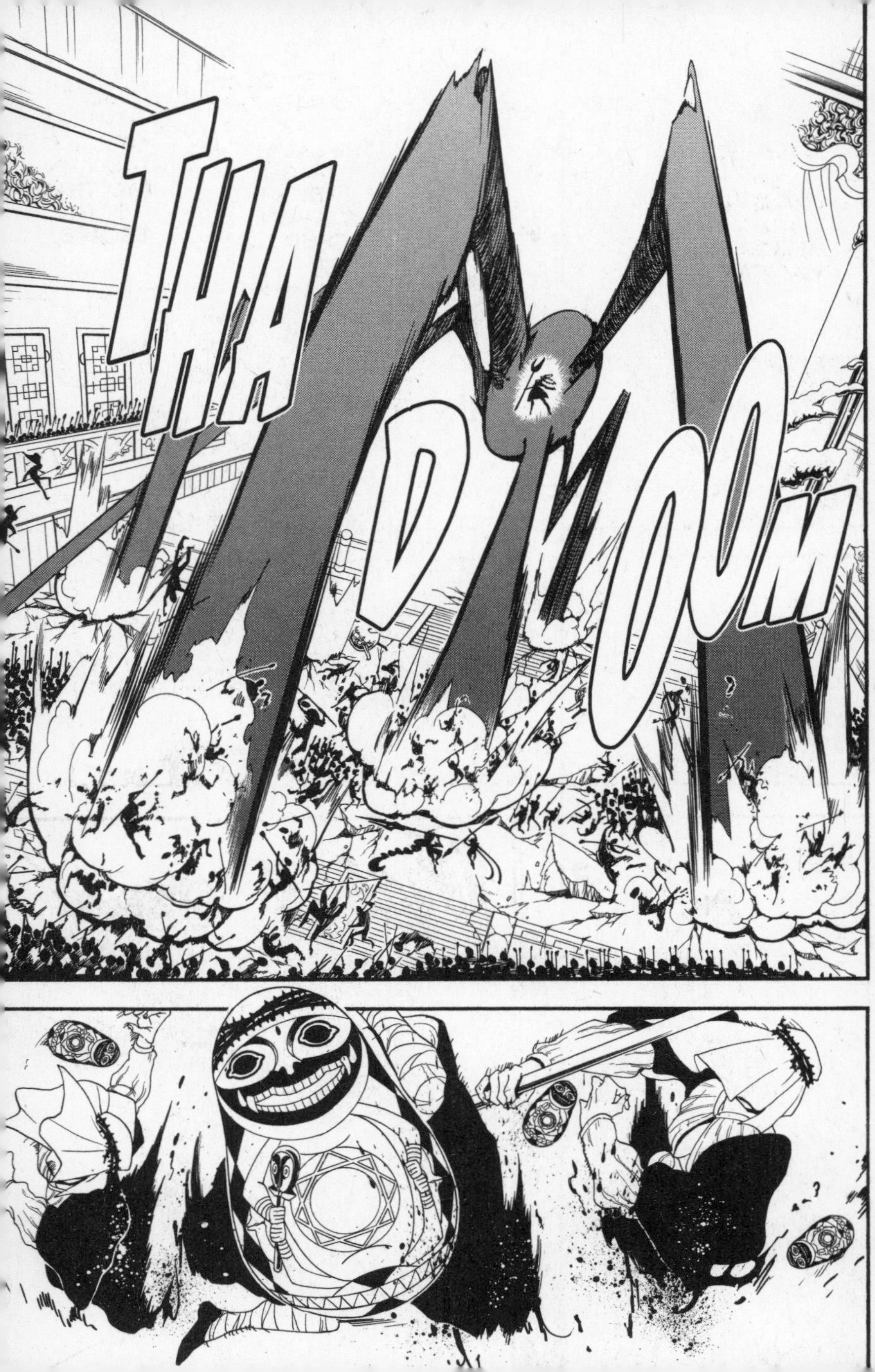
THA DOOM

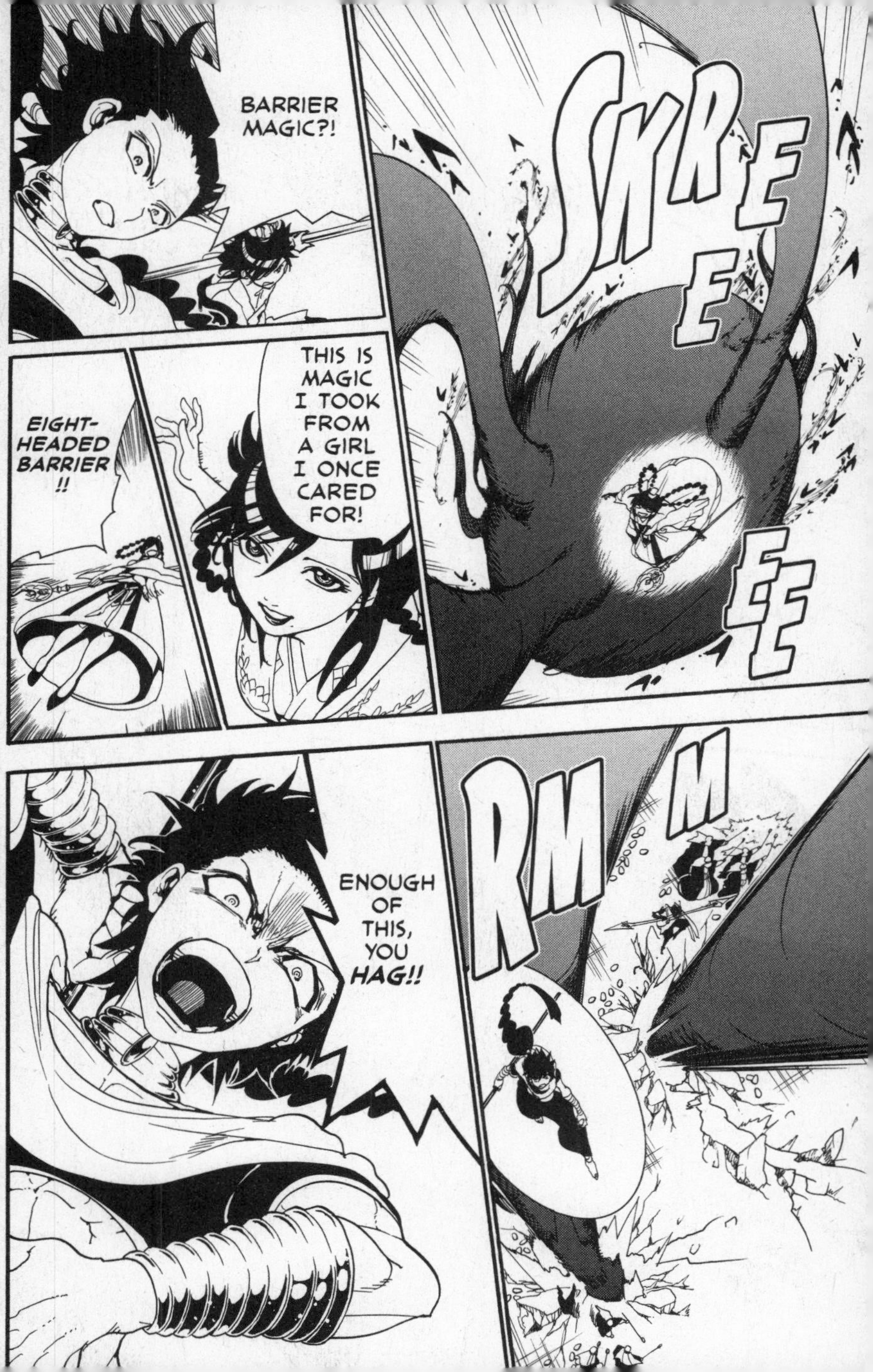
SKREEEEEE
BARRIER MAGIC?!
THIS IS MAGIC I TOOK FROM A GIRL I ONCE CARED FOR!
EIGHT-HEADED BARRIER!!
RMMM
ENOUGH OF THIS, YOU *HAG!!*

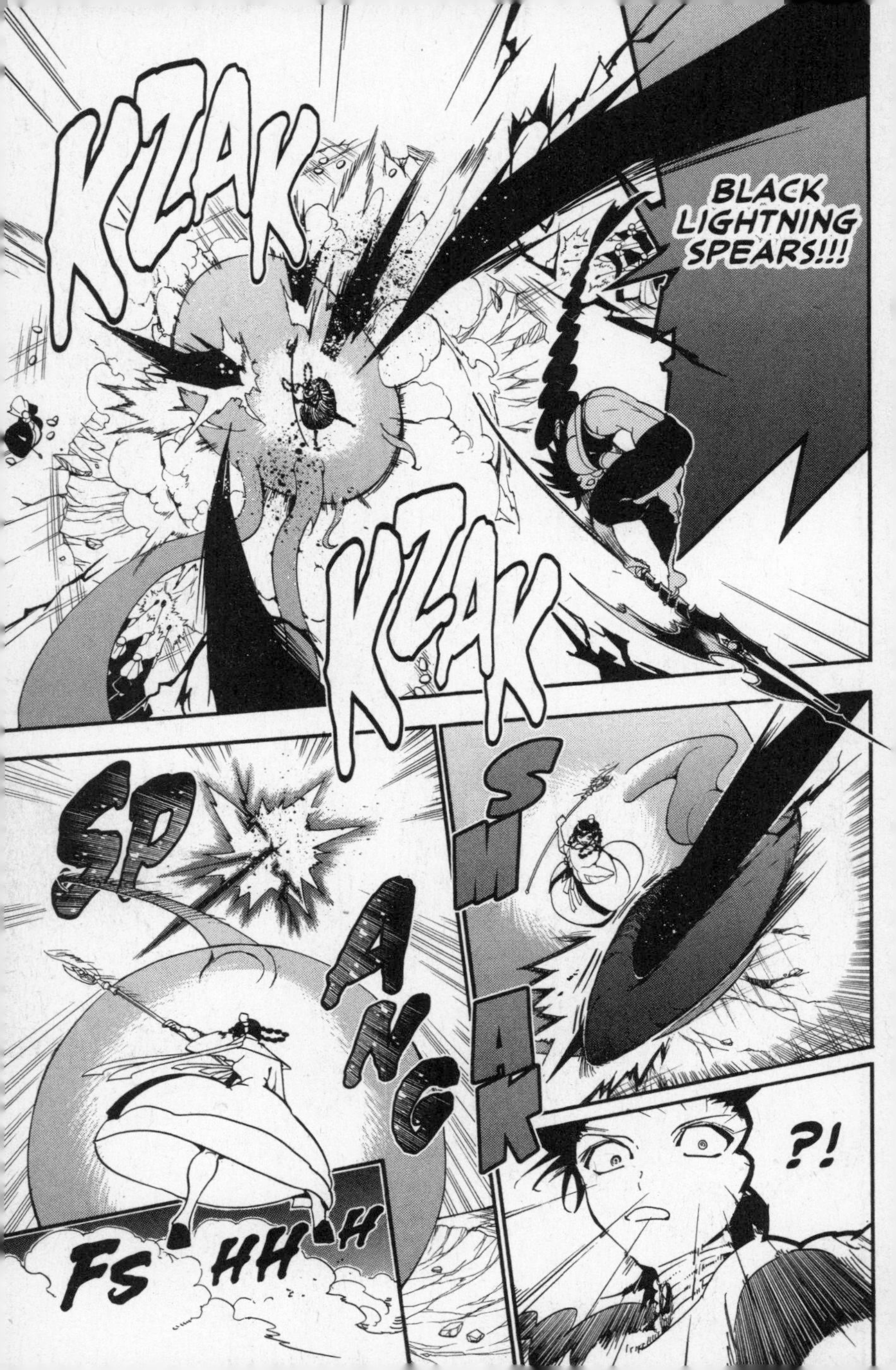
BLACK LIGHTNING SPEARS!!!
KZAK
KZAK
SMAK
?!
SPANG
FSHHHH

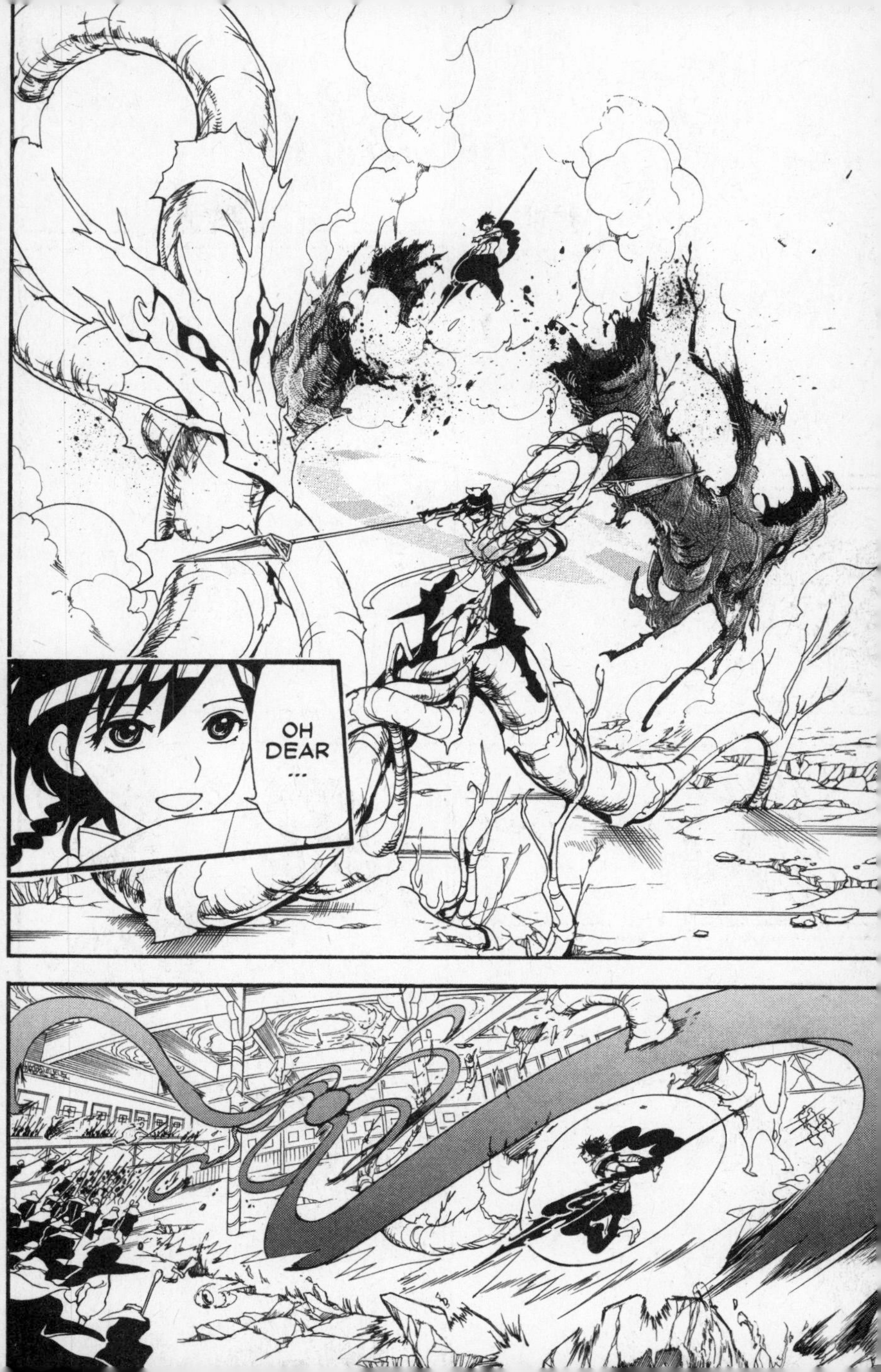
OH DEAR ...

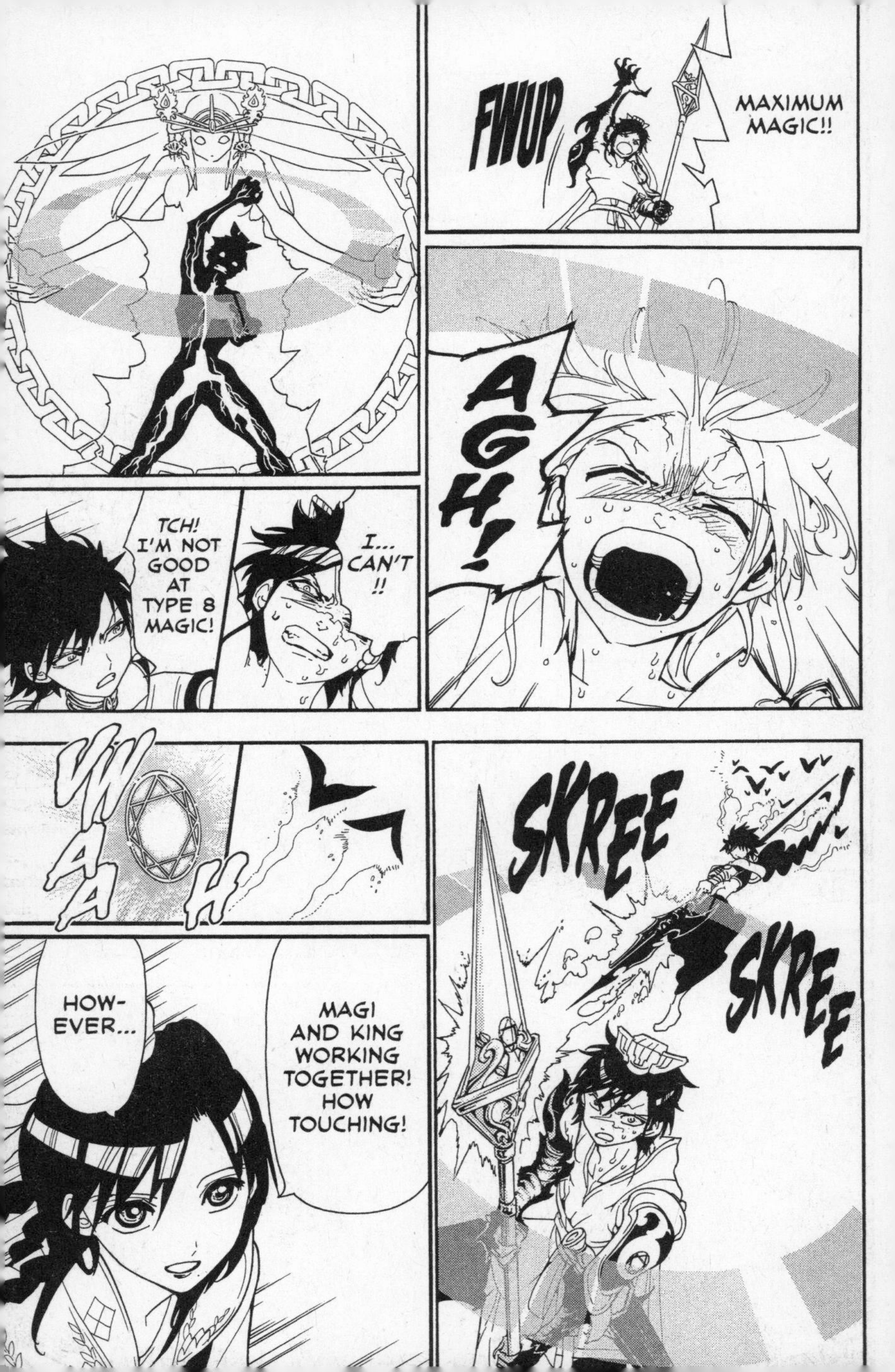
FWUP
MAXIMUM MAGIC!!
AGH!
I... CAN'T!!
TCH! I'M NOT GOOD AT TYPE 8 MAGIC!
SKREE
SKREE
VWAAH
MAGI AND KING WORKING TOGETHER! HOW TOUCHING!
HOW-EVER...

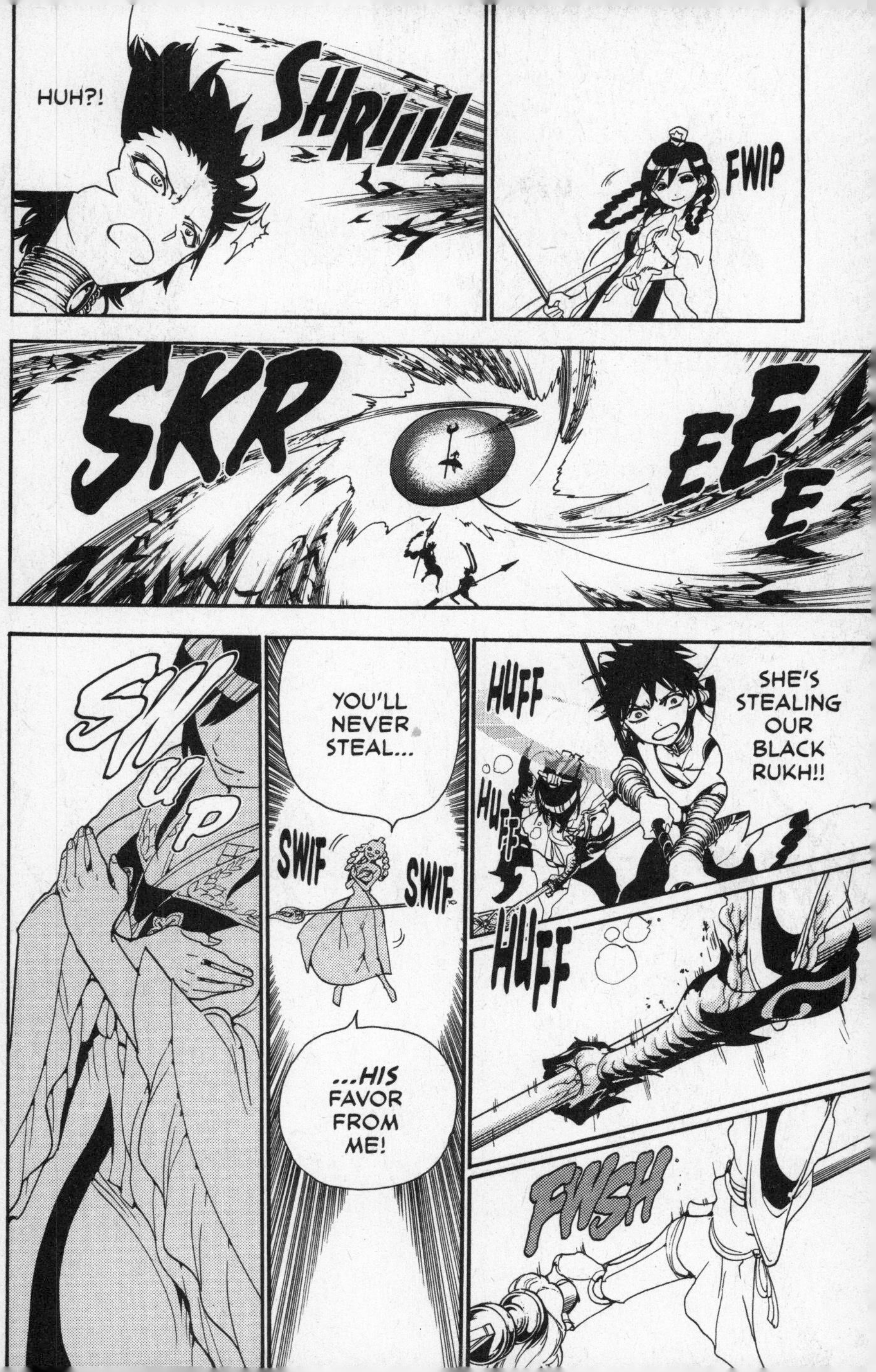
FWIP
SHRIIII
HUH?!
SKR
EEE
E
SHE'S STEALING OUR BLACK RUKH!!
HUFF
HUFF
HUFF
FWSH
YOU'LL NEVER STEAL...
SWIF
SWIF
...HIS FAVOR FROM ME!
SHUP

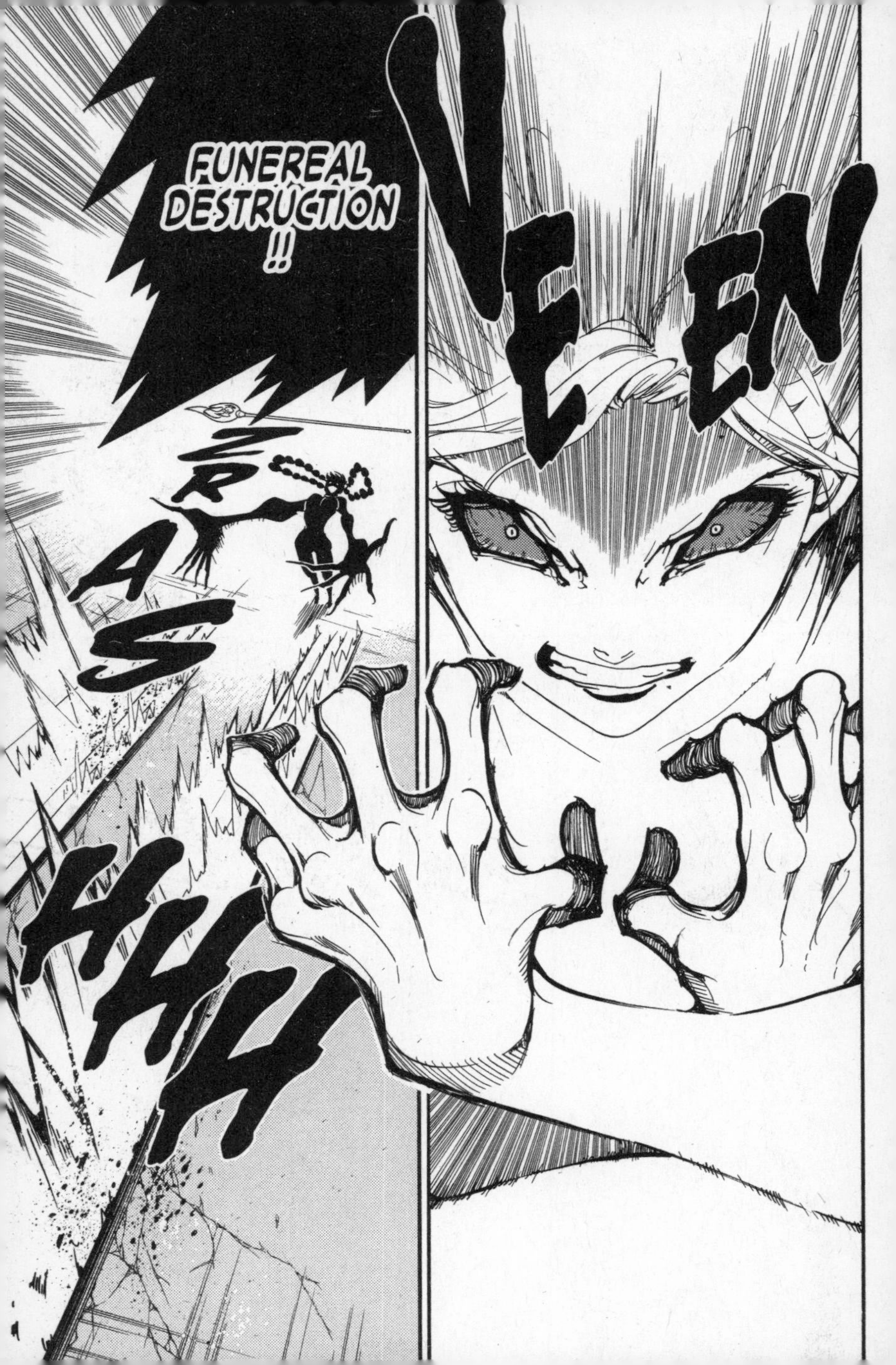
VEEN
FUNEREAL DESTRUCTION !!
ZRASHHH

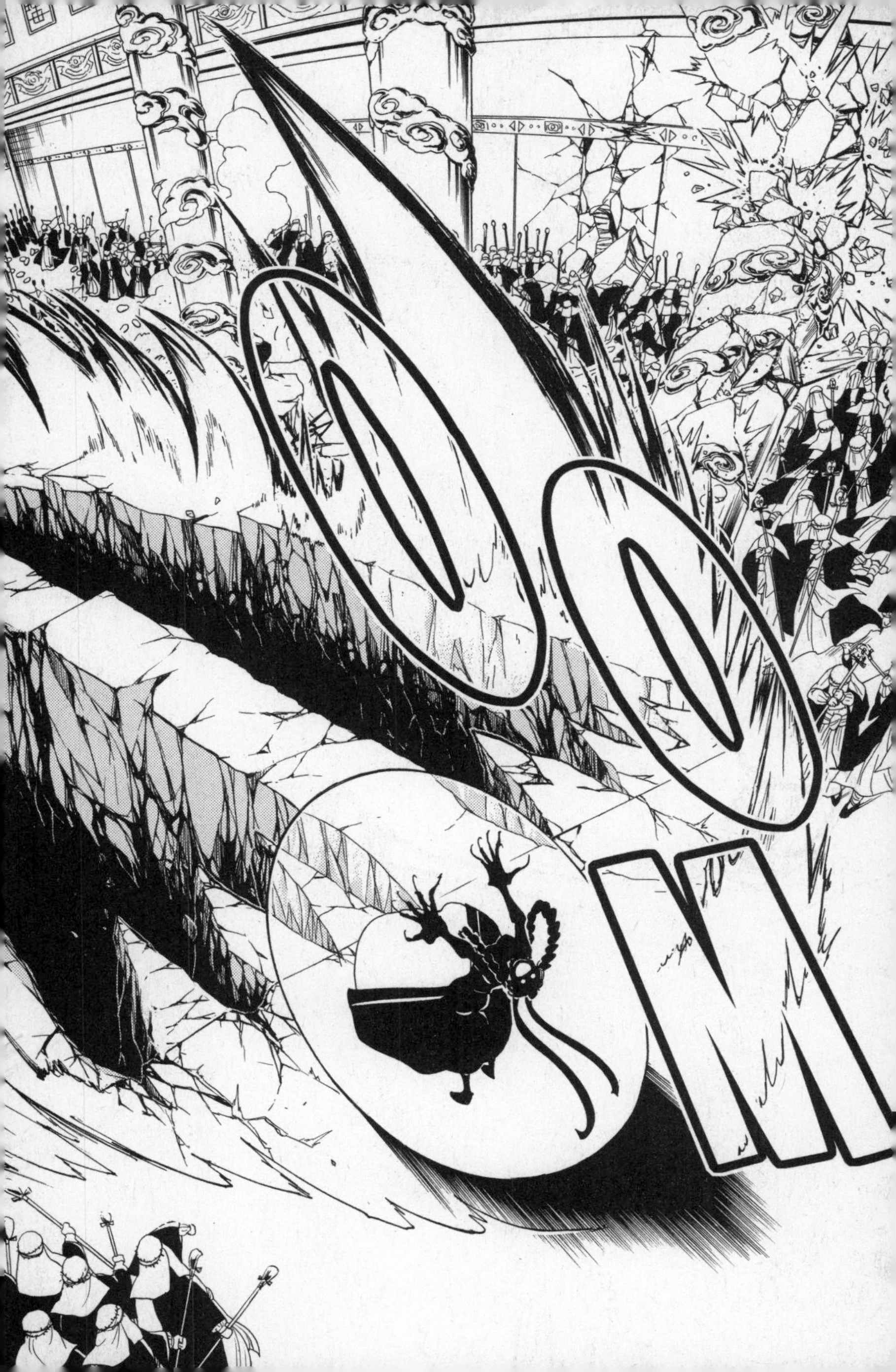

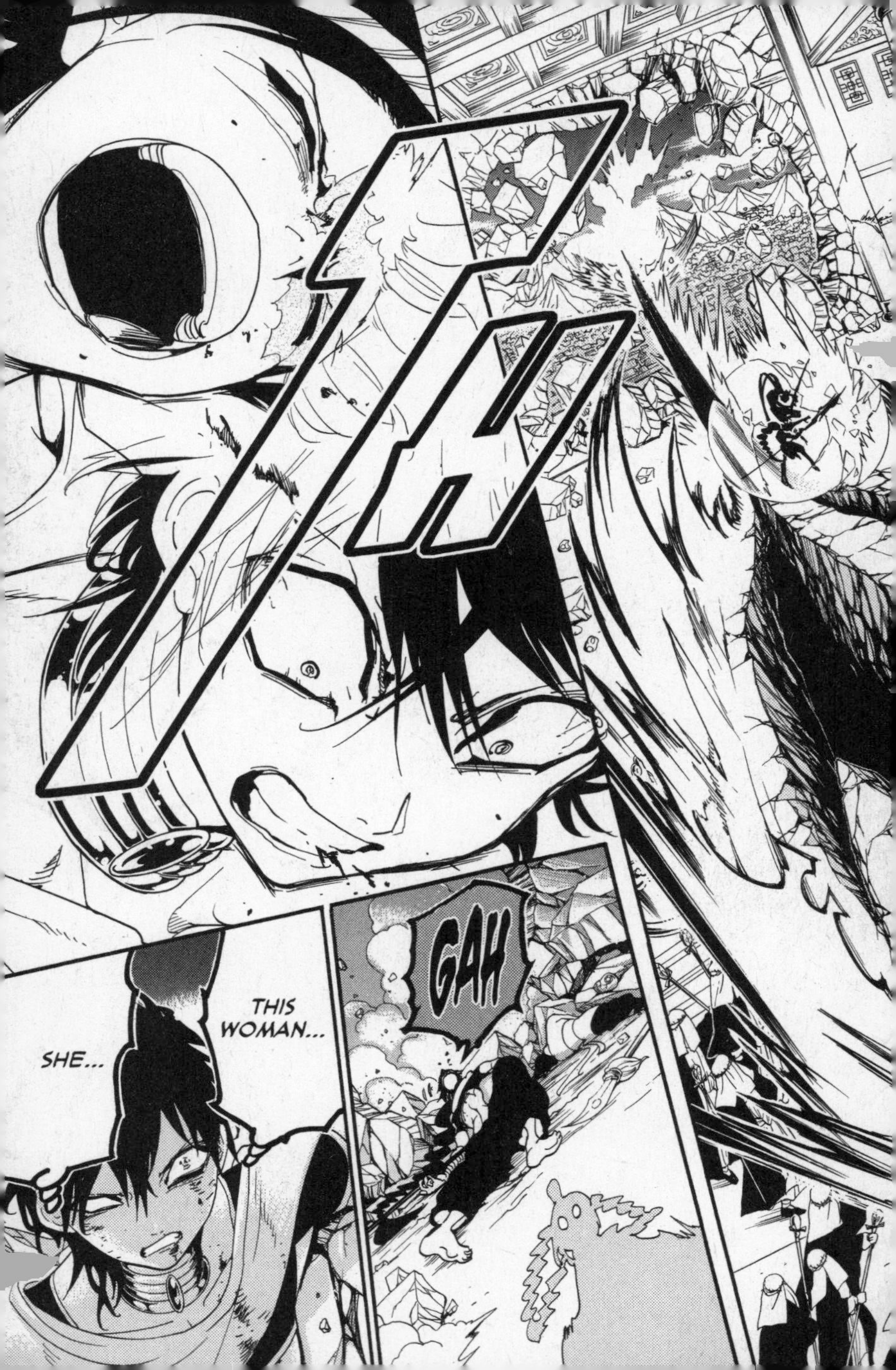
GAH
THIS WOMAN...
SHE...

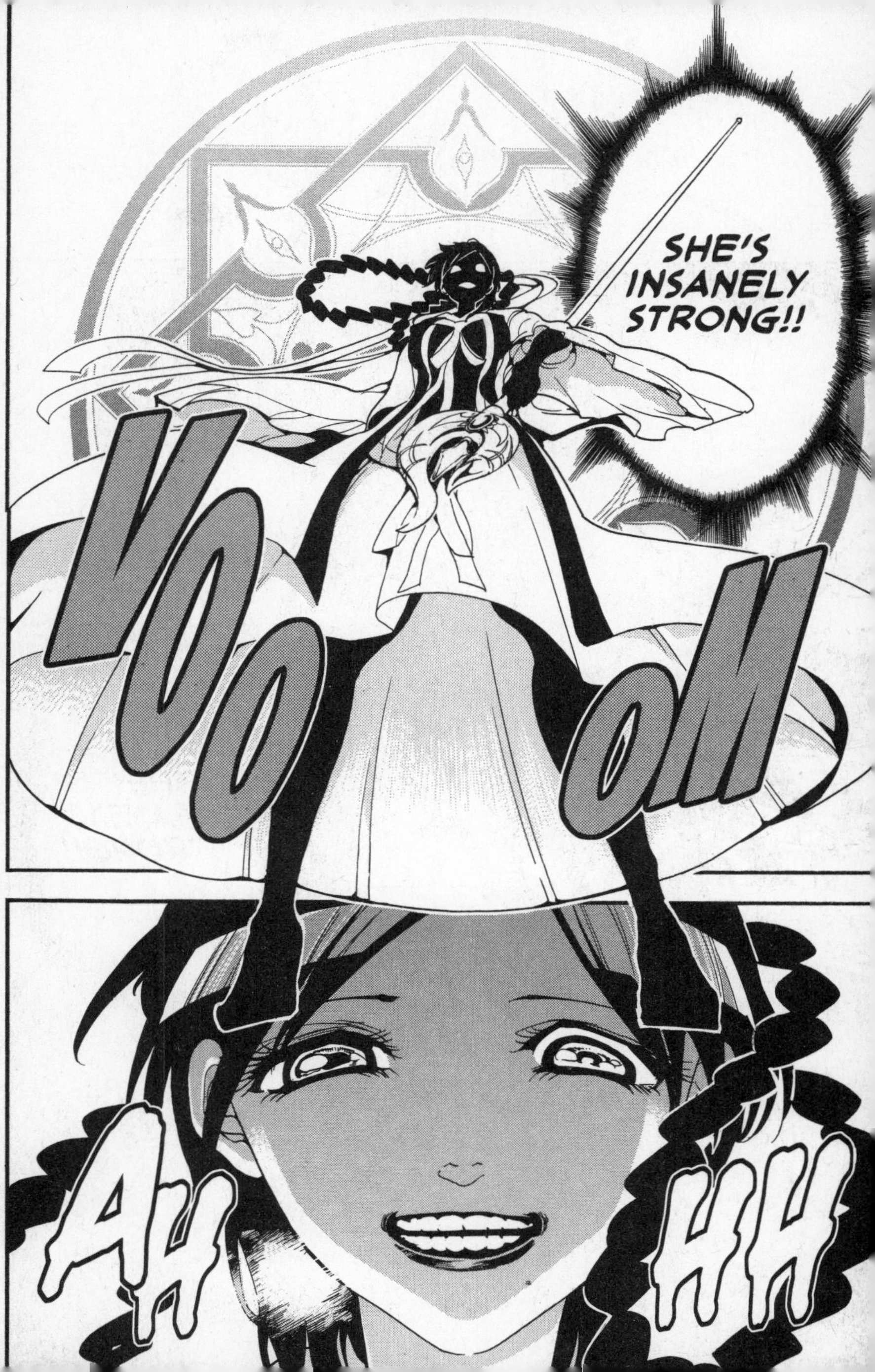
SHE'S INSANELY STRONG!!
VOOOM
AHHH

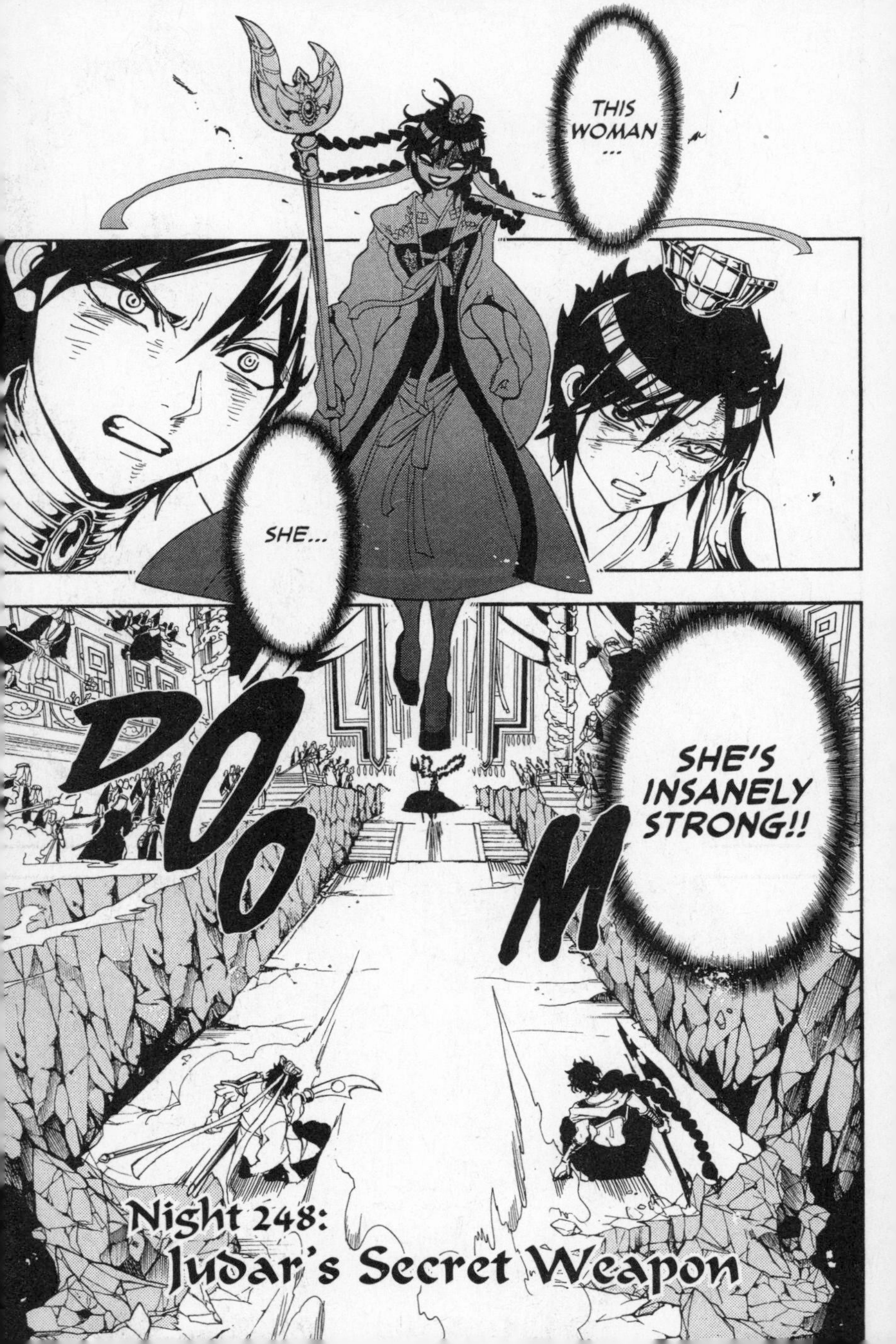
THIS WOMAN...
SHE...
SHE'S INSANELY STRONG!!
DOOM
Night 248:
Judar's Secret Weapon

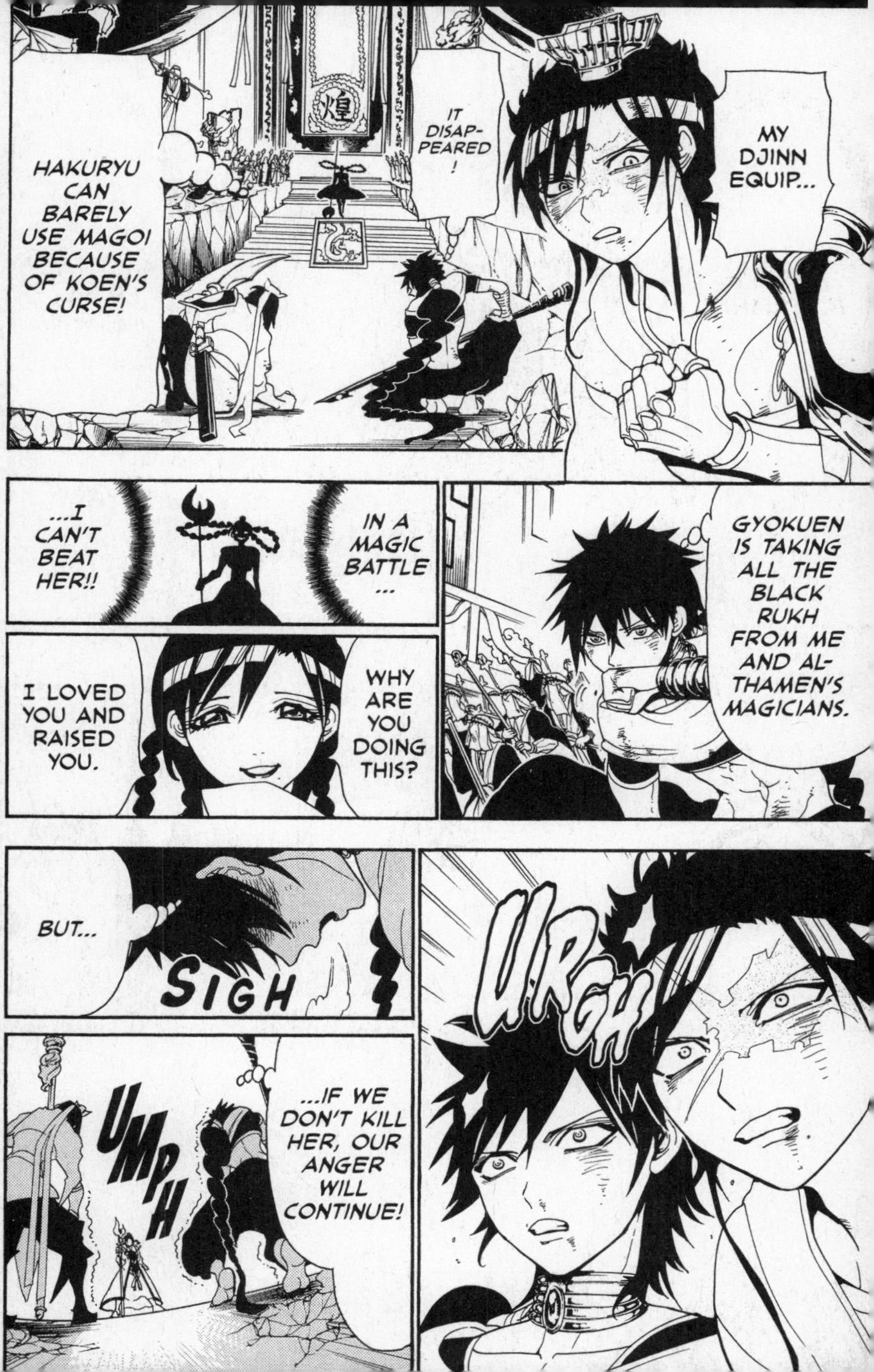
MY DJINN EQUIP...
IT DISAPPEARED!
HAKURYU CAN BARELY USE MAGOI BECAUSE OF KOEN'S CURSE!
GYOKUEN IS TAKING ALL THE BLACK RUKH FROM ME AND AL-THAMEN'S MAGICIANS.
IN A MAGIC BATTLE...
...I CAN'T BEAT HER!!
WHY ARE YOU DOING THIS?
I LOVED YOU AND RAISED YOU.
URGH
BUT...
SIGH
...IF WE DON'T KILL HER, OUR ANGER WILL CONTINUE!
UMPH

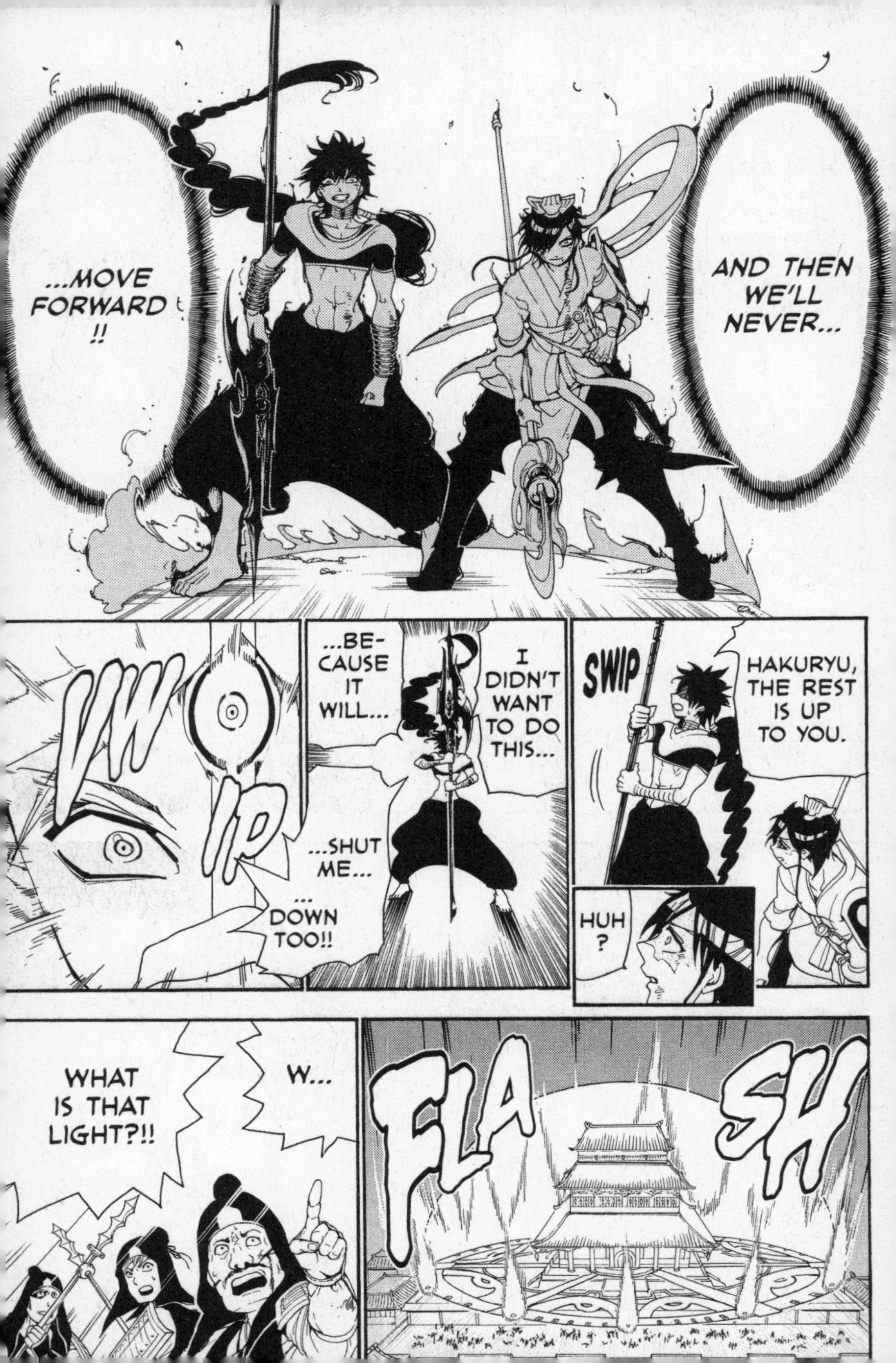
AND THEN WE'LL NEVER...
...MOVE FORWARD !!
SWIP
HAKURYU, THE REST IS UP TO YOU.
HUH ?
I DIDN'T WANT TO DO THIS...
...BE-CAUSE IT WILL...
...SHUT ME...
...DOWN TOO!!
VWIP
FLASH
W...
WHAT IS THAT LIGHT?!!

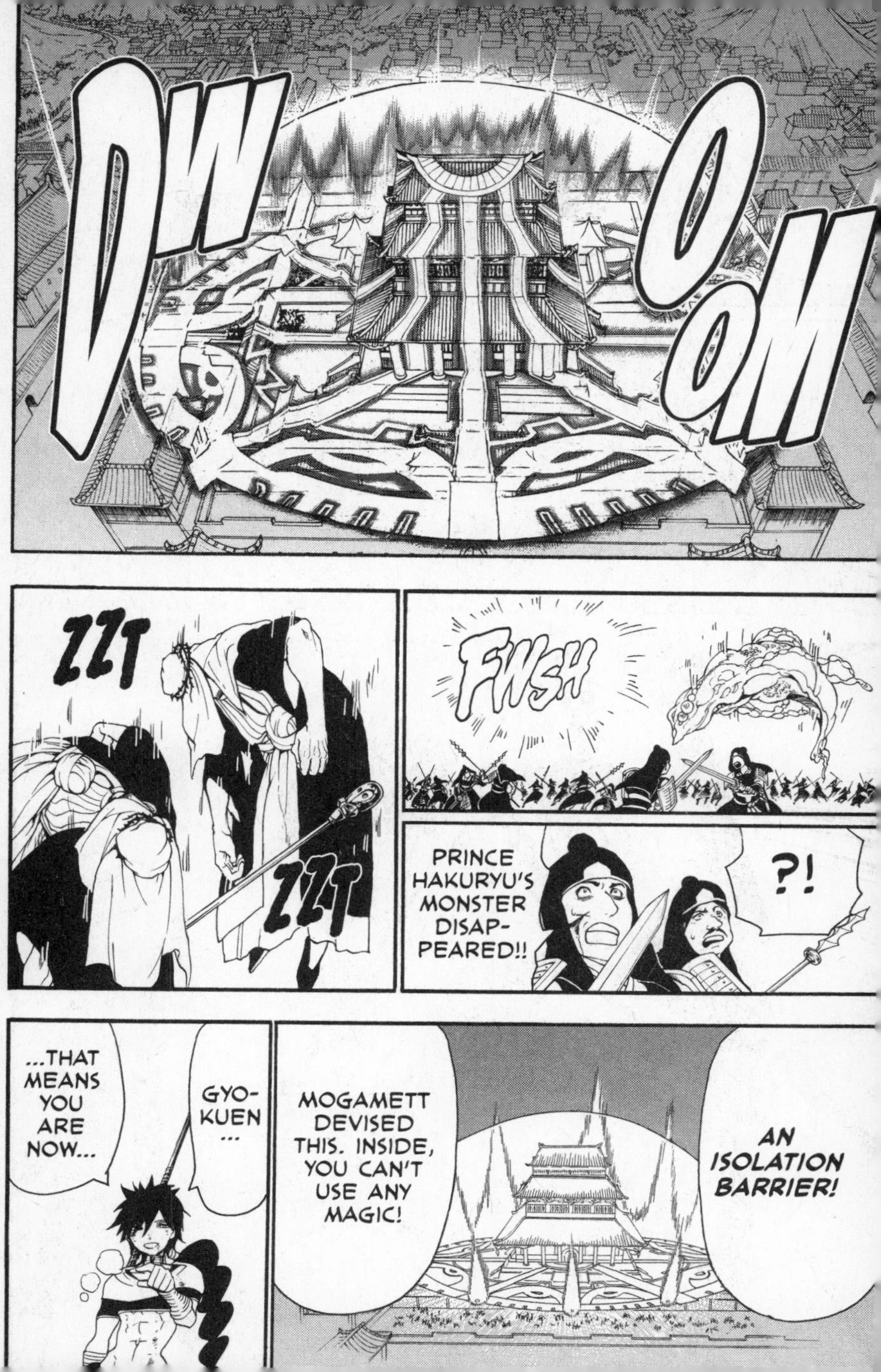
DWOOM
FWSH
?!
PRINCE HAKURYU'S MONSTER DISAPPEARED!!
ZZT
ZZT
AN ISOLATION BARRIER!
MOGAMETT DEVISED THIS. INSIDE, YOU CAN'T USE ANY MAGIC!
GYOKUEN...
...THAT MEANS YOU ARE NOW...

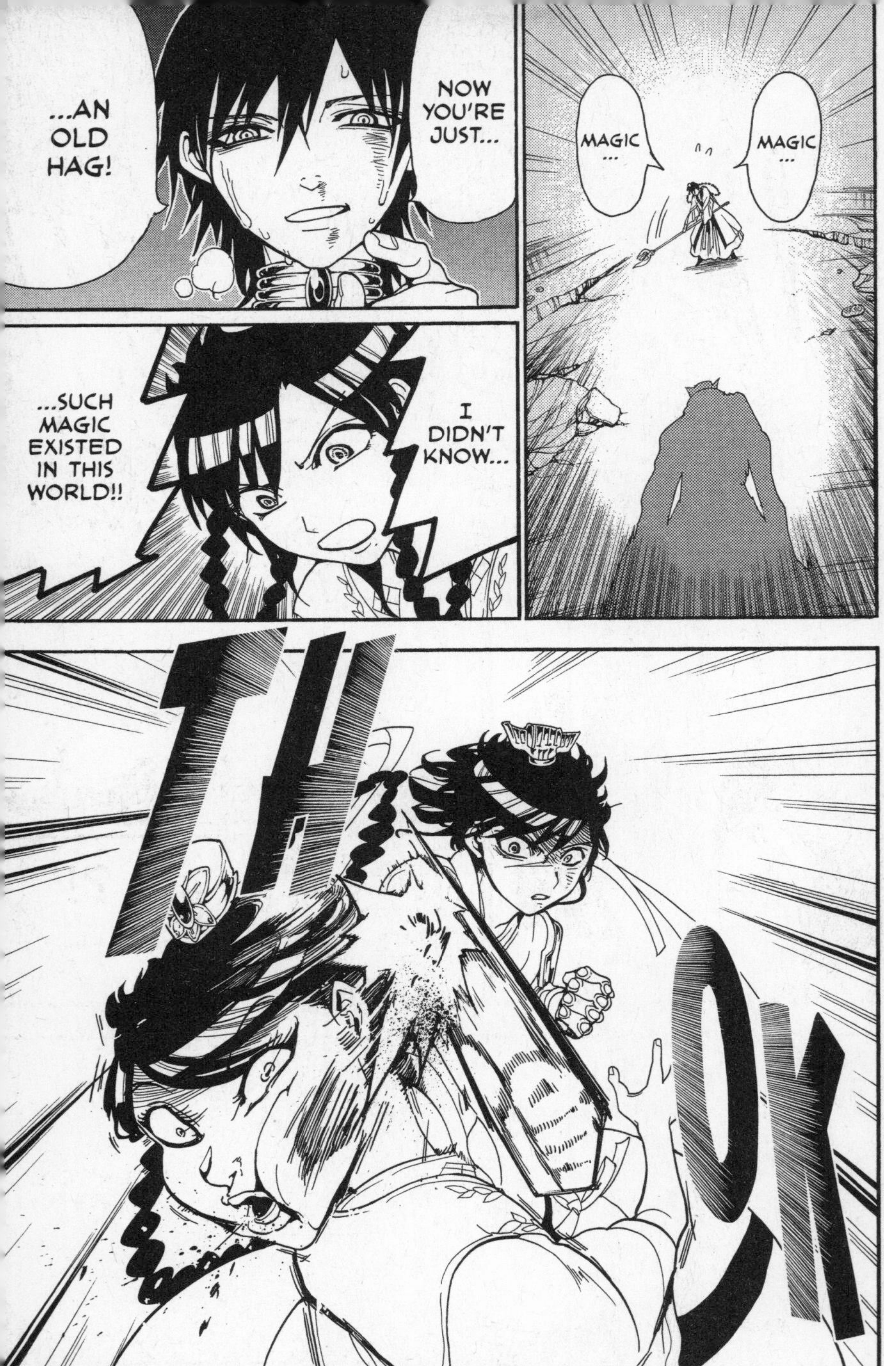
MAGIC...
MAGIC...
NOW YOU'RE JUST...
...AN OLD HAG!
I DIDN'T KNOW...
...SUCH MAGIC EXISTED IN THIS WORLD!!
THOK

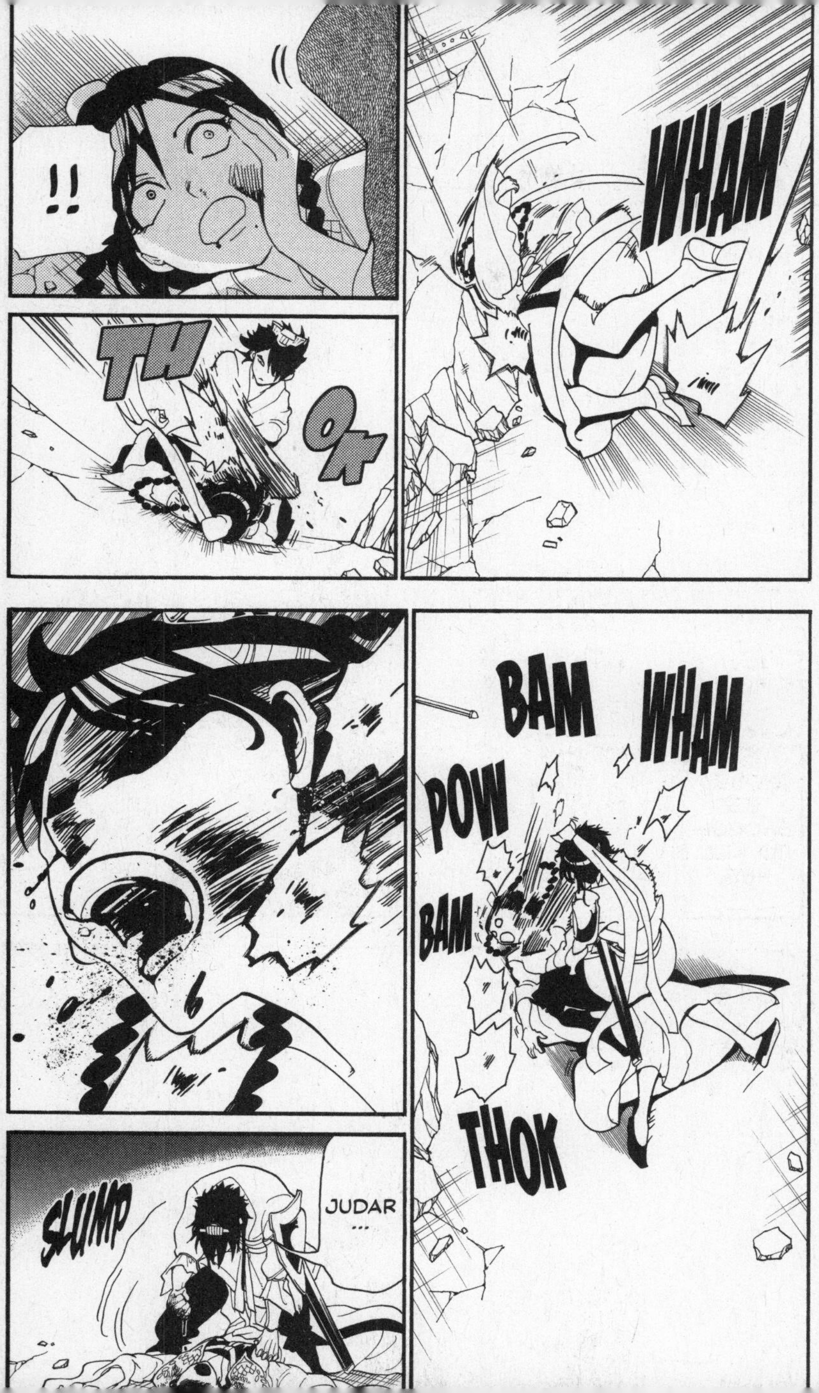
WHAM
!!
TH OK
WHAM
BAM
POW
BAM
THOK
JUDAR...
SLUMP

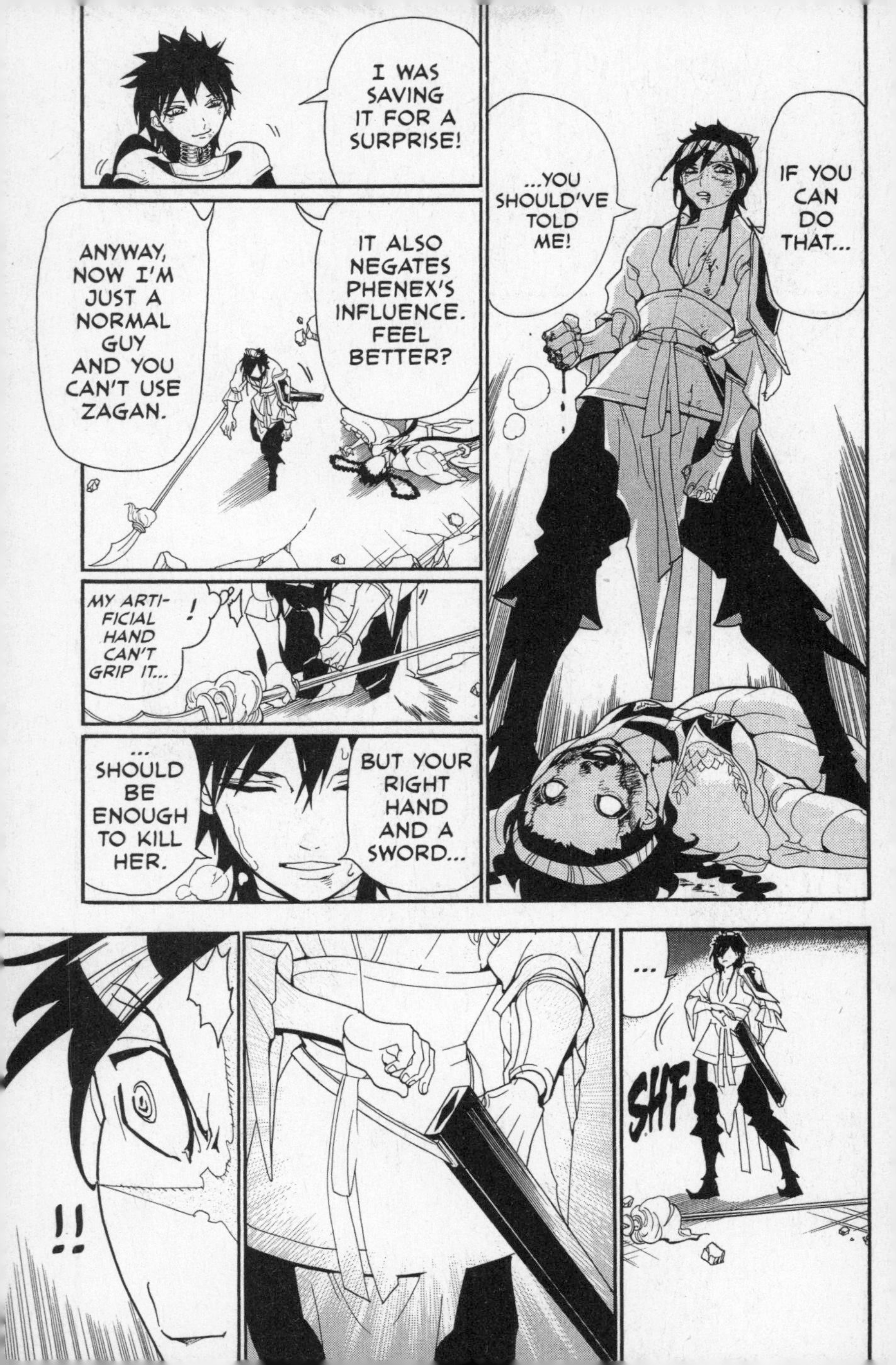
IF YOU CAN DO THAT...
...YOU SHOULD'VE TOLD ME!
I WAS SAVING IT FOR A SURPRISE!
IT ALSO NEGATES PHENEX'S INFLUENCE. FEEL BETTER?
ANYWAY, NOW I'M JUST A NORMAL GUY AND YOU CAN'T USE ZAGAN.
!
MY ARTI-FICIAL HAND CAN'T GRIP IT...
BUT YOUR RIGHT HAND AND A SWORD...
...SHOULD BE ENOUGH TO KILL HER.
...
SHF
!!

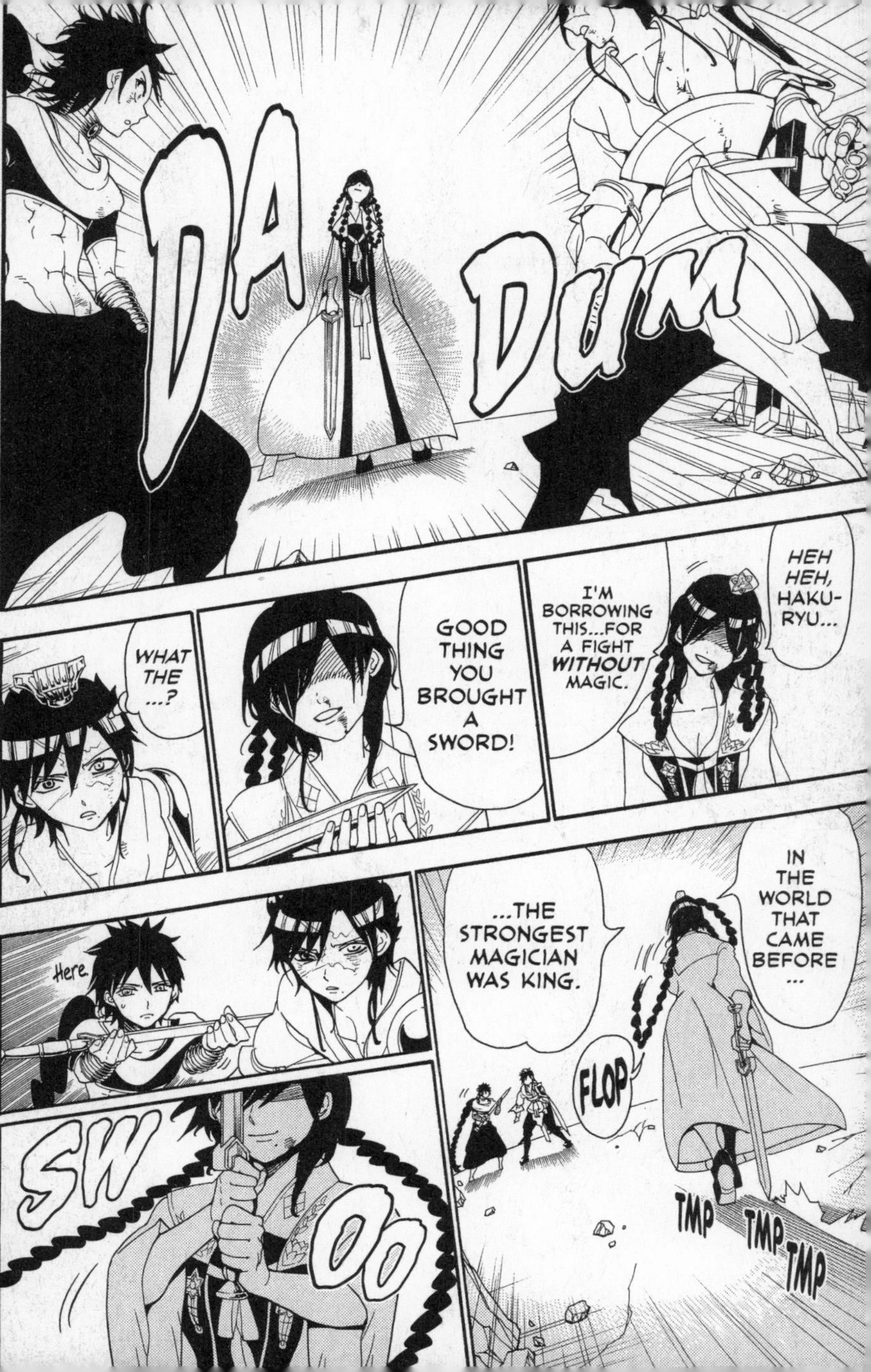
DA DUM
HEH HEH, HAKURYU...
I'M BORROWING THIS...FOR A FIGHT *WITHOUT* MAGIC.
GOOD THING YOU BROUGHT A SWORD!
WHAT THE ...?
IN THE WORLD THAT CAME BEFORE ...
...THE STRONGEST MAGICIAN WAS KING.
FLOP
TMP TMP TMP
Here.
SWOO

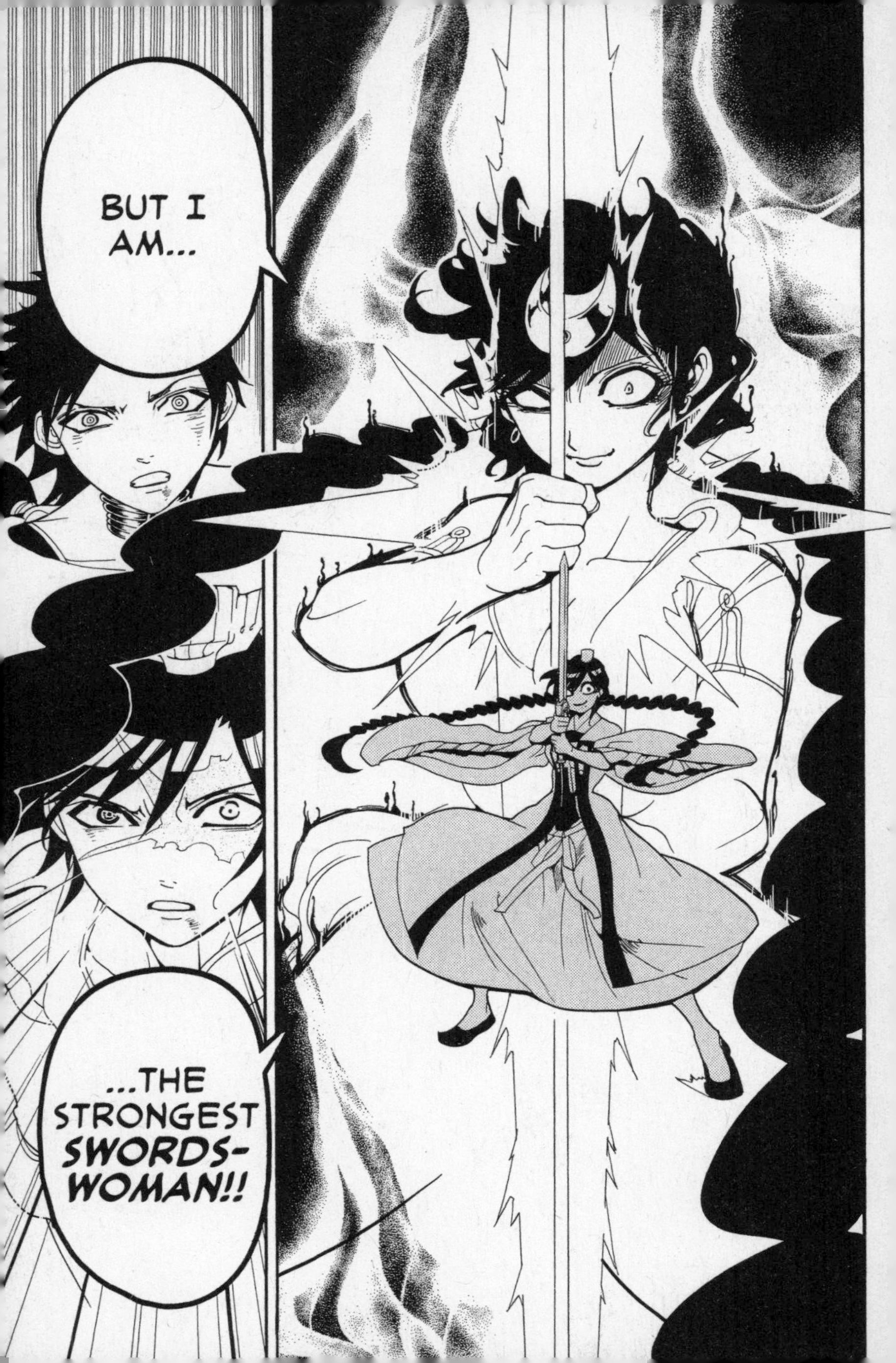
BUT I AM...
...THE STRONGEST SWORDS-WOMAN!!

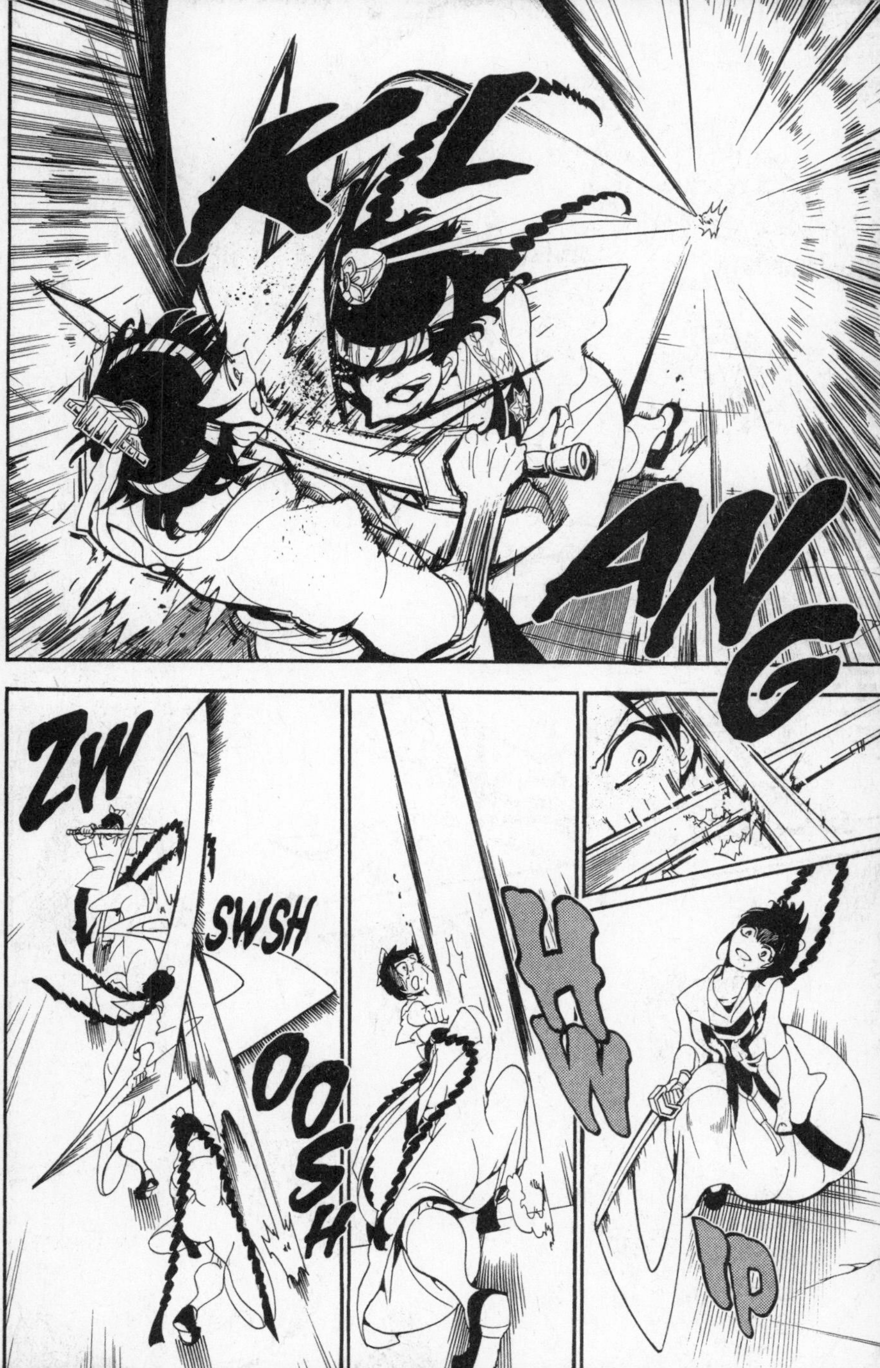
KLANG
WHIP
ZWOOSH
SWSH

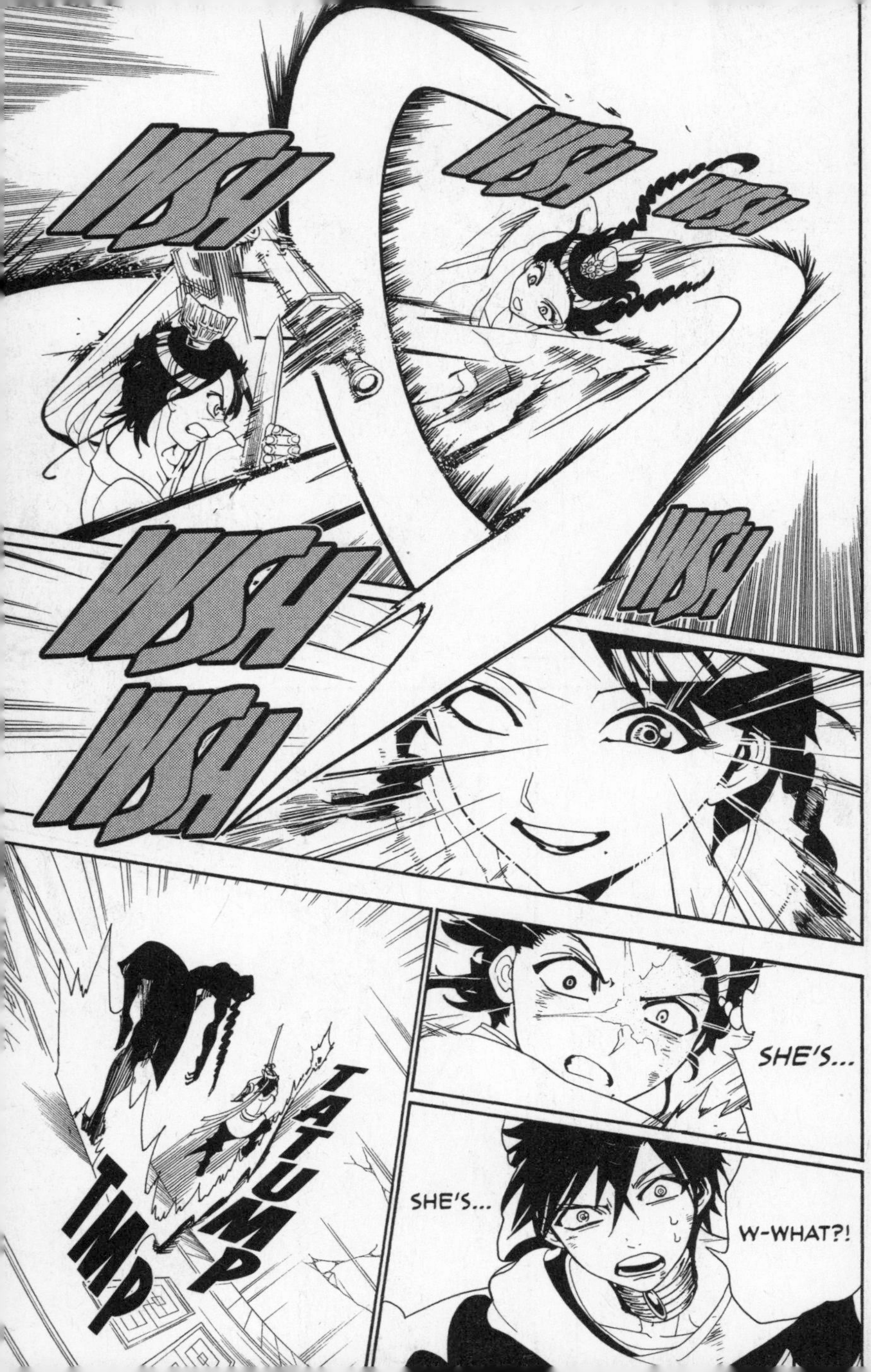
WSH
WSH
WSH
WSH
WSH
WSH
SHE'S...
SHE'S...
W-WHAT?!
TATUMP
TMP

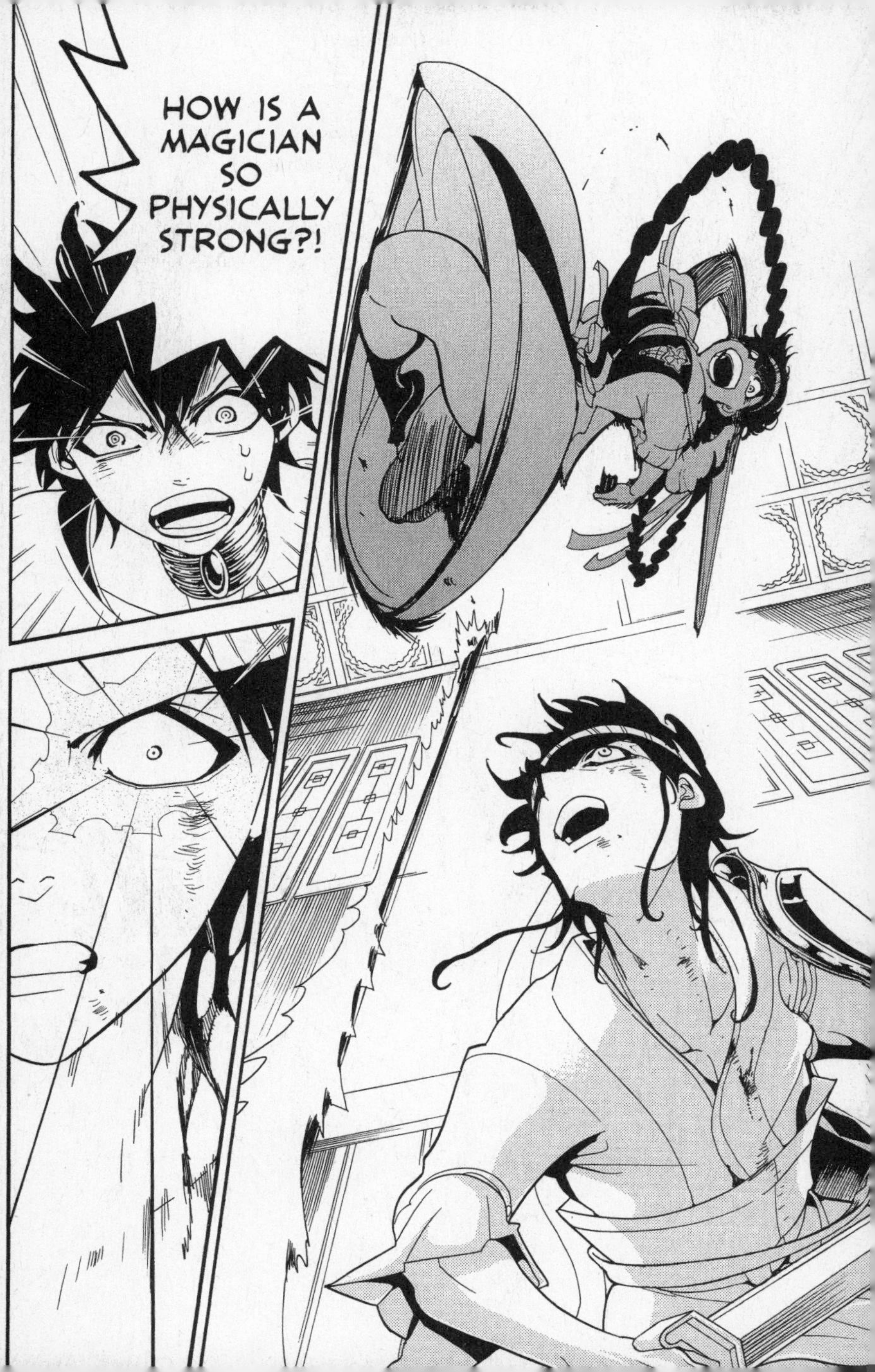
HOW IS A MAGICIAN SO PHYSICALLY STRONG?!

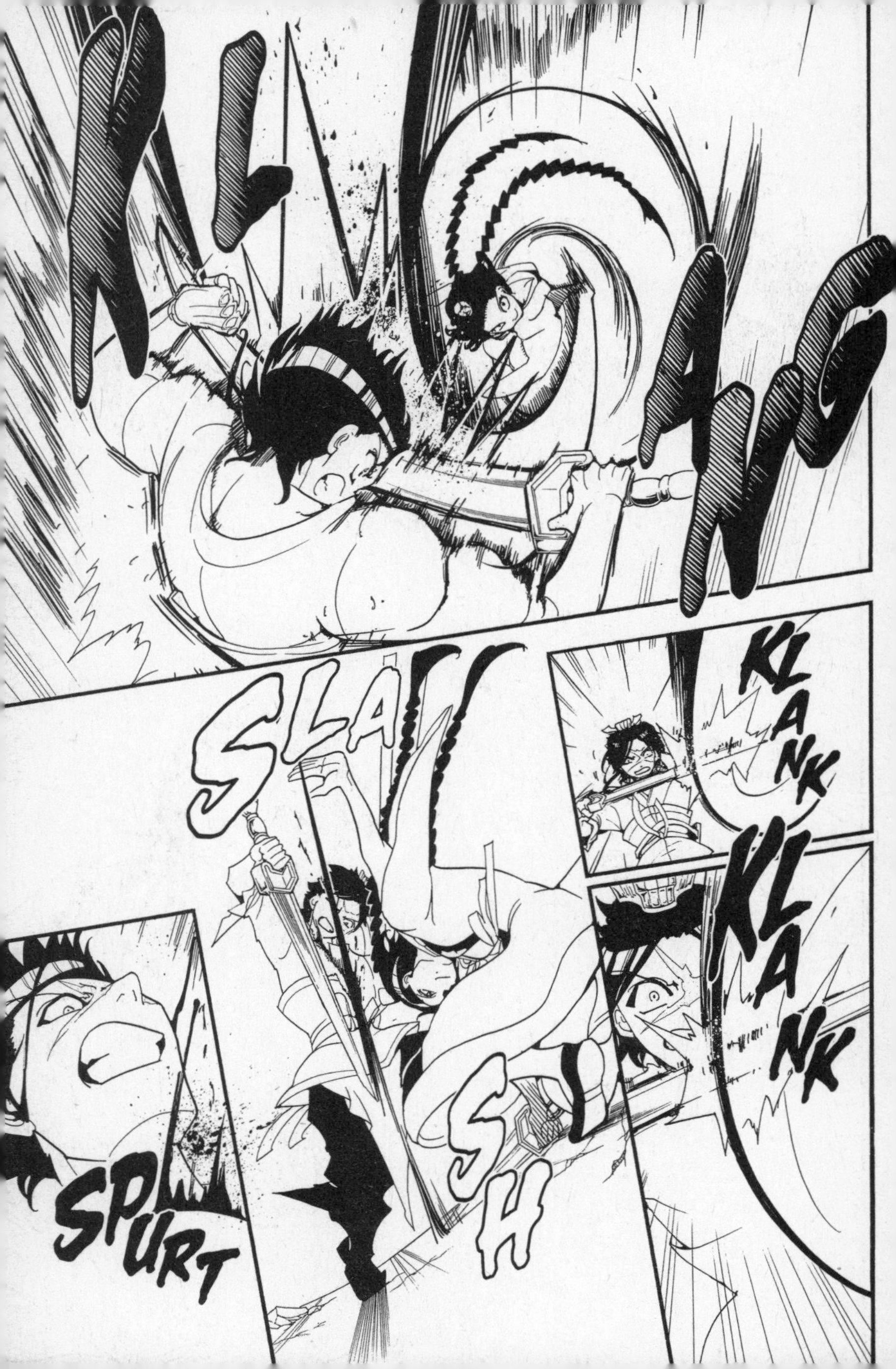
KLANG
KLANK
KLANK
SLASH
SPURT

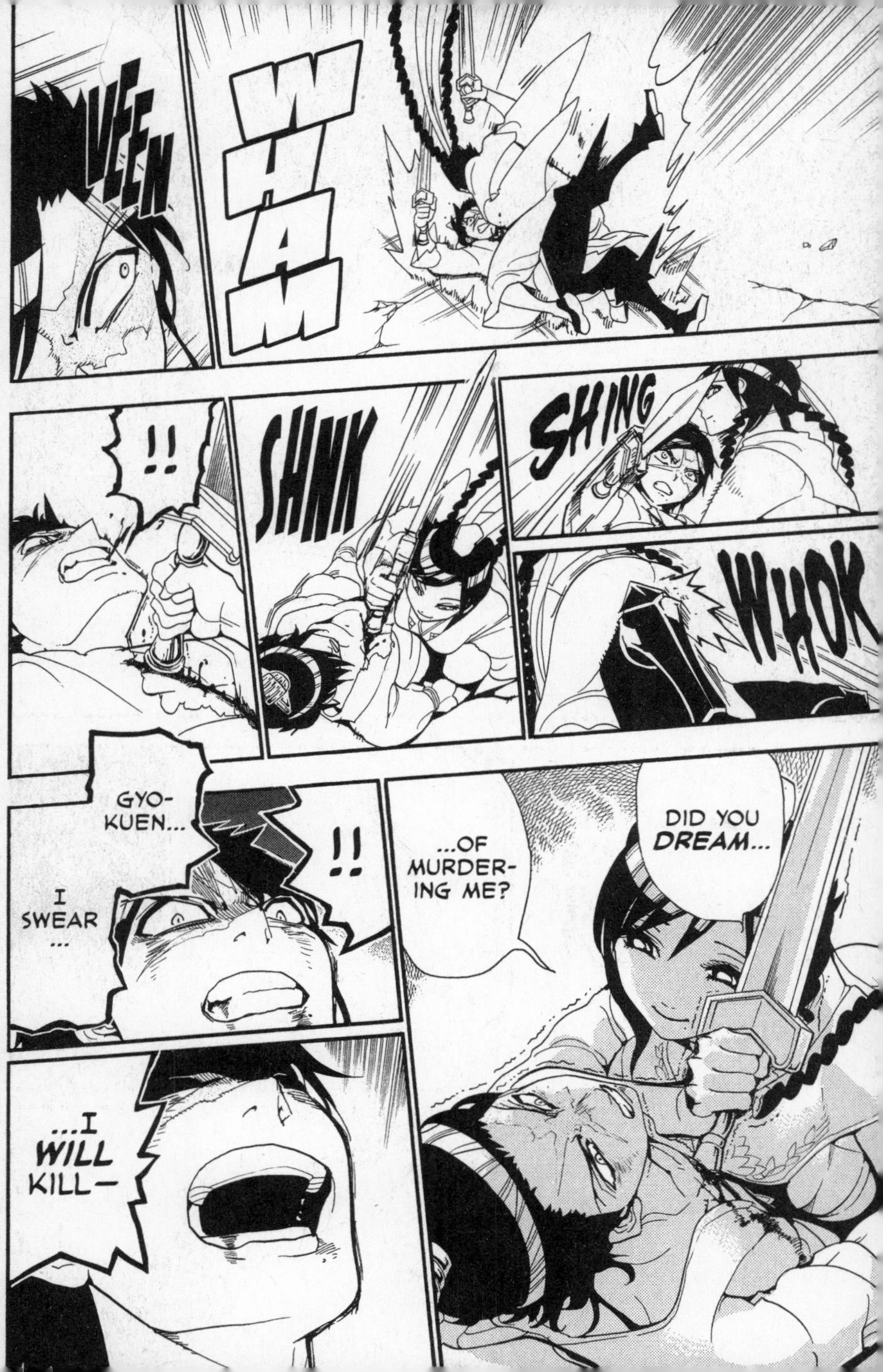
WHAM
VEEN
SHING
WHOK
SHNK
!!
DID YOU DREAM...
...OF MURDERING ME?
!!
GYO-KUEN...
I SWEAR ...
...I WILL KILL—

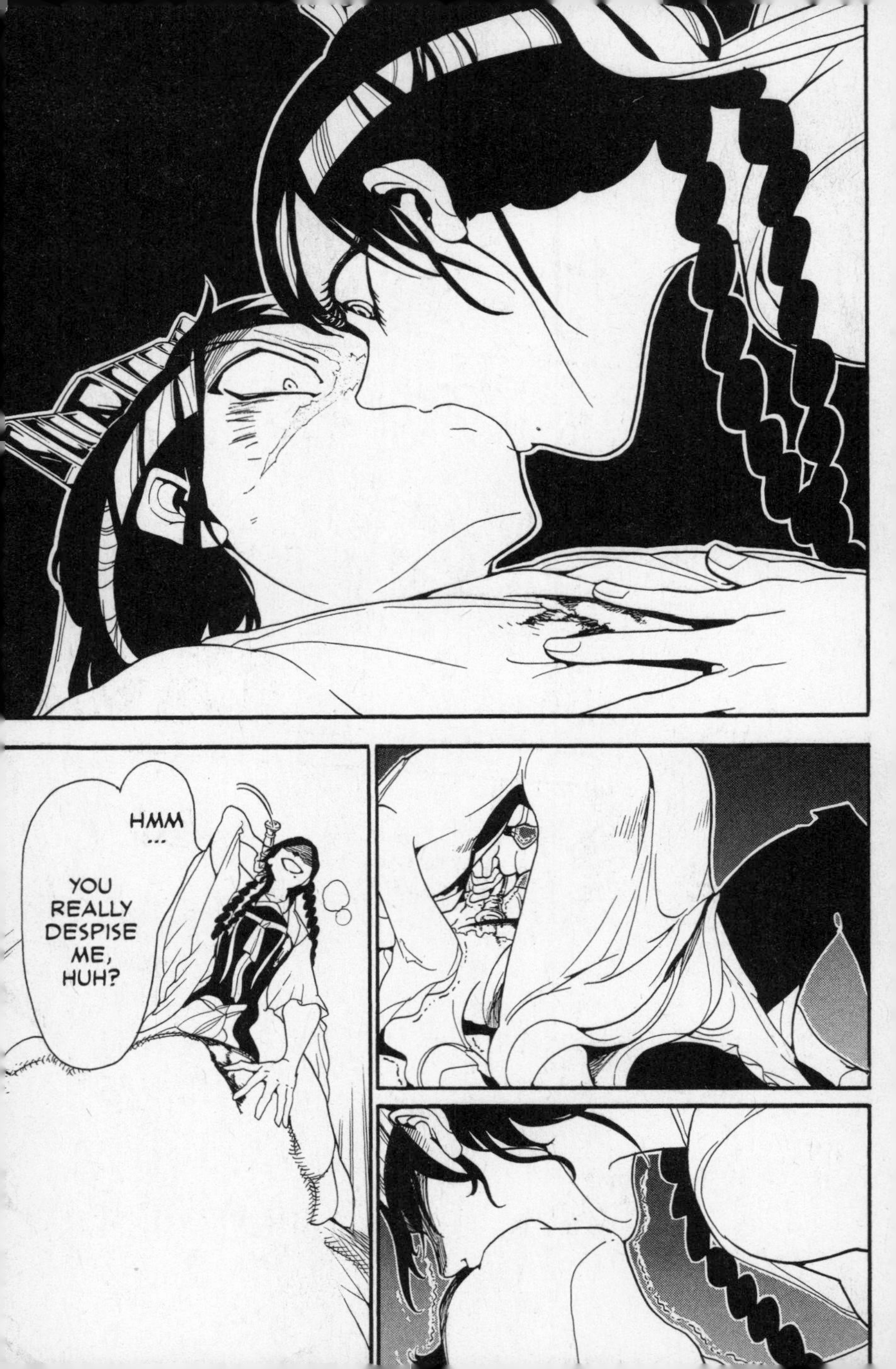
HMM ... YOU REALLY DESPISE ME, HUH?

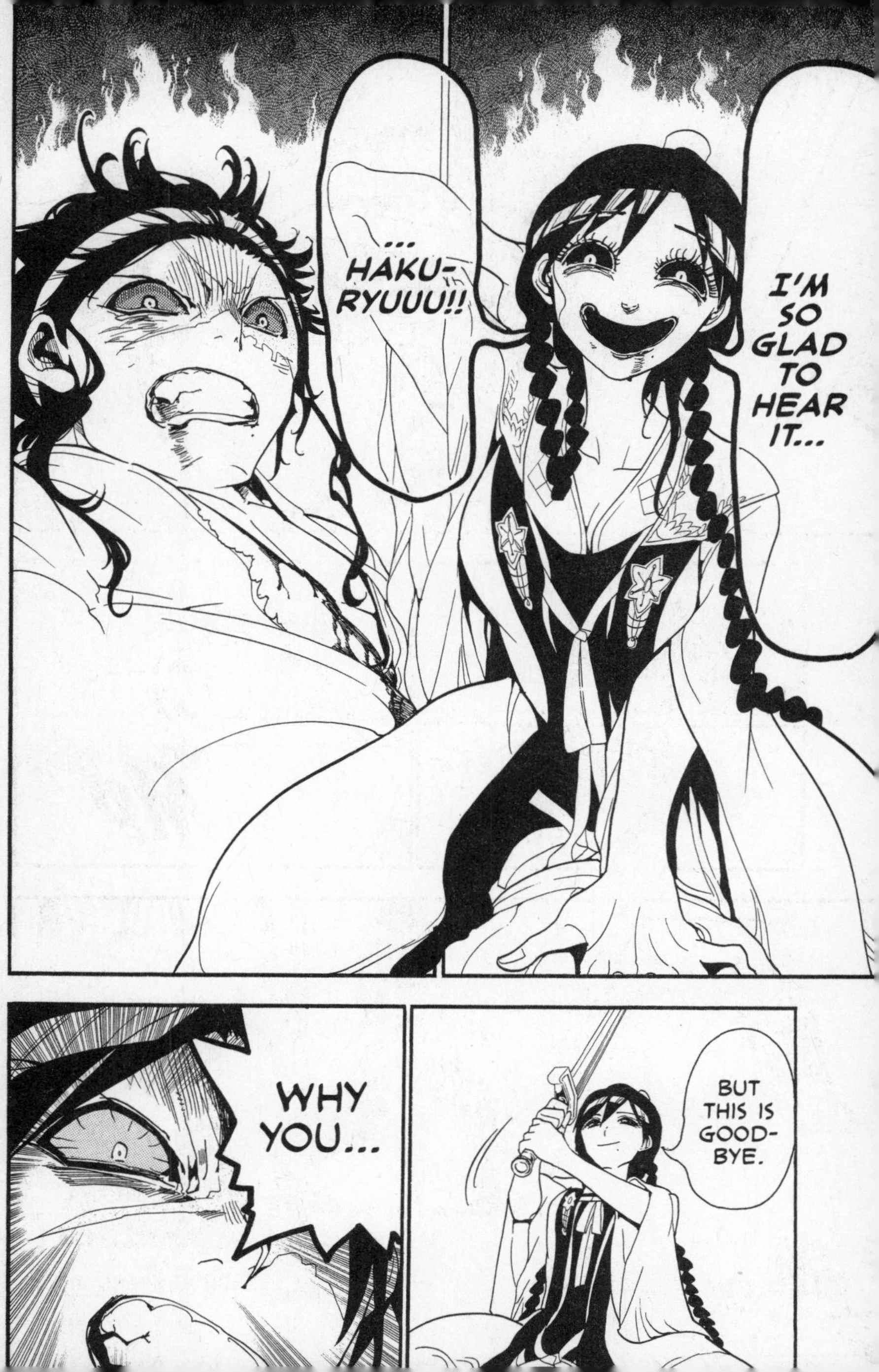
I'M SO GLAD TO HEAR IT...
... HAKU-RYUUU!!
BUT THIS IS GOOD-BYE.
WHY YOU...

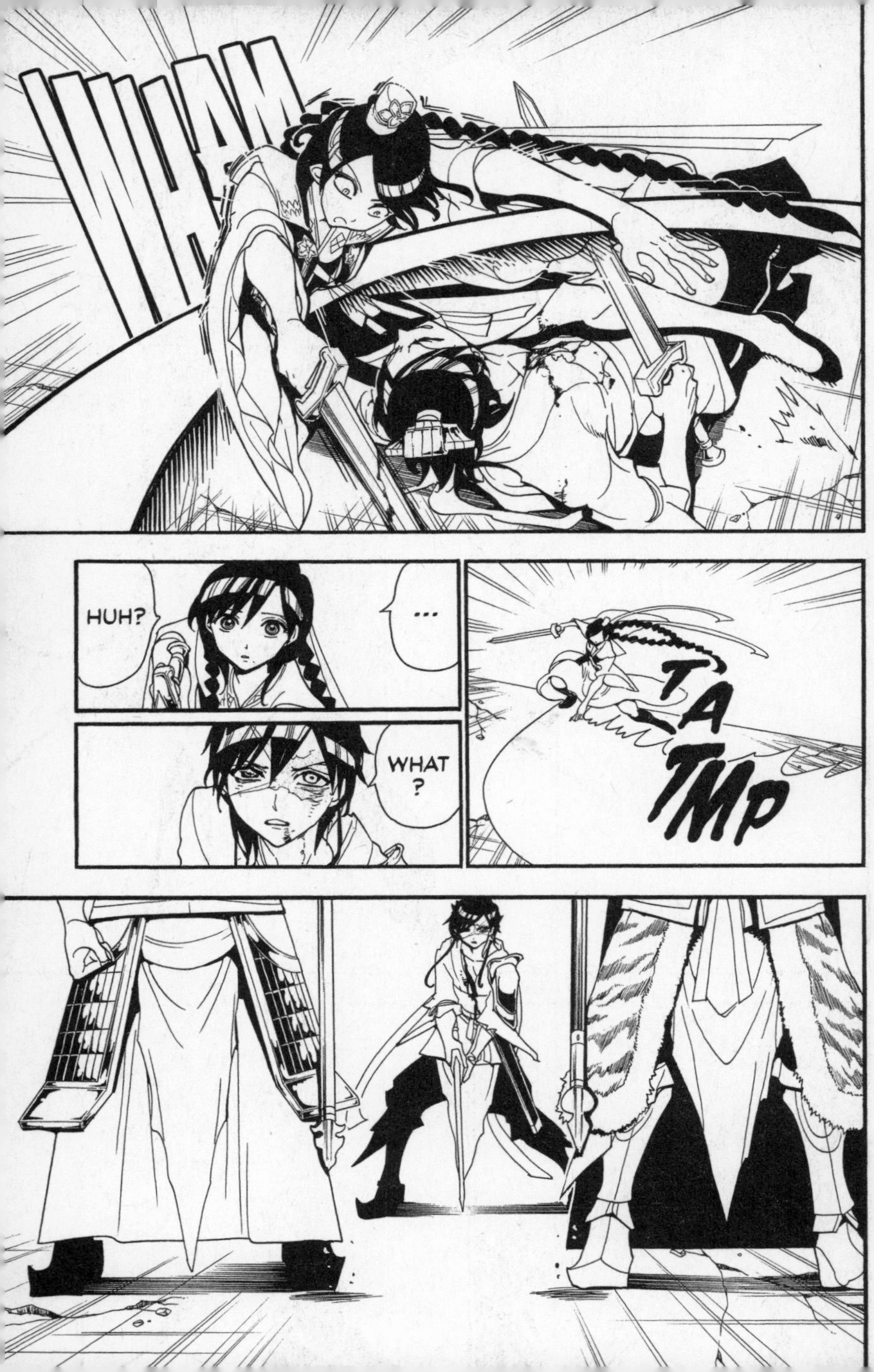
WHAM
TA TMP
...
HUH?
WHAT?

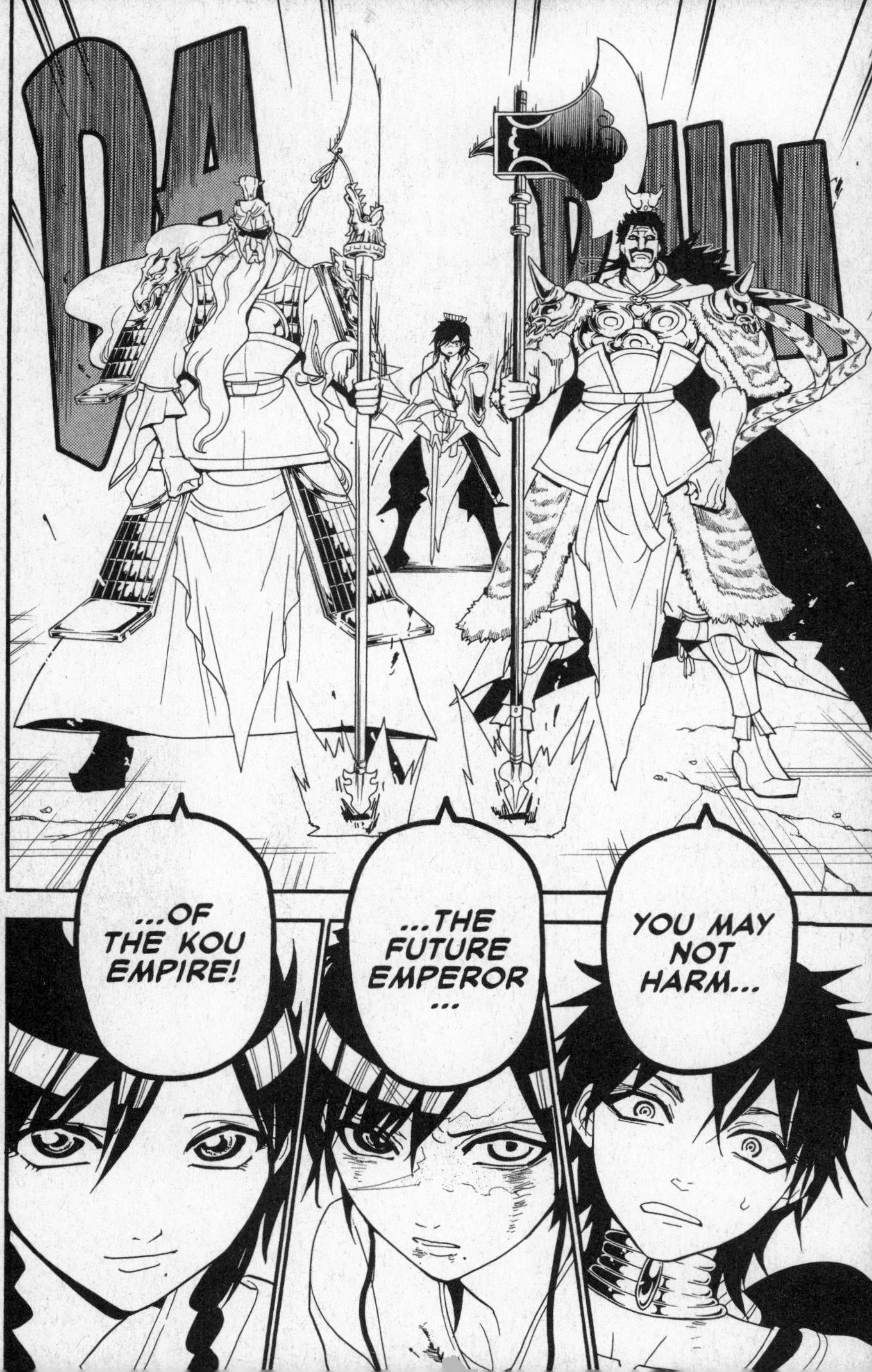
YOU MAY NOT HARM...
...THE FUTURE EMPEROR ...
...OF THE KOU EMPIRE!

MAGI
The labyrinth of magic
25

Staff

■ Story & Art
Shinobu Ohtaka

■ Regular Assistants
Hiro Maizima

Yuiko Akiyama

Megi

Aya Umoto

Mami Yoshida

Yuka Otsuji

■ Editors
Kazuaki Ishibashi

Makoto Ishiwata

■ Sales & Promotion
Tsunato Imamoto

Yuta Uchiyama

■ Designer
Yasuo Shimura + Bay Bridge Studio

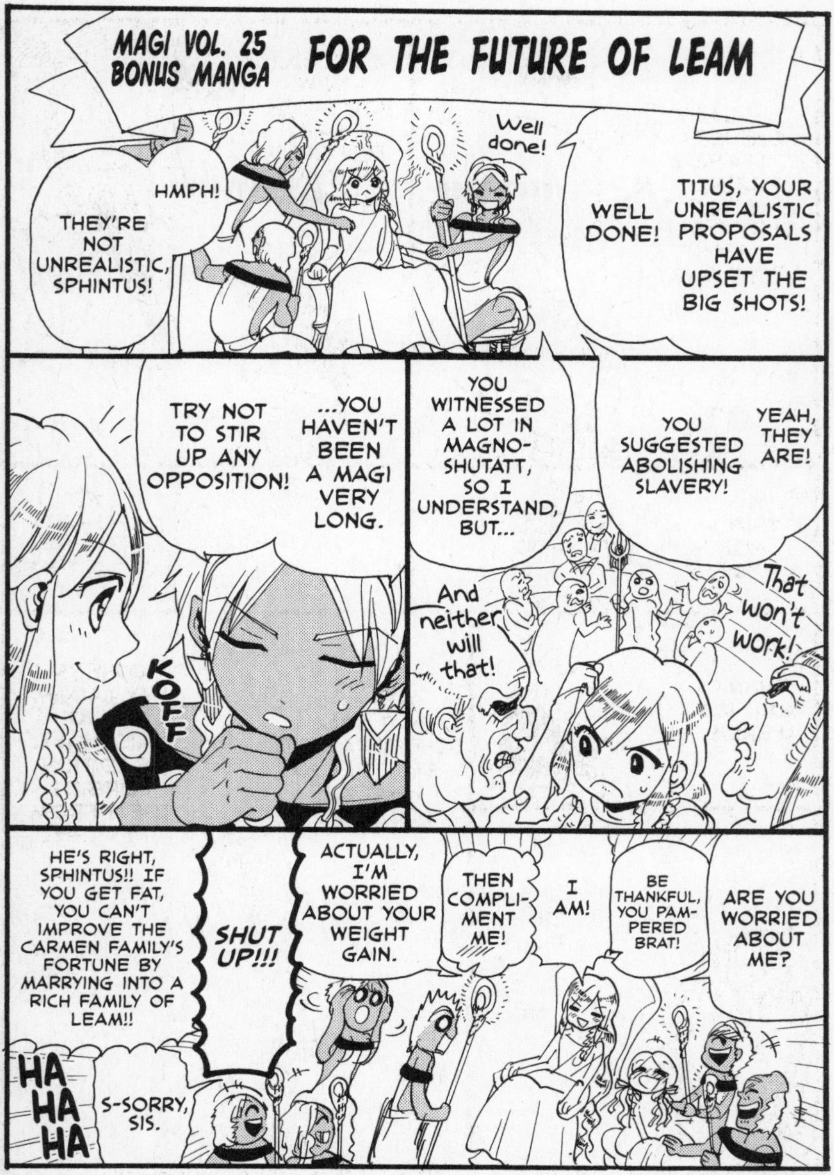
MAGI VOL. 25 BONUS MANGA
FOR THE FUTURE OF LEAM
TITUS, YOUR UNREALISTIC PROPOSALS HAVE UPSET THE BIG SHOTS!
WELL DONE!
Well done!
HMPH!
THEY'RE NOT UNREALISTIC, SPHINTUS!
YEAH, THEY ARE!
YOU SUGGESTED ABOLISHING SLAVERY!
That won't work!
And neither will that!
YOU WITNESSED A LOT IN MAGNO-SHUTATT, SO I UNDERSTAND, BUT...
...YOU HAVEN'T BEEN A MAGI VERY LONG.
TRY NOT TO STIR UP ANY OPPOSITION!
KOFF
ARE YOU WORRIED ABOUT ME?
BE THANKFUL, YOU PAMPERED BRAT!
I AM!
THEN COMPLIMENT ME!
ACTUALLY, I'M WORRIED ABOUT YOUR WEIGHT GAIN.
SHUT UP!!!
HE'S RIGHT, SPHINTUS!! IF YOU GET FAT, YOU CAN'T IMPROVE THE CARMEN FAMILY'S FORTUNE BY MARRYING INTO A RICH FAMILY OF LEAM!!
S-SORRY, SIS.
HA HA HA

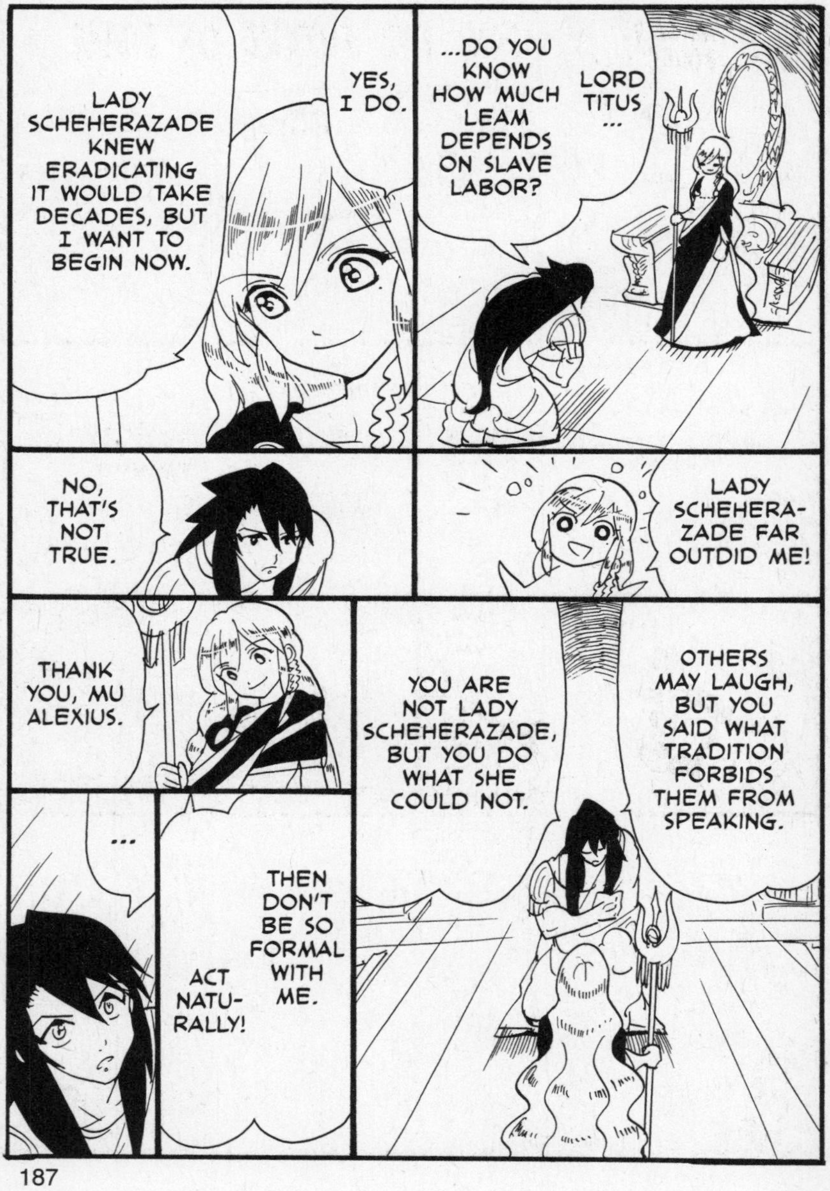
LORD TITUS ...
...DO YOU KNOW HOW MUCH LEAM DEPENDS ON SLAVE LABOR?
YES, I DO.
LADY SCHEHERAZADE KNEW ERADICATING IT WOULD TAKE DECADES, BUT I WANT TO BEGIN NOW.
LADY SCHEHERAZADE FAR OUTDID ME!
NO, THAT'S NOT TRUE.
OTHERS MAY LAUGH, BUT YOU SAID WHAT TRADITION FORBIDS THEM FROM SPEAKING.
YOU ARE NOT LADY SCHEHERAZADE, BUT YOU DO WHAT SHE COULD NOT.
THANK YOU, MU ALEXIUS.
THEN DON'T BE SO FORMAL WITH ME.
ACT NATU-RALLY!
...

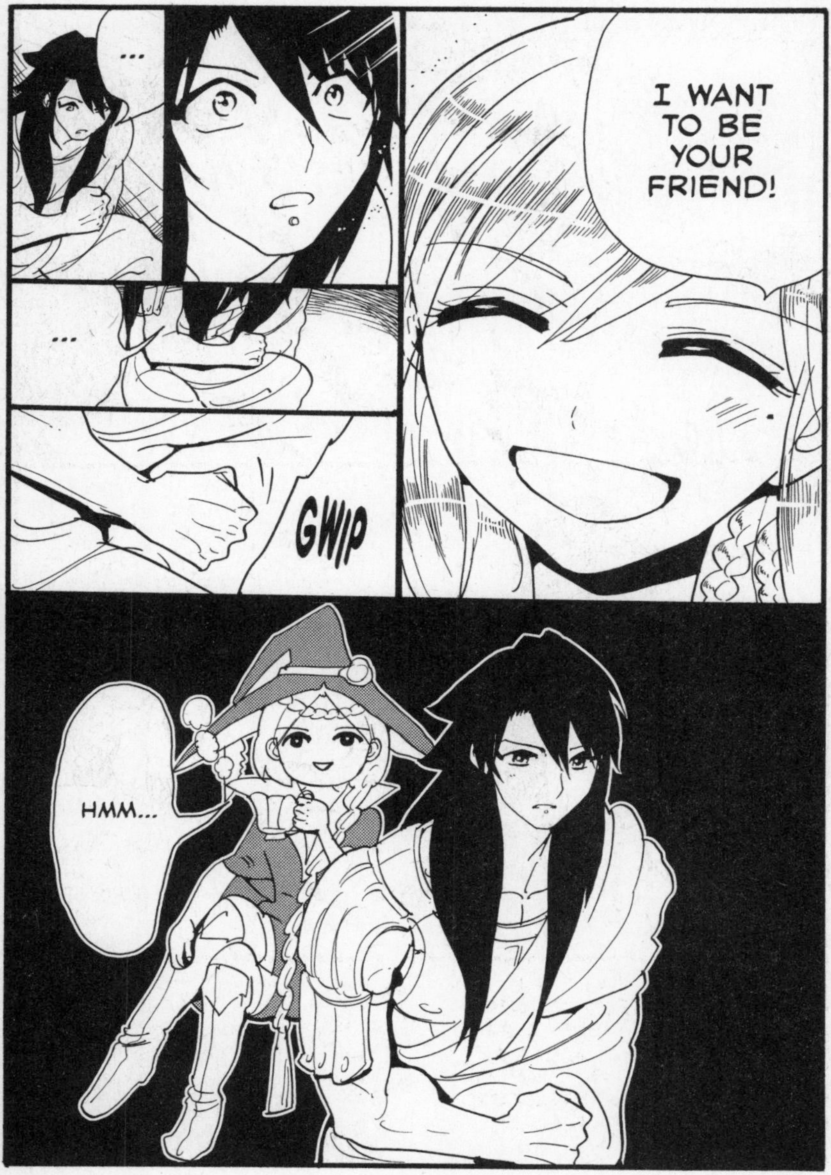
I WANT TO BE YOUR FRIEND!
...
...
GWIP
HMM...

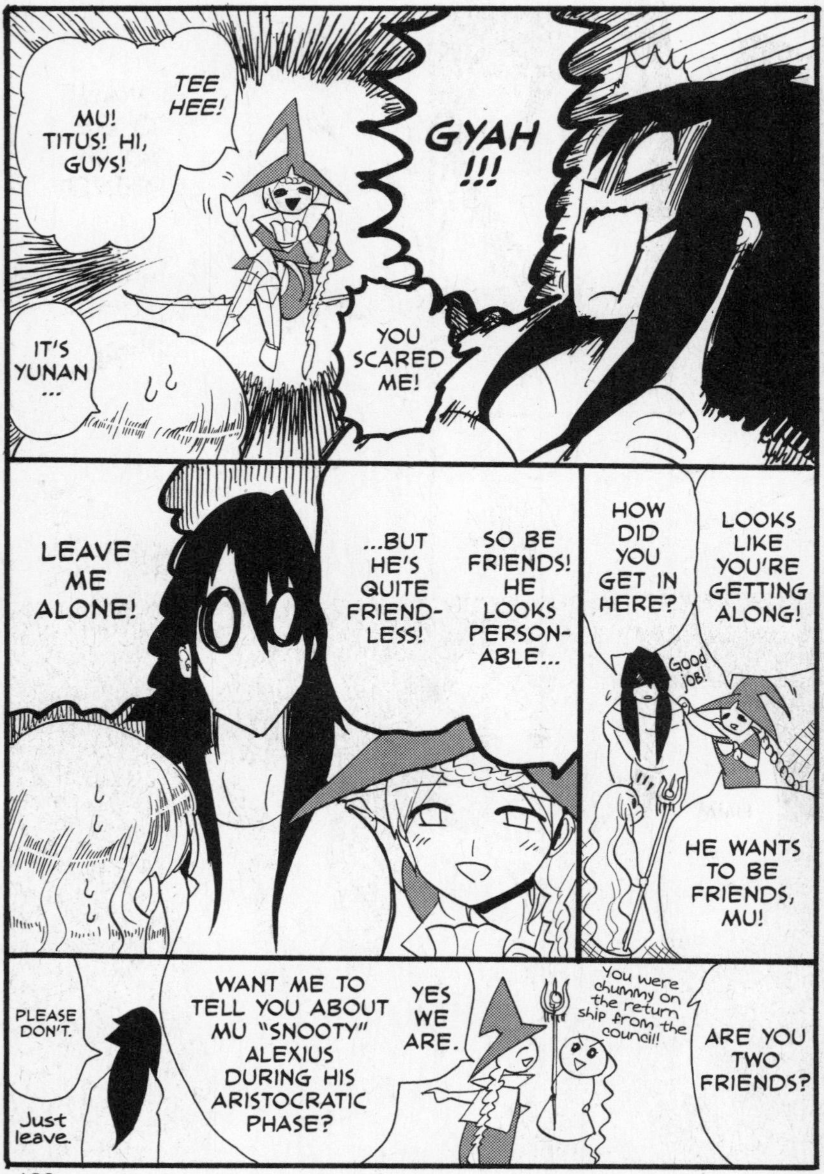
GYAH !!!
YOU SCARED ME!
TEE HEE!
MU! TITUS! HI, GUYS!
IT'S YUNAN...
LOOKS LIKE YOU'RE GETTING ALONG!
HOW DID YOU GET IN HERE?
Good job!
HE WANTS TO BE FRIENDS, MU!
SO BE FRIENDS! HE LOOKS PERSONABLE...
...BUT HE'S QUITE FRIENDLESS!
LEAVE ME ALONE!
ARE YOU TWO FRIENDS?
You were chummy on the return ship from the council!
YES WE ARE.
WANT ME TO TELL YOU ABOUT MU "SNOOTY" ALEXIUS DURING HIS ARISTOCRATIC PHASE?
PLEASE DON'T.
Just leave.

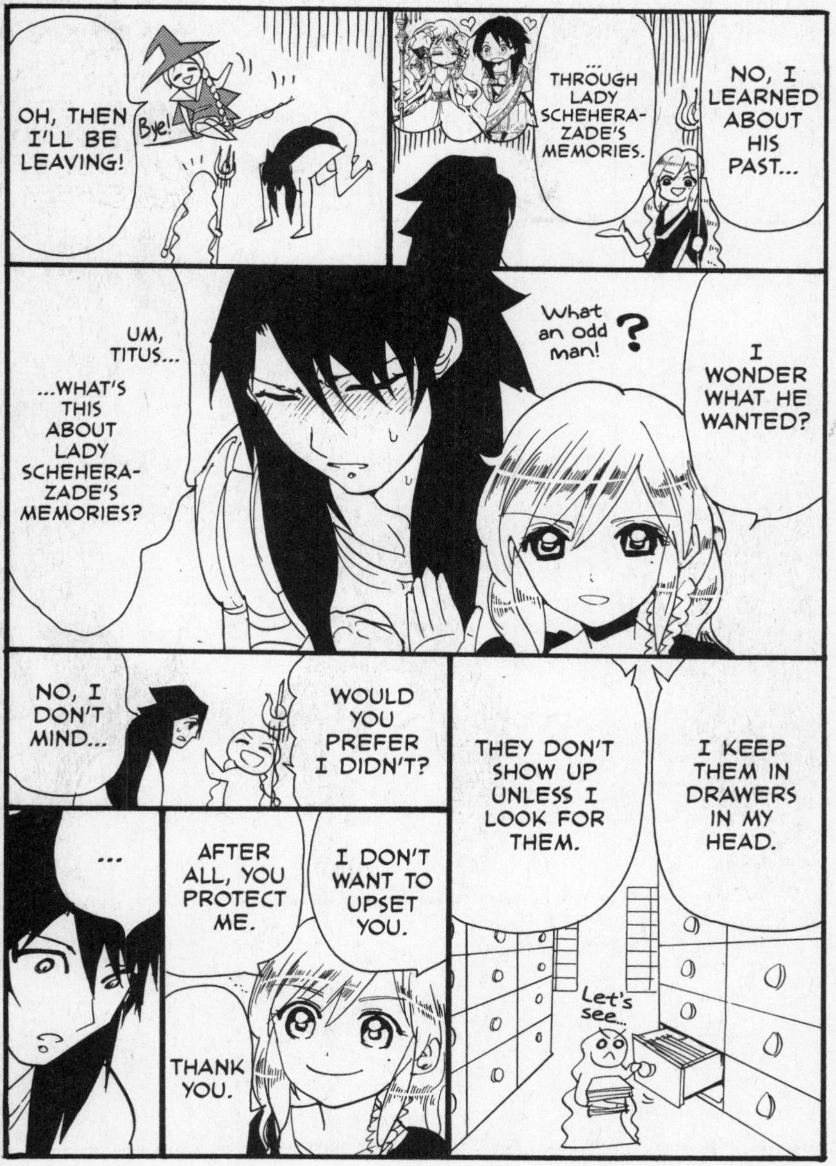
NO, I LEARNED ABOUT HIS PAST...
...THROUGH LADY SCHEHERAZADE'S MEMORIES.
OH, THEN I'LL BE LEAVING!
Bye!
I WONDER WHAT HE WANTED?
What an odd man!
UM, TITUS...
...WHAT'S THIS ABOUT LADY SCHEHERAZADE'S MEMORIES?
I KEEP THEM IN DRAWERS IN MY HEAD.
THEY DON'T SHOW UP UNLESS I LOOK FOR THEM.
Let's see...
WOULD YOU PREFER I DIDN'T?
NO, I DON'T MIND...
I DON'T WANT TO UPSET YOU.
AFTER ALL, YOU PROTECT ME.
THANK YOU.
...

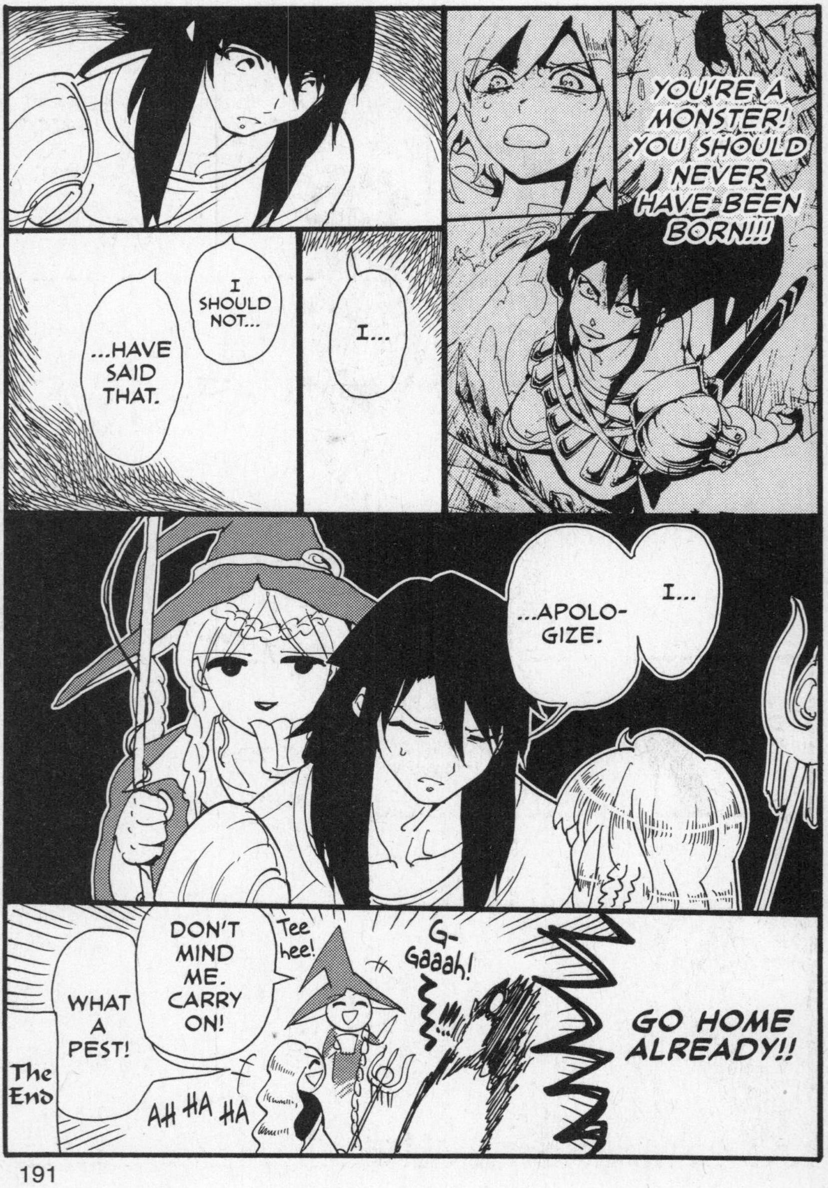
YOU'RE A MONSTER! YOU SHOULD NEVER HAVE BEEN BORN!!!
I...
I SHOULD NOT...
...HAVE SAID THAT.
I...
...APOLOGIZE.
GO HOME ALREADY!!
G-Gaaah!
Tee hee!
DON'T MIND ME. CARRY ON!
WHAT A PEST!
AH HA HA
The End

You're reading the
WRONG WAY

MAGI reads from right to left, starting in the upper-right corner. Japanese is read from **right** to **left**, meaning that action, sound effects, and word-balloon order are completely reversed from English order.

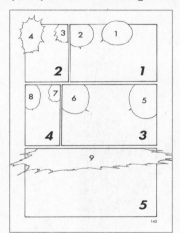

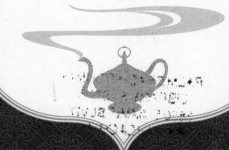